MINORITY RIGHTS IN THE 'NEW' EUROPE

MINORITY RIGHTS IN THE 'NEW' EUROPE

Edited by

Peter Cumper
Lecturer, Law School, Leicester University, United Kingdom

and

Steven Wheatley
Senior Lecturer, Department of Legal Studies,
University of Central Lancashire, United Kingdom

MARTINUS NIJHOFF PUBLISHERS
THE HAGUE / LONDON / BOSTON

A C.I.P. Catalogue record for this book is available from the Library of Congress.

ISBN 90-411-1124-7

Published by Kluwer Law International,
P.O. Box 85889, 2508 CN The Hague, The Netherlands

Sold and distributed in North, Central and South America
by Kluwer Law International,
675 Massachusetts Avenue, Cambridge, MA 02139, USA

In all other countries, sold and distributed
by Kluwer Law International, Distribution Centre
P.O. Box 322, 3300 AH Dordrecht, The Netherlands

Printed on acid-free paper

Printed and bound in Great Britain by Antony Rowe Limited

Table of Contents

Foreword

In a euphoric atmosphere at the summit of the Heads of State and Government meeting in Paris in November 1990, the participating States of the then Conference for Security and Cooperation in Europe signed the *Charter of Paris for a New Europe*. This meeting and Charter represented at one and the same time both the end of the dark days of a divided continent and the beginning of a united and peaceful Europe. Indeed, the Heads of State and Government effectively launched a campaign towards collective peace and prosperity.

Unfortunately, the euphoria was all too soon replaced by a collective anxiety in the face of the bloody dissolution of the former Yugoslavia. It became rapidly apparent that the declarations of the Paris Charter would require prompt and energetic action to transform them into meaningful words for the people of Europe. Some important steps were taken. But, almost a decade later and on the cusp of the new millennium, we are still discovering all that the 'New' Europe means and requires.

While some of the lessons were learned decades and even centuries ago, we are only now coming to terms with the complex issues of diversity within and between democratic States. These issues present themselves in all States, but they are only more apparent and acute in the countries of central and eastern Europe where decades of totalitarian government effectively suppressed minority interests and claims or dispersed them through the then prevailing ideology. The resurfacing of these interests and claims now poses special and dangerous problems for countries which are undergoing already difficult transitions from authoritarian to democratic governance and from planned to market economy. Tension and instability in this regard also pose problems for neighbouring States and for Europe as a whole.

There are today increasingly worrying signs of renewed or developing tensions involving national minorities in several States. Evidently, we have failed to move far or fast enough in addressing the root causes of minority-related problems. Significant success has been achieved in establishing new standards of minority rights, in particular through elaboration of the June

P. Cumper and S. Wheatley (eds.), Minority Rights in the 'New' Europe, vii–ix
© 1999 *Kluwer Law International. Printed in Great Britain.*

1990 Copenhagen Document of the CSCE Conference on the Human Dimension and, subsequently within the Council of Europe, the November 1992 European Charter for Regional or Minority Languages and the February 1995 Framework Convention for the Protection of National Minorities – the last two treaties just recently having entered into force. However, this important progress in standard-setting has in many situations yet to be met with sufficiently robust implementation at the national level, much less at the local level. As such, the minority rights concepts and specific entitlements of the 'New' Europe remain less than tangible for a large part of the intended beneficiaries – even in established democracies. There remain, in fact, significant obstacles (including stiffening opposition in certain situations) to full respect for many minority rights.

It has been evident at least since the end of the Cold War that all of Europe has been engaged in remarkable transitions. As the transitions in the 'New' Europe unfold, it becomes increasingly clear that respect for the Rule of Law and human rights, including the rights of persons belonging to national minorities, is vital to collective security and prosperity. It also becomes clear for the new or restored democracies that much of good and democratic governance is really about processes which are based upon principles of equality, freedom, tolerance and mutual respect, inclusion and integration. For such a system to work, it requires a common and collective understanding of, and commitment to, basic values. This is exactly what the 'New' Europe is all about – a commitment to the common European values of democracy, human rights and the market economy where individual talents, skills and interests may be pursued in conditions of fairness to the benefit of each and everyone. But, in order to hold fast to these common European values, we must act constantly with vigilance to ensure their respect everywhere and for everyone. It is on this basis in the 'New' Europe that no State may any longer plead 'non-interference in internal affairs' when responding to concerns over respect for human rights, including the rights of persons belonging to national minorities. It is also partly on this basis that we speak increasingly in Europe about 'good governance' (not simply 'democratic governance'), meaning that government must be for the benefit of the whole population and not merely the majority or that part of the population who voted for those in power. Indeed, it is in this relation that the 'effective participation' of persons belonging to minorities in decision-making processes is a 'right'.

Evidently, the complex problems posed by the 'New' Europe require careful attention and a developed sense of our own values together with a principled approach to problem-solving. We know, of course, that democracy is not an end in itself, but rather a permanent project – in fact, an open-ended, evolving and unlimited process. If we are seeking to facilitate the realisation by everyone of their individual and diverse aspirations in conditions of equality and fairness, then we must think progressively and creatively and we must act carefully and energetically. The duty of good governance requires responsiveness to the needs of all – majority and minorities alike – with a view to fulfilling not merely the *minimum* standards in terms of *obligations*, but striving to fulfil the *spirit* of declarations, conventions and commitments in terms of *shared values*. Accordingly, we should think in terms of "the citizenry" rather than "the nation" – of multi-cultural society as distinguished from mono-cultural society, and we should pursue policies of social integration rather than assimilation. This no doubt requires some enlightened and perhaps courageous leadership. But, equally, it requires a popular commitment to the underlying values of equality, dignity and freedom for all.

Minority Rights in the 'New' Europe thus constitutes a timely contribution to the public consideration of important issues of relevance to Europe's development now and in the coming decades. The specific matters addressed demonstrate the diversity and complexity of the issues – along with the seriousness of the consequences of failure to respond. More hopefully, the contributions also show the way forward in dealing with existing problems. Certainly, much has been achieved, but much remains to be done. A combination of scholarly reflection and informed political action is needed. This book makes a significant contribution to this end.

Max van der Stoel
OSCE High Commissioner on National Minorities
The Hague, April 1998

Introduction: In the Strongroom of Vocabulary

*Patrick Thornberry**

"Then I entered a strongroom of vocabulary
where words like urns that had come through the fire
Stood in their bone-dry alcoves next a kiln

And came away changed . . . "[1]

THE STRONGROOM OF HUMAN RIGHTS

The contents of this volume testify to the weight of contemporary scholarship devoted to the issue of minority rights. Scholarly treatments of minority rights were profusely offered in the era of the League of Nations, and before.[2] Minority rights were an organic part of the body of international law, one of its uncommon humanitarian principles, if operating for the benefit of specified groups, and not others. But in the early UN decades, intellectual effort devoted to minority rights might have been regarded as self-indulgent nostalgia, as exegesis of arcane mysteries,[3] as valuable as the speculations of Flann O'Brien's great de Selby, scientist and savant.[4] Minority rights were not in fashion; the agenda had collapsed with the League. Human rights were the new vogue. The great project was person-centred, the premises universal, the concerns transcendent. The UN agenda of the 1950s and 60s was different from what it is now. It was dictated to a degree by the raft of new members seeking to recover the lost voices of Africa and Asia, prickly about slights to their sovereignty, using the General Assembly of the UN as their legislature.[5] The new States entered the sanctum of international law and sought change from the inside. They changed it in aspects unfavourable to the development of minority rights. They were devoted to nation-building. What else could they do, left to cope with the ridiculous demarcations of the colonial powers, those straight lines drawn on the map of Africa invisible to satellite reconnaissance?[6] Hence the laborious business of making territories into nation-States, omelettes from eggs, with overborne groups of many kinds

1

P. Cumper and S. Wheatley (eds.), Minority Rights in the 'New' Europe, 1–14
© 1999 *Kluwer Law International. Printed in Great Britain.*

as the raw ingredients. The Western States for the best Liberal reasons were also uninterested, although there were exceptions, and some fitful arrangements of a bilateral nature.[7] The USA, so influential in drafting the UN Charter and transcribing the message of individual human rights, showed little concern about minorities, except perhaps religious ones, groaning under the Soviet yoke. Perhaps the USA had never understood the notion of treating with collectives rather than individuals, unmindful of its history of dealings with indigenous nations.[8] Or perhaps it only aspired to keep a distance from such questions, anxious to maintain differences with Bolshevism and collectivism. Other Western States were concerned with Empire, with suppressing and then accommodating liberation movements. Their interest was more or less limited to playing the minorities card – or the indigenous suit – to beat off the ideologues of decolonisation.[9] The Soviet Union was at once the great champion of collective rights and a fortress of imprisoned peoples. Soviet enthusiasm for collective rights spilled over into a theory and praxis. The Soviet minority rights model was available for export, hence the title of inspiring works such as "How the Soviet Union Solved the Nationalities Problem".[10] The Yugoslav model was also available, hence their sponsorship of UN initiatives in this field.[11] The first UN products – the Charter and the Universal Declaration of Human Rights – did not deal with minority rights, but with non-discrimination, after the fashion of the USA, further shaped by the expanding international struggle against Apartheid.[12] The Council of the Europe had the term "national minority" in Article 14 of the European Convention on Human Rights,[13] but almost to the present day has done little with it; the Council's further exercises in standard-setting were a long way off.[14]

ENTERING THE STRONGROOM

From, say, the late 1970s, things were changing. The minority rights international law programme was in process of development, spurred by the publication of the Capotorti report in 1977 with associated academic writings.[15] The International Covenants were in force, with the crucial Article 27 of the Covenant on Civil and Political Rights [ICCPR] waiting to be explored – a process which produced *Lovelace v Canada*[16] and other cases,[17] proving that Article 27 could, after all, have some uses. The international community witnessed the slow if not stately progress towards a UN Declaration on Minority Rights. A makeover was imminent for the highly assimilationist ILO Convention 107 on Indigenous and Tribal Populations.[18] The CSCE/OSCE had made reference to minorities in the

Helsinki Final Act. Liberals were becoming more curious about minority rights.[19] Perhaps the universal rights/non-discrimination package was insufficiently nuanced for every group everywhere. The take-off point for international law on minority rights did not arrive until the end of the 1980s. By that time, the concern with political decolonisation in Africa and Asia had largely ebbed away and shifted focus on to economy and development. The unravelling of the Soviet Union and Yugoslavia contributed to the realisation that the amorphous masses submerged in grand conceptions such as the *homo sovieticus* were in reality discrete peoples, with sharply differentiated identities. Identity and culture emerged as key post-modern themes, overriding consciousness of class as the authentic mediator of social relations. The politics of ethnicity and nationalism were the surrogate bodies, the carriers of the new consciousness into social action. The results were inspiring and terrifying. Liberals finally woke up.[20]

As the burgeoning number of entities revealed themselves, international organisations competed to 'do something about' minorities; the CSCE/OSCE and the UN were quick, the Council of Europe painfully slow. The ILO put in place its empowering and underrated Convention 169 on Indigenous and Tribal Peoples. Even a Convention on the rights of children contained identity references, obligatory in 1990.[21] The new consciousness can be measured by considering the drafting of the UN Declaration on Minority Rights. Early drafts were presented to the UN in 1978 and 1979. By 1989, there was virtually no agreed text. By 1990, a full text had been given a first reading; the second reading was complete to all intents and purposes by December 1991. The General Assembly ratified the drafting work and adopted its declaration in December 1992.[22] The interval between first and second reading was, in UN terms, the blink of an eyelid. Something had changed.

. . . Words like Urns . . .

Inscribing this relatively new opulence of minority rights in international law has its own difficulties. There was no bright white space on which to make marks entitled "minority rights". The rights, and those of the indigenous, are not a single issue enthusiasm.[23] They have made their way into international law through the usual channels.[24] They interconnect with the other principles of human rights and the norms and structures of international law. This is not the League of Nations revisited. In that period, there was a blank space outside the minorities system; an absence of rights. In our new system, it is difficult to say where minority rights begin and end. General human rights apply to members of minorities as they apply to everyone. Genocide picks out the most vulnerable, usually the minority, though they are not named as objects of genocidal process by the Genocide Convention.[25] Minorities participate – or should – in general self-determination processes, though they are again not named as the holders of the right.[26] The edge between minorities and indigenous peoples is not well honed, but indigenous peoples, who have greater possibilities of an empowering code than other groups, have pushed forward the boundaries of minority rights.[27] The articles or paragraphs on minority rights in the general texts such as the ICCPR[28] or the UNESCO Convention on Discrimination in Education must read coherently with all the rights.[29] The pre-existing format of human rights and the minority rights superimposed on it generate a host of questions, many of which are explored in the present volume. While no area of rights is immune to controversy, these new rights generate more controversy than most. They have as much force as other rights, and like all rights, exist in a state of (one hopes, creative) tension with the rest, including generalised principles such as non-discrimination.[30] The relationship between principles will occupy lawyers and theoreticians for a time to come. For international law, it is not a question of moving from a norm of non-discrimination to one of minority rights. Both norms are simultaneously valid; mutually supportive interpretations are needed. Conceptualising the relationship between minority rights and general human rights is lawspeak against funda-mentalism. The rights of one group or one person will not be allowed to override or subdue into insignificance the rights of others. Rights may trump interests,[31] not other rights, and certainly not fundamental rights imprinted in the canon of international law.

. . . THAT HAD COME THROUGH THE FIRE . . .

This last-mentioned lapidary principle is to be applied at inter-individual and inter-communal levels, and accounts for some of the most demanding issues. One is the relationship between the individual and the collective. Human rights law insists that collective rights should not undermine individual rights; but the converse is also true. This leads, in *Lovelace, Kitok*[32] and other cases, to emollient metaphors of 'balance' between the rights, even though considerable pain may be caused on both sides of the argument. Just as individuals may be destroyed by exclusion from community, so are communities destroyed by excessive exercises in self-identification by those claiming membership of particular communities. If we believe in the principles of individual self-identification, can anyone join the Yanomami, or the Gypsies or the Sami? If we believe in the right of a community to continue in existence, or communal as opposed to individual self-identification and self-determination, can the community expel individuals who disturb and disrupt? Can the individual reject the community? Are communities permitted to discriminate in terms of gender, or disability? Are they to be comprehended in a monistic manner, or does this conceal inequalities and oppression, disparities of power; are they perhaps only revealed to us through the eyes of elites?[33] All of these questions bring in reflection on rights which are recognised in one way or another in contemporary international law: the communal right to exist-ence[34]; the individual right to self-identify[35] – though the self-identification may not necessarily result in the legal consequences desired by the individual, and the right not to be discriminated against. The texts also tell us that individuals may not be compelled to use minority rights.[36] International law is against cultural determinism – the systemic locking-in of individuals to communities against their will. But personal self-expression has limits.

Such arguments are organically linked to questions of value.[37] Why do we value the rights of communities, or claim to do so? Is it because cultural diversity is like biodiversity? Have cultures and religions and languages something like intrinsic value? Or can they only be viewed through the eyes of individuals who compose these societies here and now, without regard to forebears or generations to come? International law, as might be expected, insinuates diverse answers. It affirms the value of cultural diversity,[38] and of individual choice,[39] and cultures as contexts of choice.[40] It also affirms the conditions for the continuance of cultures, and the nexus between individual and collective identity. There may perhaps be a delicate reordering of values at work in favour of the collective – in the area of minority rights, and more so of indigenous peoples, and peoples' rights generally. The UN Declaration on Minority Rights has quietly recognised the value of collective existence and identity. While it has retained the language of individual rights, there is a subtle amplification of the collective dimension of those rights. The collective language is more dramatic in ILO Convention 169, where rights are recognised directly as belonging to the peoples. This has led commentators to assert that we must move to collective rights to affirm the value of collectives.[41] But collective interests can also be advanced through the language of individual rights – which still constitutes the framework of international law. Hence for example, the anti-assimilationist thrust of contemporary texts is expressed in provisions which disapprove of assimilation against the will of individu-als;[42] in such cases, any accompanying lament for the disappearance of cultures is played on muted strings. The truer collective interest may not be the interest of the collective alone, but the collective conceived as part of a whole, with the good the common good. The privileging of 'ourselves alone' by any group, however threatened, has only limited appeal.

. . . STOOD . . . NEXT A KILN . . .

So which minority rights have been brought to human rights and which have not? Minority rights enriches human rights through developing the language of existence and identity and principles of participation in cultural, social, economic and public life. Participation is to be secured and the marketing of identities is to be related to the rights and interests of legal subjects. Development processes and the concept of development are also affected by the movement in minority rights.[43] The new law greatly concerns itself with questions of education and language. It demands respect for traditions and customs unless specific practices within them contravene international standards.[44] While the monistic integrity of cultures is respected, international law will dissect them when the occasion demands to uncover and condemn unacceptable practices. The legal register approximates to the view of Charles Taylor: it is reasonable to suppose that:

> cultures that have provided the horizon of meaning for large numbers of human beings . . . that have . . . articulated their sense of the good, the holy, the admirable – are almost certain to have something that deserves our admiration and respect, even if it is accompanied by much that we have to abhor and reject.[45]

The law promotes mutuality of respect among diverse population groups, processes which require education of society as a whole, striving to go beyond the promotion of tolerance. As the Human Rights Committee reminds us, culture manifests itself in many forms,[46] and the various manifestations are accommodated in one way or another by the newly installed norms.

The texts have also sought to revalue the importance of names to individuals and communities.[47] In this, an important spatial extension of minority rights can be confirmed. When the Human Rights Committee made its remark on the manifestations of culture, it also noted the relevance of land to culture. For many groups – mainly but not exclusively indigenous – land is a part of culture. It is their territory where they practice their specific modes of economy. Land may be the temple of a people, the source of their spirituality, as Delphi with its *omphalos* was the navel of the world. As the Committee recognised, some groups may have no existence outside a territory.[48] Denial of access, deforestation, logging and mining by outsiders or manipulated by outsiders may therefore be potentially ethnocidal. For many others, and the more usual minority configuration, territory may have been shared. Minority rights law suggests that they be permitted to make their marks upon the territory by naming it in their language. They may not 'own' the spaces as in an autonomy (below), but they share it, and this sharing is entitled to some recognition.[49] The spatial extension of minority rights also brings with it an enhancement of rights in the public spheres of language recognition, its use before public authorities, its use in the educational process. The impact of all this on traditional international law is considerable. Politics, diplomacy, public administration in the widest sense, the economy, are all areas where relevant authorities are obliged to take the ethnic factor into their calculations. Minority rights are increasingly inopportune for casual or neglectful arrangements by state authorities; they require action, and they require resources.

The resources question is a problem for human rights in general. The debate over resourcing minority rights can enrich the arguments. All human rights 'consume' resources – they cannot be put in place without action by the State and by civil society. Even the elimination of torture requires instruction and education of officials, and training rarely comes cheap. Minority rights threaten to consume more resources than many other human rights. Take the New Guinea Question; or make it easier and take the Papua New Guinea Question. According to the new World Directory of Minorities, 840 distinct languages are used in the PNG.[50] So what is the duty of the State in terms of succouring or salvaging the languages, bearing in mind that most will qualify as minority languages? The Committee on Economic, Social and Cultural Rights insists that even a minimal duty to take steps to develop rights requires that steps should be taken. Steps should be deliberate, concrete and targeted.[51] Some minority rights look like process rights (the development of identity and culture, the education continuum); others look like civil and political rights – speech, worship, participation, names, contacts across frontiers. But the resources issue is not met by answering that the State has no resources. What resources it has can and must be amplified by engaging the international community to widen the pool.[52] And lack of resources does not excuse the lack of a principle to allocate resources. Minority rights law gives ample indications on resource and rights allocation in terms of need and demand mediated by principles of proportionality solidarity and equality. There are gaps. Standards refer to numerical strength of groups as one factor to be take into account.[53] This does not necessarily result in easy calibrations of competing claims of small vulnerable language or other cultural groups and those larger groups entitled to more on a taxpayer argument (the more taxes, the greater payback expected) but whose language rates high on a scale of linguistic vitality. So international law makes demands on States, but provides significant if not exhaustive principles and guidelines for respecting and ensuring rights. They are signposts on the way to determining the cash value of minority rights.

Minority rights do not trespass on the territory of the international law principle of self-determination, though again, some reconfigurations are implied. If participation is to have a meaning and minorities have rights to participate democratically in processes which shape and determine the future of nations, our understandings of self-determination should accommodate this.[54] Minorities may not have the right to self-determination, which is recognised as belonging to peoples,[55] but they have a part in it which must not be ignored. As a collective movement, only indigenous peoples have mounted a frontal challenge to the orthodoxy of self-determination. They insist on the concept as the best vehicle to carry their claims and aspirations.[56] States may be fearful and cry "Bosnia" in response. But indigenous peoples did not create or destroy Bosnia, and their approach to self-determination as respect for their historicity, presence and difference is potentially valuable for all others. States created the image of self-determination as a Frankenstein's monster of perpetual secession, come to devour its creator. There are other meanings, and other uses.

Neither do the rights appropriate the spaces of autonomy, that notion of accommodation so often grudgingly offered and ungratefully accepted.[57] Autonomy is referred to in key texts such as the CSCE/OSCE Copenhagen Document, with a thin watery applause not a ringing cheer in the auditorium of minority rights. It is not mandated by international law as a solution to minority problems, and many would reject it for reasons similar to a rejection of self-determination, even though the two are not the same. In some areas of the world, such as Central Europe, the word "autonomy" carries an electric charge.[58] If autonomy is a good thing, as most concede that it is, it may still be strategic to practise autonomy in stringent circumstances under alternative conceptual banners.

In the specific context of indigenous peoples, as represented by ILO 169, the terminology of autonomy is not adopted but there are functional equivalents in its portfolio of collective rights. The draft Declaration on Indigenous Peoples only dabbles in the currency of autonomy – as noted, self-determination is the preferred discourse. So, actually or prospectively, the indigenous participate in a broader rights discourse than minorities.[59]

. . . And came away changed . . .

Minority rights, and the rights of indigenous peoples, offer a challenge to many orthodoxies, as heresiarchs among the faithful, who in course of time may become the new orthodox. It is clear that few areas of international law, and not only human rights, will remain unaffected by the developments. International law constantly discovers or uncovers new foci of oppression and undertakes fresh readings of social reality. Despite impressions to the contrary, minority rights are not a focus for Eurocentricity. There is something positive in the rights for the vast ramifications of inter-communal relations, wherever the communities are located. Like international law itself, or human rights, origins are not crucial. What is crucial is the development of a common language by which situations and processes can be addressed as lived aspects of our common humanity. The prescriptions of minority rights can be translated into global and regional space. They can be valid for Africa and Asia. The instruments do not require that the precise vocabulary of minority rights be adopted in every State whatever its history or cultural proclivities. What it does require is that the underlying rights are respected. States will find it difficult. The rights do not only challenge the national community to provide space for minority identity, they also transfigure the identity of the nation itself. Many governments and peoples will find this disturbing, uncanny – the nation is familiar and strange at the same time. The State is not what it was, with the new identity conception superimposed on the old – consider the map of Australia before Mabo[60] and after.[61] Minority rights and the rights of the indigenous pose a challenge to international law as have the rights of women and perhaps the assertions of cultural relativism.[62] Of course they intersect with these perspectives – not always coherently – and read local, national and international affairs through their special dialect. The essays in the present volume reveal many of the opportunities and perplexities of the new canon, in terms of setting standards, conflict resolution and conflict avoidance. There is more to come in standard-setting, to elaborate what is, and to rectify mistakes – the reflection will continue.[63] Standard-setting in minority rights, and the other uses to which the rights may be put, are not only for the universalists. Bilateral and limited multilateral arrangements also have their place,[64] as well as the vital translation of rights into domestic law. The evolution of minority rights and the thinking and practice that goes with it has the potential to transform legal and social routine. The intergovernmental organisations are presently making a considerable effort to translate law into practice. Civil society follows suit. The hope is that the new prescriptions grafted on to the old will percolate through to the mundane and the everyday, to the stuff of existence. The hope is that the exploded energy of ethnicity and religious passion will burst into affirmative practices through the matrix of a reformed discourse.

AND AFTER THE CHANGED WORDS, THE MILLENNIUM?

The millennium gone has seen the emergence of rights discourse, through theology, natural law and the remorseless advance of secular philosophy. This oratory found its way into universal international law only recently. It is always challenged by new *'isms'*, but the flow continues. The assertion of rights was never congruent with the practice of rights. The ideal is always one step ahead of the real world and oppression is a sad constant in human affairs. Minorities feel the force of this truth. But the language of human rights is perhaps the only transcultural legal language we now possess. After a hiatus, minority rights have entered the discourse of human rights and this is important.

Italo Calvino characterised the next millennium as lightness, quickness, exactitude, visibility and multiplicity.[65] He was discussing literary values but we can adapt his phrases to our subject. In minority rights language – millennially – our approach to culture and language may become lighter as the heaviness of State-building lifts off, quicker as experience is shared and good rights practices emulated, more exact as we understand better the requirements of rights language and the full meaning of the interpolation of minority rights. Minorities are increasingly visible, societies multiple. The greatest defect of recent international law – and the domestic law which suggested and mimicked it – was the extra weight it laid on the shoulders of weak and vulnerable groups struggling for existence. It gave little understanding or assistance to resist the evils of forced assimilation, genocide, ethnic cleansing and all the rest. Human rights were for everyone, but for no one in particular. That was the plague of the absence of minority rights, the heaviness. It is a little better now, if still speculative and hesitant, with evidence of generosity and parsimony.[66] The reformation of international law in progress has the promise to assist in developing the understanding and the means to lighten the burden and encourage the survival of cultures over the millennium bridge. Then they can be light and quick and multiple. It will be too late for some groups, some languages, not destined but forced to disappear, in the cruel continuum of ethnocidal practices, though many will survive the crossing.

NOTES

*Professor of International Law, University of Keele

1.   Seamus Heaney, "To A Dutch Potter in Ireland", in *The Spirit Level* (1996).
2.   P. Thornberry, *International Law and the Rights of Minorities* (1991), Part I.
3.   Hence the title of an early speculative article by the author, "Is There a Phoenix in

the Ashes ? – International Law and Minority Rights", *15 Texas International Law Journal* (1980) 421-58.

4. See for example Flann O'Brien's *The Third Policeman* and *The Dalkey Archive* for some ruminations of the great thinker.

5. For a review, see A. Cassese, *International Law in a Divided World* (1986), *passim*.

6. For a reconnaissance of effects of the demarcations on the principles of self-determination and minority rights, see A. Cassese, *Self-Determination of Peoples; A Legal Reappraisal* (1995); C. Tomuschat (ed.), *Modern Law of Self-Determination* (1993).

7. Some of the longstanding bilateral arrangements are included in a relatively early UN document, *Protection of Minorities; Special Protective Measures of an International Character for Ethnic, Religious or Linguistic Groups* (New York: United Nations, 1967), UN Sales No.: 67.XIV.3.

8. R.A. Williams Jr., *The American Indian in Western Legal Thought; The Discourses of Conquest* (1990).

9. Hence the development of the "Belgian Thesis", discussed by the present author in "Self-determination, Minorities, Human Rights: A Review of International Instruments", 38 *International and Comparative Law Quarterly* (1989) 867-89.

10. By A. Nenarokov and A. Proskurin (1983). The Bolsheviks were great "experts" on nationality questions, with lamentable historical results, see J. Stalin, *Marxism and the National Question* (1950); V. I. Lenin, *The Right of Nations to Self-Determination* (1947, seventh printing, 1979).

11. The original draft for the UN Declaration on Minority Rights was presented by Yugoslavia: UN Doc. E/CN.4/L.1367/Rev.1, 2 March 1978; see also the revised and consolidated draft, UN Doc. E/CN.4/Sub.2/L.734, 2 July 1980.

12. Reflected, among many expressions of international disapproval of the Apartheid regime, in the International Convention on the Suppression and Punishment of the Crime of Apartheid, 1973.

13. Article 14 of the Convention prohibits discrimination on the grounds, *inter alia* of "association with a national minority".

14. The most notable is the Framework Convention for the Protection of National Minorities, opened for signature on 1 February 1995; the Convention entered into force in February 1998. For a discussion of the genesis and attributes of the framework Convention, see A. Spiliopoulou-Åkermark, *Justifications of Minority Protection in International Law* (1997), chapter 8; F. Benôit-Rohmer, *The Minority Question in Europe; Texts and Commentary* (1996).

15. F. Capotorti, *Study on the Rights of Persons Belonging to Ethnic, Religious and Linguistic Minorities*, UN Doc. E/CN.4/Sub.2/384/Rev.1, 1979, UN Sales No. E.78.XIV.1.

16. Communication No. 24/1977, Views of the Human Rights Committee in UN Doc. A/36/40 (1981).

17. Spiliopoulou-Åkermark, *supra* n. 14, at 157-74.

18. L. Swepston, "A New Step in the International Law on Indigenous and Tribal Peoples: ILO Convention No. 169 of 1989", *15 Oklahoma City University Law Review* (1990) 677-714.

19. Developments are captured in V. Van Dyke, *Human Rights, Ethnicity, and Discrimination* (1985).

20. An excellent spectrum of essays is presented in W. Kymlicka (ed.), *The Rights of Minority Cultures* (1995).

21. Notably Article 30 of the United Nations Convention on the Rights of the Child [1990] dealing with the children of minorities and the indigenous.
22. The chronology is detailed in P. Thornberry, "The UN Declaration on the Rights of Persons belonging to National or Ethnic, Religious and Linguistic Minorities: Background, Analysis, and an Update", in A. Phillips and A. Rosas (eds.), *Universal Minority Rights* (1995) 13-76.
23. The point is made sharply in I. Brownlie, edited by F.M. Brookfield, *Treaties and Indigenous Peoples* (1992).
24. In this essay, I have not attempted to speculate on the nature of the rights constituencies suggested by "minority" and "indigenous". A paper carrying the title "Who is Indigenous ?" will be published in 1998 by the Northern Institute for Environmental and Minority Law at the University of Lapland in Rovaniemi.
25. The Convention applies to certain depredations directed against "a national, ethnical, racial or religious group" – Article II.
26. See the essay by the present author in Tomuschat (ed.), *supra* n. 6.
27. See A. Spiliopoulou- Åkermark, *supra* n. 14.
28. Article 27.
29. Article 5(1)c.
30. See N. Lerner, *Group Rights and Discrimination in International Law* (1991).
31. I adopt the notion expressed by R. Dworkin in *Taking Rights Seriously* (second edition, 1978).
32. Before the UN Human Rights Committee, *Kitok v Sweden*, Communication No. 197/1985, Views of the Committee in UN doc. A/43/40 (1988).
33. See the useful discussion in M.J. Perry, "Are Human Rights Universal ? The Relativist Challenge and Related Matters", *19 Human Rights Quarterly* (1997) 461-509.
34. See, for example, Article 1 of the UN Declaration on the Rights of Persons belonging to . . . Minorities, promulgated by UN general Assembly resolution 47/135, 18 December 1992.
35. Article 1(2) of ILO Convention No. 169 on Indigenous and Tribal Peoples in Independent Countries provides: "Self-identification as indigenous or tribal shall be regarded as a fundamental criterion for determining the groups to which the provisions of this Convention apply".
36. See, for example, Article 3(2) of the UN Declaration on Minority Rights; and Article 3(1) of the Council of Europe's Framework Convention, both of which relate to the exercise of rights by members of minorities as matters of choice by individuals. Paragraph 32 of the Copenhagen Document of the OSCE Human Dimension bites deeper in providing that "To *belong to a national minority* is a matter of a person's individual choice and no disadvantage may arise from the exercise of such choice" (present author's emphasis).
37. There is an interesting discussion of some key issues in Spiliopoulou-Åkermark, *supra* n. 14, chapters 3 and 4.
38. According to Article 1(1) of the UNESCO Declaration on the Principles of International Cultural Co-Operation: "Each culture has a dignity and value which must be respected".
39. See the citation in n. 35, *supra*.
40. Article 3(1) of the UN Declaration on Minority Rights: "Persons belonging to minorities may exercise their rights, including those set forth in this declaration, individually as well as in community with other members of their group, without any

discrimination". The point on cultures as contexts of choice echoes W. Kymlicka, *Multicultural Citizenship: A Liberal Theory of Minority Rights* (1995).

41. N. Lerner, "The Evolution of Minority Rights in International Law", in C. Brölmann, R. Lefeber and M. Zieck (eds.), *Peoples and Minorities in International Law* (1993) 77-101; and the remarks to the contrary by M. Nowak, in Brölmann *et al* (eds.), *ibid.*, 103-18.

42. For example, Article 5(2) of the Framework Convention.

43. These *topoi* emerge and re-emerge in the instruments on minority rights – the UN Declaration on Minority Rights carries most of them.

44. For some typical issues, see the *Follow-up Report on Traditional Practices Affecting the Health of Women and Children*, Special Rapporteur Mrs. Halima Embarek Warzazi, UN Doc. E/CN.4/Sub.2/1997/10.

45. C. Taylor, "The Politics of Recognition", in A. Gutmann (ed.), *Multiculturalism and the Politics of Recognition* (1992), cited by M. J. Perry, *supra* n. 33, at 489.

46. Paragraph 7 of the General Comment No. 23 (1994) of the Human Rights Committee on Article 27 of the International Covenant on Civil and Political Rights, in UN Doc. A/49/40, Vol. I, 107-110.

47. Notably Article 11 of the Framework Convention.

48. "There is no place outside the Tobique reserve where such a community exists" – Human Rights Committee in *Lovelace*, *supra* n. 16, at paragraph 15.

49. This theme emerges very strongly in the Council of Europe Framework Convention on National Minorities, *supra* n. 14.

50. Minority Rights Group (ed.), *World Directory of Minorities* (1997) 682-84.

51. General Comment 3 (13) can be read in *Manual on Human Rights Reporting* (1991), 83-85. For a more recent compilation of General Comments, see *Compilation of General Comments and General Recommendations Adopted by Human Rights Treaty Bodies*, UN Doc. HRI/GEN/1/Rev.3, 15 August 1997.

52. General Comment 3 of the Committee on Economic, Social and Cultural Rights. For broader comment, see M.C.R. Craven, *The International Covenant on Economic, Social, and Cultural Rights: A Perspective on its Development* (1995).

53. See, for example, the recent elaboration by experts of international legal principles in *The Hague Recommendations Regarding the Education Rights of National Minorities* (1996).

54. The collection of essays in *Tomuschat* (ed.), *supra* n 6, still represents the most comprehensive elaboration of the ramifications of this relationship.

55. Common Article 1 of the International Covenants on human Rights is only one in the enormous number of elaborations of this principle.

56. Article 3 of the UN draft Declaration on the Rights of Indigenous Peoples, UN Doc. E/CN.4/Sub.2/1994/2/Add.1.

57. H. Hannum, *Autonomy, Sovereignty, and Self-Determination – The Accommodation of Conflicting Rights* (1990).

58. Hence the famous "1201 question" – a reference to that recommendation of the Parliamentary Assembly of the Council of Europe, which contained, in Article 11, a guarded affirmation of a right to autonomy. Hungarian diplomacy in particular attempted to transcribe 1201 into its bilateral treaties with neighbouring States and convert it into binding domestic law. Various strategies were adopted in the ensuing rows to downgrade the importance of the recommendation.

59. And some minorities such as the Boers would like to get in on the act. It is possible

that international law will develop rules of closure to prevent the undue appropriation of the larger ground by minorities, perhaps in the form of stringent definitions.

60. *Mabo v State* of Queensland (1992) CLR 1; Native Title Act 1993. Native title claims may cover a considerable part of the Australian landmass in the light of Mabo: see Minority Rights Group, *World Directory of Minorities, supra* n. 50, 658-64.

61. J. Jacobs and K. Gelder, "Uncanny Australia", *2 Ecumene* (1995) 71-84. Consider the 1996 cases of *The Wik Peoples v The State of Queensland and The Thayorre People v The State of Queensland before* the High Court of Australia: http://www.austlii.edu.au/au/cases/cth/high_ct/unrep299.html.

62. See the copious extracts from recent work in H. Steiner and P. Alston, *International Human Rights in Context: Law, Politics, Morals* (1996), chapters 4 (cultural relativism) and 13 (rights of women).

63. To follow The Hague Recommendations, *supra* n. 53, the Foundation on Inter-Ethnic Relations completed a set of recommendations on the language rights of national minorities.

64. There has been an explosion of bilateralism in Central and Eastern Europe in association with the Balladur Initiative and the Stability Pact. Many of the new treaties have significant sections on minority rights, and some instruments are devoted entirely to this issue. The Budapest-based Constitutional and Legislative Policy Institute will shortly publish a compilation and analyses of the treaties and declarations under the editorship of Prof. A. Bloed. The present author has contributed a chapter on Hungarian treaties and declarations. See, also, F. Benoit-Rohmer, *supra* n. 14, chapter 6.

65. I. Calvino, *Six Memos for the Next Millennium* (1996).

66. As expressed in limiting interpretations of "minority" entered by some States in ratifying the Framework Convention, and the emulation of the denial by France of the existence of minorities on its territory (for purposes of the ICCPR and the CRC) by Venezuela and Turkey - comment by the author in A. Phillips and A. Rosas, *supra* n. 22, at 21.

Minority Rights in the 'New' Europe: An Introduction

Steven Wheatley and Peter Cumper

As we approach the new millennium and commentators cast their minds back to the tumultuous events which dominated Europe in the twentieth century, it is hard not to be struck by the number of conflicts involving the persecution, or alleged mistreatment, of ethnic, racial, linguistic or religious minority groups: the events in the Balkans which precipitated the First World War, Hitler's aggression in the name of protecting the German speaking minorities of Eastern Europe, the Holocaust, successive Soviet Pogroms, and, more recently, ethnic cleansing in Bosnia and civil war in Chechnya and Kosovo.

At the start of the 1990's, it was assumed that such tragedies might prove to have been a thing of the past. The much hailed, and ultimately short lived, 'New World Order', celebrated in the aftermath of the collapse of the Soviet Empire, had began in Europe with the symbolic demolition of the Berlin Wall. Totalitarian regimes collapsed across the continent. The leaders of Europe's democracies hailed the triumph of liberal 'Western European' values, including individualism, pluralism and cosmopolitanism. Inevitably, efforts were made in this 'New' Europe to resolve the 'issue of minorities', which traditionally had blighted efforts at creating a peaceful and stable continent. Within most European states, there was a general acceptance that not only *human* rights, but also *minority* rights, had to be respected both in theory *and* in practice. International standards relating to human rights and the rule of law came to be recognised as the essential prerequisites for international legitimacy, internal stability and economic success in this 'New' Europe, and certain policies were regarded as incompatible with its ethos: those which fostered totalitarianism, racial hatred, anti-Semitism, xenophobia and discrimination or persecution on religious and ideological grounds.[1]

The governments and peoples of this 'New' Europe were, therefore, expected to be tolerant of diversity and respectful of difference. However, perhaps in view of the region's violent and bloody past, all of these grand hopes proved unrealistic and the 'New' Europe has, at least so far, failed

15

P. Cumper and S. Wheatley (eds.), Minority Rights in the 'New' Europe, 15–28
© 1999 *Kluwer Law International. Printed in Great Britain.*

to fulfil the expectations of those who had thought that the end of the Cold War might usher in a period of unprecedented co-operation and peace. The re-emergence of latent nationalisms and xenophobia has, as Boris Yeltsin (President of the Russian Federation) noted, created the very real danger of Europe "plunging into a cold peace".[2] Most notably, in those states in Central and Eastern Europe which have, in the past, witnessed tensions between minorities and other groups, the re-awakening of national consciousness has meant that individuals have associated themselves increasingly with the group to which they and their families have traditionally belonged, thereby rejecting notions of civic identity derived from citizenship of the state. This assertion of national identity, sometimes, but not always, accompanied by irredentist rhetoric, provoked in many instances – or at least provided the excuse for – repressive measures on the part of certain state authorities in Central and Eastern Europe, which were fearful of secessionist claims. The conflicts which resulted from these clashes between the state and minority groups led to a deterioration of relations not only within such states, but also with neighbouring states, particularly where the neighbouring state shared some ethnic, or other, allegiance with the minority – the so-called 'kin states'.[3] The clearest failings of the 'New' Europe occurred where a political elite, in many instances former Communist rulers, sought to retain power by adopting nationalistic policies, promoting the interests of the majority populations at the expense of those of the minority. Indeed, in the former Yugoslavia much of the blame for the conflict and subsequent disintegration of the State may be blamed on the pursuance of such policies by the Croatian and Serbian political elites, who, at the time of writing, are still in power.

One of the many lessons which may be learnt from the conflict in the former Yugoslavia, and other states experiencing similar problems, is that the violation of the rights of the minority groups within the state may, in many cases, be part of a wider problem of a lack of respect for human rights *per se*. A state which disregards the human rights of all its citizens is unlikely to be greatly concerned with the particular rights of its minority communities. Whilst most of the governments of the 'New' Europe may pay lip service to the desirability of appropriate human and minority rights protection,[4] the reality is one of less than perfect compliance.[5]

In the many states which have recently gained their independence (either *de facto* or *de jure*), but particularly in the states of the former Soviet Union, except Russia, the nations' political leaders have generally been much more willing to promote the creation of a clear and visible identity for the State – notably in the drive to replace Russian as the official language – than in the adoption of measures to protect and guarantee the rights of what may be seen as 'troublesome' and 'irredentist' minorities. This is perhaps understandable in those states where the 'indigenous' national culture was denigrated at the expense of the Russian culture and language during the period of the Soviet Empire, and where the culture of that state may be seen as vulnerable within a wider contemporary European context. But such understanding cannot, and should not, be seen in any way as legitimising discriminatory treatment against that part of the population associated with the former political elite. The Russian minorities in the states of the former Soviet Empire also have rights. In particular, the restrictions placed on the acquisition of citizenship in such states, which have created large numbers of stateless peoples and disenfranchised the Russian minority populations from the political process, have, quite rightly, been the source of much concern and criticism.

The challenge of striking a fair and equitable balance between the rights of the minority and the majority population are, of course, not peculiar to the final decade of the twentieth century, nor to Europe: the reality of the global community has, in recent times, been one in which the multi-ethnic state is the norm. Attempts to create homogenous states at the end of the First World War out of Europe's nationalities palpably failed (and indeed such attempts are being seen to fail today – most strikingly in the former Yugoslavia), as did the scheme adopted to provide minority guarantees for those individuals who remained outside of their 'nation'. It is probably unsurprising therefore that, following the Second World War, the United Nations and the Council of Europe concentrated, not on minority rights but upon human rights for all, seeking to guarantee minority rights through provisions on non-discrimination. Any specific or explicit reference to minority rights was absent from the United Nations Universal Declaration on Human Rights (1948), and from the provisions of the Council of Europe's European Convention on Human Rights (1950). Indeed it was not until 1966, with the adoption of the International Covenant on Civil and Political Rights (ICCPR), that minority rights were given recognition within the corpus of the international legal regime:

> In those states in which ethnic, religious or linguistic minorities exist, persons belonging to such minorities shall not be denied the right, in community with the other members of their group, to enjoy their own culture, to profess and practice their own religion, or to use their own language (Article 27, ICCPR 1966).

The (minority) right contained in Article 27 is, like all other minority rights, individual in character, granting each individual the right to choose to identify him/herself with the group, and this identity may not be imposed.[6] However, once the group has been identified, the members of that group enjoy the right, individually and collectively,[7] to the protection and promotion of the identity of that group to which they belong. This right to identity, provided for in Article 27 of the ICCPR, has been elaborated upon, both by the UN Human Rights Committee,[8] and in a number of international documents and instruments such as the Council of Europe's Framework Convention on the Rights of National Minorities (1994), the OSCE's (CSCE) Copenhagen Document on the Human Dimension (1990) and the United Nations General Assembly Declaration on the Rights of Persons Belonging to National or Ethnic, Religious and Linguistic Minorities (1992). (A selection of extracts form international instruments concerned with minority rights may be found at the back of this book.) Taken together, these instruments provide a body of principles which give meaning to the general right to identity. The key rights in this context relate to issues of language,[9] educa-tion,[10] culture[11] and unimpeded contacts (irrespective of territorial borders) with those whom the group shares an ethnic, or other, bond,[12] as well as the right to participate in the decision making process, where the decision is likely to have an impact upon the group.[13]

Notwithstanding the symbolic value of such rights, they may be considered 'minimalistic', and unlikely, in reality, to assist in the preservation of a minority's culture and identity. Few minority groups have the financial resources themselves (or the patronage of an economically wealthy 'kin-state') to support private educational institutions[14] or thriving cultural societies or festivals. Such groups require financial, and other, assistance from the state. However, the international mechanisms grant a wide discretion to the state in its adoption and application of minority rights provisions, with the consequence that the extent to which minority rights are recognised remains, in most cases, a legitimate and exclusive aspect of state policy. In this context minority rights may be termed *aspirational* – not in the sense of economic, social and cultural rights, whereby the state must 'take steps' progressively to achieve the full realisation of the rights, but that these are 'rights' to which a minority may *aspire*. For this reason, amongst others, it is clearly of great importance that the minority group is able to influence the determination of state policy, either through the adoption of some form of power sharing within government, the establishment of autonomous regimes, or the creation of a genuinely inclusive pluralist democracy. In other words, the guarantee of the right of the minority group to effective political participation may be just as important as the substantive provisions contained in the international instruments.

Whatever the limitations of the provisions on minority rights, in the 'New' Europe it is recognised that ethnic, religious and linguistic minority groups enjoy a right to self-realisation and, in contrast to the inter-war scheme, that minority rights are universal and not specific to a limited number of groups. Minority rights are those rights which are granted to members of minority groups in recognition of their difference from the general population, for the purpose of protecting and promoting that difference.[15]

One of the perennial problems associated with any inquiry into minority rights is the question of definition: what is a 'minority' group for the purposes of protection under international law. As well as the seeming division between 'minorities',[16] 'national minorities',[17] and 'peoples',[18] the term 'minority could legitimately include, for the purposes of this present collection, persons defined as belonging to minority groups by reference to such factors as sexuality, disability and gender.[19] This work, however, does not seek to deal with the latter groups, but instead concentrates upon the jurisprudence developed in respect of ethnic, racial, linguistic and religious minorities within the 'New' Europe. The reasons for this are two fold: the constraints of space, and the fact that the international community, rightly or not, responds more readily to conflict which have been caused by ethnic differences rather than (violent) conflicts within society as the result of discrimination against other minority groups on the basis, *inter alia*, of class, sexuality, disability and gender. The main consequence of this has been the development of a more comprehensive body of rules and principles in relation to ethnic, linguistic and religious minorities, which may, in turn, be examined.

And what of the regional coverage of this book? The 'New' Europe in the title of this work is political, not geographical. It refers to those states which are members of the Council of Europe and the Organisation for Security and Co-Operation in Europe (excluding the United States and Canada), thereby encompassing all states within Central, Eastern and Western Europe as well as those states within Central Asia which were formerly part of the Soviet Union. However, notwithstanding the breadth of its ambit, it is not intended that this book should provide a survey as to the situation facing the differing minority groups within Europe, a task which has been undertaken more effectively by the Minority Rights Group in their *World Directory of Minorities*.[20] The areas covered here reflect the fact that the Council of Europe and the OSCE have, almost uniquely in international law, developed a comprehensive body of principles which may be applied in the resolution of minority issues, although the adoption by the General Assembly of the Declaration on the Rights of Minorities[21] may auger in a more 'universalist' regime.

The aim of this book is four fold: first, to examine the institutional response to the protection of minority rights in the 'New' Europe; secondly, to consider the development of minority rights, in general, in this area; thirdly, to analyse their application to particular situations and to consider what lessons can be learnt for the future, and finally to consider the relationship between minority rights and conflict resolution, in which the primary aim of any agreement between the minority and the state will be the resolution of the conflict. In the latter, it is inevitable that the mechanisms which are adopted in the resolution of the conflict may be less than ideal and should not be regarded as any 'blueprint' for minority rights protection generally, but rather as temporary measures to be adopted until the full realisation of a peaceful, heterogeneous democratic society may be achieved.

The book is split into six sections, including this introductory one. We are particularly grateful to Max van der Stoel, the OSCE High Commissioner on National Minorities, for writing the *Foreword* to the collection, and to Professor Thornberry for the introductory remarks (P. Thornberry, *Introduction: In the Strongroom of Vocabulary*). Both pieces enable the reader to place the aspects of minority rights, considered in the following chapters, within their wider context. The subsequent sections deal with the following issues relating to minorities in the 'New' Europe: the institutional response; the content of certain minority rights; the challenges posed in the exercise of state building; and finally, the issue of minority rights generally, and conflict resolution. Finally, at the end of the book, a collection of documents, which complement these chapters and are relevant to minority rights in the 'New' Europe, can be found.

The attempts of the 'New' Europe to deal with the question of minority rights through both its legal and political institutions, the Council of Europe and the Organisation for Security and Co-Operation in Europe, are considered in the section entitled *The Institutional Response of the 'New' Europe*. The workings of the OSCE institutions with regard to minority rights are examined initially (*Minority Protection and the Organisation for Security and Co-operation in Europe*, María Amor Martin Estébanez). Estébanez considers the role of the OSCE in the development of international standards relating to national minority groups, and the unique mechanisms for ensuring the effective implementation of the standards adopted. Moreover, she examines the workings of the primary organs of the OSCE, and concludes that whilst the institutions may be required to develop their role in this context, the OSCE nevertheless remains a crucial international institution through which minority rights may be effectively protected.

The Council of Europe, on the other hand, has been more tentative in its approach to the issue of minority rights protection, particularly in its rejection of an additional protocol on minority rights to the European Convention on Human Rights (1950), instead concluding the Framework Convention (1994), whose "weak obligations and weak monitoring render [it], as it stands, almost worthless as a means of guaranteeing minority rights within the Council of Europe" (G. Gilbert, *Minority Rights Under the Council of Europe*). In his chapter Professor Gilbert examines the jurisprudence developed by the institutions of the Council of Europe, notably the European Court and the Commission [on Human Rights], for the protection of minorities under the European Convention on Human Rights. He concludes that, despite some tentative successes, the OSCE's mechanisms, in particular the office of the High Commissioner on National Minorities, are better designed and equipped to achieve the effective protection of minority rights, in view of the lack of political will amongst states to conclude effective legally binding agreements on the issue. The workings of the Framework Convention are further examined in the context of the enforcement mechanism which have been adopted (G. Oberleitner, *Monitoring Minority Rights under the Council of Europe's Framework Convention*). Oberleitner considers the monitoring mechanism adopted under the Framework Convention and, through consideration of the workings of other reporting mechanisms, the necessary pre-requisites for its effective operation. He argues that it is unfortunate that the Council of Europe did not take sufficient account of the experiences of other reporting systems when working out the details of the reporting mechanism adopted, and concludes that the Committee of Ministers of the Council of Europe – the body entrusted with overseeing states' compliance with the Framework Convention – will have to demonstrate through the working practices which it adopts (particularly in the role and functions it assigns to the Advisory Committee) whether, or not, it is serious about monitoring minority rights in Europe.

The following chapter examines the tentative steps undertaken by the European Union in its dealings with minority groups, both inside and outside of the Union (A. Biscoe, *The European Union and Minority Nations*). Biscoe argues that the European Union's approach to minority nations has been rather ambiguous, in that the EU has supported the 'group rights' of minority nations out-side of the European Union, but that within the EU it has been much more committed to an 'individual rights' approach. He concludes his examination of the measures undertaken by the European Union, in seeking to protect minority rights, by questioning the ability of an organisation which emphasises de-regulation and is pre-eminently concerned with the rights of individuals to provide effective protection for its own internal minority 'nations'.

Whilst clearly not part of the 'institutional' response of the 'New' Europe, the role of states themselves in establishing bilateral mechanisms for the protection of minority rights is a significant new development which is considered appropriate for consideration at this point (I. Pogany, *Bilateralism versus Regionalism in the Resolution of Minorities Problems in Central and*

Eastern Europe and in the Post-Soviet States). Pogany considers the principal advantages of bilateralism, examining Hungary's Bilateral Treaties with Slovakia and Romania. He argues that a bilateral approach to minority rights protection is a useful supplement to the universalist approach of the UN and the regional approaches of the Council of Europe and OSCE, in that it provides for greater specificity in the elaboration of minority rights, recognises the reality that certain minority issues have a bilateral dimension and provides a means of enhancing the confidence of the group.

The Content of Rights in the 'New' Europe considers the developments and application of certain key minority rights: non-discrimination, preferential treatment, the rights of religious minorities and cultural rights. In the first chapter, in this section, the attempts of the United Kingdom Government to deal with allegations of discrimination within Northern Ireland are considered by Professor Hadfield, who considers the operation of Part III of the Northern Ireland Constitution Act 1973 (B. Hadfield, *The Northern Ireland Constitution Act 1973: Lessons for Minority Rights*). Professor Hadfield reviews the operation of the Act in detail, and notes the deficiencies of a system which relies upon individual, rather than institutional, enforcement. She concludes that, even when taken with other provisions the legislation may not be taken to "add up to a Charter of Human Rights" for Northern Ireland.

Measures aimed at dealing with the problem of discrimination in the past are then considered in the next chapter, where the issue of preferential treatment for members of ethnic and other minority groups is addressed by Professor Edwards (J. Edwards, *Preferential Treatment and the Rights to Equal Consideration*). He examines the moral and ethical claims for preferential treatment, arguing that such practices may be criticised on both practical and philosophical grounds. Professor Edwards considers, however, that the main criticism of such schemes is that the right to preferential treatment is one which attaches to the group. In other words, as it is the group which enjoys the right to compensation for the past discrimination, such a right cannot, in any meaningful way, be attached or transferred to an individual beneficiary. The adoption of any practice of preferential treatment therefore, he argues, must recognise that the benefit achieved, as a result of the practice, may well be at the expense of the individual right to equal consideration.

The rights of religious minorities, and in particular new religious movements, are considered by Cumper (P. Cumper, *The Rights of Religious Minorities: The Legal Regulation of New Religious Movements*). He suggests that the ways in which unorthodox and controversial religious movements are treated can be one way by which the tolerance of the 'New' Europe to minorities may be measured.

The final chapter in this section considers the legal status of the cultural rights of national minorities (W. Mannens, *The International Status of Cultural Rights for National Minorities*). Mannens examines the nature of cultural rights, and the initiatives adopted by the international community in determining the nature and scope of the right of such groups to their 'culture'. He argues that despite much work previously undertaken, the international community must redouble its efforts to elaborate the exact content of what is meant by 'culture', which Mannens considers to be synonymous with identity, if that right is to have any real meaning.

The third section, *The Challenges of State Building in the 'New' Europe*, examines issues of power sharing, democratic government and the development of autonomous regimes as methods by which the internal organisation of the state may be altered to achieve a resolution of disputes involving minority groups; the section also examines the particular problems of Ukraine, in its development as a modern state. Wheatley considers recent developments in international practice concerning the introduction of power sharing regimes, and seeks to examine why such schemes are incompatible with the proper and effective protection of human rights (S. Wheatley, *Minority Rights, Power Sharing and the Modern Democratic State*). He then examines how a more inclusive concept of pluralist and participatory democratic government may assist the minority group in achieving its basic and other needs, concluding that, certainly in the case of larger national minority groups, the state should establish formal mechanisms and institutions for consultation with the group. Rehman, on the other hands, considers how the introduction of autonomous regimes by the state may assist in the solution of minority problems (J. Rehman, *The Concept of Autonomy and Minority Rights in Europe*). He examines the conceptual problems in defining what is meant by autonomy and examines the history of its application in Europe, including consideration of its inclusion (or lack thereof) in the recently adopted instruments. Rehman considers that the association – at least in the minds of governments – of autonomy with secession has led to a reluctance on the part of states to introduce a right to autonomy within the corpus of the international jurisprudence on minority rights.

The issue of minority rights in the post-Soviet state of Ukraine is examined in two chapters: M. Antonyvch, *The Rights of National Minorities in Ukraine*: An Introduction; and W. Bowring, *New Nations and National Minorities: Ukraine and the Question of Citizenship*. In her work, Antonyvch, considers the history of minority rights protection in Ukraine this century, examining past and present attempts by this state, in which more than 100 nationalities exist, to accommodate the differing demands and claims of such groups. She examines the legislation which has been adopted, and concludes that, notwithstanding present difficulties, Ukraine has been more successful in dealing with the issue of minorities than most of the other states of the former Soviet Union. One of the minorities mentioned in Antonyvch's chapter, the Crimean Tartars, are considered in some detail by Bowring, within the context of minority rights protection more generally in Europe. The Crimean Tartars, a people deported *en masse* in 1944 – when 40 per cent of the population died – are today, in many cases, prevented from acquiring Ukrainian citizenship as the result of restrictive citizenship laws. In his consideration of the claims of the Crimean Tartars to citizenship, for all members of the group, Bowring argues that the liberal, individualistic view of minority rights (the prevalent view amongst legal scholars) is unable to deal with such situations, as it fails to recognise the collective rights of such groups. Consequently, he concludes that a radical transformation and extension of existing legal instruments is required to take account of group rights and demands, which can provide a framework within which the successful resolution of minority issues may be achieved.

The final section of the book considers the issue of *Conflict Resolution and Minority Rights*. In her work on the Dayton accord, Mertus examines the similarities between the scheme adopted at Dayton and that imposed in the aftermath of the First World War (J. Mertus, *The Dayton Peace Accords: Lessons from the Past and for the Future*). In doing so, she explores the role that national identity played in the break up of the former Yugoslavia, and the attempts by those concluding the settlement to impose new identities on the peoples of Bosnia-Herzegovina – a state geographically and constitutionally divided along ethno-nationalist lines. She argues, however, that it will not be the success of the legal innovations adopted at Dayton, nor their similarities to those in past history, which will determine the success, or otherwise, of the accord, but rather the political will of those involved which will make the agreement work.

In a chapter which further draws upon the experiences of the former Yugoslavia, and in particular the impact of the recourse of the various parties to international rules and principles – in this case territorial integrity and self-determination – Basic, *et al.,* seek to examine, through the use of game theory, how the present operation of the international legal system exacerbates minority/majority disputes, and how such conflicts almost inevitably lead to conflict (N. Basic, D. J. Fleming and W M. Vaughn, *International Legal Order and Minority/Government Conflict*). They further consider how the international legal system may be restructured, through the introduction of an element which demands that both sides respect the human rights of the other, to encourage the parties to make rational choices which will reduce the likelihood of conflict in the future

The issue of the clash of international legal principles is also considered in the final chapter of the book, in the context of Northern Ireland where the issues of territorial integrity, self-determination and human/minority rights are considered in their potential application to this conflict (C. Bell, *Minority Rights and Conflict Resolution in Northern Ireland*). In her chapter, Bell argues that the application of 'neutral' principles of international law to such tribal situations may be expected to achieve a more just resolution of the dispute, than one which relies upon a negotiated settlement, where the agreement is concluded as the result of a series of concessions and counter-concessions – irrespective of the merits of the claims being made, or of the concessions granted.

Most of the chapters in this book are based on versions of papers which were first delivered at a conference, in November 1996, at the Institute for Advanced Legal Studies in London. Although the book's editors are both legal academics from the British Isles, the contributors' backgrounds are diverse and varied, originating from a number of different countries, with expertise in a wide variety of areas.

And finally, as the 'New' Europe approaches the next millennium, the words of a British Prime Minister bear repeating:

> We shall never sheath the sword which we have not lightly drawn . . .
> until the rights of the smaller nationalities of Europe are placed upon
> an unassailable foundation.

Not Tony Blair in the late 1990's, but Herbert Asquith at the outset of the First World War. It is ironic how similar the sentiments expressed in the 'New' Europe are to those expressed earlier in the century, most notably after the Treaty of Versailles and the ill founded optimism associated with the creation of the League of Nations. In the years immediately after 1918, it appeared as if 'democracy' had won; but disillusionment with liberal democracy paved the way for totalitarianism, and this should provide present generations with a warning against complacency. Until the leaders of Europe can manage to devise a way of protecting all of the rights of minorities in Europe, the battles of previous years will continue to be re-fought by present and future generations, inevitably leading to conflicts, deaths, the mistreatment of innocent civilians, ethnic cleansing and the de-stabilisation of the regions in which they occur.

Although minorities have, in the past few years, been accorded unprecedented recognition under international law, the problem of balancing majority and minority rights remains. Not surprisingly, there are no clear or easy answers to this conundrum. It is, however, the hope of the editors that this book will, at least in some small way, contribute to the debate as to the challenges facing the 'New' Europe in terms of the protection it offers to minority groups.

NOTES

1. Document of the Copenhagen Meeting of the Conference on the Human Dimension of the CSCE (1990), 29 *ILM* (1990) 1318, at para. 40: "The participating States clearly and unequivocally condemn totalitarianism, racial and ethnic hatred, anti-semitism, xenophobia and discrimination against anyone as well as persecution on religious and ideological grounds. . .".

2. *Newsweek*, 19 December 1994.

3. These are what Mullerson calls 'Motherland' states. He notes that such states, which share an ethnic similarity with a minority group resident in another state, have no greater rights than any other under international law. They are, however, more likely to take an interest in issues relating to those minorities, and be more willing to make representations and even undertake interventions on behalf of that minority: R. Mullerson, "Minorities in Eastern Europe and the Former USSR: Problems, Tendencies and Protection", 56 *Modern Law Review* (1993) 793, at 808.

4. See, on this point, the unanimous adoption of the Copenhagen Document, *supra* n. 1, by the states of the (then) CSCE; the member states, at the time, were as follows: Austria, Belgium, Bulgaria, Canada, Cyprus, Czechoslovakia, Denmark, Finland, France, the German Democratic Republic, the Federal Republic of Germany, Greece, the Holy See, Hungary, Iceland, Ireland, Italy, Liechtenstein, Luxembourg, Malta, Monaco, the Netherlands, Norway, Poland, Portugal, Romania, San Marino, Spain, Sweden, Switzerland, Turkey, the Union of Soviet Socialist Republics, the United Kingdom, the United States of America and Yugoslavia.

5. On the position of the minorities within the 'New' Europe, see Minority Rights Group (ed.), *World Directory of Minoriites* (1997), chapters 3, 4 and 5.

6. The Framework Convention for the Protection of National Minorities (1994), Council of Europe, Stasbourg, 8 November 1994, 34 *ILM* (1994) 351, Article 3(1): "Every person belonging to a national minority shall have the right freely to choose to be treated or not to be treated as such . . . ". The Framework Convention was adopted in Strasbourg, on 8 November, 1994 and opened for signature on 1 February 1995, coming into force 1 February, 1998 (for purposes of consistency it will be referred to, in this work, as the Framework Convention for the Protection of National Minorities (1994)). As of 20 July 1998 the following States had ratified the Convention: Austria, Croatia, Cyprus, the Czech Republic, Denmark, Estonia, Finland, Germany, Hungary, Italy, Liechtenstein, Malta, Moldova, Romania, San Marino, Slovakia, Slovenia, Spain, 'the former Yugoslav Republic of Macedonia', Ukraine, and the United Kingdom.

7. See the Declaration on the Rights of Persons Belonging to National or Ethnic or Religious Minorities (1992), General Assembly Resolution 47/135, adopted 18 December 1992, Article 3 (1): "Persons belonging to minorities may exercise their rights, including those set forth in the present Declaration, *individually as well as in community with other members of their group*, without any discrimination (*emphasis added*)".

8. See, on this point, Thornberry, "*Introduction: In the Strongroom of Vocabulary*" (this work), at nn. 16 and 17, and accompanying text.

9. The General Assembly Declaration on Minorities, *supra* n. 7, Article 2(1): "Persons belonging to national or ethnic, religious and linguistic minorities . . . have the right . . . to use their own language, in private and in public, freely and without interference or any form of discrimination". See, also, Article 4 (3): "States should take appropriate measures so that, wherever possible, persons belonging to minorities may have adequate

opportunities to learn their mother tongue or to have instruction in their mother tongue".

10. The General Assembly Declaration on Minorities, *ibid.*, Article 4(4): "States should, where appropriate, take measures in the field of education, in order to encourage knowledge of the history, traditions, language and culture of the minorities existing within their territory. . .".

11. The General Assembly Declaration on Minorities, *ibid.*, Article 4(2): "States shall take measures to create favourable conditions to enable persons belonging to minorities to express their characteristics and to develop their culture, language, religion, traditions and customs, except where specific practices are in violation of national law and contrary to international standards".

12. The General Assembly Declaration on Minorities, *ibid.*, Article 5: "Persons belonging to minorities have the right to establish and maintain . . . free and peaceful contacts with other members of their group and with persons belonging to other minorities, *as well as contacts across frontiers* with citizens of other States to whom they are related by national or ethnic, religious or linguistic ties (*emphasis added*)".

13. The General Assembly Declaration on Minorities, *ibid.*, Article 2(3): "Persons belonging to minorities have the right to participate effectively in decisions on the national and, where appropriate, regional level concerning the minority to which they belong or the regions in which they live . . . ".

14. The Framework Convention, *supra* n. 6, provides: " . . . [T]he Parties shall recognise that persons belonging to a national minority have the right to set up and to manage their own private educational and training establishments. *The exercise of this right shall not entail any financial obligation for the Parties* (Article 13, *emphasis added*)".

15. The Framework Convention, *supra* n. 6, contains a great deal of ambiguity as to when exactly state parties should apply its provisions, particularly when contrasted with the Parliamentary Assembly of the Council of Europe's Recommendation 1201 (1993), granting an almost absolute discretion on the state as to the implementation of the minority rights contained within the Framework Convention. See, for example, Article 14: "In areas inhabited by persons belonging to national minorities *traditionally or in substantial numbers*, if there is *sufficient demand*, the Parties *shall endeavour to ensure, as far as possible* and within the framework of their education systems, that persons belonging to those minorities have *adequate opportunities* for being taught the minority language or for receiving instruction in this language (*emphasis added*)".

16. 'Minorities' are protected under Article 27 of the International Covenant on Civil and Politcal Rights (1966). The term is inclusive of those groups who share a common culture, religion and/or language, is not restricted to the citizens of the state, nor to those permanently resident in the state. It would include, for example, migrant workers: see the Human Rights Committee General Comment 23 (on Article 27) (Fifteenth Session, 1994), at paras. 5.1 and 5.2.

17. The concept of a 'national minority' is more restrictive than the term 'minority', *ibid.* Such groups are also protected under Article 27, but further enjoy the protection of the rights outlined in the General Assembly Declaration on Minorities, *supra* n. 7, and the Council of Europe's Framework Convention, *supra* n. 6. The definition of "national minority" suggested by the Council of Europe's Parliamentary Assembly is worthy of note: "the expression "national minority" refers to a group of persons in a state who: a. reside in the territory of that state and are citizens thereof; b. maintain longstanding, firm and lasting ties with that state; c. display distinctive ethnic, cultural, religious or linguistic characteristics; d. are sufficiently representative, although smaller

in number than the rest of the population of that state or of a region of that state; e. are motivated by a concern to preserve together that which constitutes their common identity, including their culture, their traditions, their religion or their language (Article 1)", Recommendation 1201, *supra* n. 15.

18. They are protected under Common Article 1 of the ICCPR and ICESCR (both 1966) and thus enjoy the right to self-determination. The most usually employed definition is that employed by the UNESCO meeting of experts: a *people* is a group of people (who identify themselves as a group) who enjoy some or all of the following characteristics of (i) common historical tradition; (ii) racial or ethnic identity; (iii) cultural homogeneity; (iv) linguistic unity; (v); religious or ideological affinity; (vi) territorial connection, or, (vii) common economic life: *Final Report and Recommendations of an International Meeting of Experts on the Further Study of the Concept of the Right of People for UNESCO* (1990), SNS-89/CONF.602/7.

19. The latter, of course, not being in most societies numerically a minority group, but sharing a number of the characteristics of such groups, notably that of being disenfranchised from political power.

20. *Supra* n. 5.

21. The General Assembly Declaration on Minorities, *supra* n. 7.

The Institutional Response of the 'New' Europe

Minority Protection and the Organisation for Security and Co-operation in Europe

María Amor Martín Estébanez[*]

INTRODUCTION

One of the main features of the Organisation for Security and Co-operation in Europe (OSCE), even from its earliest days, has been its 'comprehensive approach' to international peace and security. This has led the OSCE participating States to consider not just the issue of security, but political, military, economic, environmental and so called 'human dimension'[1] issues as relevant to security in Europe and as being closely interconnected.[2] The protection of minorities has always been an important aspect of this 'comprehensive approach' and the OSCE's undertakings in this area have hardly been matched by that of any other international organisation. This is illustrated, not only by the OSCE's contribution to standard-setting in the field of minority rights, but also to the implementation of relevant international standards. The emergence of the 'New' Europe has allowed the OSCE to develop from being a mere forum for dialogue, into becoming an organisation which actively fosters co-operation between its members.[3] This emergence has also provided the OSCE with new security challenges. Inter-ethnic relations and conflicts have become a primary focus of international concern. In the midst of this the OSCE has devoted particular attention to the prevention of conflicts, and to monitoring the implementation of international standards relating to the protection of minorities. The OSCE has contributed to the process by which minority protection has become an essential object of day-to-day multilateral dialogue and inter-State co-operation in Europe.

THE OSCE AND MINORITY PROTECTION STANDARDS IN THE 'NEW' EUROPE

It would appear that the 'political' nature of the OSCE's 'human dimension' standards has largely been responsible for the OSCE's success in adopting measures aimed at guaranteeing the protection of minorities.[4] The OSCE's

P. Cumper and S. Wheatley (eds.), Minority Rights in the 'New' Europe, 31–52
© 1999 *Kluwer Law International. Printed in Great Britain.*

standards (or 'commitments') in this area do not establish international legal obligations which are binding on participating states through either international judicial and quasi-judicial organs or through inter-state procedures. The possibility of one state referring a conflict to a Conciliation Commission under the OSCE's Convention on Conciliation and Arbitration, when another state has violated its OSCE commitments relating to the protection of minorities, whilst open, remains to be tested.[5] The concluding documents adopted in the framework of the OSCE's meetings and conferences, fail to grant subjective rights which persons belonging to a minority or minority groups as such may execute before a relevant international organ, and only rarely have the OSCE's human dimension commitments concerning minorities fully been implemented in the domestic legal systems of states.[6]

Despite this, according to the OSCE's Vienna Concluding Document (1989), the OSCE participating states 'will take all the necessary legislative, administrative, judicial and other measures and apply the relevant international instruments by which they may be bound, to ensure the protection of human rights and fundamental freedoms of persons belonging to national minorities within their territory'.[7] Similarly, in the Moscow Concluding Document (1991) the participating states called for a swift and proper implementation of the commitments, which had been adopted, concerning questions relating to national minorities.[8] OSCE participating states are under a duty to abide by the OSCE's commitments which regulate the treatment of minorities, as a constituent element of a wider package of comprehensive security measures, in order to contribute to the development of peaceful inter-state relations in the OSCE framework. The OSCE's participating states have affirmed that issues concerning national minorities, as well as compliance with international obligations and commitments concerning the rights of persons belonging to them, are matters of international concern and that they are no longer a matter for each State.[9] They have emphasised that human rights constitute the basis of the protection and promotion of the rights of persons belonging to national minorities and have recognised that questions relating to national minorities can only be satisfactorily resolved if there is a democratic political framework, based on the rule of law, with an independent judiciary.[10] Further, the OSCE has established a number of international bodies, institutions and mechanisms, in order to ensure that minority protection is made effective, at the domestic level, on a day-to-day basis. This is particularly important in view of the fact that no agreement has, as yet, been reached in terms of a comprehensive international regulation of minority rights, endowed with international judicial control.[11] The limited possibilities to guarantee minority protection under the European Convention on Human Rights and its Additional Protocols are discussed elsewhere in this book.[12]

The OSCE has taken a leading role in the international regulation of minority protection, and its standard-setting activities have served as a basis for the progress achieved in the Council of Europe's adoption of the Framework Convention for the Protection of National Minorities (1994) and the UN's Declaration on the Rights of Persons Belonging to National or Ethnic, Religious and Linguistic Minorities (1992). Although the wording of OSCE commitments is often confined to 'persons' belonging to 'national' minorities, the OSCE's documents have also included references to collective rights. Moreover, it should be emphasised that OSCE commitments have not been confined to 'national' minority issues and claims, but have addressed the ethnic, religious and linguistic aspects of the protection of minorities. In some OSCE documents, such as under the 'Basket III' section of the Final Act of Helsinki (1975),[13] and the Vienna Concluding Document (1989),[14] references to 'national minorities' have been made along with the term 'regional cultures'. However, in the OSCE framework, use has been made of the term 'national' by some states as a means of restricting minority protection provisions to the 'citizens' of the respective states.[15] Furthermore, this term has been used by some states when maintaining that 'national minorities exist' only to the extent that they are recognised by the state concerned and/or on the basis of an international treaty.[16]

Since the emergence of the "New" Europe, these restrictive approaches by a limited number of participating states has tended to be of lesser significance. Issues relating to the legal status, or economic, social and cultural rights, of persons who have become 'aliens' within the territories in which they have been living, as a result of the processes of state disintegration and reconstruction which have characterised the emergence of the 'New' Europe, have also been addressed by various OSCE structures and institutions which deal with 'national minority' questions – notably the High Commissioner on National Minorities.[17] Indeed, it may be noted that even those states which have adopted policies of 'express recognition' with regard to their 'national minorities' have discussed the status and the exercise of minority rights by their unrecognised, and seemingly non-existent, minorities under the framework of the OSCE's human dimension implementation review debates, although the situation of these minorities may not have become an object of specific concern to the OSCE's main political bodies.[18]

Attempts to include under the "national minority" concept those who originally came to participating states for work purposes, and whose descendants have been born in the host state but have not been able to acquire the citizenship of the state, has proved more difficult. 'Migrant workers' have become the object of a separate heading in the OSCE's concluding documents, which also contain specific provisions which address the situation of the migrants' families and those of 'second generation migrants'.[19] This reflects, in part, opposition within a majority of host states, as well as from many of the countries of origin, to such people being granted the full enjoyment of civil and political rights in the host countries.

A wealth of literature exists which describes the substantive steps taken by the OSCE in the setting of increasingly rigorous standards relating to the protection of minority rights.[20] Given the limited scope of this chapter, the following pages will concentrate on some strengths of the OSCE standards in relation to those recently adopted in the framework of other international organisations dealing with minority protection in Europe.[21]

One area in which the OSCE's provisions stand out is in the protection, generally, of the identity of minorities. Whilst under the Council of Europe's Framework Convention States undertake 'to *promote the conditions* necessary for persons belonging to national minorities *to maintain and develop their culture, and to preserve the essential elements of their identity, namely their religion, language, traditions and cultural heritage*',[22] in the Copenhagen document[23] the OSCE's participating states undertake to '*create the conditions for the promotion*' of the ethnic, cultural, linguistic and religious identity of minorities, and to take the necessary measures to that effect after due consultations, including contacts with organisations or associations of such minorities, in accordance with the decision-making procedures of each state.[24] These OSCE provisions also go further, substantively, than the corresponding article of the 1992 UN Declaration (Article 4(2)). The provision of the Copenhagen document dealing with the possibility of learning the mother tongue or of receiving instruction in the mother tongue,[25] is less affected by escape clauses than the corresponding provision of the Council of Europe's Framework Convention,[26] and this also applies to the use of the mother tongue in dealings with administrative authorities.[27] The establishment and maintenance of cultural and religious institutions, organisations or associations, provided for in the Copenhagen Document as a subjective right,[28] has not been similarly reflected in the Council of Europe's Framework Convention which, in relation to religious institutions, organisations and associations, only addresses the 'establishment' aspect.[29] The 1992 UN Declaration, in Article 2(4), also refers only to a subjective right to establish and maintain minority 'associations'. Furthermore, the Copenhagen Document supports the activities undertaken in the framework of the minority educational, cultural and religious institutions, to seek voluntary financial and other contributions as well as public assistance;[30] a similar provision cannot be found in the Council of Europe's Framework Convention. The substantive 'right to participate fully . . . in the political, economic, social and cultural life of their countries including through democratic participation in decision-making and consultative bodies at the national, regional and local level . . . ' which is established in the Helsinki Document (1992),[31] is not matched by the corresponding provisions which are found in Article 15 of the Council of Europe's Framework Convention and Article 4 of the 1992 UN Declaration. Finally, another important aspect in which the OSCE's commitments stand out relates to the reference, contained in paragraph 35 of the Copenhagen document, to the establishment of 'appropriate local or autonomous administrations' as one of the possible means 'to protect and create conditions for the promotion' of the identity of certain national minorities, in the context of the facilitation of effective minority participation in public affairs. There is no analogous reference in the Council of Europe's Framework Convention or in the 1992 UN Declaration.

THE OSCE's BODIES, MECHANISMS AND INSTITUTIONS AND MINORITY PROTECTION

The consideration of minority issues as a distinctive element of security deserving specific consideration has influenced the OSCE's institutional development in the context of the 'New' Europe. This is particularly well illustrated by the establishment of the High Commissioner on National Minorities.[32] Reciprocally, the institutional development of the OSCE in recent years has also influenced the approaches of this organisation to minority protection. The initial stage of the emergence of the 'New' Europe has been characterised by the development of formal and often mandatory or semi-mandatory procedures for inter-state dialogue in the OSCE's framework which are still available.[33] These procedures rely mainly on the initiative of individual participating states, and do not require much institutional support. The establishment of the 'Human Dimension Mechanism', which has frequently been used to deal with disputes concerning minority protection among the OSCE States, serves to illustrate this stage. The 'Human Dimension Mechanism' consists of a series of mandatory and formalised procedures for dialogue on human dimension issues between OSCE states,[34] including requests for: (i) information; (ii) the holding of bilateral meetings; (iii) the invitation of missions of experts 'to address or contribute to the resolution' of questions relating to the 'human dimension';[35] and (iv) the sending of missions of rapporteurs to 'establish the facts, report on them and give advice on possible solutions to the question raised'.[36] It should be noted that in the evolution of the mechanism, increasing impetus has been given to the OSCE's Institutions and, in particular, to the Office for Democratic Institutions and Human Rights (ODIHR),[37] to serve as a channel of information among the

participating states in relation to the Mechanism's procedures and as a venue
for the holding of bilateral meetings, in order to support the establishment
of the expert and rapporteur missions.[38] Similarly, it is now possible that the
OSCE's main political bodies, namely the Permanent Council (PC)[39] may
activate the Mechanism and establish missions of experts or rapporteurs, as
well as take follow-up action based on the rapporteur's reports.[40] Nevertheless,
the highly political use made of the mechanism soon after its establishment,
led to it gaining a reputation as a 'confrontational' instrument of dialogue
on human dimension issues.[41] A report of the ODIHR, in October 1995,
found that since July 1992 there had only been four uses of the Moscow
Mechanism,[42] all of them in relation to the protection of minorities.[43] During
the 1994 Budapest Review Conference,[44] references were made by various
States to the Estonian and Moldovan cases as examples of "constructive use"
of this instrument.[45] In both cases there had been a self-activation of the
mechanism by a participating state, that is, an invitation, at the initiative of
the State concerned, of an OSCE mission of experts to assist it. The activation
of the Human Dimension Mechanism by another participating State tends
to be perceived as an unfriendly act, rather than as a positive instrument
which promotes inter-State dialogue and co-operation on human dimension
issues. The attempts to increase the use of the mechanism following the
emergence of the 'New' Europe, which include successive calls to this effect
in OSCE documents,[46] have not prevented its use being infrequent. The views
recently expressed by the participating States, suggest that they consider the
mechanism only to be a subsidiary source of inter-state dialogue.[47]

In the present context of inter-State co-operation, the OSCE's participating
States prefer to channel their inquiries about compliance with human
dimension standards through ever more institutionalised, and at the same
time flexible, mechanisms of dialogue, rather than being involved in rigid,
and formal inter-State procedures. The individual State's initiatives, and those
concerning minorities in particular, now tend not to be pursued in isolation,
but rather to be channelled (and thus, screened) through multilateral, political
bodies of collective decision-making. The OSCE Chairman-in-Office (CIO),
"perceived as the embodiment of the consensus of the OSCE states",[48] has
seen its power of initiative strongly promoted. In addition, the OSCE has
made it possible for a number of common institutions[49] which, although
acting in support of the OSCE's main political bodies, enjoy varying degrees
of independence, to bring issues relating to minorities falling within their
respective mandates to the attention of the main political bodies. Furthermore,
the OSCE has been engaged in a process to create the tools which are necessary
to ensure its presence on the ground, particularly in areas where there are
international security concerns. This has enabled the OSCE to address and
become directly involved in situations where minorities face problems, making

it possible for the OSCE's instruments and institutions to channel information, relating to these situations, to the OSCE's main political bodies for further action.

THE ROLE OF THE MAIN POLITICAL BODIES

Although the OSCE's Meetings of Heads of State or Government and Ministerial Councils[50] continue to hold the main responsibility for decision-making and the setting of general policy guidelines, the Permanent Council (PC), composed of the permanent representatives of the OSCE's states, has become the most important and regular OSCE body for political consultation and decision-making. The PC meets regularly, usually on a weekly-basis, in Vienna.[51] The OSCE's participating states have decided that human dimension issues will be regularly dealt with by the PC.[52] However, discussions 'on' the human dimension have not, so far, been a pre-fixed item on the agenda of the PC[53] and this also applies to minority protection. In this connection, an important decision has recently been adopted to the effect that in the future the CIO will organise each year, in the framework of the PC, as a rule, three informal Supplementary Human Dimension Meetings.[54] These meetings, which will last one working day, will serve to discuss key substantive concerns raised at the previous Human Dimension Implementation Meeting or Review Conference, and to ensure follow-up for them as well as for the OSCE Human Dimension Seminars.[55] Questions of minority protection are likely to become the object of attention at such meetings. So far minority protection issues have often been addressed by the PC, and these issues have come to the forefront of PC discussions in relation to situations of crisis, and to gross violations of human dimension commitments relating to minorities. In these situations the OSCE has often sent *ad hoc*, short-term, fact-finding missions, normally under the initiative and leadership of the CIO, to gather information, to establish initial contacts with the relevant State authorities, and frequently also with the minorities involved. These contacts have occasionally led to the establishment of Long-Term Missions.[56] It is possible that decision-making by consensus within the PC (the norm with the OSCE's main political bodies) may be overturned in circumstances which evidence cases of clear, gross and uncorrected violations of OSCE commitments,[57] of which minorities have frequently become the main targets. The possibility has also been opened for breaking the consensus rule in taking decisions whether or not to send rapporteur missions to the territory of the State concerned in cases of 'very serious violations of human rights'.[58] Thus far the PC involvement in these situations of crisis has most often given rise to the exertion of political pressure and to formal or informal requests for the adoption of specific measures by the States concerned.

The role of the CIO, the Foreign Minister of the OSCE State which holds the annual OSCE presidency and is vested with overall responsibility for executive action,[59] is of the utmost importance in relation to the approach taken by the OSCE's main political bodies to minorities issues. The CIO is responsible for establishing the agenda of the main political bodies. Although in the Budapest Document (1994)[60] the CIO is 'encouraged' to inform the PC of serious cases where there is alleged non-implementation of human dimension commitments,[61] there is no reference made to the threshold for a case of alleged non-implementation to become 'serious' or to the extent to which this information must lead to an in-depth consideration and discussion in the PC. The power of evaluation in this area seems to remain in the hands of the CIO. The possibility that the CIO may appoint personal representatives to deal with specific situations of crisis or conflict,[62] allows the CIO to obtain additional and targeted information. These personal representatives can pay frequent visits to the areas of tension and establish direct contact with the parties involved. Additional possibilities for information of the CIO and dialogue with the parties to tensions as well as political endorsement of the CIO's initiatives have been provided through the increasingly active role of the OSCE's Troika, consisting of the acting, preceding and succeeding CIO. Moreover, *ad hoc* steering groups of the OSCE's states have been established to monitor specific situations of tension,[63] or to work to settle particular situations of conflict, such as the Minsk Group, which deals with the Nagorno-Karabakh conflict.[64] Similarly, the CIO receives support and information from the increasingly 'active involvement in all aspects of the management of the OSCE's Secretary General.[65] Occasionally, the CIO has taken the initiative to organise informal meetings, normally on the day preceding PC meetings, in which NGOs have been invited to present issues relevant to minority protection, particularly with regard to situations of gross violations of the rights of persons belonging to minority groups. These initiatives have been significant in view of the fact that the deliberations of the main political bodies had been closed to NGO participation. As it comes to formal OSCE meetings, only the annual reviews of implementation of the human dimension commitments and the Human Dimension Seminars had provided for NGO participation, until the recent decision to the effect that the CIO will organise Supplementary Human Dimension Meetings to which NGO's having relevant experience in the field of the human dimension will be invited.[66]

Moreover, in the Budapest Document (1994), particular reference is made to the information from the Office for Democratic Institutions and Human Rights (ODIHR), the reports and recommendations of the High

Commissioner on National Minorities (HCNM), the reports of the Head of an OSCE mission,[67] and the State concerned, as the basis upon which the CIO is 'encouraged' to inform the PC where there are serious cases of alleged non-implementation of human dimension commitments.[68] This provision does not seem to have resulted in a limitation of the powers of the CIO in determining the OSCE agenda. However, the activities of the institutions and bodies mentioned earlier, together with the sporadic initiatives taken by some participating states, have contributed positively to both the way and the frequency in which minority issues have been addressed by the OSCE's main political bodies, particularly by the PC.

THE ROLE OF THE OFFICE FOR DEMOCRATIC INSTITUTIONS AND HUMAN RIGHTS (ODIHR)

The approach of the High Commissioner on National Minorities (HCNM) to the implementation of its mandate, together with fact that the wide substantive scope of the ODIHR's mandate is not supported by sufficient resources,[69] have contributed to a 'de facto' distribution of responsibilities between the HCNM and the ODIHR, which is the main OSCE institution of the human dimension, with regard to questions of minority protection.[70] Those minority protection issues which rank highly within the OSCE's security agenda, have usually been addressed by the High Commissioner. However, the activities of the ODIHR[71] have also played an important role in minority protection. Given the limited scope of this chapter, attention will focus here the role of the ODIHR in integrating the human dimension in the work of the PC; the co-operation of the ODIHR with the CIO; the assistance of the ODIHR to the Long-Term missions, and the activities of the Contact Point for Roma and Sinti Issues.[72]

According to the Budapest Document (1994), the ODIHR, 'in consultation with the CIO, will, *acting in an advisory capacity,* participate in discussions of the Senior Council and the Permanent Council, *by reporting at regular intervals on its activities and providing information on implementation issues* . . . acting in close consultation with the Chairman-in-Office, the Director of the ODIHR may propose further action'.[73] Although the ODIHR provides the PC with information on its activities regularly,[74] it is not as active as the HCNM in bringing specific minority situations to the attention of the PC. The initiative to make use of the information available at the ODIHR on failures to implement minority protection standards, and to bring these situations to the attention of the main political bodies, still relies largely on the participating states. Instead of promoting minority rights issues in the PC, the ODIHR seems mainly to have developed a low-key approach to minority protection.[75] The formal and informal contacts initiated by the ODIHR with the authorities of various States, where human dimension commitments concerning the protection of minorities are not respected, is evidence of this approach.[76] In addition, during 1996, the ODIHR prepared two reports on human dimension issues for discussion by the PC. One of them was devoted to violence and discrimination against the Roma.[77] Several other reports dealing with issues which are particularly relevant to minority protection are presented by the ODIHR at the annual reviews of the implementation of human dimension commitments,[78] and thus made available to the members of the PC.[79] A final aspect of the ODIHR's mandate deserves special attention: the possibility that the ODIHR may propose further action, 'acting in close consultation with the CIO'. When it comes to minority protection, and besides the recommendations made by the ODIHR under the reporting activity previously mentioned, this competence of the ODIHR seems to have been interpreted restrictively. Such competence does not seem to have resulted in proposals for further action by the ODIHR to the PC 'in close consultation with' the CIO. Instead, such competence seems to have been limited to the provision of information by the ODIHR to the CIO on issues of concern or to an information exchange between the ODIHR and the CIO. In 1996 the ODIHR prepared four 'early warning' reports, which were sent in strict confidence to the CIO, and have in all cases have resulted in direct action by the CIO. The limited description of these reports provided by the ODIHR suggests that at least some of them may have been directly concerned with minority protection issues.[80]

Finally, the activities of the Contact Point for Roma and Sinti issues (CPRSI), established within the ODIHR in accordance with the Budapest Decisions (1994), must be considered. The CPRSI has taken a pro-active approach to the implementation of its mandate.[81] One year after the establishment of the CPRSI, its programme of activities has included: the recording and communication of all reported instances of violence to the national institutions with responsibilities for Roma and Sinti issues; the provision of legal assistance, mainly through training programmes; the identification of national mediation bodies; support for the promotion of co-operation between Roma and Sinti associations; the establishment of regular meetings on Roma and Sinti issues; and the broad dissemination of information on the Roma and Sinti communities.[82] However, due to the resource constraints of the ODIHR, these initiatives have not been conveniently developed.

THE OSCE's LONG-TERM MISSIONS

The long-term OSCE missions are considered as the main embodiment of 'The OSCE's long-term involvement in conflict prevention and crisis management activities on the ground'.[83] Together with the so called 'Other OSCE Field Activities' they ensure a continuous OSCE presence in the areas where they have been established, and where there have normally been situations of inter-ethnic tensions and questions relating to the protection of minorities which cause international security concerns. The promotion of human rights, as well as the development of democratic institutions, has been a common feature of the OSCE's missions' mandates, and occasionally the missions have been given a role in fact-finding in relation to human rights violations concerning minorities.[84] Specific references to the minority question have often been included in the mandates of missions and, even when no such references have been included, the missions have dealt with minority concerns. The mission members have been involved in political mediation at the highest level with state authorities in relation to inter-ethnic tensions, and have also maintained contacts with the representatives of political movements, local populations and NGOs, including those in 'break-away' regions of countries such as Georgia or Moldova.[85]

The OSCE missions have also sometimes provided expert advice on the drafting and implementation of new constitutions where minority questions have been addressed, and this has often taken place with the support of the ODIHR.[86] The missions have also offered assistance in dealing with questions of regional status, autonomy and other forms of local self-government. Some of the missions have been specifically mandated with the task of providing assistance and expertise in the implementation of legislation in areas relating to the protection of human rights and minority protection.[87] The role of the missions to Latvia and Estonia, in assisting with the implementation of bilateral agreements and in implementing legislation which affects the Russian-speaking minority living in those countries, has been highlighted by the Ministerial Council.[88] Similarly, some of the missions have been involved in providing assistance to the human rights institutions existing in their respective countries. The missions to Bosnia and Herzegovina, and to Tajikistan, have each been given the task of providing co-operation and assistance to the Human Rights Ombudsmen institutions established in those countries. Similarly, the Assistance Group to Chechnya and the Mission to Tajikistan (as well as more recently the Mission to Croatia) have been required to monitor the human rights situation of the returning refugees and internally displaced persons and to assist the state authorities in facilitating their return,[89] while some of the missions have also been involved in the provision of humanitarian assistance to members of minority groups.[90]

The level of attention paid to minority issues in the reports of the missions to the PC has been influenced, not only by their particular mandate, but also by the sensitivity of the mission members (and the Head of Mission in particular) towards the situation of minorities in the countries where the missions have been deployed.[91] It has also been influenced by the decision taken to the effect that the ODIHR should follow-up the mission reports, and the fact that the missions must designate a mission member to liaise with the ODIHR and with NGOs on human dimension issues.[92] The HCNM's involvement in the countries where the missions have been established, has also played an important role.[93]

THE ROLE OF THE PARLIAMENTARY ASSEMBLY

In contrast to the diplomatic and rather low-key approach to minority rights issues which have traditionally been synonymous with the activities of the OSCE's main political bodies and institutions, the OSCE Parliamentary Assembly (PA), which enjoys an independent status and involves members of parliament of all OSCE participating States, has been active in highlighting and publicising issues relating to the protection of minorities.[94]

In all of the PA's Annual Plenary Sessions, which are considered to be the 'backbone of the Assembly',[95] and which take place in a different OSCE participating State each year, attention has been devoted to minority questions. Of the three chapters or main sections in which the declarations and resolutions resulting from the Annual Sessions of the PA have normally been divided,[96] it has been Chapter III, entitled 'Democracy, Human Rights and Humanitarian Questions', where minority issues have occupied the most prominent position.[97] However, the treatment of minority issues under Chapter III has not followed a constant pattern.[98] Apart from the detailed treatment of the situations in Turkey and Yugoslavia, the Assembly Declarations have hardly referred to any specific country situations concerning minorities and their approach to the minority question seems to have responded more to public opinion concerns than to an attempt to provide a thorough and continuous follow-up to the situation of minorities in the OSCE States.

When it comes to an analysis of the situation in particular countries, special reference must be made to the decisions of the Assembly to send missions of parliamentarians to the former Yugoslavia and to Turkey.[99] The Assembly's missions have provided for an alternative 'soft' option as it comes to dialogue on human dimension issues, which has made it easier for the authorities in these countries to admit an OSCE presence. This is particularly important in view of the earlier unsuccessful attempts to pursue other 'harder' or 'inter-governmental' types of OSCE involvement in such countries. Two of the Parliamentary visits to Yugoslavia took place following the suspension of its participation in the OSCE. The primary

objective of these visits was to ascertain the prospects for an improvement
of the treatment of minorities as well as to provide some international
monitoring of their situation.[100] The successive calls by the Nordic states,
during 1994, for the Turkish authorities to invite a mission of experts
under the Human Dimension Mechanism, in relation to the situation of
the Kurdish minority, were dismissed by Turkey, which did, conversely,
find it acceptable to receive an OSCE parliamentary delegation. The mission
provided for a detailed picture of some of the problems facing Turkish
Kurds and it made use of the opportunities provided during its visit to the
country to appeal publicly on behalf of a number of Kurdish
Parliamentarians who were held in prison.[101]

The Parliamentary Assembly's Declarations have occasionally sought to
introduce issues relevant to minority protection in the agenda of the work
of the OSCE's main political bodies,[102] but there is no evidence of these
recommendations being successful. The CIO's duty of bringing the recommendations of the Assembly to the PC and of informing the Assembly of
the activities of the OSCE,[103] as well as the fact that the CIO addresses the
plenary sessions of the PA and replies to questions from the members of the
PA directly,[104] have increased the possibilities of holding the OSCE main
political bodies accountable to the PA in relation to their approach to minority
protection. Moreover, the increasingly active role of the more permanent
bodies of the PA which have progressively been established, and in particular
its Standing Committee and its Bureau as well as the Assembly's Secretariat,
has also created opportunities for greater accountability.[105] During the recent
visits to Armenia, Azerbaijan and Georgia by the President of the
Parliamentary Assembly,[106] in order to enhance the OSCE's 'involvement at
the inter-parliamentary level', the President met with parliamentary and
government leaders 'to discuss political issues in the region'.[107] 'Low-key'
approaches to the prevention and resolution of conflicts seem to feature
increasingly among the activities of the PA, supplementing the more 'public'
endeavours which characterised the approaches of the PA in the past.

THE REVIEWS OF IMPLEMENTATION OF OSCE COMMITMENTS

'National Minorities' have traditionally constituted a specific item on the
agenda of the working group dealing with the human dimension in the
general reviews of the entire range of activities of the OSCE; and in the years
in which these general reviews do not take place, in the context of the human
dimension, 'specific' Implementation Meetings on Human Dimension Issues
organised by the ODIHR. Problems relating to the implementation of OSCE
standards concerning minority protection have also been raised under other

agenda items, including the rule of law, tolerance, education, citizenship and displaced persons. NGO participation, which in the OSCE framework does not require the acquisition of consultative status, has been allowed in discussions relating to these and other substantive aspects of the implementation of OSCE standards relating to minority protection. During the Implementation Meetings on Human Dimension Issues, where all sessions have been opened to NGO participation, and occasionally during the general reviews (presently called 'Review Conferences' or 'Review Meetings'), NGO's have also been able to make a contribution to the review of the use of existing mechanisms and structures and the activities of the institutions dealing with the human dimension.[108] Thus, not only States, but also NGO representatives have presented claims in relation to minority protection publicly, and received replies from the governments or OSCE Institutions concerned in relation to their claims.

In the 1996 Vienna Review Meeting, the traditional, geographical linkage between the – until then biannual – review exercise of the entire range of the OSCE activities and the drafting of the final, decision-making document adopted during the Meeting of Heads of State or Government (which is the highest OSCE decision-making body) has come to an end.[109] In spite of the fact that the CIO has produced a report of the Vienna Review Meeting to the Lisbon Summit, the end of this linkage has contributed to a widening of the gap between the implementation debate and the adoption of new commitments which could provide for a follow-up to the review of implementation of existing standards concerning minority protection. In the Lisbon Document 1996, in contrast with previous OSCE concluding documents, there has not been a separate chapter on the human dimension, and no new standards have been adopted in relation to minority protection. Although the Lisbon Summit Declaration contained in this document focuses on implementation and includes references to specific minority situations, these references do not address the majority of the minority situations put forward during the Vienna implementation debate.[110] It should be noted, however, that the Lisbon Declaration on a Common and Comprehensive Security Model for Europe for the Twenty-First Century, contained in the Lisbon Document, highlights minority protection as one of its important elements. With regard to the Implementation Meetings on Human Dimension Issues held so far, they have provided a partial record of the problems concerning the implementation of OSCE minority protection standards and suggestions for their solution, but they have not produced a decision-oriented document.[111] Nevertheless, the implementation reviews continue to play a very important role, as they provide a possibility for a thorough implementation debate, and the proposal of initiatives to improve implementation which do not take place in the day-to-day response to 'attention rising' issues and emerging security threats with which the activities of the main political bodies, and namely the PC, are mostly concerned. The possibilities for long-term approaches by the main political bodies to minority protection which could be derived from the recently established Supplementary Human Dimension Meetings of the PC remain to be tested.

CONCLUSION

As a result of its readiness to create the tools necessary to respond to security threats using an unparalleled 'hands on' approach, the OSCE has become the most effective of the existing international frameworks in approaching minority protection in the 'New' Europe. The lack of 'legal character' of the OSCE's commitments in this area has been compensated by its active role in the setting of standards for the protection of minorities and the contribution to their implementation. The achievements of the OSCE in fostering inter-state co-operation with regard to minority protection remain unmatched, particularly if compared to those of other international organisations which exist in Europe.

However, notwithstanding the positive achievements, the lack of strictly legal guarantees of minority protection renders minority protection in the OSCE framework particularly fragile, as this protection can be easily counterbalanced by other security concerns. Moreover, the OSCE's political bodies tend to focus mainly on responding to emergency situations and, in particular, to gross violations of minority rights, rather than adopting 'long-term' policies to prevent conflicts. Thus, the activities of the OSCE's institutions, such as the Office for Democratic Institutions and Human Rights (ODIHR) and the High Commissioner on National Minorities (HCNM), which provide for 'long-term approaches' to security issues, should be supported and promoted. In particular, the ODIHR should be given a more active role in fostering state participation in concrete programmes of action leading to the adoption of domestic policies, whilst at the same time maintaining its independence so that it does not become bogged down by political controversy. There is a need to ensure that the knowledge derived from the OSCE field activities and reviews of implementation is actually utilised and followed by concrete programmes of action with the support of the OSCE main political bodies and the individual participating States. The OSCE's institutions, and the ODIHR in particular, should serve as the upholders of such programmes, and be provided with the adequate resources to that effect.

As long as European States continue to be unable to agree on a solid and comprehensive system of international guarantees of minority protection which is capable of having an effect at the domestic level, the need for the OSCE's activities in this field to be continued and promoted remains crucial. The activities of the OSCE and the Council of Europe have developed so far in a complementary manner, and there is no ground for restricting OSCE competencies on the basis that they could possibly be assumed by the Council of Europe. Whether the OSCE is required to continue playing the active role with regard to minority protection which it has played so far, will have an influence not only in the shaping of security in Europe in the future, but also on the possibility for adequate international minority protection regimes to be established on the continent.

NOTES

*D. Phil. Research Student, Centre for Socio-Legal Studies, Faculty of Law, Wolfson College, University of Oxford

1. The protection of human rights and fundamental freedoms has been the object of concern for the OSCE from its inception. In addition, 'human contacts and other issues of a related humanitarian character', the development of pluralist democracy, and the rule of law, have also become object of concern for the OSCE, and are included in the so called OSCE 'human dimension'. For a brief explanation of this concept see R. Brett, 'Human Rights and the OSCE', 11 *Human Rights Quarterly* (1996), 668–693, at 672.
2. See A. Bloed, 'Two Decades of the CSCE Process: From Confrontation to Co-operation, An Introduction' in A. Bloed (ed.), *The Conference on Security and Cooperation in Europe* (1993) 1–118, at 27–28.
3. At the time of writing 55 participating States including the United States and Canada, States in Western, Central and Eastern Europe and the former Soviet Republics form the OSCE. Yugoslavia (Serbia and Montenegro) is the only participating State which has had this status suspended. For an analysis of the role of the present OSCE see P. Switalski, 'An Ally for the Central and Eastern European States', 1 *Transition* (1995) 26–29.
4. See A. Bloed, 'The Human Dimension of the OSCE: Past, Present and Prospects', 3 *OSCE ODIHR Bulletin* (1995) 15–26.
5. According to S. Jacobi, the same applies with regard to the OSCE Valetta Mechanism for the Peaceful Settlement of Disputes, established in 1991. See, S. Jacobi, 'Subsidiarity and Other Obstacles to the Use of the OSCE Dispute Settlement Procedures', in M. Bothe, N. Ronzitti and A. Rosas (eds.), *The OSCE in the Maintenance of Peace and Security* (1997) 425–458, at 450. The Convention on Conciliation and Arbitration, adopted by the CSCE Council held in Stockholm in 1992, and which entered into force in 1994, is an international legally binding document establishing formalised procedures to settle disputes between OSCE States. The Convention previews the establishment of Conciliation Commissions constituted for each dispute as well as Arbitral Tribunals. See L. Caflish, "The OSCE Court of Conciliation and Arbitration: Some Facts and Issues", in *The OSCE in the Maintenance of Peace and Security, ibid.*, 381–408.
6. A recent example of the implementation of OSCE commitments relating to the protection of minorities in the domestic legal system of two OSCE participating

states is the adoption of the Treaty of Understanding, Cooperation and Good Neighbourliness between Romania and the Republic of Hungary: see A. Bloed, 13 NQHR (1995), 181–187. For comments on the treaty and the scope of its provisions relating to minorities see M. A. Martín Estébanez, 'Inter-Ethnic Relations and the Protection of Minorities', in International IDEA (ed.), *Democracy in Romania* (1997) 123–143, at 127–130.

7. See Concluding Document of Vienna (1989), Section on Principles, paragraph 18.

8. Document of the Moscow Meeting of the Conference on the Human Dimension of the CSCE, Chapter III, paragraph 37.

9. See the Report of the CSCE's Meeting of Experts on National Minorities, Geneva 1991, Chapter II, paragraph 3.

10. See the Report of the CSCE Meeting of Experts on National Minorities, Geneva 1991, Chapter II, paragraph 2.

11. See the Chapter by P. Thornberry in this book.

12. See the Chapter by G. Gilbert in this book.

13. See Chapter on Co-operation in Humanitarian and Other Fields, Section 3 on Co-operation and Exchanges in the Field of Culture.

14. See Chapter on Co-operation in Humanitarian and Other Fields, Sections on Human Contacts, Co-operation and Exchanges in the Field of culture and Co-operation and Exchanges in the Field of Education.

15. Some of the provisions of the Geneva Report of the CSCE Meeting of Experts on National Minorities (1991) would also point towards a connection between the protection of minorities and citizenship. See Chapter IV, paragraph 5 of the report.

16. See A. Heraclides, 'The CSCE and Minorities – The Negotiations Behind the Commitments, 1972–1992', in 3 *Helsinki Monitor* (1992) 5–18, at 5.

17. See generally M. A. Martín Estébanez, 'The High Commissioner on National Minorities: Development of the Mandate', in *The OSCE in the Maintenance of Peace and Security, supra* n. 5, 123–165.

18. On the human dimension implementation reviews, see further below.

19. See the Concluding Document of Madrid (1983), Chapter on Co-operation in the Field of Economics, of Science and Technology and of the Environment.

20. See V.-Y. Ghebali, "La CSCE et la Question des Minorites Nationales", in A. Liebich and A. Reyler (eds.), *L'Europe Centrale et ses Minorités: vers une Solution Europèenne?* (1993), 51–72. See also J. Helgesen, 'Protecting Minorities in the Conference on Security and Co-operation in Europe (CSCE) Process', in A. Rosas and J. Helgesen (eds.), *The Strength of Diversity* (1992) 159–186. See, generally, A. Heraclides, *supra* n. 16.

21. See, generally, M. A. Martín Estébanez, *International Organizations and Minority Protection in Europe* (1996).

22. See the Council of Europe's Framework Convention (1994), Article 5.

23. The Document of the Copenhagen Meeting of the Conference on the Human Dimension of the OSCE (1990), which was adopted in an unprecedented climate of East-West co-operation, contains some of the most advanced OSCE standards in the human rights field, and in the area of minority protection in particular.

24. See the Copenhagen Document (1990), paragraph 33. This provision reinforces the commitments undertaken in the Concluding Document of Vienna (1989), Chapter on 'Cooperation on Humanitarian and other Fields', section on Human Contacts, paragraph 59, to the effect that minorities can 'maintain and develop their own culture in all its aspects, including language, literature and religion, and that they can preserve their cultural and historical monuments and objects'.

25. The Copenhagen Document (1990), paragraph 34. The relevant provision of the 1992 UN Declaration, Article 4(3), closely resembles this OSCE commitment.
26. See Article 14(2) of the Council of Europe's Framework Convention (1994).
27. See the Copenhagen Document (1990) paragraph 34 and the Council of Europe's Framework Convention (1994), Article 10(2). It should be noted, however, that the Framework Convention contains a specific provision with regard to the use of the mother tongue in relation to the administration of justice, falling in line with Article 6 of the European Convention on Human Rights. However, the 1992 UN Declaration does not contain any reference to the use of minority languages in relations with the public administration.
28. Paragraph 32(2).
29. Article 8 of the Framework Convention (1994).
30. The Copenhagen Document (1990), paragraph 32(2).
31. Helsinki Document (1992), Chapter VI, paragraph 24.
32. See M. A. Martín Estébanez, 'The High Commissioner on National Minorities: Development of the Mandate', *supra* n. 17 at 157.
33. See A. Rosas and T. Lahelma, 'OSCE Long-Term Missions', in *The OSCE in the Maintenance of Peace and Security*, *supra* n. 5, 167–190 at 167.
34. For a detailed analysis of the evolution of this mechanism and how it functions, see R. Brett, 'Is More Better? – An Explanation of the CSCE Human Dimension Mechanism and its relationship to other systems for the promotion and protection of Human Rights', 9 *Papers on the Theory and Practice of Human Rights*, Centre for Human Rights (1994).
35. See the Document of the Moscow Meeting of the Conference on the Human Dimension (1991), Chapter I, paragraph. 5.
36. *Ibid.*, paragraph 11.
37. On the activity of this institution, see below.
38. See the Helsinki Document, Chapter VI, paragraph 7, and the Prague Council Meeting Decisions, Prague Document on Further Development of CSCE Institutions and Structures, Chapter III, paragraph 14.
39. On the activities of this OSCE main political body, see below.
40. This possibility is established in the decisions of the Rome Council Meeting, Chapter IV, paragraph 5.
41. See R. Brett, *supra* n. 34.
42. These are the procedures of the human dimension mechanism developed in the Document of the Moscow Meeting of the Conference on the Human Dimension of the OSCE (1991 – also referred to as Moscow Concluding Document), which deal with the involvement of missions of experts and rapporteurs. See paragraphs 1–16 of the Moscow Concluding Document.
43. This has included the sending of a rapporteur mission to Croatia and Bosnia-Herzegovina, at the initiative of the United Kingdom, with the support of nine other EU states; the invitations by Estonia and Moldova respectively, to receive a mission of experts; and the initiative of the Committee of Senior Officials (this main political body has ceased to exist, having been replaced first by the 'Senior Council' and then by the 'Reinforced Permanent Council'), to send a mission of rapporteurs to Serbia-Montenegro, which was stopped following the Serbian refusal to issue visas to the mission members. See further OSCE-ODIHR, 'Implementation Meeting on Human Dimension Issues', Materials for Subsidiary Working Body 2, *Review of the Human Dimension of the OSCE*

with a Special Focus on Monitoring and Enhancing Compliance with Commitments and on the Use of Existing Mechanisms and Procedures, (1995), 13–18.

44. On the OSCE Review Conferences, see further below.

45. See C. Krause, Budapest Review Conference, *Towards a Genuine Partnership*, 16 *Papers in the Theory and Practice of Human Rights* (1995), at 34.

46. See, for example, Rome Council Decisions, Chapter IV, paragraph 5. The most recent reference to this is contained in the Budapest Document (1994) Chapter VIII, paragraph 5.

47. See M. A. Martin Estebanez, 'The OSCE Implementation Meeting on Human Dimension Issues 1995', in 7 *Helsinki Monitor* (1996) 5–26, at 21.

48. See M. Harris, 'Human Rights Monitoring and the CSCE. A Perspective from Budapest', in 6 *Helsinki Monitor* (1995) 18–22, at 20.

49. The role of these institutions is described below.

50. The Ministerial Council meets, as a rule, towards the end of every term of chairmanship (that is, once at the end of the year), when a Meeting of Heads of State or Government does not take place, at the level of Ministers for Foreign Affairs of the OSCE participating States.

51. In view of the political importance which has been acquired by the Permanent Council, the previously biannual/triannual meetings of the Senior Council (formerly known as Committee of Senior Officials) have now been replaced by the 'Reinforced Permanent Councils' still attended by high-ranking officials of the Ministries of Foreign Affairs. On the functioning and role of the OSCE's political bodies, see A. Bloed, 'The OSCE Main Political Bodies and Their Role in Conflict Prevention and Crisis Management', in *The OSCE in the Maintenance of International Peace and Security*, *supra* n. 5, 35–52.

52. See the Budapest Decisions (1994), Chapter VIII, paragraph 5.

53. See M. Harris, *supra*, n. 48, at 21.

54. OSCE document PC.DEC/241, 9 July 1998. It should be noted that the Supplementary Human Dimension Meetings in the framework of the PC will be open to NGO participation.

55. On the Human Dimension Implementation Meetings, Review Conferences and Human Dimension Seminars, see below.

56. An example in this regard is provided by the fact-finding sent to Croatia in October 1995, following the events of the preceding August in particular, and which opened the ground for the establishment for the Long-Term Mission to this country. On the Long-Term Missions, see A. Rosas and T. Lahelma, *supra* n. 33.

57. Chairman's Summary of the conclusions of the Prague Council Meeting, 'Prague Document on Further Development of CSCE Institutions and Structures', Chapter IV, paragraph 16.

58. See A. Bloed, 'Two Decades of the CSCE Process: From Confrontation to Cooperation, An Introduction', *supra*, n. 2, at 19–21.

59. See OSCE Secretariat, Department for Chairman-in-Office Support, *OSCE Handbook* (1996), at 11.

60. This document was adopted in the OSCE Meeting of Heads of State or Government which followed the OSCE Review Conference held in Budapest in 1994.

61. The Budapest Decisions, Chapter VIII, paragraph 5.

62. See the Helsinki Decisions (1992) Chapter I, paragraph 22.

63. This is the case of the 'external follow-up' of the situation in Kosovo, Sandjak and Vojvodina by a 'watch group' of states, following Yugoslavia's suspension from the OSCE.

64. On the role of the Minsk Group in the settlement of the conflict, see R. Dehdashti, 'Nagorno-Karabakh: a Case Study of OSCE Conflict Settlement', in *The OSCE in the Maintenance of Peace and Security, supra* n. 5, 459–478.

65. See The Budapest Decisions (1994), Chapter I, paragraph 20.

66. PC.DEC/241, 9 July 1998. On the annual reviews of implementation of the human dimension commitments and Human Dimension Seminars see below.

67. Although the reference to 'mission' is somehow confusing, since no further qualification is made as to the type of mission this decision refers to, the preceding term 'Head' points to the OSCE's Long-Term Missions.

68. Budapest Decisions (1994), Chapter VIII, paragraph 7.

69. The need to increase the ODIHR's resources was emphasised by most delegations taking the floor to comment on the role of the ODIHR during the Vienna Implementation Meeting (1996).

70. On the HCNM see also M. A. Martín Estébanez, *supra* n. 17. For a compilation of the documents and decisions where the mandate of the ODIHR has been defined see OSCE ODIHR, *ODIHR – What It Is and What It Does* (1995), at 28.

71. For a detailed account of these activities, see OSCE ODIHR 'OSCE/ODIHR Activities in Participating States (1991–1995)' (1996). For an analysis of the activities of the ODIHR, see S. Guerra, 'The Multi-faceted Role of the ODIHR', in 4 *OSCE Bulletin* (1996), at 10.

72. See ODIHR OSCE, *ODIHR Annual Report for 1996*, (1996), REF. RM/59/96.

73. Budapest Decisions (1994), Chapter VIII, paragraph 8 (author's emphasis).

74. See *OSCE ODIHR Annual Report for 1996, supra*, n. 71, at 8.

75. According to the *OSCE's ODIHR Annual Report for 1996, supra* n. 72 'with regard to the information provided for discussions among participating States, ODIHR actively sought, and continues to collect information with respect to non-compliance with participating States's commitments in human dimension areas . . . The ODIHR has also established positive working relationships with representatives of the governments of the participating States in Vienna'.

76. A recent example is provided by the visit carried out by the Director of the ODIHR, and the Co-ordinator of the Contact Point for Roma and Sinti Issues, to the Czech Republic in order to discuss with high ranking officials the practical implementation of the Czech Citizenship Law in relation to the Roma population. During the discussions 'it was agreed that close working contacts will be maintained on issues related to the situation of Roma, in particular regarding cases of discrimination and acts of violence against Roma'. See 1 *CPRSI ODIHR Newsletter* (1995), 2.

77. *Ibid.,* at 9.

78. See below.

79. During the most recent, Implementation Review Meeting held in Vienna in 1996, this included reports on 'current trends in the OSCE Region with respect to the problems of aggressive nationalism, racism and xenophobia'; 'analysis of the problem related to basic liberties, especially freedom of religion'; and Violence and discrimination against Roma in the OSCE region. *OSCE ODIHR Annual Report for 1996, supra* n. 72, at 9.

80. *See the ODIHR Annual Report for 1996, supra* n. 72.

81. See the Budapest Document, Chapter VIII, paragraph 23. On the approach of the HCNM to the Roma, see M. A. Martín Estébanez, *supra* n. 17, at 143.

82. See the *CPRSI Newsletter*, supra n. 76 at 1–2.

83. See the *OSCE Handbook 1996, supra* n. 59, at 18.

84. According to the Budapest Decisions (1994), Chapter VIII, paragraph 11, the ODIHR

will be consulted on the missions' mandate. For an account of the recent long-term missions and the content of their mandates, see OSCE Secretariat, *Survey of OSCE Long-Term Missions and other OSCE Field Activities* (1996) REF. SEC/649/96.

85. See The Chairman's Summary of the Fifth Meeting of the Council of Ministers, Budapest (1995). Occasionally, the missions have been given a specific responsibility with regard to providing an input into the general political frameworks for a peaceful settlement of the tensions, aiming at the establishment of appropriate minority protection regimes, such as in the case of Moldova.

86. See 'OSCE/ODIHR Activities in Participating States (1991–1995)', *supra* n. 71 for an analysis of the influence of the ODIHR in such cases.

87. For example, the mission to Croatia. On this generally, see Survey of OSCE Long-Term Missions and other OSCE Field Activities, *supra* n. 84, at 24.

88. See the Chairman's Summary of the Fifth Meeting of the Council of Ministers (1995). The missions have taken up the responsibility to monitor the cumbersome naturalisation process, providing assistance and information. The activities of the Mission to Latvia have included the monitoring of the repatriation of Russian servicemen remaining in Latvia following the agreement on the withdrawal of Russian troops from the country. See 3 *OSCE Newsletter* (1996), at 27. The activities of the Mission to Estonia have included the support for the implementation of a language training programme for the members of the Russian minority willing to have access to Estonian citizenship. See 1 *OSCE Newsletter* (1994), at 5.

89. See The *Survey of OSCE Long-Term Missions and other OSCE Field Activities, supra* n. 84, at 15 and 21, respectively.

90. The OSCE Assistance Group to Chechnya has received a specific mandate in this regard. See Survey of OSCE Long-Term Missions and other OSCE Field Activities, *supra* n. 84, at 27. Also other missions, such as that to Georgia, have been involved in this kind of activity in a lower scale.

91. Written reports on the missions activities are sent normally every fortnight by the head of missions to the Chairman-in -Office, and then channelled to the PC. The Heads of Missions have also been invited to report personally to the PC, usually three or four times a year, on their missions' activities.

92. See The Budapest Decisions (1994), Chapter VIII, paragraph 11.

93. See M. A. Martín Estébanez, *supra*, n. 17 at 160.

94. Some of the activities of the ODIHR also receive publicity, as do some of the activities of the Long-Term Missions, particularly in so far as this can act as a confidence-building measure.

95. On these and other aspects of the Parliamentary Assembly, see R. Spencer Oliver, 'The OSCE Parliamentary Assembly' in 7 *Helsinki Monitor* (1996) 42–57, at 45. The Annual Sessions have so far been held in Budapest (1992), Helsinki (1993), Vienna (1994), Ottawa (1995) and Stockholm (1996).

96. Between 1992 and 1994, a specific chapter of the Declaration was devoted to the situation in the Former Yugoslavia. Since 1995, the situation there has been addressed under Chapter I, 'Political Affairs and Security', in conjunction with other specific country situations or regional issues, such as the situation in Chechnya, Nagorno Karabakh, the Baltic Region or the Mediterranean. Although under Chapter I, security arrangements relevant to minority protection have been addressed, minority protection has not been the object of specific attention.

97. The role of the General Committee of the Assembly, responsible for preparing the paper and draft resolution on Chapter III for presentation to the Plenary, Annual Session,

and of the specific Rapporteurs responsible for preparing the work of the General Committee in highlighting minority protection issues, should not be underestimated.

98. While the minority issue have been treated in a separate section of the Budapest, Helsinki and Ottawa Declarations of the Assembly, in the Vienna Declaration it was addressed under several sections dealing with: 'Self-determination'; the 'International War Crimes Tribunal'; 'Racism, Xenophobia, Anti-Semitism and Aggressive Nationalism'; and 'Migrant Workers'.

99. See R. Spencer Olivier, *supra* n. 95, at 51.

100. *Ibid.*

101. See W. Wimmer 'OSCE Parliamentary Assembly's Delegation To Turkey' (30 June 1996): <gopher:/marvin.nc.nato:int: 70/00/other_international/CSCE/PARLIAMENT/MISSION/TURKEY/Turkey.doc

102. See The Vienna Declaration (1994), Chapter III, paragraphs 21 and 29.

103. See The Budapest Decisions (1994), Chapter I, paragraph 24.

104. See R. Spencer Olivier, *supra* n. 95, at 46.

105. The Bureau of the Assembly normally meets in conjunction with the meetings of the OSCE's Ministerial Council and the OSCE's Summits. The Standing Committee Meetings are being addressed by the CIO and receive briefings on the latest OSCE developments from senior OSCE officials, including the Secretary General, the HCNM and the Director of the ODIHR. The representatives of the Assembly have contributed to the implementation review meetings, and the President of the Assembly has addressed Summit Meetings, meetings of the Council of Ministers and of the OSCE's Troika.

106. These visits included meetings with the CIO's Representative to the Minsk Conference. See 11 *OSCE Newsletter* (1996), at 8 and 13 *OSCE Newsletter* (1996), at 10.

107. During the visit to Georgia the Assembly's President met with local officials and peacekeeping forces in order to observe the work which the OSCE's Mission to Georgia had been conducting in the secessionist area of South Ossetia. See 9 *OSCE Newsletter* (1996), at 8.

108. Also a number of OSCE Human Dimension Seminars organised by the ODIHR, (including those on Tolerance, 1992; Case Studies on National Minorities – Positive Results, 1993; and the Roma in the OSCE region, 1994, which was co-organised by the Council of Europe) have brought together the participating States and NGO's in discussing questions relevant to minority protection. The same applies to the OSCE regional seminars organised by the ODIHR.

109. Although preliminary work on the concluding document already started in Vienna, most of the work was carried out in the preparatory meeting of the Summit held in Lisbon.

110. See Lisbon Summit Declaration paras. 19 and 20. In the Declaration on a Common and Comprehensive Security Model for Europe for the Twenty-first Century, the OSCE participating States reaffirm their determination to fully implement their commitments relating to minorities and to respond to requests by the participating States to seek solutions to minority issues within their territory.

111. See Helsinki Document 1992, Helsinki Decisions, Chapter VI, para. 11.

Minority Rights Under the Council of Europe

Geoff Gilbert[*]

INTRODUCTION

Almost eighty years ago, at the end of the Great War, the Allied Powers embarked on the twin tasks of redrawing the borders of Central and Eastern Europe through the peace treaties[1] and establishing the League of Nations. With regard to the former, they recreated States with a long pedigree of independence, such as Poland. They also agglomerated peoples who had been divided between the former Empires of the region for many centuries past, such as the new Serb-Croat-Slovene State, the forerunner of the former Yugoslavia. In all cases, the new boundaries were arbitrary, leaving small pockets of minority populations in these newly established States, like rockpools left behind when the tide goes out. And, as with 'rockpools', some waited for the 'tide' to return as irredentas in the new States, while others 'disappeared' through assimilation, such as the Gagauz of inter-War Romania.[2]

As for the League of Nations, the absence of the United States and the in-built tendency for tension as the League assumed responsibility for guaranteeing minority rights (provided for by those self-same peace treaties), meant that the political and economic climate of the inter-War period added little to collective stability. Another aspect of the Covenant of the League of Nations was that there was no universal guarantee of minority rights by all member States, despite the efforts of President Woodrow Wilson of the USA[3] – minority rights obligations were only for the new States and those defeated in World War I,[4] the States of Central and Eastern Europe and the Balkans, rather than those of Western Europe.

This division between East and West may be re-emerging through the advent of fresh minority rights instruments in Europe after the collapse of the former Soviet bloc. As the Council of Europe has grown eastward, so has its promotion of minority rights distinct from its long-standing guarantees of other human rights. This chapter will examine the Council of Europe's endeavours in the field of minority rights and question the appropriateness of the venture – the problem with 'dipping one's toes in

53

P. Cumper and S. Wheatley (eds.), Minority Rights in the 'New' Europe, 53–70

rockpools' is that, without having checked the rockpool carefully beforehand, one might 'stub them on the rocks[5] hidden beneath'.

It is trite to state that, partly as a recognition of the treatment certain groups received during World War II, the focus in 1945 shifted from minority to human rights. However, not only is it trite, it is too simplistic. While the Universal Declaration of Human Rights 1948 did not mention minorities, the United Nations Charter commences its Preamble with "We the Peoples . . .";[6] nevertheless, the allusion is weak, for it, too, does not refer to minorities. On the other hand, many of the minority provisions in the post-World War I treaties were non-discrimination measures for members of the group and both the Charter and the Declaration prohibit discrimination on grounds of race, sex, language or religion.[7] Furthermore, the Commission on Human Rights established a Sub-Commission on the Prevention of Discrimination and the Protection of Minorities in 1947.[8] In terms of treaty measures, the Genocide Convention 1948 protects "national, ethnical, racial or religious" groups.[9]

The Statute of the Council of Europe does not refer to minorities. Turning to the European Convention for the Protection of Human Rights and Fundamental Freedoms (ECHR),[10] it only mentions minorities expressly in Article 14, the non-discrimination clause:

> The enjoyment of the rights and freedoms set forth in this Convention shall be secured without discrimination on any ground such as sex, race, colour, language, religion, political or other opinion, national or social origin, *association with a national minority*, property, birth or other status (emphasis added).

Given that the ECHR is geared towards protecting individual rights, the protection accorded to minorities as groups through Article 14 would only ever be incidental, although individual representatives of the group would be able to bring an application to uphold the rights of members of the group under Article 25.[11] This combination of standing and interest has, on occasions, allowed the European Commission and Court of Human Rights incidentally to protect the rights of the group (see below).

The European Social Charter[12] does not refer to minorities, although it does prohibit in its Preamble discrimination in "the enjoyment of social rights" on the ground of "national extraction or social origin".[13] The phrase is peculiar and could be taken to include those persons who claim to be ethnically from another nation, whilst having the nationality of the home State, for example, ethnic Danes in Germany. Such an interpretation would be in line with one description of 'national' minorities, to be considered below. The Charter also provides for the rights of migrant workers in Article 19. The traditional view[14] is that migrant workers are not a minority for the purposes of international law. However, the Human Rights Committee's 1994 General Comment on Article 27 of the ICCPR[15] has argued that with respect to that Article, the minority population need neither be nationals of the State in question nor permanently resident there and would include migrant workers. In sum, the extent to which the European Social Charter provides protection overall to minority groups is questionable.

The Council of Europe, though, did not wholly ignore minorities before the fall of the Soviet bloc. During the early 1950s it left the issue untouched, but Parliamentary Assembly Recommendation 285 (1961), building on the work of the 1959 Struye Report, proposed protection for national minority groups in terms of them enjoying their own culture, using their own language, establishing schools and receiving teaching in their own language and professing and practising their own religion.[16] The Committee of Experts[17] eventually decided in 1973 that, following the *Belgian Linguistics* case,[18] there was no need for a protocol to the ECHR on minority rights, although there was nothing in law to prevent such a step.[19]

WHAT ARE NATIONAL MINORITIES?

European instruments promulgating minority rights have invariably protected 'national' minorities, and this is still the case post–1990, as will be seen below. Article 27 of the International Covenant on Civil and Political Rights (1966) contains no such term. A reading of the *travaux préparatoires* of, *inter alia*, Article 27 in the ICCPR and the 1973 report of the Committee of Experts on Minority Rights of the Council of Europe indicates that in United Nations documents 'ethnic' includes national, while Council of Europe documents subsume ethnic within 'national'.[20] What is certain is that there is no generally accepted definition of minority or national minority in international law.[21] Traditionally, the minority population has been seen to consist of nationals of the State, but 'national' could also be a descriptive term, like ethnic, religious or linguistic, referring to those minorities with a kin-State or which have nationalist aspirations or a sense of nationhood. The Council of Europe's Parliamentary Assembly Recommendation 1201 (1993) did attempt a definition in its ultimately rejected draft Protocol to the ECHR: a national minority would, *inter alia*, reside as citizens on the State's territory.[22] Klebes, in commenting on the

Council of Europe's Framework Convention on the Rights of National Minorities,[23] states that "it is clear from the context that 'national minority' refers to a minority on the national territory (the territory of the State)"; given that the Framework Convention imposes obligations on the State, though, it would be strange indeed if it required the State to protect national minorities resident outside its territory. While one cannot be conclusive, national minority in the European context incorporates a range of ideas which, taken together, would offer protection to most ethnic, religious, linguistic and cultural minorities in a State.

THE PROTECTION OF NATIONAL MINORITIES AT STRASBOURG[24]

The Strasbourg institutions have repeatedly reiterated that the European Convention on Human Rights contains no minority rights provision:

> The Commission finds that the situation complained of falls outside the scope of the provisions of the Convention. . .The Convention does not provide for any rights of a. . . minority as such, and the protection of individual members of such minority is limited to the right not to be discriminated in the enjoyment of the Convention rights on the grounds of their belonging to the minority (Article 14 of the Convention).[25]

Despite the failure by the Council of Europe to provide an express guarantee of minority rights in the ECHR, it is impossible to deny that the Strasbourg organs did, and still do, on occasion, protect minority groups under the ECHR. While many group rights will entail measures guaranteeing non-discrimination and other fundamental freedoms relevant to individual claims, the protection and promotion of the minority as such, will be serendipitous. A person might not suffer discrimination, but may well be denied the opportunity to assert his/her cultural identity.[26]

Nevertheless, as matters stand, applicants seeking to preserve the rights of their minority group have to rely on Article 14 of the ECHR. Article 14 is purely a non-discrimination provision. A wide interpretation of discrimination in Article 14 could, however, provide minority groups with effective protection of their collective interests. If it is read to encompass indirect discrimination and affirmative action to eradicate institutionalised discrimination, then many group rights[27] can be enforced through individualised Article 14 applications. The standard definition of discrimination is found in the *Belgian Linguistics* case:[28]

> In spite of the very general wording of the French version ('*sans distinction aucune*'), Article 14 does not forbid every difference in

treatment in the exercise of the rights and freedoms recognised. This version must be read in the light of the more restrictive text of the English version ('without discrimination').

It is important, then, to look for criteria which enable a determination to be made as to whether or not a difference in treatment, concerning of course the exercise of one of the rights and freedoms set forth, contravenes Article 14. On this question the Court, following the principles which may be extracted from the legal practice of a large number of democratic states, holds that the principle of equality of treatment is violated if the distinction has no objective and reasonable justification. The existence of such a justification must be assessed in relation to the aim and effects of the measure under consideration, regard being had to the principles which normally prevail in democratic societies; moreover, Article 14 will be violated when it is clearly established that there is no reasonable relationship of proportionality between the means employed and the aim sought to be realised.[29]

This view clearly includes direct discrimination, but, through a justified "difference in treatment" which is reasonable and proportionate, a State might be permitted to favour a minority group over the majority population, although the minority could not assert a *right* to such treatment where the State was not already providing it.

While Article 14 and other substantive articles of the ECHR are capable of bearing an interpretation that would allow for the promotion of minority rights, there have only been a few cases where this has been the result. Nonetheless, it is established case law that there should be no discrimination between similar groups within a high contracting party in the exercise of Convention rights.[30] By way of corollary, essentially different groups should not receive identical treatment.[31] Again, by analogy with the 1988 case of *Plattform 'Artze für des Leben' v Austria*,[32] a State might have to take positive measures to allow the minority group to assert its rights under the ECHR.[33] Moreover, under Article 10, a minority group may be allowed to assert its identity in public as it perceives itself, even where the State would wish to describe the group in other terms are the Slav and Turkic Muslims of north-west Thrace in Greece a different ethnic/national group or are they merely a religious minority?[34]

Going further still, the Commission observed in *Liberal Party et al. v United Kingdom*[35] that a State might design voting laws so as to enhance the election prospects of a religious or ethnic minority.[36] Such would be the case where a minority could never be represented in the legislature 'because there was a clear voting pattern along these lines in the majority'.

It would effectively amount to discrimination to continue with an electoral law which excluded minority representation, even though the minority population had the same voting rights as the majority. This view endorses the Commission's earlier decision in *Lindsay* that it is proper to discriminate, to take affirmative action, if that improves the effectiveness of a Convention right for the benefit of a minority, provided that the difference in treatment has a reasonable and objective justification.[37] Despite repeated assertions by the Strasbourg organs that the ECHR does not contain a provision guaranteeing minority rights, the upholding of domestic laws that favour a minority over the majority in so important a field as democratic representation indicates that merely having regard to the wording of the Convention is too simplistic an approach. The Strasbourg organs will, in appropriate circumstances, uphold a grant of a right by the State, although the minority group could not, in the absence of the grant, assert their entitlement to such a right.[38]

The Commission has been willing to find that Article 8 of the ECHR includes a guarantee to a minority group of its lifestyle. In *G and E v Norway*, the Commission, *obiter*, was prepared to accept that under Article 8(1):

> a minority group is, in principle, entitled to claim the right to respect for the particular life style it may lead as being 'private life', 'family life' or 'home'.[39]

In *Buckley v United Kingdom*,[40] a case concerning a claim by a gypsy woman to be able to park her caravan on her own land without planning permission, following *G and E*, the Commission held that "the traditional lifestyle of a minority may attract the guarantees of Article 8".[41] The Commission went on to decide that her rights had been violated by the imposition of domestic planning laws, but the Court reversed the decision, focusing solely on the applicant's right to a home, not to a particular way of life. These cases seem directed towards ethnic minorities, rather than, for instance, linguistic ones, but they take the Strasbourg jurisprudence beyond mere non-discrimination, as established under Article 14, and provide authority for the protection of the rights of the minority group *qua* group. Nevertheless, in both cases, it was eventually found that the State's actions were a legitimate interference under Article 8(2), although it may be that a stricter test should be applied where the State's interference affects a way of life, not just a home.[42]

Finally, to consider an issue beyond what has already been decided by the Strasbourg organs, can a minority group assert the right to self-determination under the ECHR? Such an argument is not straightforward, not least because there is no express right to self-determination in the

ECHR. However, Article 1 of the International Covenant on Civil and Political Rights (1966) does contain such a right. One might construct an argument that while self-determination in Article 1 of the ICCPR is a right of peoples (a concept referring in general to the State as an entity in its own right or to all the peoples of the State together), in one instance it might accord rights to a particular minority group, an individual people – where that group was not permitted to participate in the self-determination process. In General Comment 12(21), the Human Rights Committee (HRC) stated that "all States parties to the Covenant should take positive action to facilitate realization of and respect for the right of peoples to self-determination".[43] If a State effectively prevented political participation by a minority group,[44] then that action might violate that particular group's right to self-determination under Article 1 of the ICCPR. While *Ominayak*[45] clearly states that no claim can be brought under the Optional Protocol before the HRC in relation to Article 1 of the ICCPR, that does not detract from the fact that self-determination is a human right recognised in the Covenant – it is simply not a right open to consideration by way of a communication to the Human Rights Committee. The minority group might then seek to bring an action based upon discrimination under Article 14 of the ECHR taken together with Article 11 and Article 3 of the First Protocol (interpreted in these circumstances to include both self-determination[46] and the right to political participation[47]) on the basis that under Article 60 of the ECHR:

> Nothing in this Convention shall be construed as limiting or derogating from any of the human rights and fundamental freedoms which may be ensured under the laws of any High Contracting Party *or under any other agreement to which it is a Party*.

Thus, self-determination under Article 1 of the ICCPR would be a human right ensured under another agreement to which the State is a party for the purposes of Article 60 of the ECHR and, as such, should be read into the scope of Article 11 and Protocol 1 Article 3, in conjunction with Article 14, of the ECHR.

However, it must be noted, as a cautionary point, that most cases involving some element of minority rights fail before the institutions of the ECHR. The Commission and Court have refused to protect minority groups when interpreting substantive provisions of the ECHR, often because the issue pertinent to minority status can be ignored since the ECHR does not speak of minority rights.[48] The rights usually sought by minority groups relate to the preservation of cultural traditions or the use of language, either in education or in public life. In the *Belgian Linguistics* case, the Court dismissed the parents' attempts to preserve their minority language and culture:

> [In] so far as the legislation leads certain [French-speaking] parents to separate themselves from their children, such a separation is not imposed by this legislation: it results from *the choice of the parents* who place their children in schools situated outside the Dutch unilingual region with the sole purpose of avoiding their being taught in Dutch, . . . one of Belgium's national languages (emphasis added).[49]

The Court has found that there is no right to mother-tongue education[50] and the Commission and Court have not upheld a right to use one's mother-tongue in public life.[51] The restriction on the use of one's mother-tongue was even allowed to take precedence over democratic representation. The facts of *Mathieu-Mohin and Clerfayt* are complex: the language in which the elected representative took the oath when being sworn into the Belgian Parliament determined the regional council upon which he would sit, and with which language-bloc he would vote in Parliament. A substantial French-speaking minority in a nominally Dutch-speaking region of Belgium could elect representatives who would either join the French language-bloc, but would not then sit on the Dutch regional council which dealt with their constituencies, or who would sit on that council, but would then not be part of the French language-bloc for important constitutional votes in Parliament. The majority of the Court saw this limitation on voters' choice as justified in that it was part of an attempt to:

> achieve an equilibrium between the Kingdom's various regions and cultural communities by means of a complex pattern of checks and balances. The aim is to defuse the language disputes in the country by establishing more stable and decentralised organisational structures. This intention, which is legitimate in itself, clearly emerges from the debates in the democratic national Parliament and is borne out by the massive majorities achieved in favour [of the relevant legislation] . . . In any consideration of the electoral system in issue, its general context must not be forgotten. The system does not appear unreasonable if regard is had to the intentions it reflects and to the respondent State's margin of appreciation within the Belgian parliamentary system – a margin that is all the greater as the system is incomplete and provisional.[52]

The Court's decision, while legally justifiable having regard to the rights accorded in the ECHR and the Protocol, does not fully acknowledge political reality. The dissenting judgment in *Mathieu-Mohin*, joined by five judges, appreciated this in coming to the view that Article 3 of Protocol 1, in conjunction with Article 14, had been breached:

> In our opinion, such a situation, excluding, as it does in practice, representation of the French-speaking electorate of Halle-Vilvoorde at regional level, does not ensure 'the free expression of the opinion of the people in the choice of the legislature' as stipulated in Article 3 of Protocol No. 1, and it creates a language-based distinction contrary to Article 14 of the Convention. None of the reasons put forward to justify this incompatibility appears to us to be convincing. In the first place, it is true that the French-speakers elected in Halle-Vilvoorde could belong to the (Flemish) regional Council if they agreed to take the oath in Dutch. In that eventuality, however, the representatives concerned would lose their status as French-speakers in Parliament, and this – in addition to the psychological and moral aspect of the issue – would have important political consequences, given the role played by the parliamentary language groups.[53]

The dissenting judges have interpreted Article 14 to include principles of indirect discrimination to reach this opinion, but an express minority rights provision would obviate the need for semantic argument and allow discussion of the facts in their appropriate context.

Thus, while some decisions of the Commission and Court have protected minority groups by means of a wide interpretation of discrimination in Article 14 and an expansive view of Article 8, the general trend has been to deny that minorities are protected under the ECHR. It is timely to enquire whether the deliberative organs of the ECHR should be provided with a mechanism whereby they could directly address the needs of minority groups.

THE COUNCIL OF EUROPE AND MINORITY GROUPS: POST–1990

By 1990, the Organization for Security and Co-operation in Europe (OSCE)[54] already had all of Central and Eastern Europe and the former Soviet Union as participating States. It had drafted a politically binding set of commitments in the field of minority rights in its 1990 Copenhagen Document.[55] Unless the Council of Europe was to expand eastward rapidly in the early 1990s and implement justiciable and enforceable guarantees of minority rights, there is an argument that there should have been a *recognised* division of responsibility between the two organisations, leaving the OSCE (utilising its Vienna and Moscow Mechanisms, and its High Commissioner on National Minorities) to deal with the issue of minority groups in the region.[56] The Commission for Democracy through Law even proposed in 1991 that the OSCE should promulgate a European Convention for the Protection of Minorities;[57] (the CDL's proposal, however, was contrary to the normal practice of the OSCE, which works by politically binding commitments, rather than legally binding treaties).[58] Nevertheless, the Council of Europe, entered the fray and in the 1990s issued a series of measures attempting to provide mechanisms to protect minority rights.[59]

An effective measure would have been the proposed Protocol to the ECHR found in Recommendation 1201 of the Parliamentary Assembly of the Council of Europe. Not only did it attempt a definition, flawed though it was, but in addition to the traditional series of rights for the minority group, which in reality are for individual members of the group in community with other members,[60] the proposed Protocol provided in Article 11:

> In the regions where they are in a majority the persons belonging to a national minority shall have the right to have at their disposal *appropriate local or autonomous authorities* or to have a special status matching the specific historical and territorial situation and in accordance with the domestic legislation of the State (emphasis added).[61]

The provision may be hedged round with imprecise terms, but it acknowledged the right of minority groups to have control over their own affairs. Legally enforceable rights are inadequate on their own if minority groups are to obtain full guarantees within a State; political power has also to be allocated to them in some measure so as to provide the group with the ability to regulate its own affairs, although the State may fear that allocation of power will engender ever greater demands for further autonomy.

However, the proposed Protocol was rejected by the heads of State and Government of the Council of Europe at its Vienna Summit in October 1993.[62] Nevertheless, Parliamentary Assembly Order 484 still requires the Legal Affairs Committee of the Council of Europe to have regard to the draft Protocol when assessing new States for admission. Thus, while the Council of Europe was not prepared to create legally justiciable rights for minorities throughout its member States, including an obligation to grant autonomy where appropriate, it still requires that new applicants, that is States from Central and Eastern Europe as well as the former Soviet Union, be assessed on the demands of Recommendation 1201. The resonance with practice in the League of Nations in the inter-War period is striking. It suggests an attitude towards Central and Eastern European States that treats them as more problematic than

States in the West, yet Spain, France, Greece and the United Kingdom, amongst others, have acknowledged difficulties with the Basques, Corsicans, Muslims of north-west Thrace and the Nationalist community in Northern Ireland, respectively. This criticism is not to suggest that implementation of Recommendation 1201 would be a sufficient and proper response to minority issues within the Council of Europe, but its retention solely as a criteria for admission indicates a two-tier organization.

The one general Council of Europe agreement on minority rights is the Framework Convention for the Protection of National Minorities 1994.[63] There is not the space here to assess this instrument thoroughly, but it fails in terms of providing guarantees of rights for minority groups for three reasons: (i) its description of rights is vague and imprecise, giving States a great margin of appreciation;[64] (ii) it is a 'framework' convention, a concept that seems to impose upon States only an obligation to endeavour to implement domestic laws to put those vague and imprecise descriptions of rights into effect;[65] and, (iii) on its face, the method of monitoring State compliance is via State reports to the Committee of Ministers aided by an advisory committee of experts.[66] The combination of weak obligations and weak monitoring render the Framework Convention, as it stands, almost worthless as a means of guaranteeing minority rights within the Council of Europe.[67] The Framework Convention's weakness as a guarantee of minority rights has been recognised by the Slovak Republic, which sought to limit the obligations it owes to its Hungarian minority under a bilateral treaty with Hungary, by restricting more strongly worded measures found in Recommendation 1201 and the Copenhagen Document[68] to the level of commitment found in the Framework Convention.[69]

CONCLUSION

One aim of implementing international human rights standards should be to improve collective stability in a region. If there is a serious human rights issue to be addressed, then half-hearted and ill-thought out measures merely serve to provide States with a 'paper' response to justified criticisms. Partly because of the success of the European Commission and the European Court of Human Rights in dealing with the human rights commitments found in the ECHR, the weakness of the Framework Convention suggests a lack of political will to confront minority rights throughout the Council of Europe. There are two matters to be considered: the perceived East-West divide on this topic and the appropriateness of justiciable rights as a comprehensive solution to the needs of minority groups.

In the Summer of 1996, Umberto Bossi of the Italian political party, the Northern League, suggested that the north of Italy should establish itself as the new State of Padania.[70] To many; this might seem to be a fanciful suggestion, but the situation should be contrasted with the likely international reaction if the Pirin region of Bulgaria, abutting the Republic of Macedonia and Greece and part of what Poulton calls 'geographic Macedonia',[71] had made a similar proposal.[72] The situation is different, but part of the response to Padania is based on the idea that States in the West do not divide, whereas those in the East could 'turn into another Bosnia'. The Council of Europe is the foremost intergovernmental organisation in the field of civil and political human rights protection; the OSCE has taken the most pro-active role to protect minority groups in Central and Eastern Europe since the fall of the Iron Curtain.[73] The efforts by the Council of Europe to protect minorities add little to the commitments on paper already entered into by those same States within the OSCE, and there are none of the interventionist mechanisms which the OSCE possesses which can promote dialogue between the minority and the government.[74] And that is the essence of the second matter for consideration. The Council of Europe has done most for international human rights standards through the case work of the Commission and Court. It excels in implementation through justiciable rights. While some minority rights can be the subject of legal application to some form of tribunal, those pertaining to the group *qua* group are more likely to need political dialogue. Minority rights are a highly contentious issue which, in the first instance, should be addressed at the political level.[75] The work of the OSCE, particularly the High Commissioner on National Minorities, has achieved most in this area and it is questionable whether the Council of Europe can add to its, and his, efforts. There is a danger of duplication with, in this case, consequent dilution, as two organisations try to operate in the same field. Without evidence of a more interventionist stance on minority rights, the Council of Europe is not going to effect further advances in providing for the protection and promotion of minorities. This is not to say that the OSCE mechanisms and the HCNM currently offer an exhaustive solution to minority issues, but they are better designed and equipped to achieve that end given a political will among the participating States. It would also do much to improve human rights standards throughout Europe if the Council of Europe focused on the ECHR; one organisation dealing with civil and political rights in the whole of Europe through the decisions of the Commission and Court, can only improve adherence to those standards from Reykjavik to Vladivostok.

NOTES

*Professor of Law, Director, Human Rights Centre, University of Essex. The author is grateful to Jane Wright, Nigel Rodley and Françoise Hampson, all colleagues at Essex, for their helpful comments. The chapter also benefited from the comments of other participants at the conference who heard a more provocative version designed to encourage discussion. Needless to add, all views and errors are mine alone. The law is correct as of January 1997, but I am grateful to the editors for their generosity in allowing me to insert several updated footnotes thereafter. The European Convention on Human Rights was amended in line this chapter, but references to Articles 25, 26 and 60 should now be read to refer to Articles 34, 35 and 53, respectively.

1. *Infra,* n. 4.
2. See C.A. Macartney, *National States and National Minorities* (1934), at 380.
3. Various drafts of the Covenant of the League of Nations by US President Wilson included a provision requiring all new States seeking admission to the League to guarantee equality in law and fact to national minorities. See D. Hunter Miller, *The Drafting of the Covenant* (1928), vol. I, 60 and vol.II, 91; P. de Azcárate, *The League of Nations and National Minorities* (1945) 168; C.A. Macartney, *ibid.* at 218–20. The lack of a general provision even for new States caused difficulties when the League wished to impose obligations concerning minority populations akin to those in the Minorities Treaties on States applying to join the League later, such as Albania and the Baltic States.
4. See, for example, the Treaty of Versailles with respect to Poland, UKTS 8 (1919), Cmd 223; the Treaty of St Germain with Czechoslovakia, 1919 (UKTS 20 (1919), Cmd 479); the Treaty of St Germain with the Serb-Croat-Slovene State, 1919 (UKTS 17 (1919), Cmd 461); the Treaty of Trianon with Hungary, 1920 (UKTS 10 (1920), Cmd 896); Treaty of Sèvres with Greece, 1920, UKTS 13 (1920), Cmd 960; and Treaty of Lausanne with Turkey 1923 (UKTS 16 (1923), Cmd 1929). For a full list, see the Commission on Human Rights, *Study of the Legal Validity of the Undertakings Concerning Minorities*, E/CN.4/367, 7 April 1950, at 2–3.
5. For a geological approach to nations, see A. Smith, *Gastronomy or Geology? The Role of Nationalism in the Reconstruction of Nations*, 1 Nations & Nationalism (1995) 3, at 13.
6. Not, "We the Member States. . .".
7. Article 2 of the Declaration is broader still, and prohibits discrimination on the additional grounds of colour, political or other opinion, national or social origin, property, birth or other status. Non-discrimination is a limited understanding of minority rights, protecting members of the group from less favourable treatment, but having no concept of positively promoting the group's identity.
8. Its terms of reference may be found in UN Doc. A/CONF.32/6 paras. 114 and 115 (1949).
9. The Convention on the Prevention and Punishment of the Crime of Genocide, 78 UNTS 277, entered into force in 1951.
10. ETS 5 (1950), 213 UNTS 222. It entered into force in 1953 and is hereinafter referred to as the ECHR.
11. "The Commission may receive petitions addressed to the Secretary-General of the Council of Europe from any person, non-governmental organisation or *group of individuals . . .* (emphasis added)". See *Application No.8765/79, The Liberal Party et al. v United Kingdom*, 4 European Human Rights Reports (1982) 106, at 120–121.

12. ETS 35 (1961); 529 UNTS 89. It came into force in 1965.
13. It is arguable that on this point the Preamble is binding – *Case Concerning the Rights of Nationals of the USA in Morocco* ICJ Rep. 1952, 176. The Revised European Social Charter, adopted in Summer 1996, now includes within the body of the treaty (Part V, Article E) a general non-discrimination clause referring, *inter alia*, to 'national extraction and social origins' and 'association with a national minority'.
14. See F. Capotorti, *Study on the Rights of Persons Belonging to Ethnic, Religious and Linguistic Minorities, 1977*, published as a separate volume by the United Nations in 1991, E.91.XIV.2.
15. Human Rights Committee General Comment No. 23(50) (Article27) (Fifteenth Session, 1994), UN Doc. CCPR/C/21/Rev.1/Add.5, 1994, paras. 5.1 and 5.2.
16. See Council of Europe, *Explanatory Memorandum on the Framework Convention for the Protection of National Minorities*, paras. 1–9, appended with the Convention to H. Klebes, "The Council of Europe's Framework Convention for the Protection of National Minorities", 16 *Human Rights Law Journal* (1995) 92, at 101–102. The Convention can also be found at 34 *ILM* (1995) 351.
17. Established by the Council of Europe to look into the possibility of a minority rights protocol, but which decided to await the decision in the then pending *Belgian Linguistics* case, *infra* n. 18.
18. *Case Relating to Certain Aspects of the Laws on the Use of Languages in Education in Belgium (Merits)*, Judgment of 23 July 1968, Series A, Vol.6.
19. Recommendation 285 (1961) was based on a Protocol to the ECHR which had been proposed in 1959; see F. Capotorti 1977, *supra* n. 14, at para. 51; and P. Thornberry, *International Law and the Rights of Minorities* (1991), at 305–06.
20. See Council of Europe's deliberations from 1973, recorded in Capotorti, *supra* n. 14, at para. 51, and the United Nations' approach as set out in Capotorti at paras. 196–201. The United Nations General Assembly's 1992 Declaration on the Rights of Persons Belonging to National or Ethnic, Religious and Linguistic Minorities, GA Res.47/135, 18 December 1992, speaks of "national *or* ethnic, cultural, religious and linguistic minorities", explicitly using 'national' as a variety of minority and not as a precondition.
21. J. Packer, "On the Definition of Minorities", in J. Packer and K. Myntti, *The Protection of Ethnic and Linguistic Minorities in Europe* (1993), at 23. The OSCE instruments also fail to define national minority, although the present High Commissioner on National Minorities, Max van der Stoel, has said that whilst he may not be able to provide a definition, 'he knows one when he sees one', see J. Wright, *infra* n. 56, at 202.
22. Immediately calling into question the status of trans-border nomadic Roma.
23. H. Klebes, *supra* n. 16, at 93.
24. See G. Gilbert, "The Legal Protection Accorded to Minority Groups in Europe", 23 *Netherlands Yearbook of International Law* (1992), at 67.
25. *X v Austria, Application No.8142/78*, 18 DR 88 at 92–93 (1979). The American Convention on Human Rights, 9 *ILM* (1970) 673, also fails to refer to minority rights.
26. The position of Bretons in France who can speak French provides a good example – *K v France, Application No.10210/82*, 35 DR 203 at 207 (1983); see also, *Isop v Austria, Application No.2333/64*, 8 YB.ECHR 338 (1965). However, if minority rights were recognised as such, it is possible that Breton would be accepted as one of the national languages. The applicant had been treated no differently from any other French speaker in France, although his cultural and linguistic identity had been denied to him in public life. Bretons have fared no better when complaining to the Human Rights

Committee under Article 27 of the ICCPR – See Communication No. 220/1987 (*T.K. v. France*), declared inadmissible on 8 November 1989, paragraph 8.6 and Appendices I and II (Annual Report 1990, A/45/40, Vol. II, Annex X.A).

On the other hand, the minority might indirectly receive protection of its way of life under ECHR provisions such as: Article 8 (*Buckley, infra* n. 40); Article 9 (*Kokkinakis v Greece*, Series A, vol.260–A); Protocol 1 Article 1 (*Cyprus v Turkey, Application No.6780/74 and 6950/75*, 2 DR 125 (1975), 4 EHRR 482 (1976) Com. Rep.); Protocol 1 Article 2 (*Kjeldsen, Busk Madsen and Pedersen v Denmark* Series A, vol.23 1976, Series B, vol.21 1975); and, Protocol 1 Article 3, *infra* n. 36.

27. Group rights should be read in this context as referring to those benefits accorded to the minority population which it exercises collectively, as opposed to those rights of members of the minority which are exercised in community with other members.
28. *Supra* n. 18.
29. *Ibid.*, at 34. See also, *McFeeley v United Kingdom, Application No.8317/78*, 3 European Human Rights Reports (1981) 161, at 214–15.
30. *Supra* n. 18, at 70.
31. *Christians Against Racism and Fascism v United Kingdom, Application No.8440/78*, 21 DR 138, at 152 (1980); hereinafter, the *CARAF* case.
32. Series A, vol.139, 13 European Human Rights Reports (1988) 204, at 210.
33. The *Plattform* case, *ibid.*, concerned Article 11 which provides for freedom of association. *Cf. CARAF, supra* n. 31 and *Application No.8191/78, Rassemblement Jurassien & Unité Jurassienne v Switzerland*, 17 DR 93 (1979), where it was held that the State was allowed to take into consideration the likely reaction of the majority.
34. See Application No.18877/91, *Ahmet Sadik v Greece*, (46/1995/552/638), 25 October 1996. The Commission's decision was reversed by the Court on the basis that the applicant had not exhausted domestic remedies (Article 26). The Commission's views on the merits were not challenged and were reasserted in the joint dissent of Martens and Foighel JJ which saw this case as part of a dispute between the State and a minority group. See also, *Sidoropoulos v Greece*, (57/1997/841/1047) 10 July 1998, where the European Court of Human Rights held that the refusal by the Greek courts to register an organization calling itself "Home of Macedonian Civilization" violated Article 11 (freedom of association) of the ECHR. Given that one only had the proposed organization's aims as they had been set out in its draft memorandum of association, and those were of a wholly cultural nature, even if its true aim were to assert that there was a "Macedonian" minority in Greece and that the Greek authorities did not respect its rights, banning the organization was disproportionate (paras.43–47).
35. *Supra.* n. 11, at 123.
36. See Article 3 of Protocol 1, taken together with Article 14.
37. In *Application No.8364/78, Lindsay et al. v United Kingdom*, [1979] 3 CMLR 166, at 170–71, the Commission held: "A system of proportionate representation will lead to the minority being represented in situations where people vote generally on ethnic or religious lines and one group is in a clear minority throughout all electoral districts. Where such a situation exists only in a specific region of a country – as it does in Northern Ireland – the Commission cannot find that the application of a system more favourable to the minority in this part of the country is not in line with the condition that the people should be able to express its opinion freely. Rather on the contrary, a system taking into account the specific situation as to majority and minority existing in Northern Ireland must be seen as making it easier for the people to express its opinion freely".

The Commission was prepared to uphold this grant of preferential treatment, even though the majority in Northern Ireland would not gain as many seats as they would if the rules applying in the rest of the United Kingdom applied there.

38. For instance, while *Lindsay*, *ibid.*,shows how the nationalist community in Northern Ireland could receive preferential treatment from the State, there is no way that the Scottish or Welsh nationalists could assert their entitlement to similar treatment under the ECHR since there is no right to any particular type of electoral system.

39. *Application Nos.9278 & 9415/81*, 35 DR 30, at 35–36 (1983).

40. *Application No.20348/92*, Commission, 2 March 1995, 19 European Human Rights Reports (1995) CD 20. Buckley's complaints were, however, rejected by the Court: (23/1995/529/615), 25 September 1996.

41. *Buckley*, *ibid.*, at paras. 64 and 65.

42. In *G and E v Norway*, *supra* n. 39, the Commission found no violation of Article 8 because it was proper to take account of the economic well-being of the State. Similarly, the Court in *Buckley*, *supra* n. *40*, reversed the opinion of the Commission, saying the local authority was justified in taking the interests of the other residents of the village into consideration under Article 8(2) – see also, F. Gibb and I. Murray, "Gypsy must stop living in caravan on her own land", *The Times* , 26 September 1996, at 2. In *G and E v Norway*, the Commission also observed (at 35) that there was no express guarantee of minority rights in the Convention, only a prohibition against discrimination – moreover, as Norwegian citizens, the Lapp applicants had all the same rights as other citizens, including the right to vote. Despite there being no Lapp representation in the Norwegian Parliament, the mere fact Lapps could vote and stand for election denied their having suffered discrimination. The application was declared inadmissible.

43. Doc.HRI\GEN\1\Rev.1 at 12 (1994), para. 6.

44. For example, the banning by the Turkish Constitutional Court of the DEP, an opposition Turkish political party which drew its support predominantly from the Kurdish population, on 16 June 1994.

45. *Communication No.167/1984, Bernard Ominayak, Chief of the Lake Lubicon Band v Canada*, Views adopted 26 March 1990, UNGAOR, 45th Sess., Supp. No.40, A/45/40.

46. F.Kirgis, "The Degrees of Self-determination in the United Nations Era", 88 *American Journal of International Law* (1994) 304. I am grateful to my colleague Jane Wright for discussions on this point.

47. *Cf. KPD v FRG*, the *German Communist Party* case, *Application No.250/57*, 1 YB.ECHR 222 (1957), which, by analogy, must imply the right to political participation in normal circumstances. See, also, *TBKP v Turkey* (133/1996/752/951) 30 January 1998, para. 56.

48. In *Application No.7823 and 7824/77, Kalderas Gypsies v FRG and Netherlands*, 11 DR 221 (1977), the Commission could deal with the complaint that the father's name was not on the child's birth certificate by saying that the German Basic Law did not discriminate against illegitimate children (at 232–33), whereas the real issue concerned the failure of the FRG to recognise Gypsy marriages, a question of cultural status. (*Cf.* On the issue of recognition, see *Marckx v Belgium* Series A, vol.31 (1979), at para. 31).

The difficulties that the lack of an express minorities provision creates are also evident from the *Belgian Linguistics* case, *supra* n. 18, at 7, where what was in effect a claim to mother-tongue education had to be couched in six complaints alleging discrimination in the provision of and access to State education and funding. Since there was an educational system provided, although teaching was in Dutch, there was no effective discrimination: nonetheless, the cultural identity of the group was threatened.

49. *Supra* n. 18, at 43.
50. *Ibid.* It is not discriminatory to give education in only one State language under Article 2 of Protocol 1 taken together with Article 14:

> "Article 14 does not prohibit distinctions in treatment which are founded on an objective assessment of essentially different factual circumstances and which, being based on the public interest strike a fair balance between the protection of the interests of the community and respect for the rights and freedoms safeguarded by the Convention.
>
> This legislation . . . tends to prevent in the Dutch-unilingual region, the establishment or maintenance of schools which teach only in French. Such a measure cannot be considered arbitrary. To begin with, it is based on the objective element which the region constitutes. Furthermore, it is based on a public interest, namely to ensure that all schools dependent on the State and existing in a unilingual region conduct their teaching in a language that is essentially that of the region", at 44.

51. Under neither Articles 10 and 11 of the ECHR, nor Protocol 1 Article 3. See *Application No.10650/83, Clerfayt and Legros v Belgium*, 42 DR 212 (1985). The case finally turned on whether the Commission had jurisdiction over the procedural affairs of the various assemblies – at 222. See also, *Mathieu-Mohin and Clerfayt v Belgium*, Series A, vol.113, 10 European Human Rights Reports (1988) 1.
52. *Ibid.*, at 18.
53. *Ibid.*, at 20.
54. Formerly the Conference on Security and Co-operation in Europe.
55. CSCE Copenhagen Document, 11 *Human Rights Law Journal* 232 (1990). See also, T. Buergenthal, "A new public order for Europe", 11 *Human Rights Law Journal* (1990), at 217.
56. See J. Wright, "The OSCE and the Protection of Minority Rights", 18 *Human Rights Quarterly* (1996), at 190.
57. See G. Malinverni, "The Draft Convention for the Protection of Minorities", 12 *Human Rights Law Journal* (1991) 265, at 268. Malinverni's piece is an abridged version of his article, "Le projet de convention pour la protection des minorités élaboré par la Commission européenne pour la démocratie par le droit", 3 *Revue Universelle Des Droits de L'Homme* (1991), at 157.
58. See A. Bloed, "Monitoring the CSCE Human Dimension: in Search of its Effectiveness", in A. Bloed, *et al.*, *Monitoring Human Rights in Europe* (1993), at 51–52. Bloed cites P. van Dijk, "The Final Act of Helsinki – Basis for a Pan-European System?", 11 *Netherlands Yearbook of International Law* (1980) 110, for the proposition that although OSCE commitments are only politically binding, they are still binding on the participating States; whether a right is legally binding or politically binding only goes to the means of enforcement, not its ultimate enforceability.
59. Although only an indirect contribution to the instruments proposed by the Council of Europe to further minority rights, the 1992 European Charter for Regional or Minority Languages is primarily a cultural agreement recognising "regional or minority languages as an expression of cultural wealth" (Article 7). Notwithstanding that it is

stated to be a cultural convention, it can enhance minority rights in the field of mother-tongue education and public use, although relying, as it does, on periodic State reports to monitor State compliance does detract from its effectiveness.
60. That is, the profession of religion, the enjoyment of culture, the use of one's mother-tongue.
61. Article 1.b. of the proposed Protocol stated that a national minority is one that wishes to "maintain longstanding, firm and lasting ties".
62. See Recommendation 1255 (1995).
63. *Supra* n. 16. And see G. Gilbert, "The Council of Europe and Minority Rights", 18 *Human Rights Quarterly* (1996), at 160.
64. For example, Article 11(3) of the Framework Convention provides that:
    "In areas *traditionally* inhabited by *substantial* numbers of persons belonging to a national minority, the Parties shall *endeavour, in the framework of their legal system*, including, *where appropriate*, agreements with other States, and *taking into account their specific conditions*, to display traditional local names, street names and other topographical indications intended for the public also in the minority language *when there is a sufficient demand* for such indications". (emphasis added)
65. See paragraph 11 of the Explanatory Memorandum, *supra* n. 16.
66. Articles 24–26. The Council of Europe is currently working on the detailed rules for the mechanism and it would be fair to say that the jury is out on its effectiveness in the future. On a positive note, see A. Phillips, *Memorandum on the Composition and Procedures of the Advisory Committee to be set up under the Framework Convention for the Protection of National Minorities*, AS/Jur/DH (1996) 2, 21 March 1996, Council of Europe Parliamentary Assembly.
67. It came into force, 1 February 1998, and contracting parties on that date were: Croatia, Cyprus, Denmark, Estonia, Finland, Germany, Hungary, Italy, Liechtenstein, Malta, Moldova, Romania, San Marino, Slovakia, Spain, 'the former Yugoslav Republic of Macedonia', Ukraine and the United Kingdom.
68. *Supra* n. 55.
69. See the Slovak Parliament's understanding of the bilateral treaty at the time of ratification in May 1996 – I am grateful to my colleague J. Wright for her assistance on this point. See J. Wright, "The Protection of Minority Rights in Europe: From Conference to Implementation", 2 *International Journal of Human Rights* (1998) 1.
70. See *The Guardian*, 16 September 1996, at 1.
71. H. Poulton, *Who Are the Macedonians?* (1995).
72. It is amazing what a mere 50 years can accomplish: Italy only achieved unification around 1860, whereas it was the Second Balkan War of 1913 that decided Macedonia's borders with its Greek and Bulgarian neighbours. There is no logical reason why Italy should be seen as any more stable than Macedonia if one looks to the longevity of their international borders, but all the other factors that indicate instability in the Balkans suggest that Padania is less of a threat. Nevertheless, there is also an element of ill-informed prejudice on the part of Western governments behind this perception of Macedonia.
73. Although the High Commissioner on National Minorities' mandate is conflict prevention, not the human dimension, see J. Wright, *supra* n. 56.
74. *Ibid.*, at 198.
75. *Cf.* The Act LXXVII of 1993 On The Rights of National and Ethnic Minorities passed by the Hungarian National Assembly.

Monitoring Minority Rights under the Council of Europe's Framework Convention

Gerd Oberleitner*

INTRODUCTION

On 10 November 1994 the Committee of Ministers of the Council of Europe adopted the Framework Convention on the Rights of National Minorities, which was subsequently opened for signature on 1 February 1995 and entered into force three years later.[1] While the Framework Convention is the first legally binding instrument on minority rights, it has been the subject of heavy criticism for its shortcomings, notably the absence of a definition of "minorities" the vague character of its provisions and, in particular, the supervisory mechanism adopted.[2] The Parliamentary Assembly of the Council of Europe has called the Convention 'weakly worded' and expressed the opinion that "its implementation machinery is feeble and there is danger that, in fact, the monitoring procedures may be left entirely to the governments".[3]

The supervisory mechanism is contained in Section IV of the Framework Convention (Articles 24–26). Under it, State parties to the Convention are bound to submit periodic and *ad hoc* reports to the Committee of Ministers, which will monitor the implementation of the provisions of the Convention. The Committee of Ministers will be assisted by an Advisory Committee composed of independent experts. The European Court on Human Rights will not be involved in the monitoring of the Framework Convention.[4]

This chapter will assess the approach adopted by the Council of Europe with regard to the monitoring of implementation by State parties of the Framework Convention, and will examine the fundamental requirements and pre-requisites needed for its proper and effective functioning. The key factors that will be examined are the possible content of State reports on minority rights; the time frame for the submission of the reports (and the potential problem of inadequate and overdue reports); the composition, mandate and procedure of the Convention's Advisory Committee; the Advisory Committee's relationship with the Committee of Ministers; and

P. Cumper and S. Wheatley (eds.), Minority Rights in the 'New' Europe, 71–88

finally, the increasingly important role of non-governmental actors.[5] Any analysis of the Framework Convention's reporting system is problematic, given that both the Framework Convention and the Explanatory Report to the Framework Convention[6] only sketch the scope and content of the proposed system, leaving it to the Committee of Ministers to determine the details within one year of the entry into force of the Framework Convention.[7] Consequently, not only the Framework Convention, but also the relevant provisions (and supervisory mechanisms) of human rights conventions adopted under the auspices of the United Nations,[8] the International Labour Organisation and the Council of Europe[9] will be taken into account in order to establish the criteria against which the efficiency of the Framework Convention's monitoring mechanism may be measured.

CONTENT OF REPORTS AND TIME FRAME

The relevant provisions on the content of State reports under the Framework Convention and their frequency are contained in Article 25 of the convention:

> (1) Within a period of one year following the entry into force of this Framework Convention in respect of a Contracting Party, the latter shall transmit to the Secretary General of the Council of Europe full information on the legislative and other measures taken to give effect to the principles set out in this Framework Convention.
> (2) Thereafter, each Party shall transmit to the Secretary General on a periodical basis and whenever the Committee of Ministers so requests any further information of relevance to the implementation of this Framework Convention.
> (3) The Secretary General shall forward to the Committee of Ministers the information transmitted under the terms of this Article.

Thus the Convention makes a distinction between information on 'legislative' and 'other' measures taken by State parties which will consequently allow the monitoring bodies to be kept informed on both *de jure* and *de facto* measures undertaken by the State in accordance with its obligations under the Framework Convention, reflecting the view that a purely legalistic approach does not meet the requirements of an effective reporting system.

State reports should give an accurate picture of the human rights (in this case minority rights) situation in a given State. As noted in the Convention on the Rights of the Child: "The report shall contain sufficient information to provide the Committee with a comprehensive understanding of the implementaion of the Convention in the country concerned".[10] Taking into account the obligations under other conventions,[11] not only laws, decrees, orders and other legal norms should be included, but also all relevant administrative acts by regional, sub-original and local authorities will have to be reflected in the reports as far as they concern minority rights. Acts of the judiciary and court decisions (with an emphasis on the judgements of the highest national courts) will also have to be presented to the monitoring bodies. If the supervisory bodies of the Framework Convention (the Committee of Ministers and the Advisory Committee) follow the example of other treaty bodies, the first report required under the Framework Convention will, furthermore, have to contain basic information on the country and its legal, administrative and judicial structure.[12] In addition, the monitoring bodies of the Framework Convention will need more detailed information on national institutions which deal with minority questions, and demographic and statistical data in order to evaluate the situation of national minorities in that particular state.

Whilst the Framework Convention only refers to 'measures' undertaken by State parties, other conventions oblige States to report on the progress made towards achieving the full enjoyment of the rights contained in the respective treaties and urge States to report on difficulties they encounter in the implementation of their obligations;[13] at this point additional information from independent sources (necessary to give the supervisory bodies a balanced picture of the situation) may be of particular importance. Some conventions go further and demand information on particular matters. The Human Rights Committee (HRC) of the United Nations, for example, asks States to take into account the HRC's General Comments in their reports.[14] Under the reporting system of the International Labour Organisation, specific information is required with regard to the role non-governmental organisations play in the drafting of reports at the national level,[15] and the Committee on the Rights of the Child makes it possible for reporting States to include formal requests for technical assistance.[16]

Following the presentation of the initial report, a State party to the Framework Convention is required to furnish periodic reports at an indeterminate time frame, with the Committee of Ministers able to request *ad hoc* reports (Article 25(2)). Such *'ad hoc'* or 'emergency' reports are also provided for under other conventions (for example, the Covenant on Civil and Politcal Rights) and have indeed been requested by the treaty bodies.[17] They have, though, met with certain problems. Whilst *ad-hoc* reports allow flexible action by supervisory bodies in situations of crisis, sufficient criteria have not yet been established specifying the circumstances when such reports can be requested. The absence of such criteria may lead to accusations of double standards in the examination of States' parties conduct. Recognising the importance of emergency reports, the Committee on the Rights of the Child has undertaken work on the establishment of such criteria. Its preliminary conclusions are that such reports should be called for (or a visit to the state undertaken) whenever there is a risk that a given human rights situation might deteriorate and further violations are likely to occur. However, this should be done in a spirit of dialogue and the decision should not be politically motivated.[18] It is to be hoped that the Advisory Committee, established under the Framework Convention, will contribute to the further developments of the operation of such emergency procedures, which can significantly raise the importance of the work of supervisory bodies in the State reporting system.[19]

SUPERVISORY BODIES

It may come as little surprise that different approaches have been adopted under the various reporting systems with regard to the structure and mandate of their monitoring bodies. While the UN treaties provide for an independent expert body for each Convention, able to arrive at conclusions from the examination of State reports and in a position to bring them to the attention of the political bodies of the United Nations, the International Labour Organisation, in contrast, has applied a two-step procedure: the examination of State reports by an independent expert committee in camera, followed by a public examination of selected cases before the tripartite Conference Committee of the International Conference (composed of government delegates, employer's and employee's organisations).[20] The European Social Charter enjoys an even more elaborate system, involving an independent expert committee, a governmental committee and the Committee of Ministers, whilst assigning certain duties to the Parliamentary Assembly of the Council of Europe.

The Framework Convention adopts none of these approaches. Instead of employing a Committee composed of independent experts, the Framework Convention establishes an Advisory Body with the task of assisting the Committee of Ministers (the principal political body of the Council of Europe) in its examinations of State reports. The relevant provisions read as follows:

Article 24

(1) The Committee of Ministers of the Council of Europe shall monitor the implementation of the Framework Convention by the Contracting Parties.

Article 26

(1) In evaluating the adequacy of the measures taken by the Parties to give effect to the principles set out in this Framework Convention the Committee of Ministers shall be assisted by an advisory committee, the members of which shall have recognised expertise in the field of the protection of national minorities.

(2) The compostion of the advisory committee and its procedures shall be determined by the Committee of Ministers within a period of one year following the entry into force of this Framework Convention.

ADVISORY COMMITTEE

Before discussing the possible consequences of the adoption of the chosen mechanism under the Framework Convention, the mandate and compostion of the Advisory Committee shall be analysed. Whilst the Framework Convention leaves these matters to be determined by the Committee of Ministers, the experience of other reporting systems indicates that such issues are crucial to the effectiveness of any supervisory machinery; in particular the method of election of the members, their qualifications and independence from political interference deserve attention.

The Parliamentary Assembly of the Council of Europe has shown a keen interest in the Framework Convention and, in particular, in the Advisory Committee's mandate and composition. The Assembly has issued several Recommendations,[21] in which it stresses, in particular, the question of the independence, efficiency and transparency of the Advisory Committee's work. The Assembly, in Recommendation 1255 (1995), has argued that the election of the experts should take place along the same lines as the election of the members of the European Commission of Human Rights or the European Committee for the Prevention of Torture, whose members are nominated by the Parliamentary Assembly and elected by the Committee of Ministers.[22]

According to the rules on the monitoring arrangements of the Framework Convention, the number of experts in the Advisory Committee shall be a minimum of twelve and a maximum of eighteen with a rotation system when the number of eighteen is exceeded. Each State party may nominate at least two experts. The Committee of Ministers shall then elect one of these experts to a list of experts eligible to serve on the Advisory Committee and then appoint members from this list according to the rules on the monitoring arrangements. Once the number exceeds eighteen, the Committee of Ministers shall give priority to appointing experts from Parties of which no ordinary member has been appointed at two or more consecutive rounds of appointments immediately preceding the current one, or at the round of appointments immediately preceding the current one. Experts shall be elected for a term of office of four years, only two terms of offices are possible. "Additional members" can be appointed from the list, who participate in the consideration of the State report of their nominating State without voting rights.

As for the qualifications of the experts, the Framework Convention merely requires them to have a recognised expertise in the field of the protection of national minorities (Article 26(1)). It will be necessary for the quality and effectiveness of the Advisory Committee that States not only nominate highly qualified and truly independent experts, but also that they make sufficient use of the expertise of non-governmental and minority rights groups. The Parliamentary Assembly further stressed the importance of the expert's independence, suggesting that they should not hold positions which are incompatible with their independence and impartiality, or the demands of office;[23] indeed this is a central pre-requisite for the efficiency and credibility of any expert body.[24] The rules on the monitoring arrangements reflect these concerns. The Parliamentary Assembly of the Council of Europe also emphasises the importance of a balance of professional and cultural backgrounds of the experts serving on the Advisory Committee.[25] Such a multi-disciplinary approach is also advocated by, for example, Philips, who demands that "members should range from international lawyers to linguistic scholars and educationalists, from political analysts to anthropologists and psychologists".[26] Indeed, in attempting to evaluate the situation of minorities not only from a legal point of view, but to take into account other factors of particular importance for minorities such as language or education, such a broad composition of the Advisory Committee may be useful.

In performing its duties, the Advisory Committee will inevitably depend primarily on the information contained in State reports. However, in order to reach well-founded conclusions, other sources of information will have to be considered so as to avoid simply accepting a government's perspective on a particular issue. Consequently, the Parliamentary Assembly desires that the Advisory Committe be able to take into account information from inter-governmental organisations, scientific organisations, national and international Non-Governmental Organisations and persons belonging to national minorities.[27] The rules on the monitoring arrangements make it clear that the Advisory Committee can receive any information it wants, but needs the approval of the Committee of Ministers if it intends to invite such information or wishes to hold meetings for the purpose of seeking information from other sources. In adition to these sources of information, the Advisory Committee will also have to explore how to best co-operate with the OSCE High Commissioner on National Minorities and how to make best use of the information contained in State reports under other conventions in order to reduce the burden on reporting States. If, in addition, the Advisory Committee may consider it useful to hear comments from experts on minority rights when examining a report, it should follow the example of the Committee on Economic, Social and Cultural Rights, which has introduced a 'day of general discussion' on selected issues with the purpose of hearing experts who otherwise could not speak before it.[28]

To complement the information from State parties and other sources on which the Advisory Committee's conclusions are based, it may also wish to collect information by conducting missions to State parties. Indeed, in the drafting process of the Framework Convention a proposal was discussed which would have established a committee, similar to the European Committee for the Prevention of Torture and Inhuman or Degrading Treatment, able to conduct missions to State parties.[29] Such visits should not be targeted at problematic situations alone but should be designed as confidence building measures and be applied on a regular basis and in an impartial manner.[30]

The Framework Convention provisions of monitoring further lack explicit reference to one important feature of an effective reporting machinery: the examination of State reports in public sessions and in the presence of State representatives. Those representatives are able to present their countries' reports, provide additional information, answer expert's questions and report back to their governments. This is the core element of the reporting procedure and the visible proof that the machinery is bassed on a dialogue between State parties and the supervisory body. The need for this practice is convincing and it is now part of all reporting systems, "in fact, it is the presence of government representatives that has first given some colour and consequence to the monitoring procedure".[31] Furthermore, the negative experiences of the supervisory bodies of the European Social Charter may, to some extent, be attributed to the fact that no State representatives are present during the deliberations before the Committee of Experts.[32] Consequently, the Parliamentary Assembly has recommended that the Advisory Committee, set up under the Framework Convention, should be able to enter into a dialogue with the government of the contracting party concerned.[33] The rules on the monitoring arrangements now enable the Advisory Committee to hold meetings with State representatives, whose report is being considered. The Committee must hold a meeting if the State so requires. As the Advisory Committee has accepted the possibility of a dialogue with the State, it will, in turn, have to deal with the question of non-attendance of State representatives and will have to decide how to react to such situations.[34]

The Framework Convention does not specify how the Advisory Committee should deal with its findings and deliberations, and whether it should address recommendations to State parties. Different approaches have been adopted by other supervisory bodies. For example, the Human Rights Committee has long been reluctant to speak out on non-compliance (with the International Covenant on Civil and Political Rights), rather it has chosen to adopt general comments.[35] Through these comments the committee has tried to clarify the scope and content of the Covenant's provisions. It can be expected that the interpretation of the Framework Convention's vague and programmatic provisions will also form an important part of the Advisory Committee's work. Nevertheless the adoption of observations on a State's compliance and recommendations addressed to all State parties, a group of State parties or a single State party, is at the heart ot a reporting system; it is the very *raison d'être* of a reporting system, a fact too often neglected by other supervisory bodies, turning them into insignificant diplomatic activities and severely endangering or damaging their reputation as a means of human rights protection.[36] The supervisory bodies established under the Framework Convention will have to ensure that any examination of State reports also produces visible results in the form of concrete conclusions and recommendations to State parties.

RELATIONS BETWEEN THE COMMITTEE OF MINISTERS AND THE ADVISORY COMMITTEE

The potential relationship between the Committee of Ministers and the Advisory Committee under the scheme envisaged by the Framework Convention remains unclear. A restrictive interpretation of Article 26(1) would lead to the undesirable situation of a governmental body examining State reports with an independent expert body in an assistant capacity only. This would be particularly troublesome, given the lack of independence, transparency and expertise of the Committee of Ministers. The Committee of Ministers cannot fulfil the duties assigned to it under the Convention to examine State reports on its own, as its political character is likely to influence the exercise of the legal functions entrusted to it.[37] Indeed, the role of the Committee of Ministers has been changed by the Eleventh Additional Protocol to the European Convention on Human Rights (adopted on the 5th October 1997) in order to prevent it from examining complaints under the European Convention on Human Rights. A strong and dominant position for the Committee of Ministers under the Framework Convention would be inconsistent with this development.

The European Social Charter may serve as an example of the negative impact of political involvement. Its Governmental Committee has constantly attempted to arrogate powers which are not specifically given to it under the Social Charter and has often arrived at its own conclusions on the basis of information contained in the State reports, neglecting the work of the expert committee. By adopting its own reports (often contradictory to those prepared by the expert committee), the Governmental Committee has paralysed the reporting procedure of the European Social Charter.[38] The role of the Governmental Committee has been changed by the Amending Protocol of 1991, so that the Committee will now act only on the conclusions of the expert committee.[39]

In contrast, the monitoring mechanisms of the International Labour Organisation are often praised, although it is accepted that this model cannot simply be imitated by other organisations, given the tripartite composition of the Conference Committee.[40] The procedures of the ILO involve an examination of all State reports, identifying cases involving serious violations of ILO conventions; these cases are then brought forward to the Conference Committee. Within the Conference Committee, the presence of employers' and employees' organisations in the public sessions leads to substantive debates, with considerable pressure exerted on those governments present.[41]

The question remains whether the Advisory Committee established by the Framework Convention will be able to act in its own capacity (as do the independent treaty bodies under other human rights conventions), or if it will merely be a subsidiary body of the Committee of Ministers. In order to establish a reporting system which would not fall below the standards of existing systems, it has rightly been urged that "the Committee of Ministers' role must be in electing a good Advisory Committee and, as a matter of principle, in supporting them".[42] In order to make clear what this could mean, one should remember the history of the Committee on Economic, Social and Cultural Rights, which has evolved from simply being a working group comprised of State representatives into a fully fledged expert body. Although the Committee is not a treaty body, as, for example, is the Human Rights Committee (but was established by resolution of the Economic and Social Council of the UN and is entrusted with 'assisting' the Council), it has in practice been able to act as an independent committee. The arguments brought forward by State representatives in the process of redefining the committee's role resemble very much the concerns voiced with regard to the Advisory Committee of the Framework Convention: a technical body would be unhampered by political or other considerations; non-State parties would not be involved in the supervisory process as would be the case if the political body was already overburdened with work.[43]

The Parliamentary Assembly, having considered the potential working relationship between the Advisory Body and the Committee of Ministers, concluded the following:[44] under normal circumstances, the Committee of Ministers shall transmit the report and the recommendations made by the Advisory Committee directly and without comments to the State party concerned. Where the Advisory Committee has drawn the attention of the Committee of Ministers to a State's non-compliance in respect of the Framework Convention, a discussion shall be held by the Committee of Ministers and the conclusions submitted to the State party, together with the report and recommendations of the Advisory Committee. Only in exceptional cases should the report be referred back to the Advisory Body, but as a general rule the Committee of Ministers should not re-open the examination of state reports. It will in any case be imperative that serious cases are brought before the Committee of Ministers in order to exert pressure on States which are not in compliance with the Framework Convention.[45] Under the rules on the monitoring arrangements, the Committee of Ministers shall, following the receipt of the opinion of the Advisory Committee, consider and adopt conclusions concerning the adequacy of the measures taken by the contracting party concerned. It may also adopt recommendations and set a time-limit for the submission of information on their implementation. It should be noted that the Committee of Experts established under the European Charter on Regional or Minority Languages adopts a similar procedure. A draft report is forwarded to the Committee of Ministers (with the comments of the State parties) containing suggestions of the Committee of Experts which "shall be taken into account when the Committee of Ministers adopts recommendations to the State parties".[46]

Unlike the European Social Charter, the Framework Convention does not provide a role for the Parliamentary Assembly of the Council of Europe.[47] The Assembly itself wishes to be able to adopt opinions on the reports of the Advisory Committee,[48] a role similar to that assigned to it under the European Charter for Regional or Minority Languages, under which the Secretary General of the Council of Europe is required to submit a report on the implementation of the Charter to the Parliamentary

Assembly every two years.[49] But this role is not expressly provided for within the Framework Convention.

THE ROLE OF NON-GOVERNMENTAL ORGANISATIONS

The increasing importance of non-governmental organisations (NGOs) in the monitoring of human rights has been frequently stressed.[50] The constructive dialogue between State parties and the monitoring body as the central element within the reporting system is not restricted to discussions between these two. Dialogue must also occur on the national level, between governments on the one side, and the civil society and non-governmental organisations on the other. NGOs can contribute to both the 'input' and the 'output' of the State reporting system, including being active in the drafting of national reports. While some States reject the idea of including NGOs in the drafting process, others explicitly invite them to co-operate.[51] NGOs contribute by providing additional information for expert committees and draft counter-reports to that of the State in order to correct inaccurate information, fill gaps and clarify uncertainties; they may also assist in making the national reports more widely known by publishing them or initiating public discussion on their content. They can also – formally or informally – participate in the meetings of expert bodies and provide information and lobby experts.[52]

NGOs also play an essential role in the aftermath of a State's report having been examined by the supervisory bodies, as they are able to ensure that the findings are made available at the national level, and are translated and widely published and discussed. Such publications might contain the State report itself, submissions made by NGOs, relevant parts of the summary records of the expert bodies meetings, the views of the experts, the replies and any additional information put forward by State representatives and the concluding observations and recommendations of the experts.[53] If such exhaustive publications were the outcome of the reporting procedure under the Framework Convention, a valuable stock of information on minority rights in Europe could be compiled over the years and one of the aims of the reporting procedure (sharing information on minority questions) advanced.

Consequently, an active role for NGOs under the Framework Convention may be considered a pre-requisite for the effective operation of the monitoring mechanism.[54] The Parliamentary Assembly proposes that the Advisory Committee should be able to listen to NGOs and representatives of minorities, so that a public examination of a State report can be established in the presence of State representative, NGOs and minority representatives.[55] To some extent, the European Charter for Regional or Minority Languages may provide a model for this, as it allows organisations, which have been lawfully established in the State parties, to draw to the attention of the Committee of Experts of the European Charter on Regional or Minority Languages questions which relate to Part III of the Charter on 'measures for the promotion of the use of regional or minority languages in the public life of the State parties'. The Expert Committee under the European Charter for Regional or Minority Languages may, after consultation with the State parties, take into account such statements in the drafting of the report, and the organisations mentioned may also make statements regarding the aims and principles laid down in Part II of the Charter.[56]

The Explanatory Report to the Framework Convention states that the implementation of the Convention shall, as far as possible, be based on the principle of transparency with the publication of State reports and other related documents envisaged;[57] the full and effective participation of NGO's will help this. Moreover, the rules on the monitoring arrangements of the Framework Convention provide for the publication of the State reports and the conclusions and recommendations of the Committee of Ministers. The European Charter for Regional or Minority Languages also requires that States parties publish their reports[58] and allows the Committee of Ministers to publish the report of the Committee of Experts of the Charter together with the statements of State parties.[54]

INADEQUATE AND OVERDUE REPORTS

The reporting system provided for in the Framework Convention will increase the burden on State parties who are already required to submit reports under various other human rights conventions. Without any doubt the problem of inadequate and overdue reports will arise. From the beginning the monitoring bodies will be confronted with the question of how to deal with this problem. Provided that overdue reports are not the result of a lack of political will, a variety of different methods to deal with this problem may be, and indeed have been (by the other supervisory bodies), developed; these may involve, *inter alia*, assistance in various forms such as model reports, guidelines, handbooks,[60] training sessions for administrative officers, questionnaires[61] or a network of regional advisers (as applied by the ILO[62]).

If such technical assistance does not suffice, attempts have been made by some supervisory bodies to draw up 'black lists' of States which have not reported in time.[63] Such a 'mobilisation of shame', both on the national and international level, may make it clear to States that overdue reports are in violation of their obligations under the relevant convention. Direct personal contacts at high political level may be another possibility. As a last step, some UN treaty bodies have decided to proceed with the examination of States even in the absence of a State report on basis of the last available report.[64] An examination without any report available, however, would exceed the mandate of the supervisory bodies, as governmental information remains the basis for the examination.

CONCLUSIONS

It may be argued that the monitoring of minority rights in Europe has lost much of its momentum after the Council of Europe decided against the idea of adopting an additional protocol on minorities to the European Convention on Human Rights, under which the Convention's supervisory mechanism could have been applied. The Council of Europe now relies on the weakest system of international supervision to monitor principles and programmatic provisions laid down in the Framework Convention: the State reporting mechanism. Furthermore, the Member States of the Council of Europe could not agree to entrust a truly independent body with the task of monitoring minority rights in Europe. Rather, they entrust the monitoring of the Convention to the central political body, the Council of Ministers, an institution with which they feel comfortable. There is great concern, not only from observers but also within the Council of Europe (as the position of the Parliamentary Assembly shows), that the politicised character of the Convention's monitoring system, coupled with a potentially weak Advisory Committee, could result in a reporting system that will not meet the standards required, and thus the protection of minority rights under the Framework Convention will prove a futile undertaking. This would indeed "question the competence of the Council of Europe on an issue that is agreed is crucial to its existence and for the people of Europe".[65]

To be fully effective, the Framework Convention requires a truly independent Advisory Committee composed of renowned experts with sufficient resources to enable it to carry out its duties, which should go beyond purely 'assisting' the Committee of Ministers. The Advisory Committee must, at least, be able to act in accordance with the standards which other independent supervisory bodies at the international and regional level have set. The proceedings before this Committee must be public, transparent and seek the co-operation of non-governmental partners concerned with minority rights. The Advisory Committee must make it clear that, although its first and foremost task is to enter into a dialogue with State parties, it is not a forum to exchange diplomatic niceties; its function is to monitor legal obligations and speak out on violations of international law.

With such a supervisory body, the Framework Convention may develop into a valuable tool for the protection of minority rights in Europe, within the limits inevitably imposed by a State reporting systems. While such a system is by no means a substitute for a complaints procedure, the installation of an obligatory periodic reporting mechanism can initiate a continuing dialogue on minority rights among European States, so that minority rights can become part of routine international co-operation. State reporting under the Framework Convention may enable the international community to adopt a non-selective and impartial approach to minority issues, allowing it to respond to minorities' concerns in a pro-active and preventive sense.[66] A functioning reporting system may develop into a 'minority rights watch' and an information system open and accessible to governments, minorities and NGOs. Although the Advisory Body is not explicitly entrusted with a promotional mandate, its activities will inevitably raise awareness about the situation of minorities, the difficulties they face and the rights they claim. State reports enable the compilation of exhaustive, reliable and up-to-date information on the legal and real situation of minorities throughout Europe. A successful reporting system will lead to a constant evaluation of different national approaches towards the protection of minorities and may initiate changes in law and practice. By speaking out on violations and by adopting recommendations, the supervisory bodies can assist States in the formulation of policies and strategies and can lay the basis for further technical assistance. However, it is unfortunate that the Council of Europe, in establishing the monitoring mechanism under the Framework Convention, has not sufficiently taken account of the experiences gained by other reporting systems. In working out the details of the reporting mechanism, the Committee of Ministers of the Member States of the Council of Europe will now have to demonstrate whether it is serious about monitoring minority rights in Europe.

NOTES

*Lecturer at the Institute of International Law and International Relations at the University of Graz, Austria.

1.   1 February 1998.
2.   For the substantive provisions of the Convention, see H. Klebes, "The Council of Europe's Framework Convention for the Protection of National Minorities", 16 *Human Rights Law Journal* (1995) 1; A. Rönquist, "The Council of Europe Framework

Convention for the Protection of National Minorities", 6 *Helsinki Monitor* (1995) 1, at 38–44.

3. Recommendation 1255 (1995).
4. On the relationship between the Framework Convention and the European Convention on Human Rights, see G. Gilbert, "The Council of Europe and Minority Rights", 18 *Human Rights Quarterly* (1996) 175.
5. Some of these issues are also dealt with in a memorandum prepared by the Minority Rights Group for the Parliamentary Assembly of the Council of Europe of March 1996: A. Philips, *The Rights of Minorities. The Composition and Procedures of the Advisory Committee to be set up under the Framework Convention for the Protection of National Minorities*, Council of Europe Doc. AS/Jur/DH (1996) 2.
6. Council of Europe Doc. H (94) 10.
7. Article 26(2) of the Framework Convention. Following this provision, the Committee of Ministers' Deputies established an *ad hoc* committee of experts (CAHMEC) in March 1996 to clarify pertinent questions and to identify possible options for the supervisory mechanism. The committee has elaborated rules on the monitoring arrangements, which have been adopted by the Committee of Ministers on 17 September 1997 (Resolution (97) 10). See, in greater detail, M. Weckerling, "Der Durchfuehrungsmechanismus des Rahmenuebereinkommens des Europarates zum Schutz nationaler Minderheiten", 24 *Europaeische Grundrechtezeitschrift* (1998) 23–24, at 605–608. Presently guidelines for State reports are under preparation.
8. See for example the Convention against all Forms of Racial Discrimination (1966); the International Covenant on Economic, Social and Cultural Rights, and the International Covenant on Civil and Political Rights (both 1966); the Convention on the Elimination of Discrimination against Women (1979); the Convention against Torture and other Inhuman or Degrading Treatment (1984); and the Convention on the Rights of the Child (1989).
9. The European Charter on Regional and Minority Languages and, in particular, the European Social Charter (1961). With the Amending Protocol of Turin to the European Social Charter, ETS 142 (1991), the supervisory system of the Charter has seen considerable changes which are taken into account in this article.
10. Article 44(2) of the Convention on the Rights of the Child.
11. See Article 9(1) of the Convention on the Elimination of all Forms of Racial Discrimination and 18(1) of the Convention on the Elimination of Discrimination against Women, which explicitly refer to "legislative, judicial, administrative and other measures".
12. To ease the burden on reporting States and to prevent duplication of the work of the monitoring bodies, the UN treaty bodies are now asking for "Core Documents", containing basic information on a State party, which has to be provided only once and can be utilised by all treaty bodies. The monitoring bodies of the Framework Convention will have to consider how to make best use of this information.
13. Article 18(1) of the Covenant on Economic, Social and Cultural Rights, Article 40(1) of the Covenant on Civil and Political Rights and Article 44(1) of the Covenant against Torture and other forms of Inhuman or Degrading Treatment.
14. See Guidelines regarding the Form and Content of Periodic Reports from States Parties, UN Doc. CCPR/C/20/Rev.2/1995, Article 6.
15. *ILO-Handbook on Procedures Relating to International Labour Conventions and Recommendations* (1995), at 17.
16. Article 45(b) of the Convention on the Rights of the Child.

17. See Rule 66 of the Rules of Procedure of the Human Rights Committee, UN Doc. CCPR/C/3/Rev.4 (1997). For examples see Report of the Human Rights Committee, UN Doc. A/50/40 (1995), at para. 36, and in greater detail S. Joseph, "New Procedures concerning the Human Rights Committee's Examination of State Reports", 13 *Netherlands Quarterly of Human Rights* (1995) 1, at 13; and M. O'Flaherty, *Human Rights and the UN. Practice before the Treaty Bodies* (1996), at 45.

18. See Report of the Committee on the Rights of the Child, UN Doc. A/49/41 (1994), at para. 372–381.

19. See also in greater detail the proposals and comments made in this respect by Amnesty International, *Facing up to the Failures: Proposals for Improving the Protection of Human Rights by the United Nations*, ai-index IOR/41/16/92 (1992), at 33; and the Norwegian Institute for Human Rights, *Making the Reporting Procedure under the International Covenant on Civil and Political Rights More Effective* (1991), at 7.

20. See, for a detailed analysis of this system, V. Leary, "Lessons from the Experience of the International Labour Organisations", in P. Alston (ed.), *The United Nations and Human Rights* (1992), at 580–619.

21. Recommendation 1255 (1995), Recommendation1285 (1996) and Recommendation 1300 (1996).

22. Article 21 of the European Convention on Human Rights and Article 5 of the European Convention on the Prevention of Torture. The same procedure is also applied by the European Charter for Regional or Minority Languages (Article 17). In contrast, the Amending Protocol to the ESC provides for the election of experts through the Parliamentary Assembly (Article 25 of the European Social Charter as amended by the Protocol 1991).

23. Recommendation 1300.

24. It may be worth mentioning that the Amending Protocol to the European Social Charter goes even further and introduces a provision stating that the members of the Charter's Committee of Experts must actually be available to be regularly present at the sessions (Article 25(1) of the European Social Charter as amended by the Protocol 1991).

25. See Recommendation 1300. Philips, *supra* n. 5, at 5.

26. See Explanatory Report to the Framework Convention, Council of Europe Doc. H (94) 10, and Recommendation 1300 (1996).

27. See P. Alston, "The Committee on Economic, Social and Cultural Rights", in P. Alston (ed.), *supra* n. 20, at 493.

28. See H. Klebes, *supra* n. 2, at 94.

29. See A. Philips, *supra* n. 5, at 7. The Committee on Rights of the Child may serve as an example, as it has recognised the importance of establishing closer contacts with local NGOs and the population and has already sent missions to States parties to the Convention on the Rights of the Child. See Report of the Committee on the Rights of the Child, UN Doc, A/49/41 (1994), at para. 371–381. C. Tomuschat, "Human Rights, State Reports", in R. Wolfrum and C. Philip (eds.), *United Nations: Law, Policies and Practice* (1995), at 632. See for a more detailed analysis of the advantages of inviting State representatives, K.J. Partsch, "The Racial Discrimination Committee", in P. Alston (ed.), *supra* n. 20, at 354.

30. See the critique by T. Öhlinger, "Die Europäische Sozialcharta", in F. Matscher *et al.* (eds.), *The Implementation of Social and Economic Rights* (1991), at 351.

31. Recommendation 1300 (1996)

32. The Committee on Economic, Social and Cultural Rights, for example, proceeds with

the examination of State Reports in the absence of State representatives on the third occasion that a State fails to send such a representative, see P. Alston, *supra* n. 27, at 506.

33. See T. Opsahl, "The Human Rights Committee", in P. Alston (ed.), *supra* n. 20, at 407. It should be noted that in April 1994 the committee adopted General Comment 23(50) on Article 27 of the Covenant on Civil and Political Rights, dealing with minority rights. See Report of the Human Rights Committee, UN Doc. A/49/40 (1994) vol., (Annex V).

34. To give a particularly frustrating example, it should be noted that in decades not a single recommendation has emerged from the reporting system of the European Social Charter; see the critique by D. Harris, "The System of Supervision of the European Social Charter – Problems and Options for the Future", in L. Betten, *The Future of Social Policy in Europe* (1989) 27. With Article 28 of the European Social Charter as amended by the Protocol 1991, the Committee of Ministers will now be obliged to adopt recommendations.

35. As pointed out some years ago by P. Leuprecht, "The Protection of Human Rights by Political Bodies – The Example of the Committee of Ministers of the Council of Europe", in M. Nowak *et al.* (eds.), *Progress in the Spirit of Human Rights. Essays in honour of F. Ermacora* (1988) 107, who added that, as a general rule, the role of political bodies should be reduced to a minimum, while the independence and judicial character of international systems of human rights supervision should be developed and strengthened in the interest of the effectiveness of international human rights protection. On the Committee of Ministers' role in the protection of human rights, see A. Tomkins, "The Committee of Ministers: its Roles under the European Convention on Human Rights", *European Human Rights Law Review*, Launch Issue (1995) 49.

36. For a critique of the reporting procedure of the Charter see, among others, D. Harris, *supra* n. 34, at 22.

37. Article 27 of the European Social Charter as amended by the Protocol 1991.

38. See, for example, V. Leary, *supra* n. 20, at 580.

39. When the ILO Conference Committee undertook its work, it established "sub-reporters" to re-examine State reports already discussed by the expert committee. It soon became clear, however, that such practice was a mere duplication of work so that it has now been given up. See D. Harris, *supra* n. 34, at 17. Philips, *supra* n. 5, at 4.

40. See, for the history of the Committee on Economic, Social and Cultural Rights in detail, P. Alston, *supra* n. 28, at 478.

41. Recommendation 1300 (1996).

42. See also the respective proposals made by A. Philips, *supra* n. 5, at 8.

43. Article 16 of the European Charter on Regional or Minority Languages.

44. It should be remarked that the Assembly's role under the European Social Charter has also been cut back by the Amending Protocol of 1991 (Article 29 of the European Social Charter as amended by the Protocol 1991).

45. Recommendation 1300(1996).

46. Article16(5) of the European Charter on Regional and Minority Languages.

47. See S. Colliver, "International Reporting Procedures", in H. Hannum, *Guide to International Human Rights Practice* (1992) 174; and recently, M. Ölz, Non-Governmental Organisations in Regional Human Rights Systems, 28 *Columbia Human Rights Law Review* (1997) 308–374.

48. For examples, see A. Bayefsky, "Making the Human Rights Treaties Work", in L. Henkin et al. (eds.), "Human Rights: An Agenda for the Next Century", 26 *Studies*

in Transnational Legal Policy (1994) 233. There have been attempts to entrust national NGOs with the task of drafting reports on their own, a proposal which should be rejected by NGOs (and has been rejected by the NGO concerned), as it is the government's responsibility to give account of it's law and policies and not the duty of an NGO. See R. Brett, "The Contribution of NGOs to the Monitoring and Protection of Human Rights in Europe: An Analysis of the Role and Access of NGOs to the Inter-governmental Organisations", in A. Bloed *et al.* (eds.), *Monitoring Human Rights in Europe* (1993) 139.

49. In order to enable organisations and institutions concerned with minority rights to attend the Advisory Committee's session, the establishment of a voluntary fund has been proposed, see A. Philips, *supra* n. 5, at 7.

50. See A. Eide, "Future Protection of Economic and Social Rights in Europe", in A. Bloed *et al* (eds.), *supra* n. 48, at 219.

51. An opinion also expressed by P. Thornberry and M.A. Martín Estébanez, "The Work of the Council of Europe in the Protection of Minorities", 46 *Review of International Affairs* (1995) 1035.

52. Recommendation 1300 (1996).

53. Article 16 of the European Charter for Regional or Minority Languages.

54. Explanatory Report to the Framework Convention, Council of Europe Doc. H (94) 10.

55. Article 15(2) of the European Charter for Regional or Minority Languages.

56. *Ibid.,* Article 16(3).

57. Such for example the Manual on Human Rights Reporting, UN Doc. HR/PUB/91/1 (1991). Amnesty International has called furthermore for the preparation of "ratification advice kits" for governments and NGOs, see Amnesty International, *supra* n. 19, at 32.

58. Instead of preparing questionnaires some supervisory bodies such as the Human Rights Committee, have compiled lists of questions frequently asked by the experts, see M. Nowak, *CCPR-Commentary* (1993), at 559.

59. See V. Leary, *supra* n. 20, at 589.

60. For the relevant activities of the Committee on Economic, Social and Cultural Rights, see P. Alston (ed.), *supra* n. 27, at 505.

61. This is, for example, the practice of the Committee on the Elimination of all Forms of Racial Discrimination. See the Committee's Report, UN Doc. A/51/18, at para. 608; and of the Committee on Economic, Social and Cultural Rights, see the Committee's Report Un Doc. E/C./12/1995/18, para. 43. Philips, *supra* n. 5, at 2.

62. As demanded by G. Alfredsson and D. Türk, "International Mechanisms for the Monitoring and Protection of Minority Rights: Their Advantages, Disadvantages and Interrelationships", in A. Bloed *et al.* (eds.), *supra* n. 48, at 176. For the preventive function of the reporting systems in general see also V. Dimitrijevic, "The Monitoring of Human Rights and the Prevention of Human Rights Violations through Reporting Procedures", in A. Bloed *et al.* (eds.), ibid., at 21.

The European Union and Minority Nations

Adam Biscoe*

INTRODUCTION

In the years that followed the Second World War, the international community adopted a different approach to the way in which it sought to protect minorities in general, and minority nations[1] in particular. This was characterised by a shift from a *group* rights to a *human* rights approach.[2] However, particularly since the end of the Cold War, the international community has once again begun to take a group rights approach to the protection of minority nations.[3] Evidence of this includes the United Nations Draft Declaration on the Rights of Indigenous Peoples (1994), the UN Declaration on the Rights of Persons Belonging to National or Ethnic, Religious and Linguistic Minorities (1992), the Organisation for Security and Co-operation in Europe's (OSCE) pronouncements on the rights of minorities, and its establishment of a High Commissioner for National Minorities (1992), and the opening for signature of the Council of Europe's European Charter for Regional or Minority Languages (1992). This contrasts with the European Union's (EU) lack of detailed consideration of minority nation issues.[4] However, since the European Union, as an embryonic political system, has an increasing role in the day to day lives of its member states and their citizens and is an emerging political actor in international affairs, it is important that any comprehensive discussion of minorities in the 'New' Europe should consider the actions of the European Union.

Two ambiguities are apparent in the EU's approach. First, while there have been clear signals in favour of a group rights approach included in the Treaty on European Union (TEU),[5] in line with the concept of unity in diversity, recent policy initiatives suggest that this commitment is merely cosmetic. Secondly, there has been a much clearer approach to the recognition of minority nations outside the EU than to those within its borders. We will interpret these ambiguities in two ways: as an example of inter-institutional co-operation and conflict (the three principle European political institutions[6] – the Council of Ministers,[7] the Commission[8] and

89

P. Cumper and S. Wheatley (eds.), Minority Rights in the 'New' Europe, 89–103
© 1999 *Kluwer Law International. Printed in Great Britain.*

the European Parliament[9] – have all been active in regard to minority nations but, as we will later see, with different outcomes); and in terms of the individual versus group rights discourse, which encompasses the accommodation of minority nations and has become central to the study not only of political theory,[10] but also to everyday politics in many liberal democracies. As Nathan Glazer has argued,[11] at some point in its history, every multi-cultural[12] polity must decide whether to adopt an individual or group rights approach to the accommodation of its minorities. This chapter considers the model which the European Union has adopted, as an emerging multi-nation polity, in its accommodation of minority nations – both internal minorities within the European Union, and those external to its borders.

INDIVIDUAL VERSUS GROUP RIGHTS IN THE EUROPEAN UNION

The central concern of this chapter is whether the EU is approaching the issue of sub-state national diversity through the promotion of individual or group rights. The EU's dealings with internal minority nations, it will be argued, has at best been ambiguous: on the one hand, the European Regional Development Fund (ERDF),[13] the Committee of the Regions (COR),[14] Article 128 of the TEU[15] and a number of programmes run by four Directorate Generals (DGs) of the Commission[16] are adduced as evidence of a commitment to regional cultural diversity; on the other hand, closer inspection of the ethos of European integration indicates that regional cultural diversity is an optional extra – often sacrificed in the drive to create a single European market[17] and the (perceived) need to maintain competitiveness in the global economy. The single market identifies the individual as the key component in society, not the group.

Minority nations exist throughout Western Europe.[18] Spain contains 'three historic' nations:[19] Cataluña, the Basque Country and Galicia; the UK four – England, Northern Ireland, Scotland and Wales;[20] in France, the Corsicans and Bretons continue vigorously to resist French assimilation;[21] in Belgium, the existence of two sub-state nations was officially recognised by the 1970 Constitution, which established the Flemish and Walloon Autonomous Communities;[22] and the post-Fascist Constitution in Italy (1948) gave special status to Trentino-Alto Adige, Sardinia and Sicily.[23] Even in Europe's less populated states, there is a lack of cultural homogeneity. For example, the Åaland Islands, a predominantly Swedish part of Finland, have retained a high degree of political and cultural autonomy.[24] Given the preponderance of sub-state nations and regional cultural diversity within the European Union mosaic, any attempt to achieve political integration in Western Europe must recognise and deal with the 'issue of minority nations'.[25] At first sight, policy initiatives and institutional developments which have directly affected non-central tiers of government, such as the European Regional Development Fund and the Committee of the Regions, suggest that the EU has indeed responded to its inherent regional cultural diversity. However, as will be argued later, the EU has, in reality, done little to enhance or protect regional cultural diversity. Indeed, to the contrary, it may have even unintentionally (or otherwise) impeded it.

THE EUROPEAN UNION AND THE PROTECTION OF INTERNAL MINORITY NATIONS

Since its creation in 1975, the European Regional Development Fund (ERDF) has been one of the most significant Community policy initiatives. It has been the subject of intensive study by political scientists, but very little attention has been paid to its impact on regional cultural diversity.[26] The Fund was established "to award grants to public and private organisations in depressed or underdeveloped regions for industrial infrastructure investment",[27] in order to reduce economic disparities across the Community. It has, however, failed to correct economic disparities between the regions to the extent that was anticipated in 1975, and many sub-state nations remain economically underdeveloped.

Administered from Brussels by the Regional Policy Directorate General (DG XVI), grants from the European Regional Development Fund were distributed on an informal national quota basis from 1975 until the mid-1980s.[28] Applications for, and the distribution of, grants were channelled through member-state governments, allowing them to act as the 'gate keepers' for European regional policy, often resulting in the replacement of national funding by European funding.[29] European regional policy, therefore, remained nationalised and had little to do with addressing the regional economic disequilibrium across the EC. In an effort to gain some control over regional policy, the Commission in 1987 won acceptance from member-states of a nomenclature of territorial units for statistics (NUTS) system which separated Europe into regions based solely on economic criteria. The system did not though distinguish between functionally based regions and sub-state nations. For example, in the United Kingdom, Cornwall was designated part of the South West region, which included other much wealthier, non-Celtic, western English counties. In France, the Breton nation was divided in two, so that Bretons in the north and west of Brittany made up the Bretagne region, while Bretons in the south of Brittany were included in a region with non-Bretons.

The failure of DG XVI to distinguish between functionally based regions and sub-state nations has had important consequences for minority nations, establishing a precedent which has been repeated in other areas of Community action, and leading to national politicians and commentators often following the European Community's example of not distinguishing between functionally and nationally based sub-state authorities.

When discussing the status of minority nations, claims that the ERDF has provided a means by which minority nations have been protected are based upon three basic, yet erroneous assumptions: first, that funds from the ERDF have actually addressed regional economic disparities; secondly, that all minority nations are economically less developed; and finally, that regional funds are not purely economic in scope but have also a cultural dimension. As Amin and Tomaney point out, the first of these assumptions is not correct: regional funds have not alleviated the economic disparity between regions.[30] Indeed, the ERDF has more often been used as a means of "promoting growth and productivity towards the economic interests of the advanced regions".[31] While this has benefited the economically developed regions, which include sub-state nations such as Cataluña, European regional policy has not sufficiently redressed the under-developed economies of Europe which include a majority of sub-state nations, such as Brittany, Cornwall and Corsica. The third assumption, that the ERDF has had a cultural dimension, is also inaccurate – only with the introduction of Article 10 in 1995 did the ERDF embrace a cultural dimension.[32]

In the 1990s, the ERDF, rather than being regarded as a means of protecting regional cultural diversity, is more accurately regarded as "a concession to interventionism within an overall framework of market-led routes to prosperity",[33] i.e. the completion of the single market project, contained within the Single European Act (SEA). The SEA, ratified by member-states in 1987, has been regarded as both a cause and a consequence of the dominance of neo-liberal economics, which lays great emphasis on a deregulated market place. It requires the removal of national barriers from the free movement of goods, services, capital and labour, with the distribution of wealth in the Community regulated by the laws of supply and demand. Thus, individuals would become the key economic unit in the single market with the freedom to buy goods, provide services and to sell their labour, where ever they chose. This reduced the scope for political group activity, whether in terms of trade unions or national groups, since individuals would enter the market place as economic equals. National, social, ethnic or cultural diversity would not be recognised as a distinguishing factor in the market place. The over-riding ethos of non-intervention, is to be extended to national groups. Only those nations which were strong and decisive enough, with a good economic infra-structure, would be able to thrive in the new market.[34] Materialism and economic liberalism were the new creeds to challenge sub-state nationalism. The European Parliament has noted of the single market that:

> [it] has not been accompanied to the necessary extent by assessment of the resulting impact on the cultural dimension, unleashing commercialisation and concentration processes governed at times by the sole criterion of competitiveness without regard to the unalterable requirements of protecting pluralism and hence freedom.[35]

In contrast to the ERDF and the SMP, the Treaty on European Union (TEU), agreed at Maastricht in December 1991, appeared to reflect a change of emphasis with regard to the cultural dimension of European integration, and therefore the rights of minority nations. That this should occur in 1991, and not before, is indicative of the political and economic environment at the national, European and global level in which the Maastricht Treaty was negotiated; it was the first Community Treaty to be drafted following the end of the Cold War. Its aim was to "mark a new stage in the process of European integration".[36] A consensus existed to broaden the scope of policies included in Community competence. Across Europe, in the negotiations leading up to Maastricht, there was an awareness of the role which national diversity had played in the collapse of the Soviet Union, and was beginning to play in the former Yugoslav Federation, and a fear that 'Balkanization'[37] could spread to Western Europe. Moreover, representatives from Spanish, Belgian and German sub-central governments sought Community guarantees of their national constitutional position in respect of Community competence, especially on the issue of culture.[38] In retrospect, it is clear that regional cultural diversity was a major concern for many of the negotiators involved in the drafting of the Treaty of European Union, culminating in the inclusion of Article 128.

REGIONAL CULTURAL DIVERSITY IN THE POST-MAASTRICHT ERA

Article 128 (1) provides the following:

> The Community shall contribute to the flowering of the cultures of the member-states, while respecting their national and regional diversity.

It is important for two reasons: first, the Article recognises that member-states are not culturally homogenous and that regional diversity, in fact, exists. This can be taken to mean that minority nations, with a different culture to the dominant national state culture, have a right to the recognition of their identity. Secondly, it emphasises that Community actions should contribute to the survival and 'flowering' of regional cultural diversity, and should not undermine it. Although the Community has not taken this as a green light to interfere in the domestic political organisation of member-states on behalf of minority nations, the inclusion of Article 128 represents a major shift in the status of European sub-state nations within the Community, as it infers a group rights approach to the issue of regional cultural diversity. However, as we will see below, the impact of Article 128 on recent institutional developments and policy initiatives has been ambiguous. The contribution to a flowering of regional cultural diversity by the Council of Ministers, the European Commission and the European Parliament has been poorly co-ordinated and piecemeal.

The most important institutional development in the TEU, which might have been expected to benefit minority nations, was the creation of the Committee of the Regions and Local Authorities (COR). However, the method by which its delegates are selected has ensured that the COR is unlikely to become a European forum in which minority nations will be able to pursue their interests. Created under Article 198a of the TEU, the COR is the first European institution to be created since the Treaty of Rome (1957). It has the right to be consulted on issues which affect non-central tiers of government, an area usually referred to as regional policy (Article 198c). The 222 COR delegates are called Members, and are formally appointed by the Council of Ministers on the recommendation of national governments. The means by which Members were to be appointed was the main focus of negotiation with regard to the COR at Maastricht, and in subsequent ratification debates in national legislatures. What resulted in some countries, particularly in France and the United Kingdom, was the creation of regions which bore little or no resemblance to the boundaries of minority nations. For example, in the United Kingdom, Cornwall became part of the South West Region, along with the six non-Celtic English counties of Avon, Devon, Dorset, Gloucestershire, Somerset and Wiltshire. The first Member for this region was a Conservative Devon County Councillor (elected local government official), and the extent to which he was able to reflect a Cornish approach to regional affairs is debatable. Thus, as Christiansen argues, "[i]t is worth querying, at the very least, the actual closeness between COR Members and their reference groups at home".[39] What might have been a real opportunity for sub-state nations to be represented at the European level has not occurred, principally because of the important role of national governments in the appointment of Members. Instead, the "COR is less a Committee of the Regions than a 'Committee of Member State Representatives'".[40] The significant part which member-states play, in the selection of COR Members, and the drawing up of their 'constituencies', is similar to their previous dominant role as 'gatekeepers' in the allocation of European Regional Development funding.

It is evident that the COR has failed to develop in a way which would have permitted regional cultural diversity to flourish in a manner envisaged by Article 128 (TEU). However, the recent initiatives of various Commission Directorate Generals (DGs) have incorporated the spirit of the Article by assisting, through financial support, the "flowering" of regional cultures. In doing so they have employed paragraph 4 of Article 128, which states that "[T]he Community shall take cultural aspects into account in its actions under provisions of the Treaty".[41] Directorate General X (DG X) – 'Audio-visual, Information Communication and Culture' – funds three programmes which are clearly intended to assist minority nations protect their cultural diversity. First, the Ariane Programme,[42] introduced as a pilot scheme in 1996, aims to promote a wider knowledge and circulation of European literature and history among European citizens. It does this by financially assisting the translation of literary, theatrical and references works, not only other official languages of the Community[43], but also into the lesser used European languages. In addition, works written in lesser used languages are eligible for financial support to translate them into official and other lesser used languages. Secondly, the Kaleidoscope Programme[44] aims to provide support for artistic and cultural activities having a European dimension involving public or private organisations from at least three member-states. This European dimension may include regional cultural diversity. Finally, under the Raphael Programme,[45] DG X finances projects aimed at conserving heritage, which also incorporates reference to the importance of the "flowering" of regional cultures. These programmes are potentially important indicators of the EU's commitment to minority nations. However, because they have relatively small budgets and are limited in scope, they can not yet be regarded as significant initiatives in the encouragement of regional cultural diversity.

Programmes initiated by the Commission's DG XXII – 'Education, Training and Youth' – contrast with those of DG X in two ways: many of them were in existence prior to the TEU (the Socrates, Erasmus, Lingua and Leonardo programmes have facilitated student and employee exchanges for a number of years[46]), and certain of the programmes address, more directly, the issue of regional cultural diversity. For example, the three projects for the Promotion of Regional and Minority Languages[47] – the European Bureau for Lesser Used Languages (EBLUL), the Mercator Programme[48] and the Euromosaic Report[49] – specifically include reference to Article 128 and the importance of enhancing regional cultural diversity.

The European Bureau for Lesser Used Languages (EBLUL) established and financed on the initiative of some MEPs in 1982,[50] seeks to preserve and promote Europe's autochtonous languages and the linguistic rights of their speakers. It is this recognition, and financial support for cultural diversity at a regional level provided by DG XXII, which has resulted in Greece and France obstructing official funding for EBLUL[51] within the annual Community Budget approved by the Council of Ministers.[52] Conflict over the funding of these Programmes is indicative of the different approaches to the flowering of regional cultural diversity, and tends to confirm the uncertain status of minority nations in the European Union.

Similarly, although it might have been expected that the European Regional Development Fund (ERDF) would have included reference to the issue of regional culture, this did not occur until the introduction of Article 10 of the ERDF.[53] This provides scope for funding projects which are linked to the promotion of regional cultural diversity. Although drawing on Article 128 of the TEU, Article 10 remains very narrow in its approach focusing on co-operation in the field of culture through the development of regional and cultural heritage networks. The annual budget of Article 10 only runs to 2 million ECUs, leading a European Commission Report to conclude that "'[c]ulture and economic development is still on the fringes when it comes to the field of inter-regional co-operation, currently standing at around 2% [of the annual budget]".[54]

Article 128 has, therefore, provided an impetus to new and existing Community programmes. This is in spite of member governments' reluctance to grant to minority nations group rights. The European Commission and Parliament have adopted a positive approach, although it must be noted that the Commission has failed to develop a co-ordinated approach amongst the DGs involved to issues related to minority nations inside the EU, in marked contrast to the programmes and initiatives that the Community has established in recognition of minority nations in Eastern and Central European states outside of the European Union.

THE EUROPEAN UNION AND THE PROTECTION OF EXTERNAL MINORITY NATIONS

Events in the former Soviet Union, Eastern and Central Europe between 1989 and 1991 prompted the European Community to reassess its approach to international affairs.[55] Of immediate concern was how to encourage political and economic reforms in an environment which precluded the option of early Community membership for the former communist states.

In an effort to subvert the "right wing authoritarian and nationalist forces" warned of by Vaclav Havel,[56] the Community concluded so-called Europe Agreements with the Visigrad states (Poland, Hungary, Slovakia and the Czech Republic), Bulgaria (1992) and Romania (1993). A Commission Report on enlargement published in June 1992, which was formally accepted by the European Council at its 1993 Copenhagen Summit, established geographical, political, economic, legal and institutional criteria for membership of the Community.[57] In addition, states were expected to have a commitment to respect human rights, as laid down by the Council of Europe and in the Helsinki Final Act (1975).[58] Within this broad definition of human rights, there was a commitment to the recognition and protection of minority nations. This emphasis on human rights, and the rights of minority nations in particular, was in line with Community policy at the global level.

Article 5 of the Fourth Lomé Convention, signed in December 1989, was the first tangible demonstration of the European Community's commitment to human rights within a contractual document;[59] many subsequent agreements have made reference to "human rights as one of the foundations of the parties' relations",[60] notably in agreements with Brazil,[61] the Andean Pact countries,[62] and the Baltic states.[63] Human rights have also been at the centre of the debate concerning Turkey's application for membership of the European Community. The European Parliament has questioned Turkish accession because of its human rights record and, in particular, its treatment of the Kurdish population in Eastern Turkey. In 1996, a Customs Union Agreement between Turkey and the EU was effectively suspended by the European Parliament, in part, because of alleged human rights abuses.[64]

Of particular concern in the development of Community policy regarding external minorities have been events in Central and Eastern European Countries, where nationalism quickly re-emerged to fill the ideological void left following the collapse of communism, the example of Czechoslovakia being a case in point. Tension among cultural groups was not confined to minorities within states, so that Hungarians, for example, became concerned about the plight of fellow Magyars in neighbouring countries. The problems of cultural diversity in Eastern Europe became ever more prominent with the outbreak of hostilities in the former Yugoslavia.

The European Union's concern about human rights and the protection of minority nations, particularly those in Eastern and Central Europe, has been reflected in a number of Community initiatives. First, the Community's Association Agreements, signed with potential new member-states, require the recognition of minority nations. This is in marked contrast to the relative inaction by the Community in recognising minority nations and their rights within the EU itself. Secondly, in March 1995, the 'Pact on Stability in Europe' was approved by a Conference of 52 states. An idea first mooted in a speech by, the then, French Prime Minister Edouard Balladur, in March 1992, and reiterated in the 1994 French White Paper on Defence, it has obvious implications for human rights and, in particular, for the East European minority nations, as it makes clear that stability in Europe will be achieved "through the promotion of good-neighbourly relations, including questions related to frontiers and minorities . . . ".[65] In order to achieve this 'good-neighbourliness' in Eastern Europe, funds from the Phare Programme for Democracy have been allocated to projects to facilitate the resolution of disputes relating to minority nations. This has usually involved financing and organising bilateral meetings between state and minority nation representatives in an effort to reduce the likelihood of nationalist tensions within Eastern Europe.[66] As a result, approximately 100 bilateral agreements concerning minority rights were attached to the final Paris Declaration.[67] Similarly, the Tacis Programme for Democracy has sponsored projects in the Commonwealth of Independent States (CIS) – those countries which were formerly part of the Soviet Union.[68]

In recognition of the multi-faceted nature of the task facing the European Union with regard to human rights, a Human Rights and Democratisation Unit has been established within Directorate General 1A (DG 1A). The aim of the unit is to co-ordinate the Commission's approach to human rights, not only in relation to external actors, but also within the European Union itself.[69] With this in mind, the Unit has instituted monthly meetings with co-ordinators from other Directorate Generals, but interestingly it does not include the representatives from the programmes noted above, which support programmes assisting minority nations in the EU itself.

It is apparent that the European Union takes a different approach to minority nations in those states outside the EU, than those inside. On the one hand, the EU insists that East European minority nations must be recognised as legitimate groups within their respective societies, and must be accorded group rights; on the other, in Western Europe, within the EU, minority nations have self-evidently not been protected through the granting of group rights. This is a "contradiction which daily confronts" the Human Rights and Democratisation Unit.[70] The refusal of certain states, such as France and Greece, to countenance the existence of minority nations within their borders – and their continuing "proclaimed homogeneity"[71] – suggests that this contradiction is likely to remain.

CONCLUSION

The European Union's approach to minority nations is, at best, ambiguous. On the one hand, Article 128 of the Treaty on European Union and the various Community programmes discussed in this chapter indicate a commitment to recognising minority nations as groups, to be accorded distinct group rights. On the other hand, major policy and institutional developments in recent years suggest that the EU is more committed to individual rights, particularly in the moves to complete the single market, the application of Regional and Cohesion Policies, and the manner in which the Committee of the Regions has been established along functional, rather than cultural, lines. Decision making in these areas remains the prerogative of the Council, and therefore the member states, which have acted with little regard to the views of the Commission or European Parliament. Therefore, whilst the group rights approach, in respect of (internal) minority nations, appears to have gained some ground in recent years, it is still 'trumped' by the individual rights approach which grants all individuals the right to be different, whilst maintaining their full rights of citizenship. This is in contrast to the emphasis on the granting of group rights to minority nations outside of the European Union, which has become a feature of the EU's external policy.

In the foreseeable future, the European Union is unlikely to commit itself formally to a group rights approach in the accommodation of minority nations. Factors likely to prevent this include institutional disagreements, and different policies toward minority nations inside and outside the Community. As the EU grapples with economic and monetary union, enlargement, institutional reform and the need to remain economically dynamic in an increasingly competitive global economy, it is unlikely to change its ambiguous approach to the issue of minority nations. Concentrating on individual rights at the expense of national group rights, however, has various implications for the process of European integration. First, the recent history of the former Soviet, Czechoslovak and Yugoslav Republics indicate the perils of ignoring regional cultural diversity, as does the experience of Canada in its tense relationship with the province of Quebec. Secondly, seeking to accommodate minority nations through an individual, rather than group, rights approach provides evidence of the nature of European integration in the future. Where the efficient working of the market place conflicts with issues relating to cultural diversity, the former will prevail. Minority nations, and multi-nation states which are concerned that European economic integration has implications for their cultural diversity, should take note.

NOTES

*Lecturer in European Integration at the Department of Politics, University of Bristol. I would like to thank many colleagues at Bristol and Reading, and friends for their help and encouragement.

1. There are five objective and one subjective criteria "which can contribute to the identification of a group as a nation: territory, state (or similar political status), language, culture and history . . . and national consciousness", J. Krejci and V. Velimsky, *Ethnic and Political Nations in Europe* (1981) at 44. Nations can be distinguished from ethnic groups because the latter are not resident in their territory of national origin, and do not generally have a political agenda. Minority nations reside in multi-nation states. The term minority nation or sub-state nation is preferred to national minorities for three reasons. First, they are not so much "national" minorities as "state" minorities. For example, the Scots are a minority in the United Kingdom, but not in Scotland. Secondly, the term national minority is sometimes used in a rather derogatory sense. Thirdly, it avoids the problem of defining national minority which has persistently dogged international organisation and commentators alike. On this generally, see F. Capotorti, *Study of the Rights of Persons belonging to Ethnic, Religious and Linguistic Minorities* (1991); F. Benoît-Rohmer, The *minority question in Europe: Texts and Commentary* (1996); and P. Thornberry, *International Law and the Rights of Minorities* (1991).
2. W. Kymlicka, *Multicultural Citizenship* (1995), at 3.
3. Minority nations are the main topic of minority rights deliberations in Europe in the 1990s. See J. Preece, "Minority rights in Europe: from Westphalia to Helsinki", 23 *Review of International Studies* (1997) 75.
4. See D. Wincott, "The role of law or the rule of the Court of Justice? An 'institutional' account of judicial politics in the European Community", 2 *Journal of European Public Policy* (1995) 583, at 593.
5. Often known as the Maastricht Treaty, or simply Maastricht, the TEU amended the Treaty of Rome (1957). The Treaty was negotiated by the European Council at Maastricht in December 1991. The Treaty was signed in February 1992, but because of delays in the ratification of individual member-states it did not come into force until November, 1993. On this generally, see A. Duff, J. Pinder and R. Pryce, *Maastricht and Beyond: Building the European Union* (1994).
6. Along with the European Court of Justice, these three institutions were established by the Treaty of Rome. Over the decades, their power and role in the process of European integration has changed. The most important changes were incorporated in the Single European Act (1987) and the Treaty on European Union (1992).
7. The Council of Ministers consists of one political representative from each member-state. There are four tiers of the Council: the Committee of Permanent Representatives (COREPER), twenty or so functional or technical councils, the General Council (Foreign Ministers) and the European Council (Heads of Government or State). See E. Kirchner, *Decision making in the European Community: The Council Presidency and European Integration* (1994).
8. The Commission is composed of twenty Commissioners and the Commission President, who are nominated by the Council of Ministers and formally appointed by the European Parliament. They take an oath of allegiance to the Community as a whole and are obligated not to take instructions from any member-state. The Commissioners are supported by approximately 16,000 administrative staff, who are also sometimes

referred to as the Commission. See M. Cini, *The European Commission: Leadership, Organisation and Culture in the EU Administration* (1996), at 106–111.

9. The European Parliament is composed of 626 directly elected Members (MEPs); see F. Jacobs, R. Corbett and M. Shakleton, *The European Parliament* (3rd edn) (1995).

10. See S. Avineri, and A. de-Shalit, 'Introduction' in S. Avineri and A. de-Shalit (eds.), *Communitarianism and Individualism* (1992) 1, at 1; and S. Mulhall and A. Swift, *Liberals and Communitarians* (1992), at vii.

11. N. Glazer, *Ethnic Dilemmas 1964–1982* (1983), at 270.

12. Multi-cultural is used as an umbrella term to cover multiple ethnic groups or nations, or a combination of the two.

13. Created in 1975, the ERDF aims, through the allocation of financial grants, to reduce economic disparity between the regions and to assist economically the least-developed regions.

14. Created by the TEU, the COR is a consultative body composed of 222 representatives of local and regional authorities which must be consulted on regional policy issues.

15. Article 128 states: "The Community shall contribute to the flowering of the Cultures of the member-states, while respecting their national and regional diversity". This will be considered in more detail later.

16. There are at present 22 European Commission Directorate Generals which "are very roughly comparable to government departments", Cini, *supra* n. 8, at 102.

17. The creation of a common or single market has always been central to the European Community since the Treaty of Rome (1957). Although initial progress was fairly rapid until the mid-1960s, it once again took centre stage in the integration process following the "1992" deadline set for its completion in the Single European Act (SEA). See Lord Cockfield, "The Real Significance of 1992" in C. Crouch and D. Marquand (eds.), *The Politics of 1992: Beyond the Single European Market* (1990) 1, at 1.

18. *Supra* n. 1.

19. R. Carr, *Modern Spain: 1875–1980* (1980), at 61.

20. H. Kearney, 'Four Nations or One' in B. Crick (ed.), *National Identities: The Constitution of the United Kingdom* (1991) 1, at 1. Payton argues that there are five sub-state nations in the UK if we include Cornwall, P. Payton, *The Making of Modern Cornwall: Historical Experience and the Persistence of "Difference"* (1992), at 2.

21. M. Keating, *State and Regional Nationalism: Territorial Politics and the European State* (1988), at 235–7.

22. L. Sharpe, *The Rise of Meso-government in Europe* (1988), at 32.

23. See L. Condorelli, "The Powers of Regions in the Field of External Relations: The Italian Experience" in R. Morgan, *Regionalism in European Politics* (1986) 144, at 144; and C. Desideri, "Italian Regions in the European Community" in B. Jones and M. Keating, *The European Union and the Regions* (1995) 65, at 66.

24. *Supra* n. 3, at 83.

25. European Commission, *Euromosaic: The Production and Reproduction of the Minority Language Groups in the European Union* (1996).

26. Nagel briefly considers this issue with regard to Cataluña in K. Nagel, "The Stateless Nations in Western Europe and the Process of European Integration. The Catalan Case", in M. Beramendi, R. Maiz and X. Nunez (eds.), *Nationalism in Europe Past and Present Volume II* (1994) 545, at 565.

27. M. Keating, "The Continental Meso: Regions in the European Community" in L. Sharpe, *supra* n. 22, 296, at 299.

28. *Ibid.*, at 300.
29. *Ibid.*
30. A. Amin, & J. Tomaney, "A Framework for Cohesion" in A. Amin, & J. Tomaney (eds.), *Behind the Myth of European Union: Prospects for Cohesion* (1995) 309, at 309.
31. *Ibid.*, at 11.
32. This forms part of the 'Second Programme of Inter-regional Co-operation and Innovative Actions within the Structural Funds: 1995–1999'. See DG XVI Call for Proposals (95/38).
33. *Supra* n. 30, at 11.
34. *Supra* n. 25, at 10.
35. European Parliament Resolution A3-0396/92: O.J. n.C 42, 21 January 1993, 179.
36. Preamble to the TEU.
37. S. J. Mestrovic, The *Balkanization of the West : The Confluence of Post modernism and Post Communism* (1994), at 75.
38. Such lobbying was eventually successful. Article 146 of the TEU states: "The Council shall consist of a representative of each Member State at ministerial level, authorised to commit the government of that Member State". Germany and Belgium have interpreted the Article to send *"regional ministers to the Council of Ministers"* for discussions about culture, L. Hooghe, "Sub-national Mobilisation in the European Union", 18 *West European Politics* (1994), at 175. So far, the pleas of the Spanish Autonomous Regions for similar treatment have been ignored by Madrid.
39. T. Christiansen, "Second Thoughts – The Committee of the Regions after its First Year", in R. Dehouse, and T. Christiansen (eds), *What Model for the Committee of the Regions? Past Experiences and Future Perspectives* (1995) 34, at 58.
40. *Ibid.*, at 47.
41. Article 128 (4) of the TEU.
42. Pilot Scheme to Provide Financial Assistance for the Translation of Literary, Theatrical and Reference Works, OJC 96/C119/04. The 1997 budget, allocated for the whole of the Ariane Project, was ECU 2.7m.
43. There are eleven official languages of the European Community: Danish, Dutch, English, Finnish, French, German, Greek, Italian, Portuguese, Swedish and Spanish.
44. European Community support for Culture, 1996 Programme, OJC 96/C 114/12. The 1997 budget, allocated for the whole of the Kaleidoscope Programme, was ECU 8.55m.
45. OJC 265 12.9.1996, 4–19. The 1997 budget, allocated for the whole of the Raphael Programme, was ECU 10.6m.
46. Socrates facilitates exchanges for school students, Erasmus for University students, Lingua for language teachers and Leornardo for young employees. These programmes are not strictly limited to the eleven official languages of the Community. For example, Erasmus facilitates the learning of Catalan, because it is an *official* language of Spain. However, Luxemborgish is included in the Lingua Programme, while Catalan is omitted.
47. Budget Line B3 – 1006. A Budget Line is different from a Community Programme in that it is not part of the Community budget sent to the European Parliament by the Council. Instead, it is an addendum annually appropriated by the European Parliament for a particular subject matter of its choosing.
48. The Mercator Programme is a computer database which aims to improve the exchange and circulation of information on lesser used languages and cultures both inside and outside of the Communities themselves.
49. *Supra* n. 25.

50. EBUL is only partly financed through the European Union. Originally the European Parliament had allocated some funds for Amnesty International. Amnesty was unable to accept this money because of its long standing commitment to remain independent of all government bodies. The Parliament, looking for an alternative repository of the funds, decided therefore to establish the EBLUL.

51. Interview with an official of the EBLUL (September, 1996) and confirmed in an interview with an official of DG XXII (September, 1996).

52. All Budget Lines are under threat as the three main European institutions have agreed that they should have a *legal act* to justify them. See the *Contact Bulletin of The Bureau for Lesser Used Languages* (1996) Vol. 3, No. 3, at 1.

53. This forms part of the 'Second Programme of Inter-Regional Co-operation and Innovative Actions within the Structural Funds, 1995–1999'. See DG XVI Call for Proposals (95/38).

54. '1st Report on the Consideration of Cultural Aspects in European Community Action' (COM (96) 160 Final) Part II, at 11.

55. External political relations were first brought within the Community sphere in the SEA (1987) when European Political Co-operation (EPC) was formalised. The TEU (1992) went a stage further by establishing the groundwork for a common foreign and security policy (CFSP). However, Pillar III, as CFSP became known, was to be strictly inter-governmental – an almost exclusive preserve of the General Council.

56. Cited by D. Dinan, *Ever Closer Union? An Introduction to the European Union* (1994), at 478.

57. European Council in Copenhagen, June 21–22, 1993, Presidency Conclusions, SN 180/93, June 22, 1993.

58. F. Benoît-Rohmer, *supra* n. 1, at 29.

59. European Commission (1995) Bulletin of the European Union: Supplement 3/95 "The European Union and Human Rights in the World" (CM-NF-95-00-EN-C), at 10.

60. Bulletin of the European Union, Supplement 3/95.

61. 29.6.1992 OJ L 779/1991.

62. 23.4.1993 OJ L 25/1993.

63. Association Agreement initiated 12 April 1995.

64. See "Turkey Cries Foul over Treatment by EU" in *European Voice*, Vol. 2 No. 47, 19 February. 1996, at 8; and N. Buckley, "EU MEPs Block Aid to Turkey" in *The Financial Times* 20 September 1996, at 2; and European Parliament News, September (1996), at 4.

65. Concluding Document of the Inaugural Conference for a Pact of Stability in Europe, Paris 26–27 May 1994 para 1.5.

66. Interview with an official of the Human Rights and Democratisation Unit, DG 1A (September, 1996).

67. F. Benoît-Rohmer points out that most agreements were in fact concluded prior to the Pact being announced, *supra* n.1, at 34.

68. For a comprehensive record of the Phare and Tacis programmes, see European Commission, Directorate General for External Economic Relations, *The European Union's Phare and Tacis Programmes: Projects in Operation* (1996).

69. *Supra* n. 66.

70. *Ibid.*

71. F. Benoît-Rohmer, *supra* n.1, at 18.

Bilateralism versus Regionalism in the Resolution of Minorities Problems in Central and Eastern Europe and in the Post-Soviet States

*Istvan Pogany**

INTRODUCTION

In recent years, the elaboration and protection of minority rights has assumed increasing importance in Europe.[1] In large measure, this renewed focus on minority rights can be explained by the minorities problems which have emerged following the collapse of Soviet-type regimes throughout Central and Eastern Europe and in the post-Soviet states.[2] Predictably, democratisation in the 'East' has not proceeded entirely smoothly.[3] Along with a host of other problems, there has been a pronounced ethnification of the political process in many post-Communist states.[4] This tendency poses considerable dangers, whether for the consolidation of democratic political structures committed to the rule of law and respect for human rights, or for peaceful relations between states whose mutual suspicions and grievances were kept in check under Communism.

The attempt to create regional mechanisms to safeguard minority rights in Europe, whether involving formal legal obligations or OSCE-type political commitments, and the establishment of systems for monitoring and review, constitute important features of an emerging regime. However, they are not the only mechanisms by which the issue of minorities may be dealt with. The post-Communist states are themselves contributing to this process, principally through the conclusion of bilateral agreements dealing wholly or partially with minority rights. A Polish scholar has commented that these treaties, "constitute an important element of international legal practice, crystallizing customary rules (at least regional) and confirming developing European standards".[5]

My central concern in this chapter is to consider the extent to which *bilateralism* can make a positive contribution to the resolution of minorities problems in Central and Eastern Europe and in the post-Soviet states. However, before proceeding further, it may be useful to define a number of terms. 'Bilateralism', as employed here, signifies a process in which the

P. Cumper and S. Wheatley (eds.), Minority Rights in the 'New' Europe, 105–126
© 1999 *Kluwer Law International. Printed in Great Britain.*

states particularly concerned with a minority problem endeavour to reach an agreement concerning the rights and entitlements of the minority in question.[6] Such agreements may take the form of a treaty or may operate at a purely political level; the scope of the agreement may be confined to minorities issues or it may encompass a range of questions affecting relations between the contracting states. In principle, such agreements may involve more than two countries. In practice, issues regarding a given national minority are generally of particular concern to two states – the state in which the minority is located and the state with whose majority population the minority shares a common 'nationality', as defined by reference to language, culture, religion etc.[7] 'Citizenship' and 'nationality' are *not* coterminous in Central and Eastern Europe, or in the post-Soviet states. For example, a person may be a citizen of Romania, while belonging to the Hungarian, German or Ukrainian 'nation'.

'Regionalism', unlike 'bilateralism', represents a more inclusive process in which multilateral mechanisms, whether involving regional organisations (Council of Europe, OSCE, European Union, etc.) or multilateral treaties, are involved.[8] The participation of regional mechanisms can assume a variety of forms. Crucially, however, 'regionalism' implies that concern in respect of efforts to deal with minorities issues is *not* confined to those states which have a direct interest. In addition, 'regionalism' may mean that genuinely neutral actors, such as courts, independent committees of experts, or other bodies, are also able to become involved.

Bilateralism and regionalism do not represent the only conceivable approaches to the resolution of minorities problems in Central and Eastern Europe. 'Universalist' techniques represent a possible third approach. However, in practical terms, universalism is not a realistic option, at least as a basis for dealing with all minorities issues. Universally elaborated standards (such as those enshrined in Article 27 of the International Covenant on Civil and Political Rights[9]) are too limited in scope to satisfy large and cohesive national minorities – such as ethnic Magyars in Romania or Slovakia, or ethnic Russians in many of the post-Soviet states – and are not congenial to states such as Hungary or Russia, for whom the interests of their 'diaspora' communities are of considerable national importance.

BILATERALISM VS. REGIONALISM?

Bilateral and regional approaches to the resolution of minorities problems differ in a number of respects. However, it is not necessary to view them as mutually exclusive. In fact, they represent potentially complementary techniques and can thus be seen, at least in principle, as mutually reinforcing. Significantly, this is how they are treated by Article 18(1) of the Council of Europe's Framework Convention for the Protection of National Minorities:[10]

> The parties shall endeavour to conclude, where necessary, bilateral and multilateral agreements with other States, in particular neighbouring States, in order to ensure the protection of persons belonging to the national minorities concerned.

Previously, in the Vienna Declaration of October 1993, the Heads of State and Government of the Member States of the Council of Europe, while calling for the drafting of a multilateral convention concerned with the protection of national minorities, had simultaneously stressed, "the importance which bilateral agreements between States, aimed at assuring the protection of the national minorities concerned, can have for stability and peace in Europe".[11]

The thrust of both instruments is clear: bilateralism may serve as a useful adjunct to multilateralism. There is no inherent contradiction between the two approaches. Where a particular minorities problem has a significant *bilateral dimension*, it is entirely appropriate to acknowledge it. Indeed, as the Vienna Declaration suggests, a formal acknowledgement by the states concerned may be viewed as a necessary stage in the process of assuring "stability and peace in Europe".

THE PRINCIPAL ADVANTAGES OF BILATERALISM

Bilateralism possesses a number of significant advantages over multilateral approaches to minority issues. These render it particularly helpful in dealing with some of the minority problems that have arisen in Central and Eastern Europe and, possibly, in the post-Soviet states, especially when used in conjunction with a number of multilateral techniques. These advantages will now be considered.

Greater Specificity and Detailed Elaboration of Rights

In the first place, bilateralism allows for greater specificity and detail in elaborating the rights and entitlements of a designated minority. Thus, the specific historical, economic, social, cultural, educational – and even psychological – features of a particular minority (or of a situation involving a minority) may be taken into account in determining the rights appropriate to the minority's needs and capacities. By contrast, regional, and especially universal, norms must operate at a much greater level of generality; such multilateral norms must be capable of application to the various national or other minorities found on the territory of contracting or member states. In this sense, universal or regional norms may be regarded as laying down minimum standards which may be supplemented, as appropriate, by bilateral or other agreements.

In addition to enumerating the rights of designated minorities, bilateral agreements may also specify various additional and related duties of contracting states which may be of interest or concern to particular minorities. For example, Article 12(7) of the Slovak-Hungary Treaty provides that, "[e]ach Contracting Party shall endeavour to expand the opportunities for learning about culture, literature and language of the other Contracting Party", while Article 12(8) states that each of the Parties, "shall ensure conditions within its country for activities of cultural centres of the other Contracting Party".[12] Compliance with these provisions may be seen as of particular, though by no means exclusive, interest to the Slovak minority in Hungary and to the Hungarian minority in Slovakia.

One may, of course, question the need for specificity. Minority rights are generally viewed as a branch of human rights.[13] Arguably, therefore, they should be of universal application. However, the disparate circumstances of individual minorities suggests that a universal approach can never do more than articulate certain basic entitlements, such as those enumerated in Article 27 of the International Covenant, or in the 1992 UN General Assembly Declaration on the Rights of Persons Belonging to National or Ethnic, Religious and Linguistic Minorities.[14] In my view, 'justice' for individual minorities, as well as the need to fashion enduring political solutions in regions where minority grievances have been a chronic cause of instability, would seem to demand a highly specific approach – in addition to the complementary activities of regional and universal mechanisms.

Where Minority Problems have a Genuinely Bilateral (or Multilateral) Dimension

Bilateralism is also appropriate, and may even be imperative, in circumstances where a minorities problem has a genuine bilateral (or even multilateral) dimension. Of course, I do not wish to imply by this that certain minorities problems fall wholly within the domestic jurisdiction of individual states. It is well-established in international law that human rights, including the rights of persons belonging to national minorities, are matters of legitimate *international* concern. This is confirmed by recent state practice. For example, Article 15(1) of the above-mentioned Slovak-Hungary Treaty on Good Neighbourliness provides that:

> (1) The Contracting Parties confirm that the protection of national minorities and of the rights and freedoms of persons belonging to those minorities forms an integral part of the international protection of human rights and, as such, falls within the scope of international co-operation and, in this sense, it is therefore not an exclusively domestic affair of individual States but it is also a subject of legitimate concern of the international community.

Nevertheless, there remains an important distinction between minorities who do *not* share a common 'nationality' with the majority in any sovereign state (for example, Catalans or Basques in Spain, Bretons in France, etc.) and minorities which may be seen as an extension of a national group that constitutes a majority in another country (for example, ethnic Hungarians in Slovakia or Romania, ethnic Romanians or Slovaks in Hungary, ethnic Russians in the Baltic states, in Moldova or in Ukraine, etc.). In the latter examples, the scope of the minority problem is different. The political interests of two states rather than of one are involved. It would be unrealistic and even dangerous, for example, to deny that Hungary or Russia has a special interest in, and concern for, the condition of the Hungarian or Russian minorities located outside their respective territories. There are intimate ties of language, of culture and of history which link these national minorities with the Hungarian and Russian 'nations' and, hence, with the Hungarian and Russian states. In these circumstances, bilateralism serves as an acknowledgement of the existence of such a special interest on the part of a state other than the territorial state. Finally, as suggested above, bilateralism offers a means of elaborating the rights and entitlements of the relevant minority in some detail.

My arguments here should be understood as sociological rather than philosophical in character.[15] I am not seeking to promote some covert revisionist agenda. Nor am I unaware of some bleakly unedifying precedents in Central and East Central Europe, notably the disingenuous efforts of Nazi Germany in the late 1930's to promote the 'interests' of the German minorities beyond its borders.[16] Nevertheless, I see little point (and indeed much harm) in denying an obvious truth – that the overwhelming majority of Hungarians, whether in Hungary itself or in the neighbouring states of Slovakia, Romania, Serbia or the Ukraine, *feel* that they belong to the Hungarian 'nation'. Comparable sentiments can be found amongst most Poles, Slovaks, Romanians and Russians, whatever state they may be citizens of.

Disregarding the bilateral dimension of a minorities problem can only exacerbate relations between the 'territorial' state, in which the minority is located, and the state with which the minority shares a common 'nationality'. Such a policy can all too easily fuel irredentist ambitions on the part of politicians who believe that their 'co-nationals' are exposed to the threat of cultural (let alone physical) annihilation. A failure to acknowledge and deal with the underlying bilateral issues can undermine peace and stability in Europe.

As a Means of Enhancing the Confidence of National Minorities

Finally, bilateralism may also benefit national minorities by enhancing their confidence. Frequently, minorities in Central and Eastern Europe and in the post-Soviet states feel themselves to be beleaguered in countries which they regard as committed to the promotion of an essentially alien 'national' culture. Such feelings may or may not be justified. Some sociologists have suggested that certain minorities are prone to "minority neurosis" or to "self-victimisation".[17] Nevertheless, such fears are understandable, particularly when set against the imperfect or qualified democratisation which some of the post-Communist states have undergone to date, and the cult of 'ethnic' nationalism which, to a greater or lesser extent, has infected many of these countries since the demise of communism.[18] The apprehensions of many minority groups are also readily comprehensible when viewed from an historical perspective. Certain national groups which presently constitute minorities in states such as Slovakia, Romania and the Baltic states previously belonged to the politically, culturally and (outside the former USSR) economically dominant 'nation'. For example, Hungary exercised uninterrupted control over the territories which now constitute Slovakia and the Transylvanian region of Romania from the *Ausgleich* of 1867 until the post-World War One political settlement;[19] during World War II, Hungary briefly reoccupied some of these territories. Memories of Hungarian ascendancy over these regions make it peculiarly difficult for today's Hungarian minorities to accept their subordinate status, or for some officials, politicians and intellectuals belonging to the majority populations in these countries to recognise the legitimacy of minority rights, particularly for the Hungarian minorities. Inevitably, there is a degree of mutual suspicion, prompting many members of the dominant communities to view minority rights for ethnic Hungarians as a possible "stepping-stone" to secession and eventual union with Hungary.[20]

Such problems are compounded by the fact that, in much of East Central Europe and amongst the post-Soviet states, there is little acceptance of the idea of multiple allegiances or identities, i.e. that citizens of the Czech

Republic, Slovakia, Romania etc. may actually 'feel' themselves to be German or Hungarian. Undiluted patriotism is, all too often, expected of all citizens. This is in contrast to the experience of many Western states where ancestral, as well as civic, allegiances are taken for granted.

In such circumstances, minorities in Central and Eastern Europe or in the post-Soviet states may gain a measure of self-confidence if they feel that their problems are being 'championed' at the international level by the state with which they identify culturally and linguistically. Bilateralism may therefore diminish the sense of 'victimhood' to which such minorities are prone. Of course, this is a double-edged sword. Minorities may have exaggerated expectations of their 'patron' and may feel betrayed if the agreements concluded on their behalf fall short of their wishes.

THE HUNGARIAN MINORITIES IN EAST CENTRAL EUROPE

One of the most significant minorities problems confronting Central and Eastern Europe, following the collapse of Communism, has been that of the Hungarian minorities. The problems associated with these minorities have stemmed, in the first place, from the sheer size of the communities involved. There are up to 2 million ethnic Hungarians in Romania, 600,000 in Slovakia, 160,000 in Ukraine, 450,000 in Serbia and significant but smaller communities in Austria, Slovenia and Croatia.[21] While some of these minority communities experienced undoubted problems during the Communist era,[22] in certain respects their position has actually worsened since 1989, particularly in countries such as Slovakia, Romania and Serbia where overtly nationalist administrations have gained power for at least some of the intervening period.[23] Against a background of economic dislocation and uncertainty, widespread corruption and only limited or imperfect democratisation, the scape-goating of the Hungarian minority by certain extremist political elements has become commonplace in these countries.[24] At the same time, the nationalist tone of Hungary's first post-Communist administration, under Prime Minister József Antall, seemed to fuel the fears of Hungary's neighbours. In his keynote address to the Hungarian Parliament on 22 May 1990, after he had been appointed Prime Minister, Antall declared:[25]

> Having regard to the fact that one third of Hungarians live beyond our borders, it is the special responsibility of the state to support everywhere the preservation of the Hungarian nation, both as a cultural and as an ethnic community.

Antall also expressed the support of his Government for the right of the Hungarian minorities outside Hungary to self-government.[26] Such sentiments, combined with Antall's declaration that he was the Prime Minister of *all* Hungarians, understandably alarmed not only Hungary's immediate neighbours but also Western leaders who were concerned, above all, with the preservation of peace and security in Europe.

In many respects, the problem of the Hungarian minorities in East Central Europe is ideally suited for diplomacy at the bilateral as well as at the multilateral levels. The three principal features of bilateralism (outlined above) are all strikingly relevant to any settlement of this problem. As will be recalled, these are: that bilateralism allows for greater specificity and detail in elaborating the rights and entitlements of a designated minority; that bilateralism may be appropriate, or even imperative, in circumstances where a minorities problem has a genuine bilateral dimension; and that bilateralism may benefit national minorities by raising their confidence.

The need for specificity and detail in elaborating the rights of the Hungarian minorities in East Central Europe derives, in my view, from their very particular circumstances and history. It is worth recalling that these sizeable and long-established communities were transformed into minorities by the post-World War One political settlement which allocated Transylvania to Romania, Slovakia and Ruthenia to the newly-established state of Czechoslovakia, and the southern province of Vojvodina to the newly constituted Kingdom of the Serbs, Croats and Slovenes. As a result of these sweeping territorial changes, 1,066,685 Hungarian speakers found themselves citizens of Czechoslovakia, 1,661,805 became Romanians overnight and 452,265 were transformed into Yugoslavs (i.e. subjects of the Kingdom of the Serbs, Croats and Slovenes).[27] As Joseph Rothschild has observed, the "peace terms left truncated Hungary with only one-third of her historic territory, two-fifths of her pre-war population, and two-thirds of her Magyar people".[28]

The Hungarians who suddenly (and reluctantly) found themselves minorities within the new or reconstituted states of East Central Europe possessed long-standing cultural, educational, religious and other institutions which they were understandably keen to preserve as far as possible. These included a Hungarian-language university in Cluj, the capital of Transylvania,[29] Hungarian-language primary and secondary schools, as well as a wealth of newspapers, journals, theatres etc. The strength, diversity and historic continuity of these institutions renders the situation of the Hungarian minorities and any assessment of their legitimate needs and entitlements significantly different, in my view, to what might be appropriate in the case of smaller, less cohesive minorities, or minorities which had not already established, for whatever reason, a comparable range of institutions. Minority rights regimes in East Central and Eastern Europe should, as a minimum, ensure that thriving and successful minority cultures, of which the Hungarian minorities in Slovakia and Romania are prime examples, retain the resources and freedoms necessary for their perpetuation.[30]

No doubt, these arguments will strike some as contentious. Where a minority has exercised undue power or influence in the past (for example, the Afrikaner community in South Africa), retention of the full range of former facilities or privileges by that minority would amount to the continuation of a grossly inequitable *status quo*. It is abundantly clear that, in those areas of Slovakia, Romania and Serbia where ethnic Hungarian minorities are now concentrated, serious criticisms may be levelled at Hungary's assimilationist policies between 1867 and the end of the First World War. As a German scholar commented, in a book published in the early years of this century, "[i]n no other state of Europe has the government been so successful, and in no other except Russia so unscrupulous, in the means by which it has tried to force upon the other elements of the population the language of the dominant majority".[31] However, since the loss of much of Hungary's territory (and population) in the peace settlement that followed the First World War, it cannot be argued that ethnic Hungarians in Romania, Slovakia or Serbia continue to occupy a privileged position – politically, culturally or economically. In such circumstances, a minority rights regime which ensures the preservation of minority journals, publishing houses, theatres and other cultural or educational resources – for as long as there remains a genuine demand for them – should not be viewed as unreasonable.

That the problem of the Hungarian minorities has a genuine bilateral dimension should be abundantly clear from what has been stated already. No meaningful settlement of this problem is feasible which ignores the evident concerns of Hungary. As the statement by Antall, the former Prime Minister of Hungary, illustrates, there is a genuine and deep-rooted sense of a Hungarian 'nation' encompassing those elements of the Hungarian people lying outside Hungary's diminished frontiers.

Thirdly, there is an important psychological dimension. There is a perceptible siege mentality on the part of the Hungarian minorities in East Central Europe, who genuinely believe (sometimes with good cause) that their rights and interests are under threat from a largely antagonistic or, at the very least, indifferent national culture.[32] There is a widespread feeling of having been abandoned by the international community since the Treaty of Trianon which 'consigned' them to the various states on Hungary's borders.[33] Thus, in principle at least, bilateralism may be expected to enhance these minorities' sense of confidence.

A BRIEF ANALYSIS OF HUNGARY'S BILATERAL TREATIES WITH SLOVAKIA AND ROMANIA

At the time of writing, Hungary has entered into twelve bilateral treaties since 1989 dealing in whole or in part with minorities issues.[34] However, the following analysis will be confined to the "Basic Treaties" concluded with Slovakia and Romania in 1996. These are of particular importance because of the size of the Hungarian minorities involved, the difficulties experienced by these minorities both before and after the 'transition' from Communism, and because of the historically fraught relations between Hungary and these neighbouring states. Particular aspects of those treaties will now be considered.

The Recognition of Minority Rights as Part of a General Political Settlement

The Treaty on Good Neighbourliness and Friendly Co-Operation between Slovakia and Hungary (hereafter the Slovakia-Hungary Treaty) and the Treaty on Understanding, Co-operation and Good Neighbourliness between Hungary and Romania (hereafter the Hungary-Romania Treaty), both of which entered into force in 1996, treat the issue of minority rights as part of a broader political settlement between the respective countries.[35] As indicated above, Hungary exercised absolute control over Slovakia, Ruthenia and Transylvania from 1867 until 1918 within the framework of the Austro-Hungarian Empire, while the historic Kingdom of Hungary ruled over these territories during the Fourteenth, Fifteenth and early Sixteenth centuries.[36] After the First World War, Hungary was forced to cede Slovakia, Ruthenia and Transylvania to the newly formed Czechoslovakia and to Romania. However, Hungarian ambitions to regain these territories persisted throughout the inter-war period. Following the First and Second Vienna Awards of November 1938 and August 1940,[37] Hungary briefly recovered much of the territories in question, although it was again forced to relinquish them after World War II. In view of this complex history, a measure of anxiety has understandably persisted in Slovakia and Romania that Hungary may wish to reassert its claims to these lands at some future date. Accordingly, both the Slovakia-Hungary Treaty and the Hungary-Romania

Treaty provide firm guarantees regarding the immutability of the post-war borders. For example, Article 3(1) of the Slovakia-Hungary Treaty states:[38]

> In compliance with the principles and norms of international law, the Contracting Parties confirm that they shall respect the inviolability of their common State borders and the territorial integrity of the other Contracting Party. They confirm that they have no mutual territorial claims and neither shall they raise any such claims in the future.

The renunciation of all territorial claims by the parties *vis-à-vis* one another (the text is identical on this point in the Hungary-Romania Treaty) was of fundamental political importance for the Slovak and Romanian authorities. It allowed them to make certain concessions regarding the rights of the Hungarian minorities that might otherwise have been difficult to justify to public opinion in their own countries.

The Introduction of Multiple Legal Regimes

One of the most striking features of these treaties is that they introduce multiple legal regimes governing the treatment of national minorities. Certain entitlements are applicable to *all* national minorities located within the territory of the contracting states.[39] For example, the Slovakia-Hungary Treaty includes the right of persons belonging to national minorities, whether individually or in community with other members of their group, "to express, maintain and develop their ethnic, cultural, linguistic or religious identity and to maintain and develop their culture in all its aspects (Article15(2)(c))". Similarly, Article 15(7) of the Hungary-Romania Treaty affirms that the contracting states will respect, "the right of persons belonging to national minorities to maintain free contacts with one another and with the citizens of other countries beyond the national borders, as well as to take part in the activities of national and international non-governmental organisations".

By contrast, various rights and entitlements are reserved solely for the Hungarian minorities in Slovakia and Romania respectively, and for the Slovak and Romanian minorities in Hungary.[40] For example, under the Slovakia-Hungary Treaty the norms and political commitments contained in designated texts are to be applied as "legal obligations" with respect solely to the Hungarian minority in Slovakia and to the Slovak minority in Hungary (Article 15(4)(b)). The texts in question are the Document of the Copenhagen Meeting of the Conference on the Human Dimension of the CSCE (1990), the UN General Assembly Declaration on the Rights of Persons Belonging to National or Ethnic, Religious and Linguistic Minorities (1992), and Recommendation 1201 of the Parliamentary Assembly of the Council of Europe.

While reference to these texts is intended to confer additional rights on the specific national minorities mentioned (i.e. Hungarians in Slovakia and Slovakians in Hungary), the *content* of those supplementary rights is not articulated with any degree of precision. Nor is it immediately clear how inconsistencies between the various texts are to be resolved.

In fact, the reference to Resolution 1201 was of particular importance to Hungary who saw it as a means, albeit indirect, of insinuating into the text of the treaty the principle of autonomy, or of minority-controlled local authorities, in regions where the members of a particular national minority form a numerical majority of the local population.[41] An explicit reference to this principle would have been unacceptable to the Slovak negotiators; indeed vehement Slovak objections were expressed to such an interpretation, *inter alia*, in a statement issued by the Slovak Government on 18 March 1995:[42]

> The Government of the Slovak republic refuses, in particular, those interpretations of the Hungarian Contracting Party according to which the Slovak Contracting Party accepted the recommendation of the Parliamentary Assembly of the Council of Europe No. 1201 (1993) in the sense enabling the creation of autonomous minority self-governing bodies.

Romanian objections to the principle of autonomy for national minorities, or even to minority-controlled local authorities, prevented the inclusion of any express reference to Recommendation 1201 in the text of its Treaty with Hungary. However, Recommendation 1201 is listed in a supplement to the Treaty, along with the Copenhagen Document and the 1992 General Assembly Declaration, as a source of legal obligations for the parties. Thus, Article 15(1)(b) of the Treaty states that the parties shall apply *as legal obligations*, in their treatment of the Romanian minority in Hungary and of the Hungarian minority in Romania, the "decisive stipulations" contained in the documents listed in the supplement to the Treaty.

Apart from the three international instruments referred to above, which confer additional, if uncertain, entitlements on the Hungarian minorities in Slovakia and Romania and on the Slovak and Romanian minorities in Hungary, the Treaties with Slovakia and Romania articulate a number of specific rights on behalf of the above-mentioned communities. For example, Article 15(2)(g) of the Slovakia-Hungary Treaty proclaims that:[43]

persons belonging to the Hungarian minority in the Slovak Republic and those belonging to the Slovak minority in the Republic of Hungary shall have the right to use, individually or in community with other members of their group, orally and in writing, their minority language both in private and in public . . .

In fact, this entitlement adds little of substance to those rights which may already be inferred from the European Convention on Human Rights[44] and other instruments which, under the Slovakia-Hungary Treaty (as under the Hungary-Romania Treaty), are incorporated as a source of legal obligation for the parties.[45] Thus, the reaffirmation of these rights seems designed simply to emphasise their importance.

Lack of Legal Precision

The topic of minority rights is acutely sensitive in Hungary, Slovakia and Romania, albeit for contrasting reasons. For Hungary, the treatment of the Hungarian minorities located outside its borders represents not only an important issue of human rights but a quasi-spiritual question affecting the survival of the Hungarian 'nation'. In Slovakia and Romania, by contrast, the issue of minority rights, especially Hungarian minority rights, is frequently viewed as a potential threat to the territorial integrity and political independence of the Slovak and Romanian states. Minority rights, from this perspective, represent a possible means of undermining the cohesion and unity of purpose of these relatively 'fragile' states,[46] potentially leading to their eventual dismemberment. For these reasons, genuine consensus on the appropriate treatment of the Hungarian minorities has proved elusive.

As should be clear from the previous analysis of the Treaties with Slovakia and Romania, there is a degree of ambiguity and imprecision in the language of certain provisions. This is a direct consequence of the underlying (and partially intractable) differences between the parties concerning the scope of the rights that should be accorded to national minorities, particularly the ethnic Hungarian minorities. As already noted, both Treaties purport to apply – as a source of *legal* obligation – the Copenhagen Document, the 1992 General Assembly Declaration on the Rights of Persons Belonging to National or Ethnic, Religious and Linguistic Minorities, and Recommendation 1201 of the Parliamentary Assembly of the Council of Europe. However, at least two of these texts, the Copenhagen Document and the 1992 General Assembly Declaration, were *not* drafted with the intention of creating legally enforceable rights, and there remain important discrepancies between the individual instruments themselves.

Significantly, major differences have already arisen concerning the application of Recommendation 1201. As indicated above, the Slovak Government has rejected any interpretation of 1201 that would entail "the creation of autonomous minority self-governing bodies". By contrast, Hungary viewed the inclusion of Recommendation 1201, in its Treaty with Slovakia, as providing for the establishment of exactly such institutions. Clearly, few assumptions can be made at this stage as to how these texts will be applied in practice.[47]

Application of the Framework Convention

One of the striking features of both the Treaty with Slovakia and the Treaty with Romania is the commitment of the parties to apply the terms of the Council of Europe's Framework Convention for the Protection of National Minorities[48] to *all* national minorities located within their borders (unless the domestic law of the contracting states embodies more favourable standards). This lends weight to the view of Professor Czaplinski that we are witnessing the formation of new customary law rules, particularly within Central and Eastern Europe, concerning the treatment of national minorities.[49]

However, the impact of the Framework Convention, should not be overestimated. Various principles enshrined in the Convention, governing the treatment of national minorities, can also be found in the Treaties with Slovakia and Romania. For example, the proscription of involuntary assimilation of persons belonging to national minorities, asserted in Article 5(2) of the Framework Convention, is affirmed by Article 15(2)(d) of the Slovakia-Hungary Treaty and by Article 15(9) of the Hungary-Romania Treaty. Several rights proclaimed by the Framework Convention correspond with rights already recognised under the European Convention on Human Rights, while the enforcement machinery available under the latter instrument is vastly superior to that provided by the former.[50]

The Framework Convention is also careful to avoid the unequivocal assertion of minority rights that are likely to entail a significant financial burden for contracting states. For example, Article 14(2) states that:

> In areas inhabited by persons belonging to national minorities traditionally or in substantial numbers, if there is sufficient demand, the Parties shall *endeavour* to assure, *as far as possible* and within the framework of their education systems, that persons belonging to those minorities have adequate opportunities for being taught the minority language or for receiving instruction in this language.[51]

Nor is the equivocal character of the obligation on contracting states arising from Article 14(2) mitigated by Article 13(1). This merely requires the Parties to recognise that, "persons belonging to a national minority have the right to set up and to manage their own private educational and training establishments", while Article 13(2) states that, "[t]he exercise of this right shall not entail any financial obligation for the Parties". In the context of Central and Eastern Europe, where minorities mostly lack the financial resources required to institute or operate primary or secondary schools catering for the needs of their communities, the state represents the only realistic source of funding in the short or medium-terms.[52] The importance of education, as a means of preserving and perpetuating minority cultures, cannot be over-stated.[53]

Finally, while the principles enshrined in the Framework Convention are to be applied to *all* persons belonging to national minorities located on the territory of the contracting states, it should be emphasised that states remain free, at least in the first instance, to designate those groups which they recognise as "national minorities" for the purposes of the Convention, or those criteria in accordance with which they will establish the identity of national minorities.[54] Therefore, it remains at least theoretically possible that certain groups not recognised as national minorities by one or other of the relevant states may be denied any benefits under the Framework Convention. At the same time, designated minorities, namely Slovaks and Romanians in Hungary and Hungarians in Slovakia and Romania, are accorded different and generally *higher* levels of treatment under the Treaties with Slovakia and Romania than those available under the Framework Convention.

Ancillary Commitments of the Parties

As indicated (above) two of the principal advantages of bilateral agreements are that they enable the parties to specify those rights which they consider appropriate to the circumstances of designated minorities, while they may also indicate the ancillary duties of contracting states. Such ancillary commitments may form an integral part of an overall 'package' aimed at promoting the interests of particular national minorities. For example, Article 12(6) & (7) of the Slovakia-Hungary Treaty provides:

> (6) Each Contracting Party shall support the teaching of the language of the other Contracting Party both at the schools and in the extra-curricular institutions. To this effect, the Contracting Parties shall assist one another in linguistic training and further education of teachers.

(7) Each Contracting Party shall endeavour to expand the opportunities for learning about culture, literature and language of the other Contracting Party, and promote the Slovak and Hungarian studies at higher education institutions.

Evidently, obligations of this type relate to the particular circumstances of the Hungarian minority in Slovakia (and the Slovak minority in Hungary), as well as the general history of relations between these two nations. In view of the specificity of these provisions, which have no application whatsoever outside Slovakia and Hungary, they are appropriately dealt with through bilateral agreement between these states. Comparable provisions can be found in the Treaty with Romania.[55]

CONCLUSION

Hungary's Basic Treaties with Slovakia and Romania illustrate both the limitations and the potentialities of bilateralism as a means of resolving minorities problems. Clearly, the conclusion of these Treaties has not 'solved' all of the difficulties and uncertainties associated with the Hungarian minorities in these countries. As indicated above, those provisions of the Treaties which are concerned with the treatment of national minorities are open to criticism as lacking precision on a number of key points. However, Judge Higgins has argued that international law should be viewed "as process rather than rules".[56] From this perspective bilateral instruments, such as the Treaties with Slovakia and Romania, are of considerable *potential* importance, both as a basis for on-going dialogue and the normalisation of relations between neighbouring states.

However, various other factors must also be taken into account in evaluating the prospects for the resolution of minorities problems in post-Communist societies. These include the extent to which the rule of law, democracy and respect for human rights have been realised in these countries. As indicated above, there has been persistent concern at the imperfect process of democratisation and constitutionalisation in states such as Romania and Slovakia (let alone Serbia or Belarus).[57] This has prompted spokesmen for minority groups, and other interested parties, to argue that minority rights are more important in situations where individual rights are not yet adequately or routinely safeguarded. A genuine commitment to the preservation of peaceful and orderly mutual relations by the states particularly concerned with individual minorities problems is also of cardinal importance.

The upsurge of demands for minority rights, particularly from national and ethnic minorities in Central and Eastern Europe and in the post-Soviet states, often reflects deep-seated unease amongst the minorities concerned at the tendency of post-Communist states to redefine themselves in terms of a single nationality, whether Slovak, Romanian, Lithuanian, etc.[58] Any significant increase in the nationalism of majorities inevitably encourages a corresponding increase in the nationalism of minorities – and *vice versa*. Bilateral initiatives, such as Hungary's Treaties with Slovakia and Romania, can only make a meaningful contribution to the resolution of minorities problems if the underlying tendencies in the contracting states – social, legal, political and ideological – are broadly consistent with the goal of resolving such problems in a mutually satisfactory fashion.

Finally, it is clear that bilateral approaches to the resolution of minorities problems are more likely to be successful if regional and even universal mechanisms assume a vigorous role in assuring that the parties discharge the obligations they have espoused at the bilateral level. In this way, the commitments which states assume *inter se*, with respect to the treatment of national or other minorities, can acquire a wider significance. Non-compliance is, then, no longer simply a bilateral question but a regional issue which may result in the application of credible sanctions.

NOTES

*Reader in Law, Warwick University. I should like to express my appreciation in the Airey Neave Research Trust who granted me a Research Fellowship in 1996. The research for this chapter was carried out during the course of my Fellowship. I should also like to thank the staff of the office of the Soros Foundation for an Open Society in Cluj, Romania, including its director Levente Salat, who kindly arranged a number of interviews for me in Cluj, in October 1996. I am very grateful to all those individuals, whether lawyers, sociologists, public officials and representatives of minority groups, who shared their insights with me during the course of my visits to Romania, Hungary and Slovakia during 1996. These visits were made possible by a generous grant from the British Academy. I am indented to Ms Júdit Szabó of Budapest, Hungary for her help in obtaining various Hungarian-language texts and to the editors of this book, Steven Wheatley and Peter Cumper, for their insightful comments on an earlier draft of this chapter. All translations from Hungarian, unless indicated to the contrary, are mine.

1. For analyses of the activities of various international organisations regarding minority rights, notably the Council of Europe and the OSCE, see G. Gilbert, The Council of Europe and Minority Rights and M.A.M. Estebanez, Minority Protection in the Framework of the OSCE (both this work).
2. The inter-war period witnessed the first concerted efforts to address minorities problems in Central and Eastern Europe. For an overview, see W. McKean, *Equality and Discrimination under International Law* (1983), chapters I-II; P. Thornberry, *International Law and the Rights of Minorities* (1991), chapter 3.
3. See, generally, on the underlying problems, I. Pogany, "Constitution Making or

Constitutional Transformation in Post-Communist Societies?", XLIV *Political Studies* (1996), at 568.

4. See C. Offe, *Varieties of Transition* (1996), chapter 4.

5. W. Czaplinski, "International Legal Protection of Minorities on the Universal and Regional Levels" ILA First Asian-Pacific Regional Conference (1996) 121, at 129.

6. In addition to recognising specific rights which national or other minorities may enjoy, bilateral agreements may prescribe other measures which, though not articulated in the form of rights, may prove equally important for the well-being of certain minorities. For example, Article 12(8) of the Treaty on Good Neighbourliness and Friendly Co-Operation between the Slovak Republic and the Republic of Hungary provides that: "Each Contracting Party shall ensure conditions within its country for activities of cultural centres of the other Contracting Party on the basis of a mutual agreement". For an English-language translation of the Slovakia-Hungary Treaty see the text published by the Ministry of Foreign Affairs of the Slovak Republic, June 1995. The establishment of such cultural centres, which can play an important role in preserving or in fostering minority cultures, may be of crucial importance to minorities (for example, Slovaks in Hungary and Hungarians in Slovakia) who may lack the necessary financial or cultural resources to organise such activities on their own.

7. In Central and Eastern Europe, 'national minorities' are frequently distinguished from 'ethnic minorities'. The latter comprise groups such as the Roma who do not possess a state of their own, in contrast to 'national minorities' such as Slovaks and Romanians in Hungary (or Hungarians in Slovakia and Romania) who can be identified with sovereign states. Further complications are introduced by efforts in the region, well-intentioned or otherwise, to classify Jews.

8. In fact, the OSCE is 'regional' only in terms of its focus. Both the United States and Canada are participating states of the OSCE.

9. Article 27 provides: "In those States in which ethnic, religious or linguistic minorities exist, persons belonging to such minorities shall not be denied the right, in community with the other members of their group, to enjoy their own culture, to profess and practice their own religion, or to use their own language". For the text of the Covenant see (1977) UKTS 6.

10. For the text of the Framework Convention and an Explanatory Report see Council of Europe, Doc. H (95) 10; 34 *ILM* (1995) 351.

11. Appendix II, Vienna Declaration, 9 October 1993, in Council of Europe, Information Sheet No. 33, Doc. H/INF (94) 2.

12. Similarly, Article 12(6) of the Treaty of Understanding, Co-Operation and Good Neighbourliness concluded by Romania and Hungary provides that each of the parties shall, "encourage the teaching of the language of the other country in universities, schools and other institutions", while Article 12(7) stipulates that the parties shall, "support the activity of their cultural centres and will make to a full extent use of those possibilities offered by these centres for developing mutual cultural exchanges". For the text of the Romania-Hungary Treaty, which entered into force on 27 December 1996, see 36 *ILM* (1997) 340.

13. For example, Article 1 of the Council of Europe's Framework Convention for the Protection of National Minorities asserts that, "[t]he protection of national minorities and of the rights and freedoms of persons belonging to those minorities *forms an integral part of the international protection of human rights* . . . (my emphasis)". For the text of the Framework Convention, see *supra*, n. 10.

14. For the text of the Declaration, which was adopted without vote by the General Assembly on 18 December 1992 in Resolution 47/135, see 32 *ILM* (1993) 912.
15. For my own robustly 'cosmopolitan' preferences, see I. Pogany, "Minority Rights in Central and Eastern Europe: Old Dilemmas, New Solutions?", in B. Bowring and D. Fottrell (eds.), *Minority and Group Rights: Towards the New Millenium* (forthcoming).
16. On the destabilising and cynical policies pursued by Nazi Germany with respect to the ethnic German (*Volksdeutsche*) minorities beyond its borders, most notably in Czechoslovakia, see J. Rothschild, *East Central Europe Between the Two World Wars* (rev. ed., 1977), at 127–34; G. Craig, *Germany 1866–1945* (rev. ed., 1981), at 703–07. On relations between Nazi Germany and Hungary's previously quiescent German minority, see Z. Zeman, *The Making and Breaking of Communist Europe* (rev. ed., 1991), at 214–15.
17. This was suggested to me recently by sociologists at the Babes-Bolyai University in Cluj, Romania.
18. On the distinction between 'civic' and 'ethnic' nationalisms, see M. Ignatieff, *Blood and Belonging* (1994), at 3–6. For an overview of some of the problems experienced by ethnic Hungarians in Romania and Slovakia, since the demise of Communism, see S. Griffiths, *Nationalism and Ethnic Conflict* (1993), at 21–25. On the imperfections of democratisation in Slovakia and Romania since 1990, see Pogany, *supra* n. 3, at 579–85.
19. In accordance with the *Ausgleich*, or compromise, of 1867, Hungary acquired equal status with Austria in the Austro-Hungarian Empire and full control over the eastern territories. See P. Longworth, *The Making of Eastern Europe* (1994), at 101.
20. Such apprehensions should now be at least partially allayed by the "Basic Treaties" which Hungary concluded with Slovakia and Romania in 1996. These treaties, which are examined in greater detail below, specifically exclude the possibility of territorial adjustments.
21. See S. Griffiths, *supra* n. 18, at 21. Of course, such statistics are not always free from controversy. For example, according to the 1992 census conducted in Romania, there were 1,624,959 Hungarians living in Romania: N. Edroiu and V. Puscas, *The Hungarians of Romania* (1996), at 30. However, this figure is probably an under-estimate as there are reasons why members of a minority which believes itself to be subject to discrimination or hostility may not wish to declare their minority allegiance.
22. On the problems of the Hungarian minorities in East Central Europe during the Communist period see G. Schöpflin, "National Minorities in Eastern Europe", in G. Schöpflin (ed.), *The Soviet Union and Eastern Europe* (rev. ed., 1986) 302, at 303–05, 309–12.
23. The results of the Presidential and parliamentary elections held in Romania, in late 1996, in which President Iliescu and his National Salvation Front party lost power, suggest that progressive changes are now underway in Romania. A party representing the Hungarian minority became a junior partner in the new coalition government.
24. See, generally, the sources cited *supra* n. 18. For a detailed assessment of the problems encountered by the Hungarian minority in Romania since 1990, see T. Gallagher, *Romania after Ceaucescu* (1995), especially chapters 3,5,6. For regular and authoritative updates on the difficulties experienced by the Hungarian minorities in both Slovakia and Romania, since the collapse of Communism, see the "Constitution Watch" section in the quarterly *East European Constitutional Review*.
25. The text of the Prime Minister's address is reproduced (in Hungarian) in M. Bihari,

(ed.), *A többpártrendszer kialakulása Magyarországon 1985–1991* (1992) 267, at 287.

26. *Ibid.*

27. See Table 23, in Rothschild, *supra* n. 16, at 155.

28. *Ibid.*

29. The University was amalgamated with its Romanian-language counterpart in 1959 to form the Babes-Bolyai University. However, various subjects ranging from medicine to sociology may still be studied and examined in either Romanian or Hungarian.

30. Of course, rather different questions are posed by minorities in East Central and Eastern Europe, such as the Roma, who are severely disadvantaged economically, educationally and politically, and who require assistance in order to establish thriving institutions and a greater knowledge of their own cultures. See, generally, D. Crowe, *A History of the Gypsies of Eastern Europe and Russia* (1995).

31. J. Partsch, *Central Europe* (1905), at 141.

32. See, generally, the sources cited *supra* nn. 18, 24.

33. An English-language version of the Treaty of Peace with Hungary, otherwise known as the Treaty of Trianon, was published in 1921 in Budapest by the Hungarian Ministry for Foreign Affairs.

34. Such treaties, generally described as Treaties of Friendship and Co-operation, have been concluded with the following states: France (1992, Article 3); Germany (1992, Article 19); Ukraine (1993, Article 17, and the appended "Declaration on the Principles of Co-operation Concerning the Securing of the Rights of National Minorities"); Latvia (1994, Article 15); Estonia (1994, Article 15); Lithuania (1994, Article 15); Slovenia (1994, Article 16; see, also, Agreement on the Protection of the Special Rights of the Slovenian National Minority in Hungary and of the Hungarian National Minority in Slovenia (1994); Slovakia (1996, especially Articles 14–15); Romania (1996, especially Articles 14–15); Croatia (1993, especially Article 17); see, also, Agreement on the Protection of the Hungarian Minority in the Republic of Croatia and the Croatian Minority in the Republic of Hungary (1995). In terms of Hungarian law, the Agreements with Slovenia and Croatia, dealing solely with minorities issues, are inter-governmental rather than inter-state instruments ("egyezmény" rather than "szerződés"). However, this distinction has no bearing on the legal character of these instruments under international law.

35. For details concerning the availability of English-language versions of these treaties see *supra* nn. 6, 12.

36. On Hungary's borders during the mediaeval period, see I. Lázár, *Hungary, A Brief History* (1990), especially at 85–99. For an account of political developments in Hungary during this period, see C.A. Macartney, *Hungary, A Short History* (1962), chapter 3.

37. On the Vienna Awards, see J. Rothschild, *supra* n. 16, at 179–84.

38. See, similarly, Article 4 of the Hungary-Romania Treaty. For details regarding the publication of this Treaty in English, see *supra* n. 12.

39. These are contained in Article 15(2),(3),(4)(a) of the Treaty with Slovakia and in Article 15(1)(a),(4),(5),(6),(7),(8),(9) of the Treaty with Romania.

40. In terms of the Treaty with Slovakia see, in particular, Article 15(2)(g),(4)(b). In terms of the Treaty with Romania see, in particular, Article 15(1)(b),(2),(3).

41. Article 11 of Recommendation 1201 states: "In the regions where they are in a majority the persons belonging to a national minority shall have the right to have at their disposal appropriate local or autonomous authorities or to have a special status,

matching the specific historical and territorial situation and in accordance with the domestic legislation of the state". Parliamentary Assembly of the Council of Europe, 44th Ordinary Session, 1 February 1993.

42. The text of this Statement is included as an appendix to the English-language translation of the Hungarian-Slovak Treaty published by the Slovak Foreign Ministry in June 1995.

43. See, similarly, Article 15(3) of the Hungary-Romania Treaty.

44. The European Convention asserts the right to freedom of expression (Article 10), while also affirming that the enjoyment of the rights recognised by the Convention, "shall be secured without discrimination on any ground such as sex, race, colour, language, religion, political or other opinion, national or social origin, association with a national minority . . . (Article 14)".

45. See Article 7(1), Recommendation 1201 of the Parliamentary Assembly of the Council of Europe. The remaining rights enumerated in Article 15(2)(g) of the Slovakia-Hungary Treaty and in Article 15(3) of the Hungary-Romania Treaty can also be found in various instruments accepted as a source of legal obligation by the parties, including Recommendation 1201.

46. The term 'fragility' may require explanation. In using the term, I simply wish to make the point that Slovakia, in particular, is a country which has had severely limited experience of statehood and which is consequently less self-assured (and perhaps less sure-footed) than many long-established states. In these circumstances, a fear of minorities and of divisions within the state can be more readily understood, if not necessarily condoned. A lack of self-assurance has also been discernible in Romania, a country which has a history of subjection to foreign interventions and dismemberment.

47. The problems which have emerged with regard to the correct interpretation of Recommendation 1201, for the purposes of the Slovakia-Hungary Treaty, have, seemingly been avoided in the Hungary-Romania Treaty. While the supplement to the Treaty with Romania lists Recommendation 1201 as a source of legal obligation, a footnote expresses the agreement of the parties that the Recommendation, "does not require the Parties to . . . secure the right to . . . territorial autonomy on the basis of ethnicity".

48. The Framework Convention recently came into force, following ratification by the twelfth member state of the Council of Europe on 1 February 1998.

49. For the views of Professor Czaplinski, see *supra*, n. 5, and the accompanying text.

50. For example, Article 7 of the Framework Convention states that the Parties, "shall ensure respect for the right of every person belonging to a national minority to freedom of peaceful assembly, freedom of association, freedom of expression, and freedom of thought, conscience and religion". Each of these rights is already recognised, and protected, under the European Convention.

51. My emphasis.

52. Analogies with religious minorities in Western Europe, such as Muslims or Jews, who have been able to fund denominational schools, are misleading. In the first place, the sheer poverty of many minority groups in Central and Eastern Europe means that they cannot realistically be expected to pay for minority schools. Secondly, only a fraction of Muslims or Jews attend denominational schools in Western Europe. Consequently, the financial burden for these communities can be absorbed in a way that would not be feasible for Hungarians in Slovakia or Romania, the overwhelming majority of whom seek education in Hungarian-language establishments.

53. Whatever the imperfections of Article 14(2) of the Framework Convention, the Hungarian minorities in Romania and Slovakia (and the Romanian and Slovak

minorities in Hungary) are in a relatively privileged position as the Basic Treaties with Romania and Slovakia accord somewhat firmer guarantees to these designated minorities regarding the right to be taught their mother tongue and to be educated in that language. It should be noted, finally, that the relevant guarantees are stronger in the Treaty with Romania than in the Treaty with Slovakia. See Article 15(3), Treaty with Romania and Article 15(2)(g), Treaty with Slovakia.

54. For example, the Republic of Macedonia, on signing the Framework Convention, declared that it would apply the Convention to "the Albanian, Turkish, Vlach, Roma and Serbian national minorities" living on its territory. See Human Rights Information Bulletin No. 40 (March–June 1997), Council of Europe Doc. H/INF (97) 4, at 29.

55. See Article 12(6),(7), Treaty with Romania.

56. R. Higgins, *Problems and Process* (1994), at 2.

57. Note should, however, be taken of the results of the legislative and presidential elections held in Romania in December 1996. As indicated previously, *supra* n. 23, these suggest that the pace and genuineness of reform are now improving significantly.

58. For example, the Act on the State Language of the Slovak Republic, adopted by the Slovak National Council on 15 November 1995, provides, *inter alia*, that Slovak is the state language and that it has "priority over other languages applied on the whole territory of the Slovak Republic" (Article 1(1),(2)). The preamble notes that "the Slovak language is the most important feature of distinctiveness of the Slovak nation, the most esteemed value of its cultural heritage and an articulation of sovereignty of the Slovak Republic" (English-language text supplied to the author by the Secretariat of the Council of Europe). I have explored these themes in greater detail in I. Pogany, *supra* n. 15.

The Content of Rights in the 'New' Europe

The Northern Ireland Constitution Act 1973:
Lessons for Minority Rights

*Brigid Hadfield**

*Brigid Hadfield**

INTRODUCTION

This chapter will focus on Northern Ireland, a region in Europe tragically synonymous with conflict between its majority and minority populations. Northern Ireland had a system of devolved government from 1920 to 1972 operating under the provisions of the Government of Ireland Act 1920. [1] Extensive legislative and executive powers were devolved to the Northern Ireland Parliament and Government, subject, under section 75 of the 1920 Act, to the overriding supremacy of the Westminster Parliament, although constitutional convention also controlled the nature of the relationship between the two Parliaments and governments. From the majority party in the Northern Ireland House of Commons the devolved government was formed exclusively and was invariably unionist[2] throughout the fifty year period. In 1920 the population balance in Northern Ireland as determined by religion was approximately two-thirds Protestant and one-third Roman Catholic. The latest figures under the 1991 census are approximately 62 per cent and 38 per cent. The voting patterns and preferences in Northern Ireland are such that a very high proportion of Protestants vote unionist, and of Roman Catholics, nationalist. Consequently, the Roman Catholic/nationalist minority was not only precluded from participation in the devolved government but was also effectively denied the hope of ever forming a government itself.

The 1920 Act had two main anti-discrimination provisions: section 5 prohibited, *inter alia*, the making of laws interfering with religious equality and section 8(6) provided that in the discharge of its responsibilities the devolved government was (subject to exceptions) precluded from giving any preference, privilege or advantage or imposing any disability or disadvantage on any person on account of religious belief.[3] In spite of these provisions, however, serious allegations of discrimination were increasingly levelled against those who held devolved power under the 1920 Act – of both active and (where the allegations involved the local councils)

129

P. Cumper and S. Wheatley (eds.), Minority Rights in the 'New' Europe, 129–146
© 1999 *Kluwer Law International. Printed in Great Britain.*

passive discrimination. The specific Roman Catholic/nationalist grievances included various aspects of the electoral law (in particular gerrymandering), unfairness in the allocation of public housing, discrimination in employment in both the public and private sector, policing, the Special Powers Acts[4] and their operation and some political bias with regard to the lower courts. These issues came to a head in the late 1960s and in the face of increasing violence,[5] the Westminster Government took over responsibility for all law and order issues in Northern Ireland and eventually for all devolved matters. The devolved system was prorogued in 1972 and formally abolished by the Northern Ireland Constitution Act 1973.

THE NORTHERN IRELAND CONSTITUTION ACT 1973

The Northern Ireland Constitution Act 1973 (NICA) provided for a new system of devolution for Northern Ireland, many of the different elements being designed to remedy some of the grievances levelled at the 1920 system.[6] The 1973 Act (and related legislation) provided for a 78-member unicameral Assembly, elected by a system of proportional representation to which was devolved (or "transferred") extensive but not absolute legislative power in the areas of education, agriculture, economic development, the environment and health and social services. Matters which had been devolved under the 1920 Act but which had been exercised, or were perceived to have been exercised, in ways that were divisive or adverse to the interests of the minority community were not devolved under the 1973 Act and remained the sole responsibility of the Westminster Parliament. These "excepted" matters included special powers, elections and all levels of judicial appointments. Devolution of the transferred matters could only take place when the Secretary of State for Northern Ireland (a member of the Westminster Cabinet) was satisfied that a devolved government could be formed which, "having regard to the support it commands in the Assembly and to the electorate on which that support is based, is likely to be widely accepted throughout the community". This requirement in section 2 is widely referred to as "power-sharing" in that it precluded single (or similar) party government. Section 25 of the Act also provided for the establishment in the Assembly of consultative committees to advise and assist the political head of each of the Northern Ireland government departments in the formulation of policy; the membership of these committees taken as a whole was, so far as practicable, to reflect the balance of parties in the Assembly. Thus at the *institutional* level the 1973 Act sought to involve in the processes of governing, on a proportionate basis, the elected representatives of the minority community. This system of devolution operated only for the first five months of 1974 because in May of that year the system was effectively terminated by the Ulster Workers' Council strike led by those opposed to power-sharing and (more particularly) to the proposed cross-border (Belfast-Dublin) Council of Ireland (on this see further below). There has been no devolution of legislative power to Northern Ireland since that time.[7] Consequently, all legislation for Northern Ireland is passed either by Westminster Acts of Parliament (mainly in the excepted areas) or – much more commonly – by way of Orders in Council, a form of delegated legislation made in accordance with Westminster's procedures for such legislation. All executive decision-making is in the hands of the Secretary of State for Northern Ireland and the "junior Ministers" of the Northern Ireland Office.

Other provisions of NICA, however, are of continuing relevance and these are the provisions of Part III of the Act, namely sections 17 to 23, which sought and seek to provide a certain amount of *substantive* protection in the field of freedom from discrimination. Section 17 of the Act renders void any legislative provision applying in Northern Ireland to the extent that it discriminates against any person or class of persons on the ground of religious belief or political opinion. This provision does not apply to the provisions of a Westminster Act of Parliament but, crucially, it does apply to Northern Ireland Orders in Council.[8] Discrimination is defined, by section 23, as being to treat any person or class of persons "less favourably in any circumstances" than other persons are treated in those circumstances. Section 19(1) makes it unlawful for public and local bodies, including local government, the statutory boards and Government Ministers "to discriminate, or aid, induce or incite another to discriminate in the discharge of functions relating to Northern Ireland against any person or class of persons on the ground of religious belief or political opinion". Section 19(2) provides that this obligation is a duty owed to any person who may be adversely affected by a contravention of subsection (1) and that any breach of that duty is actionable in Northern Ireland. Section 19(3) also provides, (whether or not damages are awarded), for the granting of an injunction in the case of continual unlawful conduct.

Section 20 provides for the establishment of the Standing Advisory Commission on Human Rights, for the purpose of advising the Secretary of State for Northern Ireland on the adequacy and effectiveness of the law in preventing discrimination on the ground of religious belief or political opinion and in providing redress for persons aggrieved by discrimination on either ground – neither of which is defined in the legislation. Section 21 relates to oaths, undertakings and declarations and makes it unlawful, subject to certain exceptions, for a public authority or body to require any person to take an oath etc. as a condition of his being appointed to or employed by that authority or body. Section 22 relates to investigations by the Ombudsman into complaints of maladministration[9] and provides that the provision in the relevant controlling legislation (which precludes the Ombudsman from conducting an investigation where the person aggrieved has or had a remedy by way of proceedings in a court of law) does not apply to the investigation of a complaint alleging maladministration involving discrimination on the ground of religious belief or political opinion or a requirement in contravention of section 21.

Section 18 (rendered in most respects redundant in the absence of devolution but of interest nonetheless) lays down a special procedure for determining the validity of legislation; it essentially enables the Judicial Committee of the Privy Council to determine the validity of those proposed or enacted legislative provisions referred to it by the Secretary of State for Northern Ireland where he believes them to be discriminatory.

Before considering the strengths and weaknesses of these legislative provisions, both then and now, the overall domestic human rights context into which they were enacted should first be addressed.

The United Kingdom has no written constitution and at the time of writing, no overall Bill of Rights (in the current civil libertarian sense of the phrase). The keystone of the constitution is the sovereignty of (the Westminster) Parliament; and although the doctrine has (arguably) been weakened by the United Kingdom's membership of the European Union, the principle that there are no legal limits to the powers of Parliament still exercises considerable and pervasive sway. Civil liberties are, therefore, protected on what is termed a residual basis – an individual citizen enjoys whatever freedoms have not been removed by Act of Parliament (and also whatever rights and benefits have been conferred by Act of Parliament). The courts have a subordinate role to play; they cannot uphold a challenge to the validity of an Act of Parliament, although through their judicial review jurisdiction (and other legal proceedings) they may develop – and have developed – legal principles which may accord respect to basic rights and freedoms.

At the time of the enactment of NICA (Part III came into force on 1 September, 1973), the United Kingdom had been a member of the (then) European Economic Community for only several months; the impact of the jurisprudence of the European Court of Justice (in the specifically pertinent domain, here, of anti-discrimination law as well as generally) would be felt later. The United Kingdom Government had accepted the right of individual petition to the European Commission of Human Rights and the jurisdiction of the Human Rights Court from January 1966. As the European Convention on Human Rights has so far not been incorporated into the domestic law of the United Kingdom, the decisions of the Commission and the Court are, therefore, of particular significance in terms of influencing the substance of United Kingdom law. The first case involving the United Kingdom, *Golder* (involving prison rules), was lodged in 1970 and the Court's judgment was delivered on 21 February, 1975. Finally the only legislation which, at this time, could be said directly to address specific civil liberties concerns were (in Northern Ireland) the Prevention of Incitement to Hatred Act 1970 and (in Great Britain) the Race Relations Acts 1965 and 1968.

The White Paper which preceded NICA[10] promised "comprehensive provisions which will constitute a charter of human rights for Northern Ireland", but the phrase promised more than was delivered. Part III of NICA itself and the Fair Employment (Northern Ireland) Act 1976 (which, extending to both public and private sector employment, made it unlawful for an employer to discriminate on the grounds of religious belief or political opinion) constituted the bulk of the "Charter". Other legislation followed later – illustrating what was the traditional United Kingdom approach of protecting rights (if at all) by specific or *ad hoc* pieces of legislation rather than through incorporation of the European Convention on Human Rights or the enactment of an autochthonous Bill or Charter of Rights. The most notable pieces of legislation passed after NICA are the Sex Discrimination Act 1975 (GB) and Order 1976 (NI), the Race Relations Act 1976 (GB), the Fair Employment (Northern Ireland) Act 1989 (which, *inter alia*, widened the definition of discrimination to include indirect discrimination), the disability discrimination legislation 1995 (UK), and the Race Relations (NI) Order 1997. Thus the main thrust of United Kingdom legislation dealing with minorities has been to protect from discrimination people or classes of people as identified by, for example, gender, race, disability, religious belief or political opinion. NICA Part III falls into this "freedom from discrimination" pattern. However, overall, this legislation has been piecemeal in its enactment, geographically variable in its extent and often covers different fields of activity in its application. Furthermore, for all the time covered by the following case-law, it has not been reinforced by comprehensive legislation requiring the positive protection or enhancement of civil liberties where the residual approach (the citizen is free to do whatever is not forbidden) still prevails. This in itself is likely to have had a not inconsiderable restrictive impact in terms of the creation of a more all-embracing "culture of compliance" with regard to the protection of minority rights in the United Kingdom, and is obviously particularly pertinent in the context of the judicial response to those cases where individuals have invoked the provisions of Part III of NICA. All this stated, however, NICA Part III possesses some very significant elements; their potential was limited by either subsequent political developments or by legislative caution in 1973, but these elements nonetheless are valuable for the future protection of minority rights in the United Kingdom and should, at the least, inform the debate which will surround the new Labour Government's decision to introduce legislation incorporating, as an interpretative principle, the European Convention on Human Rights.

It is generally accepted that the optimum enforcement of minority rights, indeed of civil liberties generally, involves the active participation of all three branches of government.[11] Part III of NICA provided for pre-legislative scrutiny by the (Westminster) Secretary of State for Northern Ireland of legislative measures proposed by the devolved Assembly and, where deemed appropriate, by the Judicial Committee of the Privy Council, where it was feared that such provisions discriminated on the grounds of religious belief or political opinion. Similar post-enactment review was also provided for. The ordinary courts too had a wide range of remedies available to them, both public law remedies and private law remedies, including damages and injunctions. Furthermore, section 22 enabled the Ombudsman to investigate alleged public body maladministration in this area without any concern that he or she would be overstepping his or her jurisdiction. The Standing Advisory Commission on Human Rights (SACHR) was also established and given a general monitoring and advisory role and (important in the context of a devolved administration where minority rights could be thought to be vulnerable) was required to submit its reports not to the devolved government but to the Westminster-based Secretary of State for Northern Ireland. All this, when coupled with the wide range of public bodies, whose administrative acts, decisions and omissions were covered by the anti-discrimination provisions, constitutes a good and (at least in British terms) innovative system of enforcement.

The potential in and of the system, however, was weakened by a number of factors. First, the devolutionary context of the anti-discrimination provisions was removed with the demise of the Assembly in May 1974. The overall Parliamentary context then became that of the Westminster Parliament where, given the centrality of the doctrine of parliamentary sovereignty, there had long been general hostility to proposals for a Bill of Rights, or to the enhancement of a "culture of rights". A further problem, particularly in terms of pre-legislative scrutiny, is the limited amount of time given in Parliament to Northern Ireland Orders in Council.[13] The absence of a Northern Ireland Assembly has had two further consequences. The arguments for a Bill of Rights for Northern Ireland specifically were largely caught within the context of the debates on a Bill of Rights for the United Kingdom generally – although there are other reasons too why this has been so.[14] Finally – and this is a point of considerable importance – the search for a new constitutional settlement for Northern Ireland has been the dominant concern at Westminster, leaving human rights issues to be addressed generally[15] as a part of an overall settlement. In many ways, therefore, the protection of human rights in the large has been regarded as a subsidiary element *dependent* upon other political or institutional changes rather than as a factor which could help to mould or influence them.

A second reason why the potential of NICA has been weakened relates to the state of the public law remedies (now termed judicial review) at the time of its enactment. Although section 19 provided for other remedies, until the reform of the public law procedure, effected in Northern Ireland by the Judicature (Northern Ireland) Act 1978 and Rules of the Supreme Court Order 53 1980 (as amended), public law proceedings were of limited (and no actual) value in the enforcement of minority rights under NICA. The reactivated (and developing) principles of review, when coupled with procedural reforms (enhancing judicial review's utility and accessibility) and a growing awareness amongst the legal profession of its overall role and value, have since 1980 led to greater use of judicial review with regard to the provisions of NICA. The fact remains, however, that the first *judicial review* application was brought more than ten years after NICA's enactment – and there has been scarcely more than a dozen such cases in total.

A third reason why the potential of NICA has been weakened relates to the statutory remit given to SACHR – a remit by which it itself has felt constrained.[16] Although SACHR has (factually but extra-statutorily) broadened its remit to address human rights issues additional to those of religious and political discrimination, its main role remains advisory to the Secretary of State for Northern Ireland with no independent legal status beyond that. A more proactive role with regard to education, strong and effective co-ordination with other human rights agencies and powers of enforcement of the statutory provisions (either generally or through individual assistance) would be of considerable value. It should also be noted in this context that the Government has not always been assiduous about consulting SACHR on proposed legislation with human rights implications; its failure to do so with regard to the removal of an accused person's "right to silence" in 1988 led to a strongly worded protest from SACHR and an undertaking that in future "in all normal circumstances" the Secretary of State would provide SACHR with the opportunity to comment on all proposed legislation with human rights implications.[17]

A fourth reason why the potential of NICA has been weakened relates, at least indirectly, to section 22 – the role of the Ombudsman. As SACHR itself pointed out in 1990:

> [despite . . .] clear indications that religious and political discrimination were to be an important focus of the work of [the Northern Ireland Ombudsman] the actual number of complaints alleging such discrimination have been relatively few. In the years from 1982 to 1988 there were a total of 39 such complaints. On an annual basis, these complaints, as a proportion of all complaints, ranged between 0.8%and 2.5%.[18]

In the subsequent Annual Reports of the Ombudsman the phrase "I received no complaints in which religious discrimination was alleged" is a regular feature.

NICA PART III: THE CASE LAW

The main provision of NICA Part III, in terms of the case law, is not unexpectedly section 19,[19] although section 17 has featured in one major case involving a challenge by Northern Ireland's Roman Catholic bishops to legislative provision made for integrated school education.[20] Only a small number of cases, however, has arisen in total in the twenty-three years since NICA's enactment, all but two of them being judicial review applications (with all the limitations of that procedure that that entails). In terms of the substantive areas involved, the cases have related to six main areas, namely:[21]

Education – *Cecil, Daly* (s.17)
Local Government – *Dallas, French* (s.22), *O'Neill, Purvis,*[22] *Quigley*
Parades – *McManus, White*
Sport – *Cleland* (s.17), *Purvis, O'Neill, Quigley*
Prisons – *Fisher* (training school), *McCartney* (Court of Appeal), *McCormaic,*[22b] *Thompson*
Security – *Lavery, McGuigan* (discovery stage only) (Court of Appeal).

Some cases are cited twice where appropriate. There was one other case – *McLaughlin* – which involved a challenge (brought by a Sinn Féin councillor, also a chairperson of Sinn Féin) to the Home Secretary's media ban on the broadcasting of certain matters, including "direct" interviews with members of Sinn Féin. This constitutes a *total* of 17 cases, only two of which reached the Court of Appeal – and of those two cases, one was an application for discovery and when this was refused the substantive application was withdrawn.[23] It is not possible in the space available to provide any detailed analysis of the cases, although one or two major points will be mentioned. In order to provide something of the flavour of the case-law, however, a very brief factual summary of each case is given.

Education

Cecil – provision of school education for non-Roman Catholic primary school children on a small island where there was only one, in effect, Roman Catholic school. *Daly* – challenge to the provisions of the Education Reform (N.I.) Order 1989 on integrated education as discriminatory against the provision of Roman Catholic schools.

Local Government

Dallas – challenge to a resolution of the nationalist majority of Derry City Council that the unionist mayor be deprived of mayoral facilities because of his participation in a road "blockade" protesting against a decision to re-route/ban an "Orange" march; that majority had previously supported Dallas's appointment as mayor. *French* – challenge to a unionist district council's resolution that councillors should not be able to attend or participate in meetings unless they had signed an "anti-terrorism" declaration (which was not, then, required by legislation). *O'Neill* – challenge to the decision of a (Protestant) majority of a district council not to open the leisure centre and swimming pool on a Sunday. *Purvis* – challenge to the refusal of a district council not to fund a Gaelic football coaching scheme (this being a sport played mainly/solely by Roman Catholics) when swimming, soccer and rugby were funded. *Quigley* – challenge to a decision of Belfast City Council not to allocate money to a playground in an area with a high level of Sinn Féin support.

Parades

McManus – challenge to a police decision to route a nationalist march away from certain parts of Belfast. *White* – the applicant sought an order directing the Secretary of State to make an order prohibiting any "Orange" parade from a Roman Catholic/nationalist part of Belfast.

Sport

Cleland – challenge to a decision to close certain roads to facilitate a motor-bike road race meeting, where the closure may have prevented the applicant from attending Vigil Mass (on Wednesday and Saturday for Corpus Christi and Sunday respectively). For *Purvis, O'Neill* and *Quigley*, see under local government.

Prisons

Fisher – Roman Catholic applicant sent to a "Protestant" training school (because of shortage of places at the "Roman Catholic" training school). He argued that this denied him access to facilities for the exercise of his religious duties and observances and exposed him to "hostilities" from people of a different religious persuasion. *McCartney* – challenge to a decision of the Secretary of State not to permit Sinn Féin elected representatives to visit prisons or prisoners other than to visit members of their immediate families. *McCormaic* – appellants to the High Court sought damages and a declaration for discrimination under section 19, with regard to non-use of the Irish language in prisons (concerning, e.g., the writing of letters, conversation, use of Irish forms of prisoners' names, delays in the admission to the prison of Irish literature), lack of facilities to play Gaelic football and the wearing of the fáinne (an emblem indicating proficiency in the Irish language). *Thompson* – applicant challenged a decision to remove him from association with other prisoners on the ground that it prevented him from attending Mass on the Sundays affected.

Security

Lavery – challenge to a decision of the Government not to provide the applicant (a Sinn Féin councillor) with financial assistance towards the cost of installing special security measures, after the applicant's home had been attacked twice, the first time occasioning the death of his son. *McGuigan* – discovery sought to assist a challenge to a decision to refuse a Sinn Féin councillor a firearm certificate for a personal protection firearm. Had the case proceeded to a substantive hearing, section 19 would have been relied upon.

Points of interest arising from the cases are as follows.

(1) On only a small number of occasions did the applicant win the judicial review application,[24] although in some cases the applicant succeeded on other grounds or the respondent in some other way sought to ameliorate the situation. The only successful applicants were those in *Purvis, French* and *Quigley*. In *Lavery*, the applicant was successful on the basis that the Secretary of State had failed to take account of his personal circumstances

and in *O'Neill* the applicant was successful on the basis that the council had imposed an unwarrantable fetter on its discretion by considering exclusively the Sunday Observance argument to the exclusion of factors such as whether the majority (or a substantial percentage) of the local population would want to avail of leisure facilities on a Sunday. In *Cleland*, the respondent arranged to permit the applicant and his family to move in and out of their home between races and in *McCormaic*, before judgment was delivered, the prison authorities had already approached the Gaelic Athletic Association to facilitate provision of Gaelic football in the prison and had removed the ban on the wearing of the fáinne.

(2) There have been cases, other than ones which specifically rely on the provisions of NICA, which are nonetheless relevant to the concerns of the legislation: for example, other cases involving the re-routeing of Orange parades, the use of the Irish language and the exclusion of Sinn Féin councillors from council sub-committees.[25] The existence of the provisions of NICA have also, it would appear, made it easier for applicants to argue that public action is unlawful because it is unreasonable as being discriminatory.

(3) In the context of those cases which involve Sinn Féin (for example, *Lavery, McCartney, McLaughlin*) it should be noted that the courts had consistently held that the expression "political opinion" does not include the belief that it is legitimate to use or to support the use of violence to achieve political ends. Since the enactment of the Elected Authorities (Northern Ireland) Act 1989 (which requires, *inter alia*, candidates at local elections to disavow by word or deed support for any proscribed organisation or for acts of terrorism connected with Northern Ireland affairs), allowance must also be made for these provisions; nonetheless this factor has had an influence on the operation of the provisions of NICA.[26]

(4) The Fair Employment Act 1976, as mentioned above, was, with NICA, a part of the Government's Charter of Human Rights. By section 16(1) of the 1976 Act, discrimination was defined as meaning discrimination on the ground of religious belief or political opinion; and section 16(2) (like section 23(1) and (2) of NICA) defined discrimination as less favourable treatment. In the Northern Ireland Court of Appeal in *Armagh District Council* v *Fair Employment Agency* in 1983[27] the then Lord Chief Justice, Lord Lowry, held that in order to establish unlawful discrimination under the 1976 Act, the complainant must show a *deliberate intention* to differentiate on the ground of religion or politics on the part of the respondent body. Indirect discrimination was not included in the fair employment legislation until section 49(1) of the Fair Employment Act 1989 amended section 16 of the 1976 Act to achieve this end.

Decisions of the Northern Ireland Court of Appeal are binding upon the lower courts in Northern Ireland including, of course, the Queen's Bench Division and the Chancery Division (which decided *Purvis*) which together have heard all the NICA cases. Decisions of the House of Lords in English cases are not technically binding on the Northern Ireland courts, although they may be and usually are very, very persuasive. In June 1990, the House of Lords decided the English case of *James* v *Eastleigh Borough Council*,[28] holding by a majority (Lord Lowry, by then in the House of Lords, dissenting) that the causative "but for" *not* the purposive (intent or motive) test applied in the domain of the similarly framed and phrased sex discrimination law. The question to be asked now is – would the plaintiff have received the same treatment *but for* his or her sex? In June 1994, the Northern Ireland Court of Appeal in *Belfast Port Employers' Association* v *Fair Employment Commission*[29] held that the decision in *Armagh* could not stand in the light of the conclusions of the House of Lords in *James* and that from henceforth the "but for" test should apply. All this had the following consequences for the judges interpreting NICA. *Armagh* was applied at first, the concept of discrimination under NICA thus being interpreted in the narrower, purposive, terms. After the decision in *James*, the judges *continued* to apply *Armagh*, both for reasons of *stare decisis* and also because they believed *Armagh* to be correct. (See, for example, *McLaughlin, McCormaic,*[30] *Cleland, Thompson, and Lavery*). After the decision in *Belfast Port Employers' Association*, the *James* test now controls the interpretation of NICA (see *Fisher*). Given that *Fisher* was decided in the autumn of 1996 (and at the time of writing there have been no subsequent NICA cases) it is too early to assess what liberating impact this may have with regard to the operation of NICA.[31]

THE EVOLVING CONTEXT OF NICA: PART III

NICA sought to balance the different interests of the two communities within Northern Ireland, hence the inclusion of what is usually termed "the constitutional guarantee" in section 1 of NICA. Under section 1, and related provisions, for as long as the majority of the people of Northern Ireland want this, Northern Ireland is and remains a part of the United Kingdom. By contrast, Articles 2 and 3 of the Irish Constitution (deemed by the Irish Supreme Court to be a "constitutional imperative") provide that the national territory consists of the "whole island of Ireland, its islands and the territorial seas" but that, without any diminution of this principle, pending the reintegration of the national territory, the jurisdiction of the Irish Government and Parliament will be confined to the Republic of Ireland. Furthermore, the minority community within Northern Ireland as identified by the Roman Catholic religion largely espouses a united Ireland. Consequently there has been increasing emphasis not only on the need to protect the minority's rights and liberties (by, for example, Part III of NICA) but also on the desirability of accommodating and protecting their "community" rights relating to national allegiance, identity and culture. The issues surrounding these latter rights (essentially constituting all aspects of legal recognition of the nationalist community) are frequently subsumed under the heading of "parity of esteem" for the two communities in Northern Ireland.[32] They are also, however, directly pertinent to the consideration of an "Irish dimension" in Northern Ireland affairs. The Irish dimension may be manifested in several forms depending partly, but only partly, on whether or not devolution is reintroduced to Northern Ireland. The Anglo-Irish Agreement of 1985 gave the Irish Government a formal consultative role on many legal, political and security aspects of Northern Ireland affairs, not least with regard to it being the guarantor of the interests of the minority community. Relations between London and Dublin (often referred to as the "east-west" axis) have been increasingly formalised with regard to Northern Ireland affairs, not least since the establishment of the Anglo-Irish Intergovernmental Council in 1981.[33] At the time of the enactment of NICA, it was intended to introduce, in conjunction with the devolved scheme it proposed, a Council of Ireland to facilitate co-operation between Belfast and Dublin (the "north-south" axis) on a wide range of matters, including the environment, agriculture, aspects of trade and industry and of public health, electricity generation, roads and transport, sport, culture and the arts. Section 12 of NICA thus empowered any (devolved) executive authority in Northern Ireland to consult with and to enter into agreements or arrangements with its counterpart in the Republic of Ireland on any matter within its competence, being thereby enabled to transfer to or receive from one another pertinent functions in the devolved areas. In the absence of devolution to Northern Ireland, such a North-South consultative and harmonising liaison is clearly not feasible, but it has long been the policy of successive British Governments to include, in any future devolved scheme at least, a similar North-South Irish dimension.

All of these elements – the conflicting territorial claims, the Irish dimension, parity of esteem and equality of treatment and of opportunity – interrelate and have an impact the one upon another. The provisions of NICA are but one part of a larger whole and should not, therefore, be viewed in isolation from the overall dynamics of the situation.[34]

CONCLUSION

An important new dimension to NICA Part III has been added by the Government's Central Secretariat Circular 5/93 on Policy Appraisal and Fair Treatment (PAFT), (which replaces Central Secretariat Circular 1/90 which advised Government Departments to consider their policies in the context of direct and indirect discrimination in the fields of religious belief, political opinion and gender). PAFT is designed to require all Government Departments and non-departmental public bodies to complement their commitment to eliminating unlawful discrimination by the active promotion of fair treatment at all levels of public policy-making, implementation and service-delivery. PAFT applies not only in the areas which were covered by CSC 1/90 but also with regard to marital status, disability, ethnicity, age and sexual orientation. Although these issues are thus currently being addressed through non-legislative means, the circular may, of course, be invoked in legal proceedings, as was done in *In re Casey*[35] where in judicial review proceedings the circular was treated as a material or relevant factor of which public bodies had to take account or as creating a legitimate expectation in individuals that public bodies would (all other matters being equal) adhere to the policy it contained. This circular (and the decision in *Casey*) when linked to the new freedom given by the removal of the constraints laid down in *Armagh* can – and should – give NICA Part III much more effectiveness. SACHR's recommendation that NICA should be amended to impose on public bodies a duty to ensure equality (or parity) of treatment and esteem for both main sections of the community in Northern Ireland may also receive increasing prominence.[36]

NICA itself, however, still bears the hallmarks of the time at which it was enacted. The provisions of Part III were largely isolated from any political context within which to operate (other than one which regarded the dominant concern as being the establishment of a new constitutional context within which protection of human rights and civil liberties could be secured). They were certainly isolated from any political will to carry the provisions forward in a legally fundamental sense. SACHR was given only limited advisory powers. The judicial contribution has also been of a limited nature – nothing approaching the ethos of a Constitutional Court, although the responsibility for this may lie as much with the *ad hoc* approach taken by Parliament as with the judges themselves. The decision in *Armagh* and the principles of precedent left NICA for its first twenty years more limited than it might otherwise have been. It is also fair to state, however, that litigants have made little use of NICA – a point which becomes of greater significance given the absence of a body with enforcement powers. Furthermore, although the private law remedies of NICA were of value, the public law aspects of non-discrimination are not necessarily best protected and furthered solely by judicial review proceedings – and for the reasons already given, the potential of the role given to the Judicial Committee of the Privy Council has not been fulfilled.

Clearly, there has been some value in NICA Part III; all else apart one should not judge such a situation only by the visible impact. However, NICA itself has not proved as valuable for the protection of minority rights as was hoped for at the time of its enactment. It, even with the other provisions, does not add up to a Charter of Human Rights. It is likely that the incorporation of the European Convention on Human Rights and (the possibility of) a new political settlement for Northern Ireland will change the scene considerably.[37]

NOTES

*Professor of Public Law, Queen's University of Belfast.

1. It is possible here only to provide a very broad outline of the relevant constitutional background. For more detailed consideration, see B.Hadfield, *The Constitution of Northern Ireland* (1989); and, more briefly, B.Hadfield, "An Introduction to the Constitution of Northern Ireland", 2 *European Public Law* (1996) 201.
2. The terms "unionist" and "nationalist" will be used generally in this chapter to refer respectively to those who support the retention of the union between Great Britain and Northern Ireland and those whose preferred political option is for Northern Ireland to be a part of a united Ireland.
3. See H.Calvert, *Constitutional Law in Northern Ireland: A Study in Regional Government* (1968), at 253-285. In 1981, it was stated on behalf of the then Secretary of State for Northern Ireland that he was "unaware" of any Acts of the Northern Ireland Parliament which discriminated between persons or classes of person on the ground of religious belief: H.C.Debs. (1981-82) vol.14, col.376. For a fuller exposition in the field of education, see E.Graham, "Religion and Education: The Constitutional Problem", 33 *Northern Ireland Legal Quarterly* (1982) 20.
4. The main Act of 1922 was passed by the Northern Ireland Parliament and was originally intended to be a temporary measure but in 1933 was made (effectively) permanent; it conferred extensive and widely-worded powers on the (NI) Minister for Home Affairs to take "all such steps and issue all such orders" as may be necessary for preserving peace and maintaining order.
5. The figures for deaths connected with "the Troubles" are: 1969, 13; 1970, 25; 1971, 174; 1972, 467; 1973, 250. The figures for injuries connected with "the Troubles" are: 1968, 379; 1969, 765; 1970, 811; 1971, 2,592; 1972, 4,876; 1973, 2,651.
6. Other reforms preceding the 1973 Act included reform of electoral law, the introduction of the "Ombudsman" to deal with complaints of maladministration causing injustice on the part of the Northern Ireland government departments (the Parliamentary Commissioner) or local and public bodies (the Commissioner for Complaints), the enactment of the Prevention of Incitement to Hatred Act (NI) 1970 (now, as amended, part of the Public Order legislation), the establishment of the NI Housing Executive (a nominated not elected body) to deal with all public authority house building and

allocation, the reform of local government (leading to very limited powers in the district councils), the establishment of an independent Police Authority, and of the Education and Library Boards and the Health and Social Services Boards.

7. The Assembly elected in 1982 (see the Northern Ireland Act 1982 and related legislation) had scrutiny and deliberative, but not legislative, powers. It was formally dissolved in 1986.

8. See the Northern Ireland Act 1974, schedule 1, para. 1(7) and NICA, section 4(3). See also NICA, section 23(3) and (4) which excludes from the operation of sections 17 and 19 legislative and executive measures with the effect or purpose of safeguarding national security or protecting public safety or public order.

9. Section 22 relates to the Parliamentary Commissioner Act 1967 (as amended), the NI Act of 1969 and the Commissioner for Complaints Act (NI) 1969. (See now the two 1996 Orders in Council.)

10. *Northern Ireland Constitutional Proposals*, Cmnd. 5259, March 1973. See especially, Part 4, paras. 90 to 105.

11. See, for example, generally Human Rights Legislation Report by The Constitution Unit, London (1996).

12. See, *ibid*, at para. 118 for a recommended form of wording to ensure that, in an era of privatisation, private bodies discharging public functions are covered by a Bill of Rights. NICA effectively defines "public body" by reference to those bodies which fall within the jurisdiction of the various Ombudsmen.

13. See, generally, B.Hadfield, *The Constitution of Northern Ireland* (1989), chapter V and B.Hadfield, "Legislating for Northern Ireland: Options for Reform", SACHR 18th Annual Report. H.C. 739 (1993) 111-128.

14. On this see the important report by SACHR, "The Protection of Human Rights by Law in Northern Ireland". Cmnd. 7009 (1977), especially chapter 6. This is a theme SACHR has continued to address; see, for example, its 18th Annual Report, *supra* n. 13, Annex C.

15. *Specific* concerns, relating to, for example, emergency powers and prevention of terrorism or to reform of the law on disability discrimination or race relations, have been considered in *ad hoc* ways. See also the British-Irish Governments' Joint "Frameworks for the Future" (1995), paras. 50 to 53, and the British Government's "Framework for Accountable Government in Northern Ireland" (1995) para. 12. It is there stated that the protection to be given to "civil, political, social and cultural" rights would have to accord with the U.K.'s existing "constitutional arrangements", although with the election of the new Labour Government this will take on new meaning.

16. See, for example, its 1977 Report, *supra* n. 14, para 6.23 and SACHR, "Religious and Political Discrimination and Equality of Opportunity in Northern Ireland". Second Report, Cm.1107 (1990), chapter 10.

17. The paper for SACHR referred to in n. 13 provides all the relevant details. The relevant legislation, the Criminal Evidence (Northern Ireland) Order 1988, was challenged, unsuccessfully, in *Re Barkley's Application* N.I.Q.B.D. (Unreported) 18 November, 1991 on the grounds that the Order dealt with an excepted matter under schedule 2 to NICA and the matter should, therefore, have been legislated on by way of Westminster Act of Parliament.

18. Cm.1107 (1990), *supra* n. 16, at para. 5.27. Note that cases involving such discrimination in the field of employment go to the Fair Employment Commission.

19. On section 21, see *In re French* [1985] N.I. 310 concerning the compatibility of a

borough council "anti-terrorism" declaration with section 21. With regard to the oath of allegiance, required to be taken by Queen's Counsel in Northern Ireland, see *Magee v U.K.* (Euro.Commission of Human Rights) EHRLR (1995) 84-86. The oath has now been brought into line with the declaration required in England and Wales. In August 1997, Martin McGuinness, Sinn Féin M.P. for Mid-Ulster, sought leave to bring a judicial review of the ruling that he (and Gerry Adams the party leader) must swear an oath of allegiance to the Queen before they can take their seats in the Westminster House of Commons. One of the grounds argued in the leave application is that the Speaker in her ruling discriminated against Mr McGuinness on the basis of his Irish republican political beliefs. See *The Irish Times*, 13 August 1997. This particular issue was not pursued at the hearing: see *In re McGuinness*, Judgment delivered 3rd October 1997.

20. *In re Most Rev. Cahal Daly* (N.I. Q.B.D.) Unreported, 5 October, 1990. In *In re Cleland* (N.I.Q.B.D.) Unreported, 17 June, 1992, the validity of a statutory rule, authorising the closure of public roads to facilitate certain motor-bike road races, was unsuccessfully challenged.

21. These cases involve section 19, unless it is otherwise specified.

22. (+*b*) Neither *Purvis* nor *McCormaic* was a judicial review case.

23. The majority of these cases are all unreported unless otherwise stated, and all are N.I.Q.B.D. apart from *McCartney* and *McGuigan*. The dates of the cases are as follows: *Purvis* [1977] N.I. 26; *French, supra* n. 19; *McCartney* [1987] 11 N.I.J.B. 94; *Cecil*, 27 January, 1989; *McManus*, 4 May, 1990; *McLaughlin* [1990] 6 N.I.J.B. 41; *Daly, supra* n. 20; *McCormaic* 11 January, 1991; *Quigley*, 11 April, 1991; *Cleland, supra* n. 20; *Thompson*, 3 December, 1993; *McGuigan* (discovery only) 29 April, 1994; *Lavery* [1994] N.I. 209 ; *O'Neill*, March 20, 1995; *White*, 11 July, 1996; *Dallas*, September 20, 1996; and *Fisher*, 11 October, 1996. Cases in which leave to bring a judicial review application was granted, but which were subsequently withdrawn (there then being no written judgment at either stage) constitute a small number of judicial review applications each year. It is not possible to ascertain how many of these cases involved arguments on NICA Part III.

24. Some of the judicial review cases are cases where leave to bring a judicial review was refused but for ease of presentation both leave applications and substantive hearings are not distinguished here. In all instances, however, written judgments were given.

25. See, for example, (on parades) *Re Murphy* [1991] 5 N.I.J.B. 72 (Q.B.D.) and 88 (C.A.), *In Re Gary Jones* (N.I.Q.B.D.). Unreported 10 July, 1996 (there are several other parades cases too); (on the Irish language) *In Re Donnelly* [1988] 8 N.I.J.B. 26; and (on council sub-committees) *In re McCann* (N.I.Q.B.D.) Unreported 13 November, 1992.

26. The Fair Employment Act 1976, section 57(3) also provides that "political opinion"does not include an opinion which consists of or includes approval or acceptance of the use of violence for political ends connected with Northern Irish affairs. See also *McKay v NIPSA* (N.I. Court of Appeal), [1994] N.I. 103, a fair employment case, in which it was held that the term "political opinion" did *not* have to be construed as to display some connection or correlation with religion or politics in Northern Ireland. See also SACHR's paper, Cm.1107, 1990, para. 4.17.

27. [1983] N.I. 346.

28. [1990] 2 All E.R. 607.

29. Unreported, 29 June, 1994.

30. See, Carswell J. (as he then was): "However one describes the purposive element which must be found, it is clear one has to look beyond the mere consequences of the

defendants' acts. It is not enough for the plaintiffs to establish that those consequences operate unfavourably to Irish Nationalist prisoners; they have to show that in doing the acts in question the defendants intended to discriminate against those prisoners on the ground of their political opinion".

31. See below on PAFT and *Casey*.

32. See most crucially here SACHR's recommendations for the reform of NICA in Cm.1107, 1990, chapter 8. See also for fuller consideration of the issues in this part of the chapter, B.Hadfield, "From the Downing Street Declaration 1969 to the Downing Street Declaration 1993", 1 *Contemporary Issues in Irish Law and Politics* (1998) 76-109.

33. The *Conference* was established in 1985 under the terms of the Anglo-Irish Agreement 1985.

34. See A. Eide, *A review and analysis of constructive approaches to group accommodation and minority protection in divided societies.* Forum for Peace and Reconciliation Dublin, Consultancy Studies Number Three (1996).

35. N.I.Q.B.D., unreported, 16 October, 1996.

36. See Cm.1107, 1990, esp. para. 8.41. The Government's then response is to be found in SACHR's Seventeenth Annual Report 1991-1992, H.C. 54, July 1992, Annex 0, 293-305, especially at 297; see, also, A.Eide, *supra* n. 34. Both the U.K. and Irish Governments have signed the Council of Europe's Framework Convention for the Protection of National Minorities, 1994. The U.K. Government ratified the Convention in 1998 and the Irish Government is now expected to ratify it shortly. In this context it is interesting to note that the reason why *O'Neill* lost on the NICA point was because: "The Council could not treat as favourably those who wanted the centre open on Sundays as those who wished it to remain closed. The opportunity for equal treatment for both did not arise. Whatever decision was taken was bound to represent a disappointment to one of the groups involved": *per* Kerr J.

37. Significant developments subsequent to the completion of this chapter include, for the UK generally, the anti-discriminatory provisions of the Treaty of Amsterdam and the Human Rights Act. This position in Northern Ireland may also be substantially changed by proposals contained in the Government's White Paper, Partnership for Equality, Cm 3890, 1998. The Agreement reached in April 1998 between the British and Irish Governments and many of the NI political parties contains a significant section on rights, safeguards and equality of opportunity; see Cm 3883, April 1998. This Agreement has been endorsed by more than 70% of the NI electorate as voting in a poll held in May 1998, and after elections to the New Northern Ireland Assembly held in June 1998, the relevant Bill is likely to be published in July 1998. One additional subsequent case invoking the provisions of NICA 1973 s19 is in *In re Hartley*, Kerr J. Judgment delivered 21 May 1998.

Preferential Treatment and the Right to Equal Consideration

*John Edwards**

INTRODUCTION: THE PREFERENTIAL TREATMENT DEBATE

The central moral dilemma of preferential treatment is that it appears to bestow social benefits on people for morally arbitrary reasons. In most western liberal democracies, we expect public and (more particularly) social policies to allocate benefits, whether in the form of cash benefits, health care, access to education, public housing or social work support, according to criteria that have moral relevance – such as having relevant needs or on the grounds of merit or in fulfilment of a welfare right.[1] We also expect employers, in both public and private sectors, not to offer jobs and promotions in an arbitrary way but rather on grounds of merit and merit alone.[2]

In pursuit of these general ends of fair allocation or social justice, we legislate against discrimination on the grounds of race, ethnicity, religion and sex. But more importantly, we try to correct racial, ethnic (and other) imbalances in socio-economic status on a scale much broader than would ever be achieved by anti-discrimination legislation. Such practice varies of course from country to country but subsequent discussion will draw on the experience of the United States, Northern Ireland, and to a lesser extent, Great Britain. We need not here document what ought to be common knowledge – that some minority ethnic groups (African-Americans, Hispanics and Native Americans in the US, and Afro-Caribbeans, Bangladeshis and Pakistanis in Great Britain)[3] tend to have lower educational qualifications, to be in lower status jobs, to be poorer, and to be more likely to be unemployed than both the majority, and some other minority populations.

If welfare resource is distributed using the criterion of need, and if some minority ethnic groups have relatively higher levels of need, then we might expect such groups to attract proportionately higher levels of welfare benefit. And this is indeed the case, though in varying degrees in different countries depending on the nature and extent of welfare provision. There are some areas of well-being however (principally education and

147

P. Cumper and S. Wheatley (eds.), Minority Rights in the 'New' Europe, 147–164
© 1999 *Kluwer Law International. Printed in Great Britain.*

employment) in which ethnic inequalities remain more intractable and it is here that we look for policy practice that goes beyond anti-discrimination measures and which, whilst maintaining the principle of merit as the only justifiable criterion for entry to jobs and places in universities, seeks to increase the numbers from minority groups who 'present themselves for interview' and are at least minimally qualified for entry or promotion. The assortment of procedures designed to effect this (outreach to minority schools and colleges, advertising positions in the minority press, compensatory education and so on) is generally referred to as affirmative action[4] and it differs in theory at least, from the cognate practice of preferential treatment insofar as it does not, like the latter, override the morally relevant criteria of merit, needs and rights.

Given the availability of this strategy for 'bending' the options in favour of minorities, there is no need (so the argument goes) for preferential treatment, nor for the harm it does by entertaining morally arbitrary criteria such as race, in the allocation of jobs and university places. And yet, preferential treatment *is* widely practised in the United States (and for rather different reasons in post-apartheid South Africa) and to a lesser extent in many other countries including Britain. We shall confine our attention to the United States however because the use of preference practice there is widely documented and it is there that the philosophical debate has been most cogently conducted.

Preferential treatment is not legally sanctioned in the US and the Supreme Court has, over the past decade, demonstrated increasing opposition to it.[5] Where employers are required to implement affirmative action under Revised Order No. 4 of Executive Order No. 11246, they must do so 'with every good faith effort' but targets for minority representation must not become quotas (i.e. stray into the realm of preferential treatment). There are no penalties attaching to a failure to reach a target (unless it is court-ordered for remedial purposes in cases of egregious negative discrimination – when it becomes a quota but is still referred to as affirmative action). And yet, despite all this, preferential treatment has become a part of the culture of most large companies and almost all universities in America.[6] We need not consider the reasons for this here (they are complex) save to say that when the costly and time-consuming apparatus that companies and universities had to put in place in fulfilment of federal affirmative action requirements proved ineffective at producing measurable results, it required no great leap to move into the (very large) grey area of practice between affirmative action and preferential treatment where results would be forthcoming. And even though federal regulations required only 'good faith efforts', the results-oriented culture that characterises most large companies was sufficient to demand *some* pay-off for the investment made.

In consequence, under the guise of affirmative action, practice moved further and further into the realms of preferential treatment and only in the past four years has there been any retrenchment.

It is in this context then that the philosophical debate about the moral justifiability of preference practice has taken place in America (and only there has it been conducted in anything like sophisticated terms). It is not our purpose however to range widely over the morality of preference in this chapter; our aim is the more closely prescribed one of attending to the difficulty that seems to be created when we use preferential treatment, which is an essentially group-based practice in fulfilment of group rights to compensation or equal opportunity when these are interpreted as rights attaching to individual members of a group (as opposed to rights held by the collectivity – an interpretation about which we shall express some reservations).

EQUAL TREATMENT AND PREFERENCE PRACTICE

There is an apparent – and probably real – contradiction between the use of preferential treatment for correcting violations of minority rights on the one hand, and on the other, one of the most fundamental of individual human rights – the right to equal consideration. If this contradiction is real, then it would seem that the promotion of minority rights can only be bought at the cost of damage to, or violations of, the right to equal consideration when this is conceived in the manner that Dworkin describes when he counterposes 'rights to equal treatment' and 'rights to treatment as equals',[7] the latter of which most closely reflects what is meant here by 'equal consideration'.

In this chapter I shall consider the difficulty for the use of a 'minority right' by using three consecutive but linked arguments. The first is an argument about whether 'minority rights' (the rights deemed to be held by a group that has identity in virtue of some common characteristic – religion, ethnicity, race and so on)[8] are, properly speaking, *group* rights and what is entailed in asserting this. We shall also need to consider whether *any* group can possess (minority) rights or only groups defined by certain characteristics.

The second consideration is the nature of preferential treatment when it is used as a practice to correct violations of minority rights, such as when its use is justified on the grounds of the need to compensate members of the group for the consequences of past harm (i.e., slavery), or to promote rights, such as when it is used to foster equality of opportunity. In this context, it will be noted that whilst preferential treatment is one of the most widely used instruments for promoting minority rights, its use is by no means always accompanied by rights-talk.

The third section examines the nature of the conflict – both apparent and real – between the use of preferential treatment as a corrective to prior rights violations, and the right to equal consideration as one of the most fundamental individual rights. Three factors come into play here. The first is whether minority rights are primarily group or individual rights (an issue around which much of the substantial discussion revolves); the second is whether preferential treatment as a group practice can impact on violations of minority rights, whether or not the latter are conceived of as group or individual rights; and the third is the degree of compatibility between the right to equal consideration on the one hand and preferential treatment on the other, both when preferential treatment is directed at rights violations as violations of *group* rights and then at rights violations as violations of *individual* rights.

Minority Rights – Real or Supposed?

In his seminal article, *Human Rights, Real and Supposed*, Maurice Cranston was at pains to argue that the 'philosophically respectable concept of human rights' had been damaged, deprived of its proper meaning, 'muddied' and had its cutting edge blunted by the inclusion in it, both in philosophical discourse and more concretely in the Universal Declaration of Human Rights (1948) and its subsequent Covenants, of many items of a logically and philosophically different kind.[9] Whatever the value of incorporating social and economic rights into the panoply of human rights, we have still to rescue a definitive and implementable notion of human rights. And this is what was at the heart of Cranston's critique – the sometimes incompatible ways in which philosophers need to discourse on rights and what those of a more legal (or positivistic) bent see to be necessary in order to get things done. A similar argument may be put in respect of 'minority rights' but my main concern here is not that habitual or casual or too inclusive usage has debased the coinage so much as that it has discomposed the meaning of the term to the extent that it now better describes a campaigning activity than a precise moral idea. And the main victim of this tendency has probably been the use, both explicitly and implicitly, of the term 'minority right' to describe something that attaches to *groups* or *collectivities*. Now whilst this is not necessarily incorrect[10] (that has yet to be established), there *is* a presumption that says some 'groups' have rights *as* groups (have a *group* right) whilst other groups do not and that such rights exist independently of individual rights (of members of a group). There are some sound arguments that go to refute these presumptions about the nature of minority rights and we shall give them an airing. But first, we need to identify what we are *not* concerned with.

There are some minority groups in respect of which the possession of minority rights, as rights of the group as a collectivity, is not problematic. These are groups that have positive statutory rights (usually to things) as a group and for whom the possession of a group right is non-controversial. Probably the most common form that such group rights take is that of 'reservations'[11] of positions in state institutions as in India[12] or Belgium. In all such cases the right attaches to the group as a whole and not to any individual member of the group (though within a reservation or set-aside, an individual member of the group might acquire rights to a position or office by virtue of 'normal' criteria such as merit or the electoral process).

Statutory group rights of these kinds create few difficulties for the arguments we shall pursue about minority rights as human rights and nothing in the subsequent paragraphs is intended to apply to group rights that are enshrined in statute, in any particular country. Our concern rather, is with the multiplicity of circumstances in which, because of alleged discrimination and oppression, minority racial, ethnic or religious groups are said to have group rights to some form of compensation or assistance. These are not posited statutory rights but *claimed* rights – on the basis of compensation, or special needs, or some other cognate ground. Thus, we might include in such 'moral' claims, the rights to compensation for past harm and rights to the enhancement of equal opportunities made by minority groups in the United States which are not specific enough to find a legal channel but which, because of their alleged enormity (and sometimes generality), such as 'racism' and 'oppression', appear to have moral weight. Rights such as these, claimed by or on behalf of minorities such as Afro Caribbeans, Bangladeshis, and Pakistanis in Britain, Hispanic peoples, African Americans and Native Americans in the USA or the Mahgreb in France, are more debatable if only because the groups to which they are attached have no legal standing and no statutory right to different treatment qua groups.[13] What is common to almost all such cases however is some form of disadvantage suffered by the group (in comparison with the majority) which is attributed to their having received (and to be currently receiving) less than equal treatment. And such disadvantage (so it is argued) gives rise to some variety of moral or human right to have the imbalance corrected.[14] Thus the language of minority rights will give voice to such assertions as: 'the rights of a minority group not to be discriminated against'; or, 'the rights of a minority group arising out of past oppression and discrimination to the group'; or, 'the rights of a minority group to equality of opportunity'; or, more substantially, 'the rights that *individuals* have because of discrimination against them *as* members of a (discriminated against) minority group'.

These are claims to moral rights of a kind, and more particularly to negative, and sometimes, positive *human rights* (in Cranston's sense of having rights to certain welfare provisions). If therefore, we wish to sustain the conception of a minority right as a *group* right (which seems to be inherent in its conventional philosophical usage) then we shall need to sustain the possibility of a *group* human right (as opposed to an *individual* human right). If it were to prove impossible to sustain a cogent argument for the existence of human rights that are *group* rights then either minority rights cannot be group rights or they are not human rights. We turn our attention next therefore to arguments about the moral standing of group rights.

Other than in the case of statutory minority rights that have already been noted, what is the nature of group rights (of which minority rights are an example) and how would the enforcement of a group right (which by definition must attach to all group members collectively) translate in practice? The first point to note (one of clarification), is that the sort of groups we are talking about are ones defined by morally arbitrary criteria; they are not, in other words, groups defined by criteria (such as disability, age and so on) which in themselves establish at least *prima facie* rights on the morally relevant basis of need. Race, ethnicity and religion do not *in themselves* give rise to rights claims of any sort and if such claims can be attached to them, it must be by virtue of morally relevant characteristics they have (harm done to them, high levels of need, due compensation etc.) in greater or exclusive measure compared with the majority, or other minority groups.[15] In the simplest of terms therefore, we must say that, for example, Bangladeshis in England do not have collective minority rights *because* they are Bangladeshis; if such rights exist, and they have them, it is because they have suffered harm and *these* circumstances have generated certain rights (to have needs met, to compensation for harm and so on). Race, ethnicity and religion do not in and of, themselves justify minority rights therefore but only characteristics that attach to such groups in certain times or places and which could in theory attach to *any* racial, ethnic or religious group. This says nothing about group rights *per se* however, only about what justifies them if they do exist. It tells us though, that a minority does not have rights as a group *simpliciter*, but only by virtue of some generalisable moral characteristic that attaches to the group.

What of minority rights themselves? In theoretical terms the least controversial of these (again excepting the sorts of statutory rights we described earlier) would be where a minority group had suffered oppression and harm of a clear and definable kind, where all members of the group had suffered and where in consequence the group *as a whole* was due compensation. The claim to reparations payments for all blacks in the US made in the Black Manifesto of 1969 by James Foreman was such an example.[16]

Such claims to group reparation tend to be more plausible and more practicable, the smaller and more clearly defined is the group and the more specific and time-limited the harm done. The difficulties that black reparations ran into included the social and economic heterogeneity of the group, the great variations in the harm suffered (and an unwillingness on the part of some whites to accept that present deprivation was exclusively the consequence of slavery), the long time-span covered by the claim and the uncertainties attaching to claims for compensation over several generations.[17] Notwithstanding these difficulties and in light of other less problematic examples of reparations, do rights to reparation for whole groups provide us with the paradigm case of *group* human rights for which we are searching? The answer will depend on how inclusive is our definition of human rights and we shall still need to accommodate group right claims that are far less 'clear cut' than Foreman's claims for black reparations.

What can be said then of group rights that are human rights of a more general kind? Perhaps the most common and forceful general argument for minority or group rights is that the wrongs of the past (and of the present) done to minorities can never be corrected by measures directed at individual rights alone. The magnitude of what needs to be done requires that corrective action be taken at the level of groups. Redressing discrimination on a one-by-one basis, it is argued, is worthy but futile.

But the very idea of a group or collective right that is also a human right is problematical for a number of reasons among the more significant of which, we may note the following. First, the harm suffered by and the compensation due to a particular racial, ethnic or religious group does not exist in a moral vacuum and cannot be calculated independently of the harm done to and the compensation due to other harmed groups. There ought, in other words, to be some parity in 'rates of compensation' and whilst not impossible, this would be an extremely difficult calculus to perform given the widely different kinds of harm done. But if this is what would be required in order to effect a proper reparation for past harm then the difficulties involved ought not to stand in the way.

The remaining difficulties are more damaging to the idea of group human rights. If a group within a country (say all Hispanics, or Afro Caribbeans or Roman Catholics) has a right to something (compensation, greater welfare resources, or to promote greater equality of opportunity), who, or what, exactly is it that holds the right? Probably the answer that springs immediately to mind is 'all members of the group'. But this will not do. 'All members of the group' (in a given country) do not constitute any kind of 'moral corporation' in which the right resides and which can pursue claims. Neither is it the case, as we shall see, that a group right vests each and every member of the group with an individual right. Thus, in this context, Sher has noted that there must be a "heavy presumption against the view that [groups] have independent moral standing".[18] A related argument concerns how, if a group has a right (such as to compensation) this right will be pursued and how compensation would be paid (and how payment would be administered). We cannot assume that an equal payment to each member will satisfy the requirements of the right since this, in itself, assumes parity of desert of every member which in turn assumes an individual right on the part of every member to an equal share. But nothing in the establishment of a *group* right will establish individual rights to any portion of whatever the group, *qua* group, has won in compensation (or whatever else it was a right to). Indeed, the moral relationship between group rights and individual rights is a complex one but I believe that a claim that group rights exist independently of the individual rights of members of the group is seriously problematic (in practice as well as in theory) as we shall see in our discussion of preferential treatment. The manner in which a group right is fulfilled in practice will almost inevitably violate some of the individual rights that members of the group have, as well as the rights of individuals who are not members of the group.

One final point in our repertoire of doubts about group rights has been put by Bayles in a much earlier discourse on preferential treatment.[19] It is that if an individual gains a benefit (a job, university place etc.) as the result of the exercise of a group right (of a group of which she is a member), it seems unlikely that she can have an *individual* right to that benefit. Now this argument is an extension of the one we made earlier about group rights not conferring any particular individual rights. But if Bayles is correct, then the rightful individual possession of the benefit (i.e., *that* university place occupied by *that particular* minority group member) is thrown into doubt. The more general consequence here is how individuals rightfully hold benefits they have obtained in virtue of a *group* right.[20]

The forgoing paragraphs have identified some important reservations about the standing of minority rights when these constitute a type of human group right. The reservations are strong and telling – to the extent that it seems more plausible that when we speak of 'minority rights' we are not referring to group rights at all but rather to the rights that individual members of the group have because some of their *individual* rights have been violated or are being violated because of their membership of the group. And the rights they have had violated are just the same individual rights that everyone has. We tend to think of them as group rights however because the violation of some individual rights, such as the right to consideration as equals, is more common among, or sometimes exclusive to, members of a definable group. We do not talk about the violation of the rights of the majority just because they suffer far fewer rights violations than do some minority groups. The rights involved however are the same, and they are individual and not group human rights.

PREFERENTIAL TREATMENT AS A GROUP PRACTICE

I am concerned here with the practice of preferential treatment rather than affirmative action. Affirmative action is usually a legally sanctioned practice and is used in many countries as a means of promoting the interests of minority groups, often in the fields of education and employment. Preferential treatment on the other hand is more widely proscribed. The single most important difference between the two practices, as we have noted, is that whereas affirmative action respects the criteria of merit and need and sets only targets, preferential treatment may override them in order to fulfil a predetermined quota. What distinguishes preferential treatment therefore is that, instead of accepting whatever racial (etc. . . .) mix comes out of the merit system, it engineers a particular mix by means of the quota. And if achieving a fixed minority representation requires accepting minority group members with lower qualifications than rejected majority applicants, then that is what must be done.[21]

It is not our purpose here to argue the moral case for and against preferential treatment – that is peripheral to our main theme and they are arguments which I have rehearsed elsewhere.[22] It is sufficient to say that in practice, the difference between affirmative action and preferential treatment is, as we have noted, a very indistinct one and a good deal of preference is practised under the guise of affirmative action (and in pursuit of diversity).[23] There is little point in being purist about this. Secondly, as I have argued elsewhere,[24] I believe that a plausible if limited case can be made for preference practice in some circumstances.[25]

Our chief purpose in considering preferential treatment is that it is probably the most well defined and extensively used *group* practice aimed at one or more minority groups. This is a crucial point in our consideration of minority rights. Preferential treatment is designed to benefit a morally arbitrary group such as African-Americans, Pakistanis, Roman Catholics, without necessarily (or usually) benefiting every member of the group (except to the extent that all members may be said to derive some psychic benefit from the perceived accelerated progress of some members of the group – the role model effect).

Finally, in these brief comments on preferential treatment, it is worth noting the main purposes of its use as group practice.[26] There are two major purposes which Goldman has characterised as 'backward' and 'forward looking'[27] and in the extent to which they have provided a justification for preferential treatment, they have (in the US particularly) had somewhat different histories. The 'backward' justification for preference practice is the necessity to compensate for past harm. Some groups in society have suffered harm in the past at the hands of the majority and other minority groups. The harm has occurred as a result of oppression, slavery, and other forms of economic exploitation.[28] An injustice will remain therefore as long as the oppression is not recognised and compensation is not paid to the group. The use of preferential treatment is one way of compensating for past harm albeit in an imperfect fashion. The logic of preference practice (and what distinguishes it from financial reparation) is that minority group members (the descendants of those originally oppressed) have not been able to take up jobs and positions which they would have filled had the oppression not occurred. And the beneficiaries of such practice are removed in time from the harm sufferers and gain positions in a sense as 'representatives' of the group. We shall return to this question subsequently.

Preferential treatment that is practised for forward-looking reasons is, to all intents and purposes, the same as that used for compensatory purposes: it is the background justification that differs. The premises are the same also – harm done to groups by oppression and discrimination, but the current practice of preferential treatment is not so much to compensate for harm done as to increase the opportunities available to minority members and their ability to exploit such opportunities. So whilst it is certainly the case that the inability to exploit opportunities is the result of previous harm from discrimination, the current strategy (so this argument goes) must be preferential treatment to promote equality of opportunity.[29]

The practice of preferential treatment is significant for any discussion of minority rights, because it is probably the single most extensively used strategy directed at morally arbitrary groups but for the correction of alleged violated rights, whether they be rights to compensation or to equality of opportunity. The final section therefore will discuss some of the difficulties and contradictions that arise between the use of preferential treatment and minority rights in their various guises.

PREFERENTIAL TREATMENT AND THE PROBLEM WITH MINORITY RIGHTS.

In an earlier section we characterised minority rights as (more likely) being individual rights rather than group rights, which conventional usage supposes them to be, and our main purpose in the last part of this chapter is to identify some of the difficulties to which this gives rise when preferential treatment is used as a corrective to violated rights. However, it also seems to be the case that even if it *were* possible to sustain a conception of minority rights as *group* rights, conflicts would still arise with the use of preferential treatment to promote them. Therefore, there are three components to the following discussion: preferential treatment as a group practice; minority rights as group rights (included here for the sake of comprehensiveness and notwithstanding the reservations we expressed earlier); and minority rights as individual rights to equal consideration. We include (and begin with) preferential treatment and minority rights as group rights, because of the conflicts they raise *even if* minority rights could be seen to constitute *group* rights, but our main concern is with conflicts arising from the application of preferential treatment for the promotion of minority rights, when these are most properly construed as individual rights to consideration as equals.

GROUP PRACTICE AND GROUP RIGHTS

It has been noted that a key component of preferential treatment is the use of a quota, representing the proportion of a workforce or student body that must be from a minority group (or several minority groups in combination).[30] The immediate practical question is then what the size of the quota should be for any given minority group – or rather, and prior to this – what principles will help to determine what the size of the quota should be. If the idea of a minority *group* right is to have value, it must surely be in just such a context. Ought we not to be able to say that a minority group (African-American, Roman Catholic etc.) has a right *as a group* to 'x' per cent of studentships in a university, in every category of employment, in every position, and so on? Just such a case has been argued by Robert Fiscus in his claim to a group right to proportionate quotas.[31] His belief is that on the (entirely plausible) assumption that in some primal state there were no genetic differences between ethnic or racial groups that would affect intelligence, or any other characteristic that might be thought to influence educational and employment performance, all racial and ethnic groups would be proportionately represented in all positions. The fact that they are not, is the result of long term oppression and discrimination against some groups by others.[32] Only factors that ought to be compensated for appear therefore, to disturb employment distributions which *prima facie* and in fact, after relevant compensation, will be the same for all groups. And from these arguments Fiscus goes on to make his claim that all groups have a right to a representation in all offices, positions, jobs, statuses and so on that is 'the same' as their representations in the population as a whole.[33]

Whilst Fiscus's derivation has the beauty of simplicity, it falls far short of establishing a set of rights for group representation across the education and employment spheres. An assumption of statistical parity cannot in itself establish a *right* that 10 per cent of doctors in America be African Americans or that 9.1 per cent[34] of philosophy professors be Hispanic. Far too much is required of such a claim, not least that all other factors which influence career paths, including culture, choice, geography and so on will have been identical and had identical effects for every group. This just is not plausible and denies what we know about multi-cultural societies and about the complex interplay of many factors in determining education and employment distributions.[35]

A second, and more sophisticated, attempt at determining 'correct' representations to which a group may claim a right is to attempt a counter-factual reasoning that would establish what the situation of different groups would now be, had the original oppression and discrimination not occurred. The difference between this counter-factual position and the current actual situation of a group would then be an indication of how much compensation is due to offset the consequences of oppression. The group, we might argue, would then have a group right to that amount of compensation (which may find expression in quotas or some other form of compensation).[36] A remedial programme might be for direct compensatory purposes or to enhance lost opportunities thereby establishing the situation that would now hold had past harm not occurred. Either route could constitute a way of fulfilling minority group rights. Unfortunately the process is virtually impossible to put into effect. The necessary counter-factual data just are not available, and if they were, it would not be possible to say what the current situation of (say) African Americans would now be had the institution of slavery never existed (they probably would not be in the US for a start).

There is a third, and far more pragmatic way of establishing 'rightful' representations of minority groups across occupation structures. These are the calculations made whenever affirmative action programmes are implemented to establish the ethnic or racial composition of a company's availability pool (the pool from which it can reasonably be expected to hire) for comparison with its actual workforce. Large ethnic or racial disparities between the make-up of the availability pool on the one hand, and the workforce on the other, then provide *prima facie* evidence of direct or indirect discrimination and of how much affirmative action is required to correct the imbalance.

Notwithstanding that the use of availability pools is an everyday matter in affirmative action procedures and that they are part of the common currency of such procedures, there seems no good reason why such pools should provide the measure of what *workforce* compositions *should* look like. As I have noted elsewhere, the ethnic or racial composition of a labour draw-area is just as subject to the legacy of past discrimination as any other grouping. There can be no grounds for thinking that what happens to be the ethnic composition of a labour draw-area at any given time provides a template of what the labour force composition ought to be, nor indeed any measure of what proportion of jobs or positions a group can claim a *right* to.[37]

There are sound theoretical and practical reasons why, if we believe that the representation of some groups in some occupations and institutions is lower (or higher) than it 'ought' to be, we should want to specify how much the 'ought' is. And, if the idea of minority group rights is to have any standing then whatever the value of the 'ought', it is to that level of representation that a minority group has a right. We have looked at three approaches to specifying what share of occupations, and so on, a minority group can claim a right to, but all three have been found wanting. At the technical or statistical level it has proved to be beyond our grasp to calculate a 'fair' representation and morally speaking it appears impossible to specify any sound basis for a group right to any particular level of representation.

The second area we shall consider under our 'assumption' that minority rights are group rights, revolves around the question of what kind of thing group rights are and what they give a right to. Some of this ground has been covered already and we need not linger over it. The least ambiguous example of a minority group right, as we have seen, is the collective right that a group may have to compensation for a specified (and specifiable) harm. This will normally take the form of appropriate reparation payments to the group as a whole to be administered for the benefit of the group as a whole, and no part of which can be claimed as a right by any individual member of the group.[38] However, apart from reparation payment for specified harm, the idea of a morally arbitrary group (such as an ethnic or racial group) having a right to something that is independent of anything that individual members of the group might have a right to (*qua* human beings) is difficult to sustain. And this is particularly the case where the benefit to which a right is claimed is not itself a collective good but rather – as in the case of preferential treatment – one that comes necessarily attached to an individual. If, therefore, we wish to argue that because of past harm a group had a group right to compensation or to enhanced opportunities, and that preference practice was the means to achieve this, we must ask what exactly does the group right give the group a right *to*?

We need also to ask whether the group has some corporate moral identity that gives it standing to pursue a claim and whether any corporate or administrative structure the group devises to administer the claim and the benefit, is one that will do so 'properly' (whatever that may mean). Some of these questions are unanswerable (at least within the scope of this chapter) and others unavoidably take us into the domain of the individual rights of minority group members and how these might prosper in the world of group rights. We turn therefore to our core concern of how compatible a right to equal consideration may be with group strategies which continue to assume that minority rights are group rights.

GROUP PRACTICE AND INDIVIDUAL RIGHTS

Suppose that a minority group had unanimously agreed (by some perfect democratic, consultative process) on the composition of a body to pursue a rights claim for the group (qua group). Suppose also that the body had been successful and had established the principle in society at large of preferential treatment for the group in education and employment. That (at least in our fantasy world) establishes the corporate and administrative standing of a unit to pursue the claim (and were it to be a claim for reparation payment, it could be the appropriate body to administer the claim). Now, how is the group right to be fulfilled? First, by its nature, preference practice takes the administration of the benefit out of the hands of the group (it will be affected by thousands of separate decisions by thousands of different personnel officers or admissions tutors in thousands of different institutions). Secondly, the group as a whole loses control over how the benefit is to operate. And thirdly, it will have no control over the distribution and impact of the benefit.

So long as we acknowledge a group right that finds expression through the group practice of preferential treatment we shall have to accept that the benefits (jobs, places in universities) will not be enjoyed by the group (except perhaps psychically) but by individual members of the group. Some members of the group, in other words, will be appointed to positions or awarded university places who otherwise would not have been awarded them. Now, in a statistical sense, this may be seen as a benefit to the group if it results in increased representations of the group in previously under-represented positions and occupations. But there are two qualifications. The first is that preferential treatment programmes will benefit only a small proportion of the members of the preferred group. Most members will see no benefit for themselves. Secondly, the preferred individuals will have obtained the benefit (a job, position, etc.) as the result of the *group* right which itself bestows no rights on them individually (i.e. the group right has not picked *them* out as having individual rights of benefit). This must result, as we have noted earlier, in the individual beneficiaries not having a right *themselves* to the position or place to which they have been appointed. Indeed, it has become a part of the argument in the United States against preference practice that an individual minority group member may have her individual right to her position based on merit and equal consideration questioned, because she is *thought* to have obtained the position through the operation of a group right.[39]

It is when a group practice is used in fulfilment of an individual right (even masquerading as a group right) that the contradictions are most manifest. Such is the case with the right to equal opportunity of minority group members. It seems fundamentally illogical to talk of 'minority rights to equal opportunity' as if these were a group right attaching to the group collectively. The opportunities that we talk about in the context of education and employment are quintessentially the opportunities open to *individuals,* and when we speak of equality of opportunity for minorities, what we mean is that all individual members of all minority groups should have opportunities that are equal to those of each individual member of the majority group (and of everyone else). Equality of opportunity also requires, in its pure form, that everyone be given equal consideration. Preference practice using quotas cannot serve the end of promoting equality of opportunity as we have defined it. Once again, the outcome of aggressive preference practice may appear to be a collective benefit but output measures of the racial and ethnic composition of workforces can tell us nothing about whether the opportunities of individual members of a group have been enhanced or if they have been dignified with consideration as equals.

CONCLUSION

There is one final and more general difficulty to which we should draw attention. If we wished to salvage the compatibility of a group right to equality of opportunity with the group practice of preferential treatment and the way it delivers benefit, we might argue that it does not matter *who* the individual beneficiaries of preference practice are; it only matters that they are members of the group and that the group has thereby benefited collectively. Such an argument, if sustainable, could keep afloat the idea of a group right (to better representation, more overall opportunities etc.) and of a group practice delivering a group benefit.

Much of what has been said in earlier paragraphs will have indicated doubts about a number of aspects of group or collective rights – in particular, whether it is possible for a group right to give an entire group a right to a particular quantum of jobs or positions or, indeed, just what it is that a group right gives a right to and to whom it gives it. There is, however, one final difficulty. The distribution of benefit between individuals that preferential treatment delivers is morally arbitrary. To say then that it does not matter *who* gets the benefits (within the group) requires that we allow the fulfilment of a group right to over-ride the individual rights that members of a group have, based on merit or compensation, for harm that *they* have suffered. It is a trade-off that many minority group members would not want to make. Furthermore, it is indicative that the right to consideration as an equal must be the victim of the aggressive pursuit of the chimera of group rights.

If, as we have argued, minority rights are in reality individual rights to equal consideration and not group rights, then there must be the potential for conflict if, in pursuit of minority rights, we use policies such as preferential treatment which assume that such rights *are* in fact group rights. We may consider that the benefits deriving from preference practice are worth the cost – but we would do well to remember that the cost may well be the violation of individual rights to equal consideration.

NOTES

*Professor of Social Policy, Department of Social and Political Science, Royal Holloway, University of London.

1. The idea of a welfare right is itself contentious however. It may be claimed as a form of human right or, more concretely, as a contractual right deriving from the claimant's status as tax and national insurance payer; see R. Plant, *Modern Political Thought* (1991), at 253; and H. Dean, *Welfare, Law and Citizenship* (1996) 24.
2. Merit is also a contestable concept, but space requires that for present purposes we accept orthodox usage. See J. Edwards, "What Purpose Does Equality of Opportunity Serve?", in 17(1) *New Community* (1990) 19–35.
3. The socio-economic circumstances of minority ethnic groups in Britain are usefully catalogued in the latest (1997) Policy Studies Institute report. See T. Modood *et al*, *Ethnic Minorities in Britain* (1997).
4. See J. Edwards, *When Race Counts: the Morality of Racial Preference in Britain and America* (1995).
5. Key findings against any practice involving minority preference have included *City of Richmond v J.A. Croson Co.* 488 US 469 (1989); *Wards Cove Packing Co. v Atonio* 490 US 642 (1989); *Northeastern Florida Contractors v Jacksonville* 113 S.Ct. 2297 (1993).
6. See J. Edwards, "Affirmative Action 'Culture' and US Equal Opportunity Practice", 34 *Equal Opportunities Review* (1990) 27–31, and J. Edwards, *supra*, n. 4.
7. See R. Dworkin, "What is Equality? Part 1: Equality of Welfare", 10(3) *Philosophy and Public Affairs* (1981) 185–246.

8. The sort of things that we call 'minority rights' which we usually attach to an oppressed or harassed group may on occasions be said to be held by a *majority* group as in Malaysia or India. See T. Sowell, *Preferential Policies : an International Perspective* (1990), at 19, 41.

9. What he had in mind were 'social and economic' rights such as the right to an 'adequate' standard of living, a pension, paid holidays, education and so on. See M. Cranston, "Human Rights, Real and Supposed", in D.D. Raphael (ed.) *Political Theory and the Rights of Man* (1967), chapter 4.

10. Lawyers and philosophers differ in the language they use and it ought to be pointed out that whilst in legal terminology 'minority rights' is far from synonymous with 'group' or 'collective' rights (minority rights often being the rights of members of a minority), our discussion here treats 'minority rights' (if they exist) as rights held collectively by a whole group. Hence the subsequent difficulties we encounter when we discuss the moral standing of benefits that accrue to an individual as the result of the fulfilment of a minority (i.e., *collective*) right of a group or collectivity of which s/he is a member.

11. 'Reservations', sometimes called 'set-asides', refer to the apportionment of (for example) a certain number of seats in a legislative assembly for one group in the population, which may be linguistically or in other ways ethnically distinct.

12. See B. Parek and S.K. Mitra, "The Logic of Anti-Reservation Discourse in India", in S.K. Mitra (ed.) *The Politics of Positive Discrimination* (1990).

13. Of course, several European countries have legislation designed to give redress for cases of *individual* discrimination. This is quite different from a *group* remedy.

14. For example, see A. Goldman, *Justice and Reverse Discrimination* (1979), chapter 3; W.T. Blackstone, "Reverse Discrimination and Compensatory Justice", in W.T. Blackstone and R.D. Heslep (eds.) *Social Justice and Preferential Treatment* (1977); and B. Boxhill, "The Morality of Reparation", in B.R. Gross (ed.), *Reverse Discrimination* (1977).

15. See J. Edwards, *Positive Discrimination, Social Justice and Social Policy* (1987); and J. Edwards, *supra* n. 4.

16. On this, see B. Bittker, *The Case for Black Reparations* (1973).

17. See B. Bittker, *ibid.*, and R.K Fullinwider, "Reverse Discrimination and Equal Opportunity", in T.P. De Marco and R.M. Fox (eds.), *New Directions in Ethics: The Challenge of Applied Ethics* (1986).

18. See G. Sher, "Predicting Performance", 5(1) *Social Philosophy and Policy* (1987) 188–203.

19. M. D. Bayles, "Compensatory Reverse Discrimination in Hiring", 2(3) *Social Theory and Practice* (1973) 301, at 302.

20. This is not an arcane philosophical affectation; it is what lies behind the familiar jibes of 'token' black (or Asian or woman).

21. See N. Capaldi, *Out of Order: Affirmative Action and the Crisis of Doctrinaire Liberalism* (1985); and N. Glazer, *Affirmative Discrimination, Ethnic Inequality and Public Policy* (1975).

22. See J. Edwards, *supra* nn. 4 and 15.

23. See J. Edwards, supra n. 4, chapter 6.

24. *Ibid.*

25. It may, for example, be permissible in moral terms to 'let race count' when the merit principle itself is unpredictive or arbitrary, or when the benefits to flow from preferential treatment are very high – as when there is a compelling need to select more minority

doctors or police officers to serve minority communities. This, it has to be said, is a circumstance much more likely to arise in the US than in Britain.

26. These purposes are common to the use of preferential treatment wherever it is used.

27. See A. Goldman, *Justice and Reverse Discrimination* (1979).

28. For examples of many accounts along these lines see Bittker, *supra* n. 16, and T. Eastland and W. Bennett, *Counting by Race: Equality from the Founding Fathers to Bakke and Weber* (1979).

29. Preferential treatment is increasingly justified on the grounds of the need to create greater 'diversity' in workforces and student bodies but in this form hardly carries the same justificatory force as the demands of compensation or equality of opportunity. 'Compensation' is less frequently used as justifying preference practice except when used by the courts in the form of imposed quotas for remedial purposes. These matters are discussed at greater length in J. Edwards, *supra* n. 4, at 167, 198. See, also, R.K. Fullinwider, *The Reverse Discrimination Controversy* (1980); R.K. Fullinwider, "Reverse Discrimination and Equal Opportunity", in T.P. De Marco and R.M. Fox (eds.), *New Directions in Ethics: The Challenge of Applied Ethics* (1986).

30. Quotas that require for their satisfaction a percentage for all minorities combined, without separate percentages for individual groups are common in the United States but they appear to have little sense or justification unless we accept the unacceptable hypothesis that all minority groups in a given country have suffered the same degrees of oppression and discrimination and all are due in consequence exactly the same amounts of compensation. Given its basis in this implausibility we shall not pursue this matter.

31. See R. Fiscus, *The Constitutional Logic of Affirmative Action* (1992).

32. *Ibid.*, at 27.

33. *Ibid.*

34. Representation of African Americans and Hispanics in US labour force (United States Bureau of the Census 1992).

35. See G. Gudgin and A. Murphy, *The Labour Market Context and Potential Effectiveness of Fair Employment Legislation in Northern Ireland* (1991); and G. Gudgin and R. Breen, *Evaluation of the Ratio of Unemployment Rates as an Indicator of Fair Employment* (1994).

36. This kind of process bears close similarities with Nozick's idea of rectification for injustice in holdings. See R. Nozick, *Anarchy, State and Utopia* (1974).

37. J. Edwards, "On What 'Ought' To Be: The Flaw in Employment Equality Practice for Minorities", 23(2) *New Community* (1997) 233–248.

38. The question of *who* benefits from collective reparation payments and whether it is possible for an entire group (in the sense of all individuals of the group) to benefit is unfortunately beyond the scope of this chapter.

39. See N. Capaldi, *Out of Order: Affirmative Action and the Crisis of Doctrinaire Liberalism* (1985), and S. Steele, *The Content of Our Character* (1990)

The Rights of Religious Minorities: The Legal Regulation of New Religious Movements

Peter Cumper*

INTRODUCTION

The eminent human rights lawyer, Paul Sieghart, once observed that: "homo sapiens appears to be unique in displaying a consistent pattern of persecuting its members for their heterodox opinions or beliefs, especially when these are systematically manifested in the form of a religion or philosophy".[1] The past millennium is replete with examples of minorities suffering persecution for their faith – even today the protagonists in many of Europe's perennial conflicts, such as those in the Balkans, Northern Ireland, and the Caucasus region, are separated by differences of religion. The close link between ethnicity, race and religion has undoubtedly increased tensions, but few commentators, if any, would claim that the people of these lands have suffered as a result of conflicts fought only in the name of 'religion'.

In contemporary Europe, however, there are groups who claim to still face persecution merely on the grounds of 'faith'. These groups are often described as 'cults',[2] a term which will be avoided because of its pejorative connotations,[3] and instead the value neutral expression 'new religious movement' (NRM) will be employed. It will be argued that the real significance of NRMs lies not in their numerical strength, for NRMs in Europe have traditionally failed to emulate the success of their counterparts in the United States,[4] but rather to the extent in which they demonstrate Europe's tolerance of religious diversity. Thus, the central thesis in this chapter is that public, governmental and institutional attitudes to unorthodox minorities, such as NRMs, will be a yardstick by which the 'New' Europe's commitment to human rights can be measured, particularly in the next millennium.

At the onset, it is important to recognise the limitations of the expression 'New Religious Movement'. After all, it is sometimes used to describe groups which are neither 'new' (eg., Paganisms) or traditionally thought of as being 'religious' (eg., Transcendental Meditation). Moreover, as James

165

P. Cumper and S. Wheatley (eds.), Minority Rights in the 'New' Europe, 165–183
© 1999 *Kluwer Law International. Printed in Great Britain.*

Beckford points out, the term NRM was originally only applied in the singular to describe "the 'new religious movement' of freshly observed groups".[5] Of course, it is important to stress that there are significant differences between NRMs[6] but, for the purposes of this chapter, 'New Religious Movement' will be used as an 'umbrella term' to cover those groups which tend to be stigmatised and have yet to be recognised as bona fide 'religions' in Europe. By this one thinks of groups such as, the Church of Scientology, the Unification Church, the Children of God and the Order of the Solar Temple. However, this chapter will avoid categorising longer established movements, such as the Jehovah's Witnesses, Mormons and various 'Christian' denominations as NRMs, for it is submitted that, whilst still fairly new in Europe, these groups have managed to establish themselves as bona fide 'religions' in most European countries.[7] Thus, attention here will be focused on those groups which the press and public often describe disparagingly as 'cults',[8] as they tend to be the NRMs which are most unpopular and at greatest risk of persecution.

In contemporary Europe new religious movements seem particularly vulnerable to persecution, as they often face opposition from a range of forces including the state (which may see them as socially divisive), the public (usually wary of NRMs as a result of sensationalist and inaccurate press reporting) and longer established religions (fearful that NRMs will 'poach' their members). Therefore, this chapter aims to examine the challenges presented for the 'New Europe' by the creation of a plethora of new religions in the second half of the twentieth century. Consideration will be given to the characteristics of these diverse and varied groups, the problems they face, and the extent to which the European Commission and Court of Human Rights have recognised their legitimate interests. It will be argued that the Strasbourg human rights institutions have been slow to protect unconventional systems of belief and have tended, on the contrary, to accord priority to those faiths which have had a long history in Europe.

THE PHENOMENON OF NRMS

A report to the Parliamentary Assembly of the Council of Europe on 'sects and new religious movements' in 1991 claimed that, "[a]s the 21st century approaches, sects [in Europe] are proliferating".[9] Its author, the British Conservative member Sir John Hunt, concluded that while this "phenomenon may not be a new one . . . it is growing and spreading internationally".[10] Two reasons were provided for the increase of interest in non-traditional religions. First, "a waning of interest in and support for churches of the traditional kind", which has left "a yawning gap in the field of spiritual quest".[11] And secondly, the public's failure "properly" to consider "secular alternatives to religion", which has "left an ethical void".[12] Thus, Sir John concluded that in Europe, "sects have taken advantage of the vacuum left by waning interest in the traditional institutions".[13]

Notwithstanding the numerous explanations offered as to why people join new religious movements,[14] as was noted earlier, the membership of NRMs in Europe remains rather low. Indeed, the relative lack of success of many NRMs has led sociologists such as Barker to comment that it is "possible that the reaction to the movements is more significant than the movements themselves".[15] Most MRMs have received much more attention than their numerical strength would ordinarily warrant and perhaps the most obvious explanation for this is that the public in Europe has often been wary of, and even hostile to, the emergence of NRMs. The reasons for this will be considered.

First, the press has tended to give the impression that NRMs are not merely psychologically manipulative, but also physically harmful to their members. James Beckford has noted how the "sensationalist approach [of the British press] helps to cement the public perception of cults as, at best, weird, and, at worst, destructive".[16] Beckford accuses "the messenger of fermenting mischief by relentlessly peddling negative stereotypes of new religious movements",[17] and it would appear that the press and media's fascination with events such as the Jonestown massacre,[18] the siege at Waco,[19] and the frequent deaths of Solar Temple members in Europe,[20] foster the myth that membership of an NRM is invariably damaging to an individual.

Certainly, a number of writers (particularly in the US) have warned that NRMs (or 'cults' as they prefer to term them) are socially harmful.[21] It is not the aim of this chapter to comment on the veracity of these claims but, despite strong evidence to the contrary,[22] it is not only large sections of the public which appear to accept the press cultivated image of 'NRM brainwashing.' In *Kokkinakis v Greece*, when the European Court considered the case of a Jehovah's Witness challenging his conviction for unlawful proselytism under a Greek law, only one member of the Court (Judge Martens) avoided mentioning the dangers of unscrupulous groups using 'brainwashing', or similar techniques, to gain new converts.[23] Thus, as James Richardson comments: "so the myth goes, once a Moonie (or a Hare Krishna, or Divine Light Mission, or Children of God) recruiter 'looks you in the eye,' you are a 'goner,' destined to live out your life as virtually a slave to the omnipotent group leader".[24]

The power and status accorded to the central figures in NRMs has been a second source of controversy. The claim that the 'cult' leader is "a Svengali figure who forces his followers to act contrary to their own wishes" has been rejected by Goldgerg, who points out that these leaders could "never attract a large following if they were not encountering youth who were actively seeking lapses from reality".[25] Nevertheless, in the public mind NRMs have traditionally been synonymous with charismatic leaders, who abuse their power and lack any accountability for their actions. This, combined with press reports of ostentatious lifestyles (the Baghwan Rajneesh's fleet of Rolls-Royces), sexual excess (David Koresh), and financial impropriety (the Rev. Moon's conviction in the US for tax evasion) reinforces stereo-typical attitudes and 'cult' leaders appear to be amongst the least popular of all public figures in contemporary society.[26] Moreover, the fact that some leaders portray themselves as 'father figures' and emphasise that the primary duty of members is to the group, has led to charges that NRMs are socially divisive and disrupt the traditional family unit.[27] Representatives of the German Government have claimed that the Church of Scientology "engenders a marked friend-foe mindset in its members" which may lead to a severance of social and family ties,[28] while it would appear that in France the "real opposition" to NRMs comes from the families of group members since "belonging to an NRM seems to imply both a rejection of the family and a questioning of its social role".[29]

Thirdly, the fact that many NRM members come from relatively privileged social backgrounds is another reason why NRMs have attracted controversy.[30] In Western Europe, the NRM member is typically white, unmarried, reasonably well educated, from a middle class background and between 20-35 years old.[31] Thus, as Beckford points out, those who feel that friends or family members have been 'stolen' by NRMs usually have the connections and influence to ventilate their grievances successfully in the public arena.[32]

Finally, other reasons why NRMs are controversial tend to include, their aggressive proselytising techniques,[33] a frequent reliance on Asian philosophies[34] (a factor which arguably fuels latent European cultural xenophobia) and Beckford's point that the mere appearance of so many NRMs at the same time generated public fears of a "new invasion of the body snatchers".[35]

In seeking to explain the disproportionate amount of unfavourable publicity generated by NRMs in Europe, it is important to remember that Europe is not a single entity. There are significant differences between European states, as religious, cultural, social, political and historical factors would all appear to predetermine societal responses to 'new' religions. Thus, NRMs in some European countries will invariably face greater opposition than in others. In a survey of the reactions of the public and governments to NRMs in four Western European states, Richardson and van Driel concluded that Netherlands was the most tolerant "followed by

England, France, and Germany in that rough order".[36] The legacy of
Fascism and a post-war suspicion of extreme ideologies may be one reason
why a number of Germans appear to believe that NRMs "pose a threat
to the individual and society".[37] Certainly, Germany has been frequently
criticised for its treatment of NRMs and thirty four Hollywood film stars
and celebrities even sent an open letter to former German Chancellor,
Helmut Kohl, condemning Germany's treatment of the Church of
Scientology, accusing it of "a shameful pattern of organised persecution",
and comparing the treatment of Scientologists to that of the Jews under
Hitler.[38] Like other European governments accused of violating the rights
of Scientologists, the administration in Bonn denied these allegations and
responded by pledging to launch an 'information offensive' so that (in the
words of former Foreign Minister, Klaus Kinkel) "these false assertions
do not surface in the future".[39] In order to get to grips with the complexities
of this situation, it is necessary to examine the main grievances of the
Church of Scientology and other NRMs in Europe which have attracted
controversy. Special consideration will be given to two factors: the reluctance
of many European states to recognise NRMs formally as 'religions'; and
the imposition of restrictions on the civil and political rights of NRM
members.[40]

NRM Grievances in Europe

Organisational grievances: non-recognition as 'religions'

In Europe, a number of NRMs are involved in campaigns to win official
recognition from the state as a bona fide religions. The advantages of this
may range from tax benefits (eg., charitable status) and making it easier
to hold public meetings (eg., in a few European countries, places of religious
worship must be registered with the state), to intangible benefits, such as
a higher public profile, an improved image, and welcome publicity for the
group. In Western Europe, the battle to win recognition as a 'religion' is
perhaps being fought most vigorously by the Church of Scientology.
Claiming to have a 8 million members attending 2,318 churches, in 107
countries,[41] Scientology's President, Heber Jentzsch, says that it is a "sincere
and genuine religion in all respects" and that "the Church is both organised
and operated exclusively for religious and charitable purposes".[42] Pointing
to the fact that "experts and scholars in theology and comparative religion
have rendered their learned opinions that Scientology more than satisfies
any academic or philosophic definition of religion", the Human Rights
Office of the Church asserts that "there is no legitimate issue as to the
'religiosity' of Scientology".[43]

Such arguments have impressed courts in the US[44] and Australia,[45] but they have been usually less well received in Europe[46] and, in particular, Germany. The German Government has denied that Scientology is a religion, on the ground that its "goals are clearly oriented to economic activity and its claim to be such a denomination or community is simply a pretext",[47] as it is "straightforward profit [rather than religion or faith] which lies at the heart of Scientology".[48]

Within Europe generally, the Church of Scientology is not alone in struggling to establish its religious identity. In a number of countries, NRMs have suffered as a result of measures introduced by suspicious governments, often with the support of the leaders of Europe's 'traditional' faiths who are wary of the NRMs recruiting members of their own congregations.[49] In 1995, a report submitted to the UN Commission on Human Rights found that the Jehovah's Witnesses (Austria), the Salvation Army (Belarus) and the Federation of Evangelical Churches (Belgium), had all allegedly been refused official registration as religious groups.[50] Even more recently it has been claimed that NRMs have been discriminated against and denied privileges in Latvia, Bulgaria, Poland, Rumania and Lithuania by laws which distinguish between officially recognised religious groups and those which are not so classified.[51]

Actions such as these, particularly in Eastern Europe, reflect the concerns of many Governments and leading Orthodox Churchmen, that new religions constitute a real threat to the social fabric and *status quo* of their societies.[52] Perhaps the most graphic illustration of this is the Russian law, passed in September 1997, which restricts full legal status to Russia's traditional religious faiths (the Orthodox Church, Islam, Judaism and Buddhism), and only recognises faiths and denominations that have been registered in Russia for fifteen years. Supporters of this law claim that it is necessary to restrict the activities of dangerous groups such as Aum Shinrilyo, which was responsible for the sarin gas attack on the Tokyo subway in 1995,[53] but there seems little doubt that it will affect innocent, law abiding NRMs, who will (amongst other things) have curbs placed on their freedom to spread their message and ability to recruit followers. These measures have been attacked by human rights organisations[54] and when cases are finally brought against Russia under the ECHR, it will be interesting to see how the European Court reacts to this legislation.

Individual grievances: allegations of discrimination

In the transition from Communism to democracy, it was perhaps inevitable that some Eastern European countries would experience problems accommodating the interests of religious minorities. The proliferation and influence of NRMs in Eastern Europe, vividly illustrated by the fact that at Moscow State University one of the old Marxist-Leninist Lecture Halls has been re-named in honour of Scientology's founder, L. Ron Hubbard,[55] was bound to create difficulties for new regimes lacking a heritage of religious freedom. However, what is much more surprising is the fact that some Western European countries, which during the 'Cold War' asserted the primacy of civil and political rights, find themselves today accused of persecuting religious minorities. The Rutherford Institute, an international human rights organisation working in this field, has charged a number of Western European states with culpability in this area,[56] and of these Germany has been the most widely criticised, particularly for its treatment of Scientologists.

The Church of Scientology claims that its members in Germany are the "targets of systematic discrimination in every strata of society as part of an insidious exclusionary policy initiated, encouraged and sanctioned by the government".[57] For example, the state government of Bavaria has introduced a requirement that applicants for positions in the Bavarian Civil Service must divulge whether they are connected with the Church of Scientology. Those found to be members may be subject to disciplinary proceedings,[58] while private enterprises hoping to win contracts from the state, and enterprises offering educational courses, must declare that they are not influenced by Scientology's principles.[59] It has been claimed that similar measures have been taken throughout Germany[60] and as a result of these, and calls by the Federal Minister of Labour for Scientologists to be banned from all occupations which "intersect with society",[61] Scientologists protest that they are at risk of dismissal if their religious affiliation becomes known.[62] Thus, the Church of Scientology insists that discrimination is experienced "on a daily basis by Scientologists in Germany"[63] and it ranges from discrimination against companies which are controlled by Scientologists,[64] to the exclusion of Scientologists from membership of the main German political parties,[65] and the imposition of restrictions on artists merely because they are Scientologists.[66]

Not surprisingly these measures have aroused the interest of the international community. They have come to the attention of the UN's Special Rapporteur on Religious Intolerance,[67] while the US Congress has debated a motion condemning the German Government's persecution of "minority religions",[68] and the US State Department has accused it of harassing and intimidating members of the Church of Scientology "merely as a result of their belonging to that organisation [and] not because . . . of any actions they've taken".[69] Despite this, the German Government has denounced these criticisms as "untenable" and has pointed out that "under international complaints procedures [these allegations] have been rejected time and again".[70] This may be so but such a statement, rather than endorsing the measures taken against the Church of Scientology in Germany, perhaps reveals more about the possible defects of these international procedures. Press reports suggest that Scientologists are planning to utilise Europe's most foremost complaints procedure, the ECHR,[71] presumably only after all domestic remedies have been exhausted in Germany,[72] and we will now proceed to consider the extent to which the European Convention is likely to be of assistance to them and other religious minorities.

NRMs AND THE ECHR

The most obvious remedy for any NRM formally denied the status of a 'religion' is the European Convention on Human Rights. Article 9 of the ECHR provides that:

(1) Everyone has the right to freedom of thought, conscience and religion; this right includes freedom to change his religion or belief and freedom, either alone or in community with others and in public or private, to manifest his religion or belief, in worship, teaching, practice and observance.
(2) Freedom to manifest one's religion or beliefs shall be subject only to such limitations as are prescribed by law and are necessary in a democratic society in the interests of public safety, for the protection of public order, health or morals, or for the protection of the rights and freedoms of others.

At first sight, it would appear that members of Europe's new religions are well protected under the ECHR. The European Court of Human Rights has affirmed that Article 9 is not merely "one of the most vital elements that go to make up the identity of believers", but that it is "also a precious asset for atheists, sceptics, and the unconcerned".[73] Therefore, in theory, Article 9 covers a range of beliefs which include pacifism,[74] veganism,[75] and opposition to abortion.[76] However, in practice, Article 9 has been interpreted restrictively by both the European Commission and the Court of Human Rights. For example, following the entry restrictions which were imposed by the British Government on members of the Church of Scientology in the late 1960s, the European Commission held that as the case was brought by the Church it would fail since only a natural person, and not a legal body, could rely on Article 9(1).[77] This rule has been amended and now a church or association with religious and philosophical objects is capable of exercising rights under Article 9,[78] so that its interests (and not merely those of its members)[79] may be protected.

Despite this, the ECHR's institutions have tended to interpret Article 9 quite cautiously, and this is illustrated in at least five ways. First, the European Commission and Court of Human Rights have refrained from defining, or even listing, the essential criteria of the word 'religion'; secondly, they deliberately have avoided categorising certain NRMs as 'religions'; thirdly, they have tended to accord 'traditional' religions much greater deference and respect than 'non-traditional' faiths; fourthly, both the Commission and Court have often been reluctant to make reference to Article 9 of the ECHR, preferring instead to refer to other Convention articles; and finally, on occasions when the Strasbourg institutions have invoked Article 9, they generally have interpreted it in such a way that states retain considerable discretion and enjoy a wide margin of appreciation.

THE INTERPRETATION OF ARTICLE 9 OF THE ECHR

Definitions of 'Religion'

The reluctance of the European Commission or Court formally to define the word 'religion' is understandable. Any definition would need to be flexible enough to satisfy a broad cross-section of world faiths, yet also sufficiently precise for practical application in specific cases. Such a balance would be almost impossible to strike and explains why definitions of religion have also been avoided in the past by the Human Rights Committee of the International Covenant on Civil and Political Rights 1966 (ICCPR)[80] and the UN's Special Rapporteur on the Elimination of Religious Intolerance.[81] Even in the United States, where judges have tended (in general) to display a greater willingness to recognise NRMs than their European counterparts, there has not been any formal definition on the ground that "[t]he determination of what is a 'religious' belief or practice is more often than not a difficult and delicate task".[82]

Identifying particular NRMS as religions

Whilst the unwillingness of the European Commission and Court to define 'religion' in a narrow or rigid sense is reasonable, perhaps the same may not be said of their failure to list, in general terms, the characteristics of a 'religion'. This has been done in the past by the members of an Australian Court,[83] but the Strasbourg human rights institutions seem disinclined to offer such guidance. Indeed, there has even been a reluctance to state whether specific NRMs, in particular cases, are 'religious'. For example, in *X v UK*,[84] the European Commission refrained from classifying Wicca as a religion, in the case of a prisoner who claimed to be one of its adherents and protested that he had been denied the necessary facilities to exercise his faith. This was in spite of the fact that Wicca has long been accepted as a religion of the ancient Celtic people of Northern Europe.[85] Moreover, in two other cases the European Commission gave judgment and still managed to avoid deciding whether Druidism[86] and the Divine Light Zentrum (DLZ)[87] are 'religions'. In the former, the Commission specifically noted that it was not necessary, in considering the case, to decide whether Druidism was a religion,[88] while in the latter it described DLZ not as a church, but as "an association with religious and philosophical objects".[89] And finally, when the European Commission considered the sale of a religious artefact in *X and Church of Scientology v Sweden*,[90] it refrained from commenting on whether Scientology is a religion.

Of course, the mere fact that a NRM is not categorised formally as a 'religion' does not exclude its adherents from relying on Article 9(1),[91] and the complainants in the previously cited cases were still able to invoke it, albeit unsuccessfully on the facts. Nevertheless, the Commission's failure to recognise these NRMs as 'religions' is regrettable for two reasons. First, the formal designation of many groups as bona fide religions would be of considerable symbolic value, particularly for those NRMs in Eastern Europe which often face persecution. And secondly, those who would restrict the use of word 'religion' only to those groups which have a long shared history should remember that, to some extent, every religion in the world originally started life as a 'sect' or a 'cult'.[92]

A Christian bias?

The extent to which the Strasbourg human rights institutions are likely to be influenced by these considerations seems remote, for their previous case law would appear to reveal a bias against non-traditional religions. No NRM (as narrowly defined for the purposes of this chapter) has ever successfully petitioned the European Commission[93] and proceeded to the European Court. Of course it must be borne in mind that relatively few cases have been brought, but even NRMs which are regarded generally as having the status of bona fide 'religions' (e.g., the Jehovah's Witnesses),[94] minority religious groups with a long history (e.g., Wicca,[95] Druids[96]) and adherents of major 'world religions' (e.g., Islam,[97] Buddhism,[98] Sikhism[99]) have all struggled to obtain redress under the ECHR. This contrasts sharply with the deference accorded to state churches[100] and, in particular, to adherents of Christianity by the European Commission[101] and the Court.[102]

There are a number of possible explanations for this reluctance to guarantee the same rights to NRMs as those which traditionally have been accorded to the Christian religion. First, the long history of Christianity and its influence on the jurisprudence of most European states' legal systems certainly helps explain why Christian denominations have experienced far fewer problems in Europe than NRMs and other faiths. Secondly, the constitutional status of the Christian Church, in some members of the Council of Europe, perhaps accounts for the deference of the Strasbourg institutions to the principles of this faith.[103] Thirdly, as noted earlier, NRMs have often been viewed with considerable suspicion, so there has been little public support for an unconditional affirmation of the rights of religious minorities. Fourthly, the concern felt by many governments about the proliferation of NRMs in Europe may have tempered any enthusiasm of the Commission and Court for boldly protecting such groups.[104] And finally, the fact that the activities of some NRMs clearly have been detrimental to the public good and obviously need to be curtailed,[105] perhaps has led the Commission and the Court to view most of such groups with suspicion. These factors explain, rather than justify, the attitude of the Strasbourg human rights institutions to NRMs, but it is hoped that this will change and that there will be a proper recognition of the rights of unorthodox religious minorities in today's multi-faith Europe.

Reluctance to utilise Article 9

Judging by the previous case law in this area, there is perhaps not great cause for optimum. It has been suggested that not merely has the European Court a "dismal record"[106] in considering Article 9 claims, but it even appears "to do all it can to avoid them".[107] This claim is perhaps a little harsh, but there is no doubt that the Court has often given the impression that it prefers to decide cases with a religious element, by making reference to Convention provisions other than Article 9. A good example of this is *Hoffman v Austria,*[108] where the European Court relied on Articles 8 (the right to a family life) and 14 (the prohibition of discrimination) rather than Article 9, in resolving a dispute over the custody of children between warring parents, one of whom was a Jehovah's Witness and the other a non-Jehovah's Witness.

The European Commission has also tended to avoid fully utilising Article 9. In *Church of Scientology v Sweden,*[109] on the question of whether the Church of Scientology could advertise a controversial religious artefact called an 'E-Meter', the Commission decided that this was a matter of "commercial" or free speech and not the manifestation of religious belief, while in a case involving a student demonstration, the Commission held that the principle of freedom of thought and conscience is subsidiary to freedom of assembly.[110] Indeed, the Commission generally has interpreted Article 9 rather cautiously,[111] with the result that very few cases in this area have proceeded to the European Court,[112] and even when such cases have managed to get there, the Commission's approach has often been more restrictive than that of the Court.[113] A significant exception to this, however, was a recent decision involving a woman who claimed that she had been unable to regain custody of her child because she belonged to a NRM called the Warriors of Christ. Rather than adopting the *Hoffman* approach, by deciding the case under Articles 8 and 14, the Commission accepted the applicant's claim that she had been under indirect pressure in order to change her beliefs to obtain custody of the child, so her complaint was declared admissible under Article 9.[114] Taking this together with the Commission's ruling in *Catholic Church of Chania v Greece*,[115] (where the question of a church's capacity to institute legal proceedings was declared admissible under Articles 14 and 9, rather than Article 6) and the Court's ruling in *Manoussakis v Greece* [116] (where Article 9 was violated in a case about the authorisation of a place of worship for Jehovah's Witnesses) these are signs of a hitherto unknown willingness to utilise Article 9 of the Convention.

Freedom of Religion and the Margin of Appreciation

The margin of appreciation is the principle that, since states are likely to be in a better position to decide certain matters than international judges,[117] governments should be permitted an element of discretion, subject to the general supervision of the European Court.[118] The margin of appreciation has been used in the interpretation of a number of ECHR Articles,[119] and tends to be associated with areas where "there is little common ground"[120] between the contracting parties. Perhaps, therefore, it is not surprising that the European Court has allowed states a wide margin of appreciation in this area as "it is not possible to discern throughout Europe a uniform conception of the significance of religion in society".[121] For example, in *Otto-Preminger-Institut v Austria,*[122] the European Court upheld the state's ban on a film which had offended the local Catholic community with its portrayal of Jesus as a simpleton and the Virgin Mary as sexually immoral, while in *Wingrove v UK,*[123] the Court held that the UK's refusal to grant a certificate permitting the distribution of a film about a nun's erotic visions of Christ on the cross, was justified by the need to protect the sensibilities of Christians. Thus, the lack of any European consensus on matters relating to religion generally is likely to encourage the Court's continued reliance on the margin of appreciation.

For those intending to challenge the restrictions imposed by Germany on its Scientologists, the margin of appreciation is clearly a formidable, though not an insurmountable obstacle. If German Scientologists exhaust domestic remedies and bring a complaint to Strasbourg, they are likely to rely on *Vogt v Germany*,[124] where a German teacher, who had been dismissed on the ground that her active membership of the Communist party was considered incompatible with her duty of political loyalty as a civil servant, challenged her dismissal successfully before the European Court. In seeking to distinguish the *Vogt* case from any application involving Scientologists, the German Government has two obvious arguments. First, that *Vogt* is of limited relevance as it was decided on Articles 10 and 11, and not Article 9 of the ECHR. And secondly, that while the ban on Communists working in the Civil Service is no longer necessary, following the end of the cold war, Scientology constitutes a present threat, in view of its plans "to take over key positions in society, in business life and in politics".[125]

Even though Germany's measures against Scientologists would appear to violate Article 9(1), it will argue that it has acted in accordance with Article 9(2) of the ECHR. Therefore, Germany may claim that the restrictions on Scientologists have a legitimate aim (that of curbing an organisation which "exploits people's fears"[126]), based on the ground of "public safety" (the "dangers" of Scientology[127]) and that these actions are "necessary in a democratic society" (that there is a "pressing social need"[128] for curbs to be imposed on the activities of Scientologists). This last point is likely to be particularly crucial in any future legal proceedings.

In the absence of any previous case law directly on this area, it is impossible to predict how the European Court will balance these conflicting arguments. However, what seems clear is that, even if the Church of Scientology is unsuccessful, it should be encouraged by the United States experience which suggests that the more powerful a NRM becomes, and the longer it remains in existence, the harder it will be for a state or a court (either domestic or international) to justify the imposition of discriminatory measures against it.[129]

CONCLUSION

On a global level the Human Rights Committee, which interprets the International Covenant on Civil and Political rights 1966, has stated that it "views with concern any tendency to discriminate against any religions or beliefs for any reasons, including the fact that they are newly established".[130] With the proliferation of NRMs in Europe, it is hoped that the newly constituted European Court[131] will tackle fairly and imaginatively the challenges posed by these new faiths. As was made clear at the beginning of this chapter, significant differences exist between Europe's NRMs. Therefore, there is a need for the European Court to offer guidelines so that law abiding and credible NRMs are able to enjoy the same rights and privileges as the longer established faiths in Europe.

As this century draws to a close, it is worthwhile remembering the advice of one of its most influential figures, F.D. Roosevelt. He warned that "[n]o democracy can survive which does not accept as fundamental to its very existence the recognition of the rights of minorities".[132] These words are of no less relevance for Europe in the next century, as they were for a pre-war United States society which was polarised by racial division. Thus, the commitment of the 'New Europe' to human rights will be measured in its treatment of minorities, particularly groups such as Europe's NRMs, which arouse suspicion and court unpopularity by rejecting traditional societal norms.

NOTES

*Lecturer, Law School, Leicester University.

1. *The International Law of Human Rights* (1983), at 324.
2. The theoretical and historical development of the term 'cult' has been traced by James Richardson who suggests that, because of its negative connotations in contemporary society, it should not be used in academic scholarship: "Definitions of Cult: From Sociological-Technical to Popular Negative", 34 *Review of Religious Research* (1993), June, 340, at 348.
3. Terms such as "'sects', 'cults', 'heresies', 'nonconformity' and 'deviations'", all convey "a mixture of doctrinal, historical, cultural and social judgments of relative 'abnormality'": J. Beckford and M. Levasseur, "New religious movements in Western Europe", in J. Beckford (ed.), *New Religious Movements and Rapid Social Change* (1986), at 29.
4. On this generally, see F. Bird and B. Reimer, "Participation Rates in New Religious Movements", 21 *Journal for the Scientific Study of Religion*, (1992) 1–14.
5. J. Beckford, *Cult Controversies: the Societal Response to the New Religious Movements* (1985), at 14.
6. This point is made by E. Barker, in "Religious Movements: Cult and Anticult since Jonestown", 12 *Annual Review of Sociology* (1986) 329–346.
7. Of course, such groups often continue to face persecution in certain parts of Europe. For example, in *Manoussakis and Others v Greece* (1997) 23 EHRR 387, the European Court of Human Rights described Jehovah's Witnesses as "members of a movement whose religious rites and practices are widely known and authorised in many European countries". However, the Court's use of the word "many" is an implicit acknowledgement

that Jehovah's Witnesses still face persecution in a minority of European states, and perhaps it is also significant that the Court described Jehovah's Witnesses as a "movement" and not a "religion".

8. Although the word 'cult' is open to a number of different interpretations, Robbins has suggested that it is usually associated with groups where there is: "(1) authoritarian and centralized leadership revolving around a charismatic figure; (2) communal and 'totalistic' organization; (3) aggressive proselytising; (4) systematic indoctrination processes; (5) recent development or importation to the United States; and (6) largely middle class and youthful clientele": T. Robbins, "New Religious Movements on the Frontier of Church and State", in T. Robbins, W. Shepherd, and J. McBride (eds.), *Cults, Culture and the Law: Perspective on New Religious Movements* (1985), at 22. The NRMs which form the basis of the discussion in this chapter would appear to satisfy the majority of these criteria.

9. Parliamentary Assembly Report on Sects and New Religious Movements, Rapporteur: Sir John Hunt, 29 November 1991, Doc. 6535, at 4.

10. *Ibid.*

11. *Ibid.*

12. *Ibid.*

13. *Ibid.*

14. On this generally see, A. Nicholi, "A New Dimension of the Youth Culture", in 13 *American Journal of Psychiatry* (1974), at 396.

15. E. Barker, "New Religions and Cults in Europe", in *The Encyclopaedia of Religion* (ed. M. Elide) (1987), at 409.

16. J. Beckford, "Cults, Conflicts and Journalists", in R. Towler (ed.), *New Religions and the New Europe* (1995) 109.

17. *Ibid*, at 108.

18. On 18th November 1978, 914 followers of Rev Jim Jones were found dead at Jonestown, Guyana.

19. On 19th April 1993, David Koresh and 82 of his Branch Davidians (of whom 33 were British) were killed following a gun battle with US federal agents at Waco, Texas. For an analysis of this, see S. Wright (ed.) *Armageddon at Waco* (1995).

20. In October 1994, the burnt bodies of 48 Solar Temple members were found in Switzerland. Solar Temple suicides were also reported in December 1995 (France) and in March 1997 (Canada).

21. On this generally, see L. Kahaner, *Cults that kill* (1988), and T.W. Keiser and J.L. Keiser, *The anatomy of illusion: Religious cults and destructive persuasion* (1988).

22. For example, see J. Richardson, "Psychological and Psychiatric Studies of New Religions", in L. Brown (ed.) *Advances in the Psychology of Religion* (1985) and J. Richardson, "Assessment of Participants in New Religions", 5 *International Journal of Psychology of Religion* (1995), at 145.

23. *Kokkinakis v Greece* (1994) 17 EHRR 397, at 438.

24. J. Richardson, "The 'Deformation' of New Religions: Impact Of Societal And Organizational Factors", in *Cults, Culture And The Law*, T. Robbins, W. Shepherd and J. McBride (eds.) (1985), at 164.

25. C. Goldberg, *"Courage and Fanaticism: The Charismatic Leader and Modern Religious Cults"* in D. Halperin (ed.) *Religion, Sect and Cult* (1983), at 163.

26. For example, see J. Richardson, "Public opinion and the tax evasion trial of Reverend Moon", 10 *Behavioral Sciences and the Law* (1992) 39–52.

27. For example, the Unification Church has often been accused of pressurising converts

into severing ties with their biological families. It lost a libel action in the United Kingdom against the Daily Mail, following the paper's publication of allegations that the Unification Church was responsible for brainwashing converts and splitting up families: *The Times* 1 April 1981.

28. *The Scientology Organization*, paper submitted by the German Delegation at the OSCE Seminar on Religious Freedom, Warsaw, 16–19 April, 1996, at 5.

29. J. Beckford and M. Levasseur, "New religious movements in Western Europe", in J. Beckford (ed.), *New Religious Movements and Rapid Social Change* (1986), at 47.

30. See J. Beckford, "The Public Response to New Religious Movements in Britain", 30 *Social Compass,* (1983) 49–62.

31. J. Beckford and M. Levasseur, in J. Beckford *supra* n. 29, at 40. It would appear that there are no links between any NRM and ethnic or racial minorities: *ibid.*, at 41.

32. J. Beckford, *supra* n. 30, at 54.

33. In *Kokkinakis v Greece*, dissenting Judge Valtiocs warned of those who are guilty of the "rape of the beliefs of others", *supra*, n. 23, at 430.

34. See R. Hummel and B.Hardin, "Asiatic Religions in Europe", 18 *Concilium* (1983), 23–28.

35. J. Beckford, "Cults, Conflicts and Journalists", in R. Towler (ed.), *New Religions and the New Europe* (1995), at 100.

36. "Modern Anti-Cultism in Europe", in *Anti-Cult Movements in Cross-Cultural Perspective*, A. Shupe and D. Bromley (eds.), (1994), at 161.

37. Rev F.W. Haack, a well known German opponent of NRMs, as cited in Richardson and van Driel, "Modern Anti-Cultism in Europe", *ibid.*, at 150.

38. "US stars accuse Bonn of Nazi view on Scientology", *The Daily Telegraph,* 10 January 1997, at 7.

39. "Media blitz launched in Germany's religious war", *The Independent*, 13 November 1997, at 14.

40. It should be borne in mind that, in addition to the issues covered in this chapter, other areas where members of NRMs frequently experience problems include: restrictions on proselytism; curbs on religious festivals; the non-recognition of religious holidays; the refusal of charitable status; and controversies surrounding the education and upbringing of children.

41. "Message from the President of the Church of Scientology", http://www.scientology.org.

42. *Ibid.*

43. The Human Rights Office of the Church of Scientology, <http:/hatewatch.freedom mag.org/gerwpap/fore.htm>.

44. *Founding Church of Scientology v United States* 409 F.2d 1146 (D.D. Cir. 1969) and *Hernandez v Commissioner of Internal Revenue* 109 S. Ct. 136 (1989).

45. *Church of the New Faith v Comr for Pay-roll Tax* (1983) 57 ALJR 785.

46. For example, in *R v Registrar General, ex parte Segerdal* [1970] 2 QB 697 at 704, Lord Denning described the Church of Scientology as "more a philosophy of the existence of man or of life, rather than a religion".

47. German Government submission to the OSCE Seminar on Religious Freedom, *supra* n. 28, at 6.

48. *Ibid.*

49. For example, see "Parliament and priests unite to keep cults out of Russia", *The Times*, 21 July 1993, at 10.

50. Report submitted by Special Rapporteur, Abdelfattah Amor, to the UN Commission on Human Rights, 15 December 1995, UN Doc E/CN.4/1996/95, para 44.

51. P. Moreno, *The Status of Religious Freedom in OSCE Countries*, (The Rutherford Institute) 1997.

52. See "Cunning patriarch propels Christianity to the heart of the state", *The Independent*, 7 January 1998, at 12.

53. *The Times*, 23 July 1997.

54. For example, see *Rutherford International,* vol 1, issue 3, 1997, at 1.

55. *The Times* 21 July 1993.

56. "The New Europe: Sects, Orthodoxy and Discrimination by the State", paper presented by the Rutherford Institute to the OSCE Human Dimension Seminar on Constitutional and Administrative aspects on the Freedom of Religion, Warsaw, 16–19 April 1996, at 4.

57. *Scientology: Religious Apartheid 1996*. <http://hatewatch.freedommag.org/gerwpap/intro.htm>.

58. *Nene Juristische Wochenschrift*, no. 46/96, 2.12.96.

59. *Ibid.*

60. See *Constitutional, Legal and Administrative Aspects of Freedom of Religion*, submission of the Church of Scientology to the OSCE Seminar on Religious Freedom, 16–19 April 1996.

61. "Scientology-The Profit Making Sect", Norbert Blum, *Die Woche,* May 1995.

62. See Submission of the Church of Scientology to the Warsaw Conference, *supra* n. 60.

63. *Scientology: Religious Apartheid* 1996, *supra* n. 57.

64. See report submitted by Abdelfattah Amor, Special Rapporteur on Religious Intolerance, to the UN Commission on Human Rights, 22 December 1994, E/CN.4/1995/91

65. *Ibid.*

66. For example, the US jazz musician Chick Corea was prevented from performing in 1993 (Baden-Wurttemberg) and could only play subject to certain conditions in 1994 in Hessia because he is a Scientologist: *Scientology: Religious Apartheid* 1996, *supra* n. 57.

67. Report submitted by Abdelfattah Amor, 15 December 1995, E/CN.4/1996/95.

68. *The Independent* 13 November 1997.

69. *The Independent* 30 January 1997.

70. "The Scientology Organization", *supra* n. 28.

71. *The Guardian*, 28 January 1997.

72. Scientologists are likely to argue, in the German Courts, that the measures taken against them contradict the principle of religious freedom as guaranteed under Articles 3(3) and (4) of the German Basic Law (1949) and Article 136 of the 1919 Constitution, which is an integral part of the Basic Law.

73. *Kokkinakis v Greece, supra* n. 23, para 31.

74. *Arrowsmith v UK Application No. 7050/75* (1978) 19 DR, 5.

75. *H v UK* (1993)16 EHRR CD 44.

76. *Knudsen v Norway* (1986) 8 EHRR 45.

77. *Church of X v UK Application No. 3798/68* (1969) 12 Yearbook 306. The British Government lifted its restrictions on Scientologists in 1980.

78. *X and the Church of Scientology v Sweden Application No. 7805/77* (1979) 16 DR 68.

79. *Chappell v UK Application No. 12587/86* (1987) 53 DR 241.

80. Human Rights Committee, General Comment 22, Article 18 (Forty-eighth session, 1993) paras 1,2.

81. *Study on the Elimination of All Forms of Intolerance and Discrimination Based on Religion or Belief* 1989, E.89.XIV.3.

82. *Thomas v Review Board*, 450 U.S. 707 (1981), at 714.

83. See *Church of the New Faith v Commissioner for Pay-roll Tax (Vic)* (1983) 154 CLR 120, at 132, per Mason ACJ and Brennan J and at 173, per Wilson and Deane JJ.

84. 11 DR, at 55.

85. On this generally, see S. Gilly and W. Shiels (eds.), *A History of Religion on Britain: Practice and Belief from Pre-Roman Times to the Present* (1994).

86. *Chappell v UK Application No. 12587/86* (1987) 53 DR 241.

87. *Omkarananda and Divine Light Zentrum v Switzerland Application No. 8118/77* (1981) 25 DR 105.

88. *Supra* n. 86, at 246.

89. *Supra* n. 87, at 117.

90. *Application No. 7805/77* (1979) 16 DR 68.

91. For example, in *Kustannus Oy Vapaa Ajattelija AB et al v Finland,* a company which was created to publish and sell books promoting the aims of freethinkers could, in principle, possess and exercise rights under Article 9(1): *Application No. 20471/92* (1996) 22 EHRR 69.

92. This claim is made even more forcefully by J. Ogloff and J. Pfeifer, "Cults and the law: A Discussion of the Legality of Alleged Cult Activities" in 10 *Behavioral Sciences and the Law* (1992), at 117.

93. For example, see *Omkarananda and DLT, supra,* n. 87; *ISKON v UK Application No. 20490/92* (1993) 76-A DR 90 ; and the Scientology cases, *supra* nn. 77 and 78.

94. For example, note the applicants' failure in *Grandrath v FRG Application No. 2299/64* (1967) 10 YB 626 and in *X v Germany Application No. 7705/76* 9 (1978) DR 196. However, it should be pointed out that Jehovah's Witnesses submitting petitions under the ECHR have been more successful in recent cases such as *Hoffmann v Austria* (1994) 17 EHRR 293, *Kokkinakis v Greece* (1994) 17 EHRR 397, *Manoussakis and others v Greece* (1997) 23 EHRR 387, and *Tsirlis and Kouloumpas v Greece* (1996) 21 EHRR CD 30.

95. *Application No. 7291/75* (1978) 11 DR 55 .

96. *Chappell v UK* (1987) 53 DR 241 .

97. *X v UK Application No. 8160/78* (1981) 22 DR 27 .

98. *X v UK Application No. 54421* (1975) DR 41 .

99. *X v UK Application No. 8231/78* (1982) 28 DR 5 and *X v UK Application No. 7992/77* (1978) 14 DR 234 .

100. The European Court has held that "[a] State Church system cannot in itself be considered to violate Article 9 of the Convention": *Darby v Sweden* Series A, No.187 (1991) 45. On religious taxes see *Gottesmann v Switzerland Application No. 10616/83* (1985) 40 DR 284 .

101. See *Choudhury v UK, Application No. 17349/1990* (1991) 12 HRLJ 172 and *Gay News v UK* (1982) 5 EHRR 123.

102. See *Otto-Preminger Institute v Austria* (1995) 19 EHRR 34, and *Wingrove v UK* (1997) 24 EHRR 1.

103. *Ibid.*

104. For example the findings of a report commissioned by the French Government into "the phenomena of sects", was recently published. See A. Gest and J. Guyard, *Les Sectes en France*, Rapport fait au nom de la Commission d'Enquete sur les sectes, le 10 Janvier 1996, 82.

105. For example the allegations in the past of child abuse in David Berg's The Children of God or the frequent suicides of members of the Solar Temple (Temple du Soleil).

106. J. Richardson, "Minority Religions and the Law", 18(2) *University of Queensland Law Journal* (1995), at 195.

107. *Ibid.*, at 195.

108. *Hoffman v Austria* (1994) 17 EHRR 293.

109. *Application No. 7805/77*, (1979) 16 DR 68.

110. *Application No. 19601/92* (1985) 80 DR, 46.

111. For example, see *Arrowsmith v UK, Application No. 7050/75,* (1978) 19 DR 5 and *Logan v UK, Application No. 24875/94* [1997] 1 EHRLR 83.

112. It was not until *Kokkinakis v Greece* (1994) 17 EHRR 397, that the European Court had the chance to examine a case specifically under Article 9.

113. The restrictive approach of the Commission in *Manoussakis v Greece, Application No. 18748/91* (1996) 21 EHRR, CD 5, can be compared with that of the Court (1997) 23 EHRR 387.

114. *Application No. 27496/95*, (1996) 22 EHRR CD 101.

115. *Application No. 25528/94*, report of September 3, 1996.

116. (1997) 23 EHRR 387.

117. *Handeyside v UK* (1976) Series A, 24, para 48.

118. On the margin of appreciation generally, see D.J. Harris, M. O'Boyle and C. Warbrick, *Law of the European Convention on Human Rights* (1995) 12–15.

119. The margin of appreciation is particularly synonymous with the interpretation of Articles 8–11, and Article 15.

120. *Rees v UK*, (1986) Series A, 106, para 37.

121. *Otto-Preminger Institute v Austria* 19 EHRR 34, at 57, 58.

122. (1995) 19 EHRR 34.

123. (1997) 24 EHRR 1.

124. *Vogt v Germany* (1996) 21 EHRR 205.

125. *The Scientology Organization, supra* n. 28, at 4.

126. *Ibid.*

127. *Ibid*, at 5.

128. See *Handyside v UK, supra* n. 117, at paras 48–49.

129. After more than thirty years of conflict the US Government granted charitable status to the Church of Scientology in 1993: *The Times* 15 October 1993.

130. General Comment on Article 18, adopted 14 July 1993. CCPR/C/48/CRP.2/Rev.1.

131. Protocol 11 created a new Full Time European Court of Human Rights, which came into force on 1st November 1998.

132. US President Franklin D. Roosevelt, in a letter to the National Association for the Advancement of Colored People, 25 June 1938.

The International Status of Cultural Rights
for National Minorities

*Wolf Mannens**

INTRODUCTION

In July 1992 the UN Sub-Commission's Special Rapporteur, Danilo Türk, in his final report on the realisation of economic, social and cultural rights, noted that, "the time for the human rights community to take a stand supporting the right to culture is surely upon us".[1] The momentum for the recognition of cultural rights continued in December of that year with the establishment, by the United Nations and UNESCO, of the World Commission on Culture and Development (WCCD)[2] and in the adoption by the UN General Assembly of the Declaration on the Rights of Persons belonging to National or Ethnic, Religious and Linguistic Minorities. This chapter will examine the extent to which the cultural rights of national minorities are recognised under international law and the author will contend that international human rights law should recognise the need for a clear implementation of cultural rights in general, and the cultural rights of national minorities in particular.[3]

CULTURAL RIGHTS

The first question which we must consider is what is culture and what is meant by cultural rights? Culture, according to Linton is a "configuration of learned behaviour and results of behaviour whose component elements are shared and transmitted by the members of a particular society",[4] while Stavenhagen defines it as a "coherent self-contained system of values and symbols".[5] Throughout history culture has been a continuously changing phenomenon, gradually being transformed from a purely social or moral issue to one of political and even legal concern.[6] However, within international jurisprudence, there is a lack of conceptual clarity about the precise nature of cultural rights.[7] Consequently, for the purpose of this chapter, 'cultural rights' will be considered as those rights which

185

P. Cumper and S. Wheatley (eds.), Minority Rights in the 'New' Europe, 185–196
© 1999 *Kluwer Law International. Printed in Great Britain.*

assist in the preservation, maintenance and development of a culture – the specific elements of the social or cultural life of a group which contribute to the separate identity of the group.[8] Therefore, 'culture' constitutes the platform for the intended continuation of the (group) identity[9] and from this it follows that words such as 'culture', 'existence', 'identity', and even 'dignity' are very much intertwined. It is in this context that we will examine the legal protection of cultural rights and, in particular, the right of each person to be able to participate, fully and freely, in the cultural life of a community of his or her choosing.[10]

In an age of increasing 'globalisation',[11] it has been argued that a 'loyalty reaction'[12] is provoked amongst elements of the state's population, with individuals often regarding themselves as being part of a group or nation and not the State.[13] The 'cultural' aspect of this phenomenon can play a crucial role in defining a group's collective identity, as well as that of the individual. This is particularly so for those groups which have been 'culturally neglected', or have a history of suffering as the result of political persecution and oppression. A consequence of this (re-)emergence of group identities may be that the *status quo* in a particular society will be threatened – especially if, until that point, only one particular culture has been dominant. Therefore, the issue of cultural rights can be seen as yet another dilemma the international community faces in ensuring the protection of, and guaranteeing rights to, national minorities under international law.[14] Indeed, the very term 'national minority' symbolises the whole range of "marginalised or vulnerable groups who live in the shadow of governing populations with a different and dominant cultural ideology".[15] The fact that a particular group is different from the rest emphasises its uniqueness,[16] a uniqueness that is very often based on a specific culture.

This chapter is concerned with national minorities, as it is this particular category of 'minority' which has received detailed attention from a number of international organisations.[17] The term "national minority" has been said to represent:

> a group of persons who, besides the characteristics of an ethnic minority,[18] have the will to exercise as a group those rights which give minorities the possibility to take part in the policy-decisions process within a given territory or even in the national context of a state without being on an equal footing with other ethnics in this State.[19]

The post-Cold War era has seen demands from several of these national minority groups for emancipation and independence. At a time when inter-state relations were seen to be evolving (into areas of co-operation and integration), intra-state structures and relations could not remain unaltered.[20] With the process of globalisation, in which communication between different societies and groups has become easier, many communities have overcome their fear of the central State authorities and sought emancipation. This has often triggered conflict between minority groups and the State, with the result that the international community has been forced to respond to, as well as having to seek to guarantee both national and international peace and stability.[21] This chapter will now proceed to examine the extent to which the provision of cultural rights has been catered for in the 'New' Europe.

INTERNATIONAL STANDARD SETTING

Within international organisations, cultural rights have traditionally been ignored or neglected,[22] as the international community has focused its attention primarily on civil and political rights. However, this is not to say that cultural rights have not been recognised, or relevant standards formulated by international organisations.

Cultural rights, or more precisely the rights that should guarantee the existence and the continuation of a culture, constitute one of the 'dimensions' of human rights.[23] Since the end of the Second World War, several international and regional organisations have considered the issue of cultural rights. For example, the Universal Declaration of Human Rights, adopted by the United Nations General Assembly in 1948, provides that "[e]veryone . . . is entitled to realisation . . . of the . . . cultural rights indispensable for his dignity and the free development of his personality".[24] Moreover, it guarantees everyone "the right freely to participate in the cultural life of the community".[25] More generally, within the United Nations system, the United Nations Educational Scientific and Cultural Organisation (UNESCO) has enjoyed a prominent role in the development of cultural rights.[26] Although UNESCO's main focus has been on 'national' (i.e. nation-state) cultures, and not on sub-cultures or the cultures of minority groups, it has nevertheless played an important role in international standard setting, such as in its adoption of the Declaration of the Principles of International Cultural Co-operation (1966) which provides that "each culture has a dignity and value which must be respected and preserved",[27] and of the 1978 UNESCO Declaration on Race and Racial Prejudice, which emphasises the right of all *individuals* and *groups* to be different.[28] In 1982, a UNESCO World Conference on Cultural Policies in Mexico stressed the virtues of diverse cultural identities, concluding that "the assertion of cultural identity . . . contributes to the liberation of peoples".[29] Furthermore, under the auspices of UNESCO, several international meetings of experts were held during the 1980's with a mandate to examine and identify the links between the rights of peoples, self-determination and cultural identity.[30] One of the conclusions of these meetings of experts was an emphasis on the necessity of continuing the "pathfinding work of elucidation of the rights of peoples, especially within its field of competence with regard to the respect of cultural identity and cultural concerns".[31] However, it must be stressed that explicit *rights* to culture are nowhere contained within UNESCO's Conventions and Declarations,[32] and this creates an impression that, for UNESCO, culture merely 'serves' human rights and is not a right in itself.[33]

Moreover, within the United Nations system, the General Assembly has adopted a Declaration on the Rights of Persons Belonging to National or Ethnic, Religious and Linguistic Minorities (1992), providing that "States *shall* protect the existence and the national or ethnic, cultural, religious and linguistic identity of minorities within their respective territories, and *shall* encourage conditions for the promotion of that identity".[34] Furthermore, Article 2 of the Minority Declaration guarantees "the right [of persons belonging to minorities] to enjoy their own culture". Although a non-binding instrument, the fact that the Declaration was adopted without a vote provides evidence of a growing international awareness of the significance of minority needs and of related cultural issues. Such matters were further recognised in 1993 with the Declaration accepted at the World Conference on Human Rights in Vienna. The Vienna Conference provides that states have an obligation to "ensure that persons belonging to minorities may exercise fully and effectively all human rights and fundamental freedoms without any discrimination and in full equality before the law", and that "persons belonging to minorities have the right to enjoy their own culture".[35]

Of particular significance in the international standard setting for cultural rights was the adoption and subsequent entry into force of the International Covenant on Economic, Social and Cultural Rights (ICESCR),[36] and of the International Covenant on Civil and Political Rights (ICCPR). In particular, the collective right of self-determination, expressed in Articles 1 of both the ICCPR and of the ICESCR, gives, *inter alia*, all peoples the right to "freely pursue their . . . cultural development".[37] Furthermore, Article 15 of the International Covenant on Economic, Social and Cultural Rights recognises the "right of everyone to take part in cultural life",[38] whilst Article 27 of the International Covenant on Civil and Political Rights provides that persons belonging to a minority should " . . . not be denied the right, in community with the other members of their group, to enjoy their own culture". The Human Rights Committee[39] has also commented that "[a]lthough the rights protected under Article 27 are individual rights, they depend in turn on the ability of the minority group to maintain its culture".[40] Therefore, this ability to 'maintain' a culture is symptomatic of the essential relationship between the individual members of the minority and the minority group itself.

Within Europe the primary focus for human rights protection is the Council of Europe, whose member states adopted the European Cultural Convention as long ago as 1954[41] – although this Convention only refers, in general terms, to safeguarding and promoting the development of a 'total' European culture. The Council of Europe's most prominent instrument, the European Convention on Human Rights (ECHR), only deals indirectly with the (national) minority question in Article 14.[42] Its focus on individuals rather than groups, however, limits the Convention's potential impact in this context.[43] The deficiencies of the ECHR, in respect of minority rights, resulted in the Council of Europe adopting the Framework Convention for the Protection of National Minorities,[44] the first binding multilateral legal instrument to protect persons belonging to national minorities *per se*.[45] Article 5 of the Framework Convention provides that "[p]arties undertake to promote the conditions necessary for persons belonging to national minorities to maintain and develop their culture, and to preserve the essential elements of their identity, namely their religion, language, traditions and cultural heritage". However, it is rather unfortunate that the broad goals and aims formulated in the Framework Convention also give the contracting States ample room for interpretation (usually in the State's favour).

Of more significance in the enumeration of national minority rights in Europe has been the Helsinki process (previously the Conference on Security and Co-operation in Europe (CSCE), now the Organisation for Security and Co-operation in Europe (OSCE)). The Final Act of the Conference on Security and Co-operation in Europe, adopted in Helsinki in 1975, provides, in the section 'Equal Rights and Self-determination of Peoples', a right of "all peoples . . . to pursue as they wish their . . . cultural development".[46] In its concluding document, following the Vienna meeting of 1989, the CSCE emphasised the protection of human rights and fundamental freedoms of persons belonging to national minorities.[47] This renewed interest in national minorities resulted eventually in a document of the Copenhagen meeting of the Conference on the Human Dimension of the CSCE (1990), which dealt extensively with specific rights for minorities. Of particular interest in this context is paragraph 32, which provides that, "[p]ersons belonging to national minorities have the rights freely to express, preserve and develop their . . . cultural . . . identity and to maintain and develop their culture in all its aspects". Furthermore, the Charter of Paris, adopted in November 1990 following the meeting of the Heads of State, notes that "[e]veryone has the right to enjoy his . . . cultural rights",[48] and in the 'Guidelines for the Future' the participating States of the CSCE stressed their determination " . . . to foster the rich contribution of national minorities to the life of our societies", and to undertake further measures "to improve their situation".[49] Moreover, within the Helsinki process, the Geneva Meeting of Experts on National Minorities in July 1991 declared that "the preservation of the values and of the cultural heritage of national minorities requires the involvement of persons belonging to such minorities and that tolerance and respect for different cultures are of paramount importance in this regard".[50]

THE LEGAL SIGNIFICANCE OF CULTURAL RIGHTS

Having examined the international standards relating to cultural rights, the provisions appear vaguely formulated and of questionable legal status. Nevertheless, concern as to issues relating to national minorities, and to minority cultures, has clearly moved on to the agenda of international and regional organisations, albeit not as a priority. Considering that one of the purposes of the United Nations is "[t]o achieve international co-operation in solving international problems of a . . . cultural . . . character",[51] one may assume that there is room for a more vigorous implementation of this policy. The reluctance to do so can be explained by the politically sensitive nature of claims to cultural rights for national minorities; although, in contrast, the progressive role played by the OSCE in developing minority protection mechanisms and procedures is remarkable, particularly in view of the fact that the OSCE is a political organisation, and not one which adopts legally binding instruments.[52]

The fact that so very few 'binding' cultural rights have been formulated illustrates the traditional reluctance of the international community to impose limitations on states' national sovereignty and, in particular, an unwillingness to place obligations on new or 'politically fragile' states.[53] However, there are countervailing and encouraging developments in some Eastern Europe countries, with the formal recognition of sub-cultures or minority cultures contained in the new constitutions of Hungary, Slovenia and to a certain extent Estonia. Furthermore, several bilateral and multilateral treaties have been specifically drafted to deal with the position and protection of national minorities.[54]

The end of the Cold War saw a greater emphasis within Europe on intra- rather than inter-state relations, with many different entities (such as peoples, groups and minorities) referring to their distinctive cultures to substantiate claims for basic human rights. Legislative policies relating to culture have often been used as instruments of domination and fragmentation, with the consequence that cultural rights have remained, in the words of Gomez, "[a]t the level of non justiciable principles of state policy".[55] Developments in international law, such as the adoption of the International Covenant on Economic, Social and Cultural Rights in 1966, have accorded only modest recognition to these rights. However, the position of cultural rights may be altering; as Eide notes, the "[r]ole of the modern nation state seems to be on the decline",[56] positioning minorities within a more global context and seeking new points of social reference. A new form of 'cultural pluralism'[57] has thus been introduced. The Report of the World Commission on Culture and Development describes this phenomenon of cultural pluralism as "an all-pervasive, enduring characteristic of contemporary societies".[58]

Analysis of the relevant international instruments demonstrates an increasing recognition of both the existence of a human right to cultural identity, or at least a guarantee of protection for 'cultural identities', and of the importance of such a recognition. Stavenhagen suggests "[t]hat the international community is moving in this direction, though the concept [of cultural identity] is open to discussion",[59] while Masini claims that "[t]here is a growing awareness of the right of every identity to survive by its own values, and of the need to find a way of respecting other identities which have the same rights".[60] Donnelly, although opposed to the creation of a 'new' or 'additional' human right to cultural identity, favours making the concept of cultural identity more explicit within the body of existing cultural rights.[61] However, it may be noted that political factors are likely to ensure that a posited right to a cultural identity remains "unexplained and undeveloped",[62] so that, in effect, it will be seen as only a right in theory, and not in practice of value to minority communities.

CONCLUSION

The protection of distinctive cultures and sub-cultures is seen increasingly today as one way of defusing tension and minimising the risk of conflict. However, existing international legal standards relating to the protection of the cultural identity of national minorities are far from perfect. Indeed, the role of cultural rights within the human rights framework remains insignificant. Recent inter- and intra-state conflicts demonstrate a need to focus on the enforcement of existing norms in the protection of national minorities, as only a continuous jurisprudence will ensure that states comply with their international obligations.[63] As Tomasevski has commented, "[i]nternational jurisprudence [also] serves to trigger off national changes".[64] Minorities demand cultural rights from states because those rights exist in international jurisprudence. The Vienna Declaration and Programme of Action (1993) stressed that economic, social, cultural, political and civil rights are universal, interdependent and indivisible.[65] Consequently, the effective implementation of cultural rights should be achievable by the international community without endangering global peace and security.[66]

The universal implications of 'culture' and 'cultural rights' can, it is contended, be used in a positive way to overcome 'state-barriers'. This author is of the opinion that history has demonstrated that national politics involving minority related conflicts are often too complex for the State concerned to solve unilaterally. A Machiavellian idea of the strict preservation of the state should, therefore, be avoided in the future. In the meantime we see national minorities slowly being transformed into 'international minorities' due to the complex legal implications of their claims. It is unfortunate that the momentum which existed towards a recognition of cultural rights at the start of this decade has faded and the status of cultural rights remains undetermined. Nevertheless, the lessons of the recent past suggest that there is a need for the international community to reaffirm its commitment to the making of progress in this area.

NOTES

*Researcher and Lecturer at the Department of Public International Law, Leiden University.

1. E/CN.4/Sub.2/1992/16, paragraph 201. See also the Statement to the World Conference on Human Rights, U.N. Committee on Economic, Social, and Cultural Rights, U.N. Doc.E/C.12/1992/crp.2/Add.1 (1992).
2. This Commission was established in accordance with 26C/resolution 3.4 of the General Conference of UNESCO and General Assembly resolution 46/158.
3. On this generally, see F. Benoît-Rohmer, *The minority question in Europe: towards a coherent system of protection for national minorities* (1996).
4. See R. Linton, *The study of man* (1936), as cited in M. Leiris, "Race and Culture", in the series: *The Race Question in Modern Science*, UNESCO (1951), at 21. Leiris distinguishes between "ornamental" culture which is just a "partial expression" like arts and sciences, and "culture in the true sense. . .comprising the whole more or less coherent structure of concepts, sentiments, mechanisms, institutions and objects which explicitly or implicitly condition the conduct of members of a group", at 22.
5. R. Stavenhagen, "Cultural Rights and Universal Human Rights", in A. Eide *et al.* (eds.), *Economic, Social and Cultural Rights* (1995), at 66.
6. J. Donnelly, "Human Rights, Individual Rights and Collective Rights", in J. Berting *et al.* (eds.), *Human Rights in a Pluralist World* (1990).
7. M. Gomez, "Social Economic Rights and Human Rights Commissions", 17 *Human Rights Quarterly* (1995), at 161.
8. For present purposes this may either be a people, a population or a minority.
9. An alternative description of the cultural group identity is given by R. Barth who states that it is not so much the content of the culture, as the social boundaries "that

define the spaces of social relationships by which membership is attributed in one or the other ethnic group". As paraphrased by R. Stavenhagen, *supra* n. 5, at 66.

10. See G. Brunner, *Nationality Problems and Minority Conflicts in Eastern Europe* (1996), at 137, who speaks in this respect of a personal autonomy (instead of the more frequently used territorial autonomy).

11. The term 'globalisation (process)' refers to "the limit of international integration, as a growing number of national economies become mutually interconnected through cross-border flows of goods, services and factors of production. Perhaps, more importantly, globalisation also describes a qualitative process of governing an increasingly complex pattern of cross-border linkages": *UN World Investment Report 1994*, TNC's employment and the workplace, chapter III, "Globalisation, integrated international production and the world economy", at 118.

12. On the issue of 'loyalty' or 'allegiance', see T. Franck, "Clan and Superclan: Loyalty, Identity and Community in Law and Practice", 90 *American Journal of International Law* (1996) 359–383. See also S. Huntington, "Clash of Civilizations?", *Foreign Affairs* (1993), 22–49, who describes two conflicting pulls, the one of tribalism and the other of globalism.

13. See M. Galenkamp, *Individualism Versus Collectivism, The Concept of Collective Rights* (1993).

14. On this generally, see J. Räikkä (ed.), *Do we need minority rights? Conceptual Issues* (1996).

15. The Report of the World Commission on Culture and Development, *Our Creative Diversity* (1995). See also F. Ermacora, "The Protection of Minorities before the United Nations", Recueil des Cours, IV (1983), at 295–296.

16. See D. Johnston, "Native Rights as Collective Rights: A Question of Group Self-Preservation", in W. Kymlicka, *The Rights of Minority Cultures* (1996), at 183.

17. On this generally, see A. Phillips & A. Rosas (eds.), *Universal Minority Rights* (1995).

18. Ermacora defines an ethnic minority "as a group with its own language, its own culture and its own history which is self-conscious as a group and whose members want to uphold its particularities": See F. Ermacora, *supra* n. 15, at 295, and the study by F. Capotorti, *Study on the Rights of Persons belonging to Ethnic, Religious and Linguistic Minorities* (1991), paragraph 568.

19. *Ibid.*, at 295.

20. See L. Khan, *The Extinction of Nation-States, A World without Borders* (1996).

21. It is worth noting that Appendix II of the Vienna Declaration (October 1993) explicitly deals with this relationship between stability and peace on the one hand, and the protection of national minorities on the other. See also R. Stavenhagen, "The Rights to Cultural Identity", in J. Berting *et al.* (eds.), *Human Rights in a Pluralist World* (1990), at 256.

22. L. Prott, "Cultural Rights as Peoples' Rights in International Law", in J. Crawford (ed.) *The Rights of Peoples* (1992), 103–104.

23. I prefer the term 'dimensions' as it implies a much more 'direct' connection between all human rights.

24. The Universal Declaration of Human Rights 1948, Article 22.

25. *Ibid.*, Article 27.

26. The purpose of UNESCO is "to contribute to peace and security by promoting collaboration among the nations through. . .culture". See Preamble to the Constitution of UNESCO, 16 November 1945.

27. Article 1(1). The explicit right and the duty of every people to develop its culture is

also stressed in paragraph 2 of Article I: "Cultural co-operation is a right and a duty for all peoples and all nations".

28. Articles 1 and 5.

29. World Conference on Cultural Policies. Final Report, UNESCO, November 1982. See R. Stavenhagen, *supra* n. 5, at 64.

30. UNESCO experts meeting, Budapest (25–29 September 1991). For Reports of these meetings see (SHS-85/CONF.613/10), SHS-87/CONF.802/7, SHS-89/CONF.602/7).

31. UN Doc. E/CN.4/Sub.2/ 1992/6 at paragraph 3f. Furthermore UNESCO was involved with the 1979 Recommendation on Participation by the People at Large in Cultural Life and their Contribution to it. Article 4(f) states: "the equality of cultures, including the cultures of national minorities and of foreign minorities if they exist, are forming part of the common heritage of all mankind". And in Article 4(g) it calls upon states to "protect, safeguard and enhance all forms of cultural expression such as national or regional languages, dialects, folk arts and traditions, both past and present, and rural cultures as well as cultures of other social groups".

32. J. Symonides, "The History of the Paradox of Cultural Rights and the State of the Discussion within UNESCO", in P. Meyer-Bisch (ed.), *Les Droits culturels, une catégorie sous-développée de droits de l'homme* (1993).

33. I. Szabo, *Cultural Rights* (1977), at 44.

34. Article 1(1) of the Declaration on the Rights of Persons Belonging to National or Ethnic, Religious and Linguistic Minorities, GA Resolution 47/135 of 18 December 1992 (emphasis added).

35. The Vienna Declaration and Programme of Action, adopted June 24, 1993, U.N.Doc. A/Conf.157/23. Paragraph 25 of the Programme of Action.

36. This covenant entered into force on 3rd of January 1976. On it generally see M. Craven, *The International Covenant on Economic, Social and Cultural Rights* (1995).

37. See the twin-articles 1 (1) of the ICESCR and the ICCPR.

38. The General Comment on article 15, that should have been due by the end of 1994, is still under consideration by the Committee on Economic, Social and Cultural Rights.

39. This Committee was established to conform with Article 28 of the ICCPR. See *Bernhard Ominayak, Chief of the Lubicon Lake Band v. Canada*, Communication No. 167/1984, adopted on 26 March 1990, paragraph 33. In an individual opinion by Judge Ando it is made clear that this right to enjoy one's own culture should, however, "not be understood to imply that. . .traditional way of life must be preserved intact at all costs". See also the appendix of this Communication, and P. Thornberry, *International law and the rights of minorities* (1991), 207–213, who deals explicitly with the *Kitok v. Sweden* and *Lovelace v. Canada* cases.

40. General Comment 23 (50), CCPR/C/21/Rev.1/Add.5, paragraph 6.2.

41. December 1954, and to be found in ETS 18.

42. Article 14 ECHR: "The enjoyment of the rights and freedoms set forth in this Convention shall be secured without discrimination on any ground such as sex, race, colour, language, religion, political or other opinion, national or social origin, association with a national minority, property, birth or other status".

43. For example see *Case No.8142/78*, D.R. 18 at 88, where the applicant wanted to belong to a Slovenian minority although he did not speak any Slovenian. Similarly note *Case Nos. 9278/81* and *9415/81*, Dec. 3.10.83, D.R. 35 at 30, where the applicants (Lapps) claimed that they were victims of discrimination by the Norwegian authorities. The fact that a nomadic community could not be regarded as an 'association' indicates the rigidity of the European Commission's interpretation of the Convention.

44. The Framework Convention on the Rights of National Minorities 34 *ILM*. (1994) 351.

45. It came into force, 1 February 1998; contracting parties on that date were: Croatia, Cyprus, Denmark, Estonia, Finland, Germany, Hungary, Italy, Liechtenstein, Malta, Moldova, Romania, San Marino, Slovakia, Spain, 'the former Yugoslav Republic of Macedonia', Ukraine and the United Kingdom.

46. The Helsinki Final Act, at paragraph 29, 14 *ILM* (1975) 1292.

47. See the CSCE Vienna Meeting (Nov. 4 1986 – Jan. 19 1989), 28 *ILM* (1989) 527, principles 18 and 19 and paragraphs 31, 45 and 59.

48. The States affirmed that, "the ethnic, cultural, linguistic and religious identity of national minorities will be protected and that persons belonging to national minorities have the right freely to express, preserve and develop that identity without any discrimination and in full equality before the law": CSCE Charter of Paris for a New Europe, Paris, November 1990, 30 *ILM* (1991) 190.

49. *Ibid.*

50. Paragraph 3 of Chapter IV of the Report of the CSCE Meeting of Experts on National Minorities, Geneva 1991.

51. Charter of the United Nations (1945), Article 1.

52. The documents produced by the OSCE are not legally binding. They are negotiated and adopted by consensus, and are therefore accepted as being politically binding. See J. Wright, "The OSCE and the Protection of Minority Rights" 18 *Human Rights Quarterly* (1996), at 193.

53. See, on the issue of cultural autonomy, G. Brunner, *supra* n. 10, 131–139.

54. For example, note the treaties between Germany and several of its neighbouring states, or between Hungary and Slovenia. See also G. Brunner, *supra* n. 10, at 72 and at 110.

55. M. Gomez, *supra* n. 7, at 161.

56. See A. Eide & A. Rosas, "Economic, Social and Cultural Rights: A Universal Challenge", in A. Eide *et. al* (eds.), *Economic, Social and Cultural Rights* (1995), at 18.

57. This state concept has changed in such a way that nowadays the claims of groups and communities are based on the plurality of cultures whereas in earlier days this concept was used from a state's perspective in order to demonstrate its well organised national policy. See W. Kymlicka, *Multicultural Citizenship* (1995), at 20.

58. See the Report of the World Commission on Culture and Development, *Our Creative Diversity* (1995), at 73.

59. R. Stavenhagen, "Cultural struggles and development in Latin America", in *The Futures of Cultures* (1994), UNESCO, at 58.

60. E. Masini, "The futures of cultures: an overview", in *The Futures of Cultures*, UNESCO (1994), at 13.

61. J. Donnelly, *supra* n. 6, at 58.

62. L. Prott, *supra* n. 22, 93–106.

63. F. Coomans, *Economic, Social and Cultural Rights* (1995) *SIM Special, No. 16*, Utrecht: Netherlands Institute of Human Rights, at 22. Report commissioned by the Advisory Committee on Human Rights and Foreign Policy of the Netherlands.

64. K. Tomasevski, "Justiciability of Economic, Social and Cultural Rights", 55 *ICJ Review* (Special Issue) (1995), at 211.

65. In this Declaration the need for elaboration of an Optional Protocol to the ICESCR was stressed as well as the establishment of an international complaints system.

Furthermore, attention was given to the development of these human rights during the UN World Summit on Social Development, Copenhagen, 1995.

66. See also in this respect the Limburg Principles on the Implementation of the International Covenant on Economic, Social and Cultural Rights, reprinted in 9 *Human Rights Quarterly* (1987) 122–135.

The Challenge of State Building in the 'New' Europe

Minority Rights, Power Sharing and the Modern Democratic State

Steven Wheatley*

INTRODUCTION

In the 'New' Europe which has followed the collapse of the Soviet Empire, the question of the central authorities' relations with internal minority groups has re-emerged in many states. Violently in the former-Yugoslavia, troublesomely in many other states of Eastern and Central Europe, and of on-going concern to Western European States such as the United Kingdom, Spain and Belgium. Difficulties relating to minority groups are not caused by the existence of different identities within a given society, but arise where the authorities adopt policies which privilege one group over another, particularly in situations where the political elite – often democratically elected – exploit ethnic differences to form 'nationalistic' governments, and demonise differing ethnic groups both within and without the state. Whether this 'question of minorities' is dealt with under the banner of human/minority rights or that of conflict resolution/prevention, there is a general acceptance that a successful resolution of disputes between minority groups and the state authorities must be grounded in a human/minority rights approach. This is reflected in the adoption of a number of Conventions and Declarations on the protection of ethno-nationalist ('national') minorities,[1] and in the work of the CSCE/OSCE. Of particular note is the work of the OSCE High Commissioner on National Minorities, whose mandate places him firmly within the conflict prevention arena, and yet whose practice has focused almost exclusively upon minority rights standard setting and implementation as the method by which tensions involving national minority groups may be reduced.[2]

The importance of standard setting and implementation of minority rights provisions (particularly those on linguistic, education and cultural rights) is not to be underestimated; however, the key issue at the heart of the 'question of minorities' remains, in most instances, one of politics and not of rights. An example of this may be seen in one of the key rights demanded by national minority groups: the right to have adequate

P. Cumper and S. Wheatley (eds.), Minority Rights in the 'New' Europe, 199–216
© 1999 *Kluwer Law International. Printed in Great Britain.*

opportunities, within the education system, to be taught in the minority language or the right to learn the minority language.[3] The right is not, for obvious reasons, absolute. It is not a right which the minority group may demand from the state without reference to other relevant factors.[4] The implementation of such a right requires the establishment of separate schooling facilities, the availability of suitable qualified teachers and provision of textbooks and resources in the minority language. Consequently, the granting of the right of the minority group to be taught the minority language, and more importantly, be taught *in* the minority language, raises questions of overall state education policy, and of education priorities, in what is likely to be a situation of limited and finite financial and other resources. It is clearly important, therefore, that the international legal regime relating to minorities provides not only broad substantive norms (within which the state policy will be determined), but that it also contains a procedural aspect, allowing the minority the right to participate in the decision making process – particularly when the decision, on for example state education policy, is likely to impact upon the members of the group. The issue of national minorities, therefore, involves not only questions of human rights (and minority rights), but also issues as to the mode of governance within a multi-ethnic state.

How is the inclusion of the minority group within the decision making process to be achieved? Two dominant trends appear within international legal theory and praxis: power sharing arrangements, whereby the minority group is formally included within the government structure; and the operation of effective pluralist and participatory democracy, in which all voices are heard and the government governs in the interests of all the people. This chapter will examine both approaches, and in doing so will conclude that arguments based on ideas of power sharing must be rejected in favour of minority rights protection through the operation of a genuinely plural and participatory democracy.

POWER SHARING ARRANGEMENTS

The writings of Lijphart have articulated most persuasively what he has called 'consociational democracy', or power sharing, where membership of the government is constitutionally guaranteed to an ethnic or other minority group. Lijphart regards this as "so obviously the appropriate answer to the problems of a deeply divided (plural) society that both politicians and social scientists have repeatedly and independently re-invented and re-discovered [it]".[5] It may be noted, in this context, that Lijphart regards the terms 'deeply divided' and 'plural' as "synonyms",[6] and he consequently concludes that there are no acceptable alternatives to power sharing schemes in the resolution of minority disputes.[7] The four elements of consociational democracy are defined as follows: grand coalition (an executive in which the political leaders of all significant segments participate); segmental autonomy (the delegation of as much decision-making as possible to the separate segments); proportionality as the basic standard of political representation, civil service appointments and the allocation of public funds; and a minority veto to protect a minorities' vital interests.[8] The intention is to protect and promote the identity and interests of the minority group from the practices and policies of the government from within, that is by making the minority group a part of the government.

The approach, it must be accepted, is superficially attractive; indeed it has gained some currency in current international practice, both in the debates as to the future constitutional arrangements in Northern Ireland,[9] and in the actual government of Bosnia-Herzegovina agreed at Dayton.[10] These are, though, highly exceptional circumstances where constitutional re-ordering may be appropriate in an attempt to end on-going inter-ethnic strife, and may properly be regarded as attempts at conflict resolution, not constitution making; a sign of the failure of democracy in a multi-ethnic State, not of its success.

Whilst regional government, appropriate autonomy and subsidiarity is to be commended, this should not be confused with a constitutional reordering intended to reflect ethnic differences within the State. Neither the ethnic 'cantonisation' of a multi-ethnic State nor any form of 'consociational democracy' is appropriate. Such schemes are misguided, and in the long term unhelpful, as they explicitly discriminate between groups on grounds like religion, language, race and national origin; moreover, they treat individuals within the given society as less than equals and are contrary to the principle of self-determination for all peoples. Power sharing schemes are concerned with the rights of groups, not the rights of individuals.[11]

In an age of human rights where "[a]ll human beings are born free and equal in dignity and rights",[12] we are aware that certain individuals, because of their membership of a particular national or ethnic group, are less able to pursue their own concept of the 'good life' than others. They are, in this context, 'born less equal'. Such a recognition does not, it is contended, validate or legitimate positive discrimination, either in terms of consti-tutional restructuring, or in other contexts,[13] to remedy the injustices of the past.[14] Such an approach is incompatible with the prevailing individualist ethos which has informed the discourse on human rights and minority rights, which rejects equality of outcome (the statistically balanced distribution of the social goods of a given society amongst the constituent groups of that society). The individualistic approach insists that issues of discrimination are dealt with through provisions on non-discrimination and equality of opportunity, with the eventual aim of equality of outcome achieved but not legislated for. To legislate for such an outcome would place the rights of the group (to equality of outcome) above those of the individual (to equality of treatment and opportunity).

This is not to suggest that the group has no place in the present discourse. Pluralist and participatory democracy, properly understood, does not view us as abstracted individuals, but as members of groups with a plurality of interests (including membership of a particular ethnic, racial, religious or linguistic group). Any procedure which singles out one of those attributes, to discriminate in a person's favour, or discriminate against them, treats that person as less than an individual, as does any scheme which views us only as individuals and not as members of particular groups. Power-sharing schemes, involving the ethnic groups within a state, would treat all members of that society as less than individuals, taking a paternalistic approach to the privileged minority, and discriminating against a resentful majority.

The right of the population of a given state to determine the form of government for that state is expressed in legal terms as the right of a people to self-determination. The right is a fundamental one, the violation of which may entail international criminal responsibility.[15] The right grants all peoples the right to "determine their political status and freely pursue their economic, social and cultural development".[16] Self-determination is an ongoing right which may be exercised by the relevant people at any and all points in time.[17] Any proposed scheme which provides for constitutionally entrenched power-sharing, or minority vetoes, substitutes self-determination for pre-determination,[18] and is unacceptable. In such circumstances, it is not the people who are determining the governance of the State (and which groups are to be involved[19]), but those who conclude the constitutional arrangement, who fix, for all time, the groups that are to share power.[20]

MINORITY RIGHTS AND DEMOCRATIC GOVERNANCE

Democracy on the face of things, popularly regarded as reflecting the will of the majority, may, on initial inspection, appear to provide little comfort for a minority group seeking to protect its identity in the face of a dominant and often hostile majority, and the government which (in the eyes at least of the minority) represents that majority. Yet, the European Ministers of Justice confirmed, at an informal meeting in June 1993, that pluralist democracy, human rights and the rule of law are, "the prerequisites for any possible solution to the problems posed by national minorities".[21] The declaration confirms that the operation of a democratic government should not subvert or challenge our concept of human or minority rights; a democratic state is obliged to implement effectively human rights to all its citizens, and appropriate minority rights to persons belonging to national minorities. Such rights provide the parameters for the political discourse within a democracy, providing the grounds upon which the political debate may legitimately be held and framing the context within which arguments may be formed. For example, no state may adopt assimilationist policies, which are forbidden under international law.[22] Political discourse on the desirability of such policies would be deemed illegitimate by international standards. Other minority rights norms accept the need to find an acceptable balance between the demands of the group and those of the wider community; for example, the UN Declaration on Minorities (1992) provides that "States should take appropriate measures so that . . . persons belonging to minorities may have adequate opportunity to learn their mother tongue or to have instruction in their mother tongue"[23] without elaborating the circumstances in which the provision of minority language tuition, or the establishment of separate minority language education institutions, would be appropriate – which would in any case, vary from situation to situation. The question, therefore, remains one of state policy on education to be determined by the authorities within the parameters provided by international minority rights norms: the state should take *appropriate* measures to ensure *adequate* opportunity for minorities to learn their language or to have instruction in it. It is, consequently, of crucial importance that the members of those groups are able to participate in the decision-making process, following which the state will adopt its policy with respect to education and minority language provision.

A general right to political participation[24] is contained in Article 25 of the International Covenant on Civil and Political Rights 1966[25] which provides that all citizens enjoy, without distinction as to race, colour . . . language, religion, political or other opinion (or) national (origin), the right "(a) to take part in the conduct of public affairs, directly or through freely chosen representatives; (b) to vote and to be elected at genuine periodic elections guaranteeing the free expression of the will of the electors". The right is self-evidently a treaty obligation, but it has also been claimed as a general rule of customary international law.[26] In the 'New' Europe the right is reflected in the work of the Council of Europe and in the Copenhagen Document of the Organisation for Security and Co-Operation in Europe,[27] and may at the very least be considered a regional custom.[28]

Whilst of general application to all citizens, the Human Rights Committee, in its General Comment on Article 25, has concluded that the right " . . . may require positive legal measures of protection to ensure the effective participation of members of the national minority in decisions which effect them".[29] Yet it is the operation of pluralist democracy, which allows all groups the freedom to enter the open market-place of ideas – where the most valuable and convincing proposals, best suited to the furtherance of the common interest, will be recognised and will prevail – which provides the potential for a "tyranny of the majority".[30] Under the traditional model of democracy, no special measures are required by the state to take into account the demands of a multi-ethnic society, in which an ethnically or linguistically distinct majority and minority must co-exist; nor is the state required to create the institutional framework for political debate, open paths to political participation which would otherwise be blocked,[31] or assure that all groups enjoy an equal ability to propagate their views. Liberal democracy, traditionally understood, allows all groups the right to compete freely for the advancement of their particular ideas and opinions.

This view of pluralist democracy is inappropriate in a multi-ethnic State. It is insufficient merely to allow the national minority the freedom to compete for resources in the face of a majority able to outvote and outbid it.[32] Truly democratic and pluralist government cannot equate the role of government with that of the 'coat holder' in some conflict awaiting for the loudest and most compelling claim to emerge. The State is not the " . . . referee in group conflict . . . [but the] custodian of the consensus".[33] As the *preamble* to the Framework Convention for the Protection of National Minorities (1994) notes: " . . . a pluralist and genuinely democratic society should not only respect the ethnic, cultural, linguistic and religious identity of each person belonging to a national minority, but also create appropriate conditions enabling them to express, preserve and develop this identity . . . .".[34]

The right to political participation, consequently, demands democratic government based on the consent of the people as a whole, in conformity with the principles of the Covenant on Civil and Political Rights.[35] Genuine pluralist democracy involves not a 'free for all', but a regulated competition for economic, political and social goods to ensure that, in general, the decisions of the government reflect the needs, desires and aspirations of all the people. The ultimate objective of the right to free elections and political participation, as the European Commission on Human Rights indicated in the *Greek* case, " . . . is not 'democracy' but a 'democratic society'. In a 'democratic society', the majority has regard to the interests of all groups and people in the state, not merely those of its supporters".[36]

DEMOCRATIC GOVERNMENT

In many ways the right to political participation is inherent in the right of all peoples to *internal* self-determination.[37] The continuing right to internal self-determination, for the people as a whole within the state, is guaranteed by the requirement in Article 25 (ICCPR) that all citizens enjoy the right to "vote and to be elected" at genuine periodic elections, guaranteeing them the right to " . . . freely determine their political status and freely pursue their economic, social and cultural development".[38] Beyond the principle of one person, one vote, no particular electoral system is prescribed by either the International Covenant on Civil and Political Rights or Article 3 of the First Protocol of the European Convention on Human Rights. The state is consequently granted a wide margin of discretion as to the electoral system it chooses,[39] provided that the system chosen is compatible with the rights protected by Article 25, in that it guarantees the free expression of the will of the electorate.

The state may, therefore, not distort the will of the electorate to favour the majority in terms of representation (through the method by which electoral boundaries are drawn up or votes are allocated[40]), although the fact that the majority population achieves a dominant position within a fair electoral system will not invalidate that system, except, arguably, where the operation of the system causes the permanent exclusion of a national minority group from electoral representation.[41] The state may, though, conversely, through its choice of electoral system (for example by adopting a system of proportional representation rather than 'first past the post') seek to ensure that minority groups are represented within the legislature, without violating the rights of the majority population, as such a 'distortion' of the electoral system would be intended to provide a more accurate representation of the 'will of the people' (taken as a whole), and would not be contrary to the right of all citizens to political participation, nor the people as a whole to self-determination.

PLURALIST DEMOCRACY

With the collapse of the socialist one party State as an effective force in world politics, it is generally accepted that the right to vote presupposes democratic pluralism – a choice of candidates, and the right to stand for election and form a political opposition.[42] These are the " . . . distinctive criterion of every truly democratic society . . .".[43] Any restriction on the choice of candidates must, therefore, be justified on objective and reasonable criteria.[44]

In the modern democratic state, the right to seek elective office further presupposes the right to stand as a member of a political party. Such a right provides the opportunity for the individual, in association with others, to seek to have common opinions and values reflected in the political decisions of the state[45] and is an " . . . essential [condition] for the effective exercise of the right to vote . . .".[46] For the members of the national minority group, however, existing national political parties may seem an inappropriate avenue through which to advance their opinions, values and beliefs; indeed the national parties may be closely associated with the majority population, and previous, and indeed present, discriminatory practices and policies. Consequently, individuals belonging to national minority groups may seek to establish ethnic parties or parties formed on the basis of religious affiliation. Such a development raises important questions as it is seemingly contrary to the precepts of a pluralist democratic society, in that the parties formed would seek to advance claims on the basis of belonging (to the ethnic group), and not on the basis of ideas and values. On the other hand, to require a national minority, disadvantaged in terms of numbers, to further weaken its electoral appeal by splitting into the differing political strands for the purposes of electoral representation would not be acceptable. Moreover, the Human Rights Committee has accepted that, in general, a party should not be excluded from the electoral process because of the opinions or policies which it advances,[47] unless the exercise of that right to political participation would have the effect of violating the rights of others persons.[48]

Accepting that members of a national minority group enjoy the right to form and operate ethnic or religions parties leaves open one interesting point. Given that all peoples enjoy a right to self-determination under Article 1 of the International Covenant on Civil and Political Rights and, further, that the rights in the Covenant may not be exercised in such a way so as destroy the rights and freedoms of others,[49] it must be potentially legitimate for the state to prohibit or exclude from the electoral process ethnic or religious parties demanding, *as a right*, separatism or independence from the state, as incompatible with a proper interpretation of the right to self-determination (which does not permit the alteration of internationally recognised borders or justify secessionist claims),[50] given that such claims would *prima facie* violate the rights of the 'people' of the state to self-determination.

Members of the minority community, therefore, enjoy the right to operate ethnic or religious parties on a temporal basis until such a the time when persons belonging to the national minority feel secure enough to participate in the public life of the state through mainstream political parties. Such an approach may be counter to the cosmopolitan instincts of many;

however, the reality remains that such ethnically based political parties enjoy the trust of their respective ethnic populations, and that faith in the civic process and democratic institutions, where parties advance themselves on the basis of ideas, will only develop over a period of time. In societies such as Northern Ireland and Estonia, where political parties are organised almost exclusively along ethnic lines, the political process must consequently and necessarily seek to be more inclusive, to ensure the effective representation of the national minority in the decision making process with the eventual aim of the creation of an effective, inclusive, civic society.

The right to pluralist democracy contains not only a substantive aspect (that is the right to stand) but also a procedural one. Pluralist democracy may only operate where there exists the free communication of information and ideas about public and political issues between citizens, candidates and elected representatives. Consequently, the "taking part" aspect of the right to political participation, the Human Rights Committee has concluded, presupposes " . . . a free press and other media able to comment on the public issues . . . [the] freedom to debate public affairs, to hold peaceful demonstrations and meetings, to criticise and oppose, to publish political material, to campaign for election and to advertise political ideas".[51] In this context the state is obliged not interfere with the right of the minority group to gain access to the media, and is required to facilitate the access of such groups to encourage as wide a political debate as possible within the media, where public opinion is formed and re-enforced. Whilst such a recognition of the need for pluralist civic debate is to be commended, it makes no allowance for the differing extent to which groups within society have traditionally been, and currently are, able to gain access to both local and national media, and the fact that the opinions and beliefs of national minority groups have traditionally been excluded from the mainstream media, or regarded as esoteric or peripheral.

The Council of Europe's Framework Convention requires, in the context of access to, and ownership of, the media, that the licensing of radio and television broadcasting be undertaken on objective criteria and without discrimination against national minority groups;[52] that persons belonging to the national minority be granted the possibility of creating and using their own media; and further prohibits (beyond the normal restrictions imposed upon all publishers) State Parties from hindering the creation and use of the printed media by persons belonging to the national minority.[53] This granting of a right of opportunity of ownership to the national minority group is not, though, complemented by a right to substantive inclusion: that national minority opinions should be reflected within the mainstream media with the aim of promoting a pluralist society. Nor does the Framework Convention mandate 'adequate' access for the national minority to the media, beyond a general obligation to " . . . adopt measures in order to facilitate access to the media for persons belonging to national minorities and in order to promote tolerance and permit cultural pluralism".[54] This absence of a clear positive obligation to promote pluralism, through the access of national minority cultural values and beliefs to the media, may be of particular concern given the acceptance by the European Commission on Human Rights that certain national minority groups (where engaged in anti-democratic activity, an example of which may include violent campaigns for secession) may be excluded from the national media.[55]

PARTICIPATORY DEMOCRACY

Governments, elected by the majority, are likely to reflect the interests of that majority. This may be true, or at the very least perceived, both in the formulation of policy and in its application, for example in the apportioning of school funding or the provision of Government spending to different regions. The right to "take part" in Article 25 requires that interested parties (including individuals belonging to the national minority) enjoy the right to seek to influence the conduct of all aspects of public administration, and the formulation and implementation of policy at the international, national, regional and local level.[56] The Framework Convention on National Minorities requires that state parties create the ". . . conditions necessary for the effective participation of persons belonging to the national minorities in cultural, social and economic life and *in public affairs, in particular those affecting them*".[57] To this end the Explanatory Report to the Framework Convention suggests measures which the state *may* adopt to ensure the effective participation of the national minority: *inter alia*, consultation by the state with members of national minorities through representative institutions when the state is contemplating administrative or legislative measures likely to have a direct effect on the national minority; involving the national minority in the preparation and implementation of regional development activity likely to affect them; and allowing effective participation by persons belonging to the national minority into the decision making process at national and regional level.[58]

The measures provided for in the Explanatory Report are consistent with an increasing recognition by the international community that questions relating to the national minority issue may only be resolved satisfactorily by the full and effective inclusion of persons belonging to the national minority in the political life of the state, and that such full and effective inclusion may only be achieved through some formal mechanism. To this end the Geneva Meeting of Experts Report of 1991 commended the establishment of " . . . appropriate democratic participation of persons belonging to national minorities or their representatives in decision-making or consultative bodies [as] an important part of effective participation in public affairs",[59] whilst the OSCE High Commissioner on National Minorities has called for the establishment of ". . . specialised organ[s] with adequate minority representation and participation . . . [with] real competencies with regard to legislation touching upon minority issues . . . ".[60] The purpose of such a body would be to establish a 'visible policy of dialogue' to ensure that rumours and speculation about prospective administrative and legislative decisions are not able to cause friction and dispute.

Such measures, it is contended, reflect a general acceptance that a successful resolution of tensions between the state and minority groups demands the effective operation of democratic pluralism, and not the introduction of any entrenched power-sharing scheme. The right to political participation, and in particular the right to "take part", does not prescribe one particular mechanism through which persons belonging to the national minority group may participate in the public life of the state, but it does demand that the right be effectively implemented. The conclusions of the international bodies concerned with the protection of the rights of persons belonging to national minorities suggest that such a right will not be effectively implemented, at least for the larger national minorities, in the absence of some formal mechanism through which the national minority may be consulted on proposed and existing Government policy.

Such mechanisms will inevitably vary from state to state, depending upon the constitutional history and institutions of that state; examples of such practice include the following: a National Commissioner on Ethnic and Language Questions to consider complaints and act as a conduit for information between the Government and the national minority in Estonia and Latvia; a specialist minorities office in Albania to have regular consultations with representatives of the Greek minority; a Round Table in the Slovak republic consisting of representatives of all national minorities groups; and, in Kazakstan, an Assembly of the Peoples of Kazakstan to report directly to the President. One should not, however, be complacent in the face of the establishment of such formal institutions. Where such mechanisms are utilised it is important that they are effective in carrying out the tasks which they are given. Many of these institutions are, at present, ineffectual 'window dressing' exercises intended to convince the wider international community that the state in question is serious about resolving tensions relating to its internal minorities; they do, however, present a potential vehicle through which the formal inclusion of the minority may be effectively achieved in the future.

The "taking part" aspect of the human right to political participation is programmatic in nature, and the full realisation of the effective right for persons belonging to national minorities will inevitably evolve over a period of time. Consequently, the development of appropriate mechanisms for the inclusion of the national minority in the political life of the state will be achieved progressively as the relationship between the central authorities and the national minority develops, reflecting their differing relationships and, in particular, the level of tensions and any associated violence involved in that relationship. Those states in which the relationship is most fraught, where there exists the greatest need to inculcate the national minority into the political process, will consequently, and inevitably, move at a slower pace towards full inclusion.

AUTONOMY AND LOCAL GOVERNMENT

It is not suggested that political participation and the operation of a pluralist and participatory democracy will solve all minority issues. The operation of an effective legal system,[61] and appropriate autonomy and subsidiarity are crucial. Many problem issues relating to minorities are created as a result of the disenfranchisement of the members of the minority group from the political process – or at the very least a *feeling* of disenfranchisement. It is clearly of vital importance that minorities enjoy some 'ownership' over the decision-making process, in particular where the decision is likely to impact upon the group. The group may still not receive funding for minority language schools, or what it considers to be adequate resources, but at least the decision will not be one taken by anonymous bureaucrats and politicians in distant places, but by officials with whom the group may have dealings with.

Most modern democratic state's devolve a certain amount of power to regional and local government, although it is to be remembered that a national minority group does not enjoy the right to self-determination but the right to self-realisation. Such groups do not enjoy the *right* to regional or local government, unless it may be demonstrated that the culture and identity of the group " . . . is closely associated with territory",[62] and autonomy is the only means by which the protection and promotion of the group's identity may be ensured; or alternately, where the group can demonstrate that, in fact, it constitutes an internal people with the right to self-determination and the "political institutions necessary to allow [it] to exist and develop according to [its] distinctive characteristics . . . ".[63]

There is a recognition by the relevant international institutions of the need to increase local democracy as a method by which the rights of national minorities may be protected. For example, the Council of Europe's European Charter of Local Self-Government (1985) calls for local authorities to be able to "regulate and manage a substantial share of public affairs under their own responsibility and in the interests of the local population (Article 3 (1))";[64] whilst the OSCE has called for persons belonging to national minorities to be allowed effective participation in public affairs, with the Copenhagen Declaration *noting* the efforts made by states to establish appropriate ". . . local or autonomous administrations";[65] and finally, the High Commissioner on National Minorities has indicated the importance of granting to national minorities powers of local government and autonomy, particularly in the fields of education and culture.[66]

The introduction of such autonomous regimes is increasingly recognised as one method by which disputes between differing peoples and groups may be resolved, both in international practice[67] and within the international institutions dealing with questions relating to minorities and minority rights. Most significantly, Recommendation 1201 of the Council of Europe's Parliamentary Assembly provides:

> In the regions where they are in a majority the persons belonging to a national minority shall have the right to have at their disposal appropriate local or autonomous authorities or to have a special status, matching the specific historical and territorial situation and in accordance with the domestic legislation of the state (Article 11).[68]

The resolution has no legal effect, and cannot be taken as implying a collective right of the national minority group to local government or autonomy where the state does not, itself, recognise such collective rights. In the words of the OSCE High Commissioner on National Minorities, it "cannot be interpreted as imposing a legal obligation . . . to introduce territorial autonomy on an ethnic basis".[69] Provisions on regional autonomy and the devolving of powers over local government remain at the discretion of the state, and any such measures must be seen as *ad hoc* arrangements in response to particular circumstances.

CONCLUSION

Participatory democracy requires dialogue, both within the civic society and between all aspects of that society and the government. The obligation of the government is not simply to listen, but to consult proactively with the relevant groups. Within such a democratic system the national minority group must be incorporated fully within the political life of the state, allowing it to advance its own interests and concerns ensuring that polices and practices determined by relevant authorities reflect the interests of the people as a whole (including the national minority), and that procedural deficiencies do not undermine public confidence in the fairness of decisions.

In the case of the larger minority groups this consultation should be formalised, and whilst the process cannot, and should not, guarantee a proportional allocation of social goods and public funding (as that relates to equality of outcome), any significant deviation from the appropriate ratio would indicate the existence of discriminatory practices within the system which the group could challenge, and answers about which the government would be required to give. Whilst the international community grants a wide margin of appreciation to states in the mechanisms which they may choose to introduce for the effective inclusion of persons belonging to the national minority, they have, as a minimum, recognised the importance of the *procedural* right of minority groups to inclusion in the decision making process; a right as important, and in some ways more important, than the substantive minority rights discourse considered elsewhere in this collection.

NOTES

*Senior Lecturer, Department of Legal Studies, University of Central Lancashire.

1. See, for example, the United Nations General Assembly Declaration on the Rights of Persons Belonging to National or Ethnic, Religious and Linguistic Minorities (1992) GA Res. 47/135, 18 December 1992; see, also, the Council of Europe's Framework Convention on the Rights of National Minorities 34 *ILM* (1995) 351. The Framework Convention was opened for signature on 1 February 1995, coming into force, 1 February, 1998. As of 20 July 1998, the following States had ratified the Convention: Austria, Croatia, Cyprus, the Czech Republic, Denmark, Estonia, Finland, Germany, Hungary, Italy, Liechtenstein, Malta, Moldova, Romania, San Marino, Slovakia, Slovenia, Spain, 'the former Yugoslav Republic of Macedonia', Ukraine, and the United Kingdom.
2. See, generally, Foundation on Inter-Ethnic Relations, *The Role of the High Commissioner on National Minorities in OSCE Conflict Prevention: An Introduction* (1997).
3. See, for example, Article 4 (3), United Nations General Assembly Declaration on Minorities, *supra* n. 1: "States should take appropriate measures so that, wherever possible, persons belonging to minorities may have adequate opportunities to learn their mother tongue or to have instruction in their mother tongue".
4. Unlike, for example, the freedom from torture (Article 7, International Covenant on Civil and Political Rights (1966)), which the state must ensure irrespective of the financial implications.
5. A.Lijphart, "Self-determination versus Pre-Determination of Ethnic Minorities in

Power Sharing Systems", in W.Kymlicka (ed.), *The Rights of Minority Cultures* (1995) 275, at 275.

6.   *Ibid.*, at 276.
7.   The alternatives (according to Lijphart's arguments) are: (i) accepting the impossibility of workable democracy in a heterogeneous society, or (ii) a peaceful pluralist democracy only where one of the ethnic parties holds a permanent and stable 'democratic' majority (for which we are given the example of Northern Ireland between 1921–1972, in which the Protestants maintained control over the devolved government of Northern Ireland). *Ibid.*, at 277.
8.   *Ibid.*, at 277–8.
9.   See C. Bell, "Minority Rights and Conflict Resolution in Northern Ireland", (this work); see also the 'Agreement reached in the multi-party negotiations (the Good Friday Accord)', which establishes a power sharing regime for Northern Ireland: http://www.nio.gov.uk.
10. General Framework Agreement for Peace in Bosnia and Herzegovina (1995), reprinted 35 *ILM* (1996) 75; see, generally, J. Mertus, "The Dayton Peace Accords: Lessons From the Past and for the Future", (this work).
11. V. van Dyke, "The Individual, the State, and Ethnic Communities in Political Theory", in W. Kymlicka (ed.), *The Rights of Minority Cultures* (1995) 31, at 31.
12. Article 1, Universal Declaration of Human Rights, adopted by the General Assembly of the United Nations, resolution 217A (III) of 10 December, 1948.
13. That is not to suggest that international law does not legitimise positive discrimination in the case of national minorities. See, for example, Article 4 of the Framework Convention, *supra* n. 1: "(2) The Parties undertake to adopt, where necessary, adequate measures in order to promote, in all areas of economic, social, political and cultural life, full and effective equality between persons belonging to a national minority and those belonging to the majority. In this respect, they shall take due account of the specific conditions of the persons belonging to national minorities. (3) The measures adopted in accordance with paragraph 2 shall not be considered to be an act of discrimination". It is important to note, however, that such measures are to be of a temporary and limited nature, intended to ensure both *de jure* and *de facto* equality of opportunity for members of the minority group to which the measure is applied, and not to ensure equality of outcome for such groups.
14. cf. V. van Dyke, *supra* n. 11, at 50.
15. Article 19(3)b International Law Commission Draft Articles on State Responsibility (1980) *ILC YbK*, Vol. II, part II, 26.
16. Common Article 1, The International Covenant(s) on Civil and Political Rights, and Economic, Social and Cultural Rights (1966); on the differing interpretations given to the right to self-determination, see F. Kirgis, "The Degrees of Self-Determination in the United Nations Era", 88 *American Journal of International Law* (1994) 304.
17. Human Rights Committee General Comment 25 (57). Adopted by the Committee at its 1510th Meeting, U.N. Doc. CCPR/C/21/Rev.1/Add.7 (1996) (hereafter General Comment 25 (57)), para 2.
18. cf. A.Lijphart, "Self-determination versus Pre-Determination of Ethnic Minorities in Power Sharing Systems", in W.Kymlicka, *The Rights of Minority Cultures* (1995) 275, at 276.
19. Such a situation is to be distinguished from situations involving power sharing agreements concluded subsequent to an election, where those representatives elected by the

people may conclude power-sharing arrangements, but which, crucially, the electorate have the right to alter/remove at subsequent elections.

20. On the tendency of such arrangements to produce corrupt and inefficient forms of government, see J. Mertus, *supra* n. 10.
21. Lugano, 22 June 1993, quoted in P. Thornberry and M. Estebanez, *The Council of Europe and Minorities*, Council of Europe, CoEMIN (1994), at 15–16.
22. See, for example, Article 5(2) of the Framework Convention, *supra* n. 1: "Without prejudice to measures taken in pursuance of their general integration policy, the Parties shall refrain from policies or practices aimed at assimilation of persons belonging to national minorities against their will and shall protect these persons from any action aimed at such assimilation".
23. UN Declaration on Minorities, *supra* n. 1, at Article 4(3).
24. See, generally, G. Fox, "The Right to Political Participation in International Law", 17 *Yale Journal of International Law* (1992) 539; and, H. Steiner, "Political Participation as a Human Right", 1 *Harvard Human Rights Yearbook* (1988) 77.
25. 999 UNTS 171, UKTS (1977) 6, Cmnd. 6702.
26. G. Fox, *supra* n. 24, at 539.
27. Document of the Copenhagen Meeting of the Conference on the Human Dimension of the CSCE (1990), 29 *ILM* (1990) 1318.
28. *Asylum Case* (Colombia -v- Peru) (1950) I.C.J. Rep. 266; although, it may be noted that the analogous right contained in Article 3 of the First Protocol (1952) of the European Convention for the Protection of Human Rights and Fundamental Freedoms (1950) only provides for State Parties to ". . . hold free elections at reasonable intervals . . . (to) ensure the free expression of the opinion of the people . . .", and not a right to "take part" more generally.
29. General Comment 25 (57), *supra* n. 17, para 7.
30. G. Fox, *supra* n. 24, at 595.
31. H. Steiner, *supra* n. 24, at 109–110.
32. R. Mullerson, *International law, Rights and Politics* (1994), at 116.
33. P. Craig, *Public Law and Democracy* (1990), at 61.
34. Framework Convention, *supra* n. 1.
35. General Comment 25 (57), *supra* n. 17, para 1.
36. D.J. Harris, *et al.*, *Law of the European Convention on Human Rights* (1995), at 550, commenting on the findings of the Commission in the Greek case (12 YB (the *Greek* case) 1, at 179) on Article 3 of the First Protocol of the ECHR.
37. See, generally, A. Cassese, *Self-Determination of Peoples* (1995), at 101–140.
38. Common Article 1, *supra* n. 16.
39. D. J. Harris *et al.*, *supra* n. 36, at 551.
40. General Comment 25 (57), *supra* n. 17, para 21.
41. See *Mathieu-Mohin -v- Belgium* A 113 (1987), where the majority of the European Court of Human Rights found no violation of Article 3 of the First Protocol, where a French speaker elected to the Halle-Vilvoorde French speaking district in Brussels was forced to choose between being a member of the French group in the national or regional assembly. A minority in the Court disagreed, providing a decision which ". . . might suggest a positive obligation to provide for minority representation, independently of any question of discrimination", (D. J. Harris *et al.*, *supra* n. 36, at 554–5). In *Liberal Party et al. -v- United Kingdom No 8765/79* 4 EHRR (1982) 106, concerning the 'first past the post' system of apportioning seats in the United Kingdom, the European Commission on Human Rights considered that where it is evident that

a minority religious or ethnic group will never be represented in the legislature 'because there was a clear pattern of voting along these lines in the majority', then the minority would suffer discrimination as a result, even though the members of the minority population enjoyed the same rights as the rest of the population.

42. General Comment 25 (57), *supra* n. 17, para 15.
43. C. Tomuschant, "Democratic Pluralism: The Right to Political Opposition", in A. Rosas and A. Helgesen (eds.), *The Strength of Diversity: Human Rights and Pluralist Democracy* (1992) 27, at 27.
44. *W, X, Y and Z -v- Belgium Nos. 6745/74, 6746/74,* 2 DR 110 (1975).
45. C. Tomuschant, *supra* n. 43, at 29–32.
46. General Comment 25 (57), *supra* n. 17, para 12.
47. *Ibid.,* para 17.
48. Article 5(1) of the International Covenant on Civil and Political Rights 1966 provides: "Nothing in the present Covenant may be interpreted as implying for any State, group or person any right to engage in any activity or perform any act aimed at the destruction of any of the rights and freedoms recognized herein or at their limitation to a greater extent than is provided for in the present Covenant".
49. *Ibid.*
50. See, generally, A. Pellet, "The Opinions of the Badinter Arbitration Committee – A Second Breadth for the Self-Determination of Peoples", 3 *European Journal of International Law* (1992) 178.
51. General Comment 25 (57), *supra* n. 17, para 26.
52. Framework Convention, *supra* n. 1, Article 9(2).
53. *Ibid.,* Article 9(3).
54. *Ibid.,* Article 9(4).
55. *Purcell -v- Ireland No 15404/89* 70 DR 262 (1991).
56. General Comment 25 (57), *supra* n. 17, para 5; see also The United Nations Declaration on Minorities (1992), *supra* n.1, which provides: "Persons belonging to minorities have the right to participate effectively in decisions on the national and, where appropriate, regional level concerning the minority to which they belong or the regions in which they live, in a manner not incompatible with national legislation" (Article 2(3)).
57. Article 15, *emphasis added.*
58. Explanatory Report on the Framework Convention for the Protection of National Minorities, Council of Europe H(94)10, Strasbourg, November 1994, para 80.
59. Section III, Geneva Meeting of Experts Report 1991.
60. Letter from HCNM to Slovak Republic, Reference No. 2556/94/L (20 June 1994); see also, Letter(s) from HCNM to Estonia and Latvia, Reference Nos. 238/93/L/Rev and 206/93/L/Rev (6 Apr. 1993).
61. Document of the Copenhagen Meeting on the Human Dimension, para. 30, *supra* n. 27; see also the International Covenant on Civil and Political Rights: ". . . any persons whose rights or freedoms as herein recognised are violated shall have an effective remedy . . . [States shall] develop the possibility of judicial remedy . . ." (Article 2(3)).
62. CCPR/C/Rev. 1/Add, 5, *adopted* 26 April 1994, *General Comment No. 23 on Article 27* of the Covenant by the ICCPR Committee on Human Rights.
63. A. Anaya, "The Capacity of International Law to Advance Ethnic or Nationality Rights Claims", 75 *Iowa Law Review* (1990) 837, at 842.
64. ETS 122.

65. Document of the Copenhagen Meeting on the Human Dimension, para. 35, *supra* n. 27.
66. Letter from HCNM to Slovak Republic, Reference No. 2556/94/L (June 20, 1994).
67. See, for example, the Israel-Palestinian Accord 33 *ILM* (1994) 622; see, generally, J. Rehman, "The Concept of Autonomy and Minority Rights in Europe", (this work).
68. Parliamentary Assembly of the Council of Europe, Forty-Fourth Ordinary Session, Recommendation 1201 (1993), on an additional protocol on the rights of national minorities to the European Convention on Human Rights.
69. Letter of HCNM to Slovak Republic, Reference 414/96/L (26 Feb. 1996).

The Concept of Autonomy and Minority Rights in Europe

Javaid Rehman*

INTRODUCTION

The rights to 'existence' and to 'identity' form the essential core of minority rights under contemporary international law.[1] However, neither general international law nor regional custom accords minorities a right to 'autonomy', 'self-government' or 'self-determination'.[2] The subject of autonomy, nonetheless, forms a vital piece in the complex jigsaw in which the minority rights regime operates at the national and international levels. Minorities and indigenous peoples claim a right to autonomy. Governments, on the other hand, are reticent to acknowledge the legitimacy of any such claims viewing autonomy as the first step towards self-determination, rebellion and possibly secession.[3]

Perceived largely as a phenomenon of political expediency, autonomy has hitherto remained a neglected area of international legal scholarship. However, the proliferation of conflicts involving minorities and indigenous peoples has led not only to a re-evaluation of the rights of minorities in international law but also to an increasing interest amongst international lawyers in utilising the concept of autonomy as a mechanism of dispute resolution.[4]

This chapter puts forward the view that while there remain serious difficulties in establishing autonomy *as a right* of minorities and indigenous peoples at the international and regional levels, recent legal developments point to movement on this issue, particularly within Europe whose minorities have had a deep and significant relationship with autonomy. The contemporary relevance to issues relating to autonomy within Europe cannot be overstated; whilst claims for autonomy and self-determination have become a political reality for states that have emerged from the aftermath of Communism, claims to autonomy remain a serious issue facing the liberal democracies of Western Europe, within or outside of the European Union.[5] Europe also has a notable proportion of indigenous peoples,[6] such as the Sami peoples of Norway, Sweden and Finland who

217

P. Cumper and S. Wheatley (eds.), Minority Rights in the 'New' Europe, 217–231
© 1999 *Kluwer Law International. Printed in Great Britain.*

treat autonomy and self-determination as inalienable and fundamental rights, rights from which modern governments cannot make any derogations.

This chapter considers the conceptual difficulties surrounding the concept of autonomy. Notwithstanding the problems involved in conceptualising autonomy, some clarification is required if further progress is to made in analysing the substantive issues. The existing literature on the subject is surveyed and formulations made as to a number of guidelines around which the subsequent analysis is based. The work then examines the development of the concept of autonomy in international practice, before making some concluding remarks.

CONCEPTUAL DIFFICULTIES SURROUNDING THE DEFINITION OF AUTONOMY

The term autonomy is a combination of the Greek words *auto* meaning self and *nomas* meaning law, and as a free-ranging concept has been utilised widely by politicians, philosophers, anthropologists and lawyers.[7] Debates over its scope and meaning have continued to be extensive though often futile, validating the comment that "on no such subject has there been so much loose writing and nebulous speculation as on autonomy".[8] While within the legal discourse autonomy is generally taken to mean 'self-government' or 'self-rule', it is the articulation and specification of the concept which remains highly ambiguous and problematic. More specifically, in the context of minority rights, lawyers and jurists disagree as to the precise content of autonomy; its relationship with federalism, regionalism, devolution; and wider concepts such as self-government and self-determination.

The existing jurisprudence on the subject fails to remove the conceptual problems associated with autonomy, although it does make allowance for some tentative views to be formulated. These are as follows: first, the key variants of autonomy in the present debate are 'general, political or governmental autonomy' which is equated to 'full autonomy' or 'self-government' as against the more "restrictive types of autonomy, e.g., cultural or religious autonomy".[9] Secondly, it is only in the narrow sense that autonomy bears a relationship to ethnic, linguistic and religious minorities. Affirming this point Professor Berndhart comments:

> In a more narrow sense, autonomy has to do with the protection and self-determination of minorities. And it is in this sense that the notion of autonomy is used in modern international law.[10]

It however needs to be noted that the protection and self-determination of which Berndhart is referring to is not to be exercised in a manner which would be inconsistent with the existing norms of international law. Thus "[a]ny attempt aimed at the partial or total disruption of the national unity and territorial integrity of a country" [11] is impermissible. Therefore, in essence, the spirit of autonomy provides for minorities and indigenous populations the possibility of moving towards "meaningful internal self-determination and control over their own affairs". [12]

Finally, whatever the nature of autonomy may be, there are no fixed rules regulating the application of autonomy within the domestic framework. As Professor Berndhart notes: "[o]rganisational as well as substantive rules for autonomous entities or groups do not follow a given and uniform pattern; the particular form will depend on the specific group, on the preparedness of the majority to grant autonomous rights and on the influence of other States and the international community in general". [13] Amidst the myriad of possibilities in which autonomy could be dispensed or indeed withheld, it is vital to consider and pronounce upon each case on its merits, and within a number of differing constitutional arrangements. [14]

In the context of minority rights, a case by case analysis of the content and quality of autonomy is particularly important. From a historical, as well as a contemporary perspective, state practice has varied considerably with the application of policies of autonomy being the exception rather than the norm. Having said that, as subsequent discussion exemplifies, the existing record presents some very interesting and colourful examples of autonomy being engineered. 'Regional' or 'Territorial' autonomy, 'Communal' or 'Personal' autonomy, are all possible variants of the phenomenon.

AUTONOMY AND THE MINORITIES OF EUROPE: THE HISTORICAL PERSPECTIVE

Religious, linguistic and cultural autonomy is not an alien concept in the vocabulary of minorities in Europe. Medieval and modern European history presents many revealing instances of the granting of autonomy to religious minorities. Autonomy and the free exercise of religion, for example, was conceded to the Protestant minority of Transylvannia by the Treaty of Vienna signed in 1607 between the King of Hungary and Prince of Transylvannia. [15] Religious autonomy was also sanctioned by the Treaties of Osnabruck, [16] the Treaty of Olivia (1660), the Treaty of Nijmegen (1678), [17] the treaty of Ryswick (1697) [18] and the Treaty of Paris (1763). [19]

A vivid example of religious, cultural and linguistic autonomy was presented by the *Millet* system employed during the currency of the Ottoman empire. The key element of the system was that of concessions by the dominant Muslims allowing Jews and Christians to organise *Millets* in which they could "maintain their own laws and customs in the personal realm, operate their own courts, administer their own schools and impose taxes on their own members".[20] This generous measure of autonomy, which allowed other religions, languages and cultures to flourish, was, according to one commentator, comparable to "the application of the right of self-determination in advance of Woodrow Wilson".[21] Indeed, it was the subsequent disintegration of the *Millets* and increasing repression of minorities which diverted the political and military interests of the Great Powers of the time into the affairs of the Ottoman Empire and sanctioned its ultimate disintegration.

Concern for minority groups in Europe was also evident during the political developments in the early part of this century.[22] Territorial readjustments (as well as the imposition of minority treaties) clearly reflected the value attached by the victorious powers to engineering policies of autonomy for certain minorities in Central and Eastern Europe, the right to autonomy being deployed as a viable substitute to self-determination.[23] The interlude between the two world wars also saw a number of imaginative attempts to realise meaningful autonomy such as the Åaland Islands, the Free City of Danzing and the Memel territory.[24] On the whole, however, the mechanisms were defective, their inadequacies providing a recipe for the future disasters which befell many minority groups prior to, during the course of and indeed in the immediate aftermath, of the Second World War.[25]

AUTONOMY AND THE POST-WORLD WAR II PERIOD

The period immediately after the Second World War was to provide a radical shift in emphasis with concern for the rights of minorities being largely absorbed into the wider concern for the protection of individual human rights. This shift in emphasis was evidenced in the failure of the United Nations Charter (1945), and the Universal Declaration on Human Rights (1948)[26] to make any reference to minorities.[27] Similarly, the European Convention on Human Rights and Fundamental Freedoms (1950),[28] the leading regional human rights treaty, reflects the psychology of the time. The European Convention lacks specific provisions relating to minority rights, although Article 14 did prohibit discrimination (in the application of the rights in the Convention) on the basis of belonging to a 'national minority'.[29]

While the individualistic conceptions of human rights led to a neglect of the issue of minority rights, the political developments during the early years of United Nations created an environment unfavourable to the propagation of a right to autonomy. The rise of the Cold-War squandered any opportunity of a constructive dialogue on the subject. The Soviet led condemnations of the treatment of indigenous peoples and minorities in the Americas and Australia were, in essence, a ploy to deflect criticisms of the violation of fundamental rights within Communists states. More detrimental to the cause of minorities and indigenous peoples was the interpretation given to the right to self-determination. At the height of the decolonisation movement the wider expression of "the principle of equal rights and self-determination of peoples",[30] as enunciated by the United Nations Charter, become almost synonymous with the granting of independence to colonial entities within the framework of existing colonial boundaries. The right of all peoples to self-determination was indeed a fundamental principle of international law, a norm of *jus cogens,* but its application was limited to the people of the whole of colonial entity; minorities and indigenous peoples within independent states could not claim to be beneficiaries of the right to self-determination.

Thus, in a political environment unsympathetic to the concept of group rights, a specific right to autonomy was seen by the international community as undesirable and a threat to the established world order. States feared that such a right would be used by irredentists as a licence to fragment the existing state structures. The difficulty in accommodating claims presented by minorities and indigenous peoples was not limited to the post-colonial world of Asia and Africa. Indeed, in many ways the position in Europe was more complex than any other region. The social, political, regional, cultural, linguistic and religious peculiarities of minorities, with their varying demands and aspirations which form part of the European mosaic, produced diverse reactions in the approaches of their states.

In states operating under the oppressive and intolerant Communist apparatus the very existence of many minority groups was threatened. State practice in Western and Northern Europe promised greater diversity and in many instances, a more accommodating and reconciliatory approach was exhibited through constitutional arrangements in the nature of federalism, regionalism and devolution – culminating in generous policies of linguistic, cultural and regional autonomy for minorities. Belgium provides an excellent example of a state responding positively to demands for linguistic and cultural autonomy. As the constitutional reforms enacted in 1993 confirm, Belgium is now a Federal state made up of three communities and having four linguistic regions.[31] The power-sharing arrangements require that, except for the Prime Minister, there should be an equal number of French-speaking and Flemish-speaking ministers in the cabinet.[32] The distinction based on linguistic backgrounds has been maintained in the legislature where three-quarters of the members belonging to one of the linguistic groups having the power to suspend consideration of a bill which is "of a nature as to gravely damage relations between the communities".[33] While cultural and communal matters are within the purview of the community councils, territorial autonomy is established through regional institutions which are accountable for such matters as planning, housing, the environment and employment.[34]

Italy's response to accommodate demands put forward by advocates of regionalism has been to create five special autonomous regions with extensive powers.[35] In the context of Italy's complex constitutional anatomy, operating within a highly charged political environment, the issue of regionalism remains a controversial one. Nonetheless the introduction of autonomy has clearly produced positive results. The South Tyrol provides a notable example of how the granting of autonomy to the German-speaking South Tyrolese minority has had the desired effect of transforming a potentially explosive national and international dispute into "one of the best examples of the protection of regional and cultural minorities in the world".[36] A similar optimistic vision emerges from Spain, where after decades of struggle the 1978 Constitution recognised and guaranteed "the right to autonomy of the nationalities and regions which make up the Spanish State".[37] The induction of the Law on Regional Autonomy granted regional governments' jurisdiction over a wide range of issues. It has been claimed that the transformation of Spain from being a highly centralised nation to one on the threshold of Federalism has not only prevented serious secessionist movements (particularly in the Basque country and Catalonia) but has also contributed to the prosperity and well being of the state.[38] However, not all disputes involving minority demands of autonomy and self-determination have been resolved amicably. Indeed, issues such as the future of Northern Ireland and Cyprus have not only produced consti-tutional crises, but have also generated serious international tensions, and in the case of Cyprus the use of military force by Turkey to protect the Turkish population in the North in 1974.[39]

Differing visions of autonomy and the right to self-determination have been put forward by the protagonists in the Northern Irish conflict. Northern Ireland reflects the case of a deeply divided and highly segregated society with a history of discrimination, deprivation and exclusion of one community – the Nationalist – from political power. On the other hand efforts to redress the balance, to initiate mechanisms of power-sharing (under the Northern Ireland Constitution Act 1973), or to introduce devolved government with regional autonomy have collapsed as a consequence of the inability and unwillingness to co-operate in such attempts on the part of both the Nationalist as well as the Unionist communities.[40]

Autonomy, as it relates to the Nationalist minority in Northern Ireland, needs be seen in the context of the 1985 Anglo-Irish Agreement, which affirms the right of all the peoples of Northern Ireland to self-determination.[41] A version of autonomy which envisages a union with the Republic of Ireland would clearly be unacceptable to the majority of the population of Northern Ireland. However, if an expression of 'external' self-determination (in the sense of a change in the political status of Northern Ireland) is not available to the Nationalist minority, this does not mean that they are excluded from the self-determination process as both the minority and majority populations are contributors to the 'internal' or democratic aspect of self-determination.[42] The Anglo-Irish Agreement, the Downing Street Declaration (1993),[43] and the recent multi-party peace agreement (1998) reflect a greater recognition of the identities and traditions of the peoples of Northern Ireland. Nevertheless, further progress needs to be made in the establishment of distinct linguistic, cultural and communal rights, protection from the abuse of emergency laws, and the introduction of measures to protect the Nationalist minority in employment, housing and political representation.

The subject of minority rights continues to provoke concern in many other parts of Western Europe, although the 'ethnic cleansing' in the former Yugoslavia and the repression and persecution in many parts of Eastern Europe has provided further impetus for a reconsideration of the inadequacies of existing mechanisms. Amidst the vacuum created by the fall of Communism, the relentless resurgence of nationalism and xenophobia have increasingly jeopardised the continuing existence of vulnerable groups.[44] Furthermore, the reshaping of the map of Europe has not produced homogeneity within states. As Dunay notes, with the exception of Albania, Armenia, the Czech Republic, Hungary, Poland and Slovenia, each of the twenty eight states of Central and Eastern Europe contain significant ethnic, linguistic, religious and national minorities.[45] It is against this background the issue of autonomy must be examined.

ELEMENTS OF AUTONOMY IN RECENT INTERNATIONAL AND REGIONAL INSTRUMENTS

There exists increasing concern over the inadequacies of the existing protection of minority rights, in particular in the individualistic approach of the relevant international instruments: the Universal Declaration of

Human Rights, the International Covenant on Civil and Political Rights (1966),[46] and the International Covenant on Economic, Social and Cultural Rights (1966).[47] Whilst both the International Covenants provide for a right of all peoples to self-determination,[48] neither is favourable to the subject of minority rights. Article 27 of the International Covenant on Civil and Political Rights is the only provision which deals directly with minority rights.[49] However, notwithstanding the burden it has shouldered in terms of developing the minority right to 'identity', debate continues as to the nature of obligations created and its value in general international law.[50]

Article 27 has been reinforced by a number of more recent initiatives. The United Nations General Assembly, in its Resolution 47/135 of 18 December 1992, adopted the Declaration on the Rights of Persons Belonging to National or Ethnic, Religious and Linguistic Minorities.[51] The Declaration is a wider and more expansive expression of minority aspirations and may be taken as a concerted effort on the part of the international community to overcome some of the limitations of international law relating to the subject of minority rights,[52] including a clear recognition that persons belonging to minorities "have the right to enjoy their own culture, to profess and practise their own religion, and to use their own language, in private and in public, freely and without interference or any form of discrimination".[53] The Declaration confirms that persons belonging to minorities also have the right to participate effectively at the national or regional levels on matters which concern the relevant minority group, to establish and maintain their institutions and to retain contacts with other members of their community across international frontiers.[54] States are, further, required to "create favourable conditions to enable persons belonging to minorities to express their characteristics and to develop their culture, language, religions, traditions and customs . . .".[55]

In spite of these provisions, the Declaration cannot, by any stretch of the imagination, be seen as a giant step in the direction of autonomy for minorities. Its limitations are apparent from its standing as a General Assembly Resolution and its conservatism is obvious from its focus upon individuals or persons belonging to minorities, rather than minorities themselves.[56] There are other drawbacks including a failure to define 'minorities' and the use of term 'national', excluding from the scope of the Declaration any non-national minority groups.[57]

Many of the substantive provisions of the Declaration are framed in general and uncertain terms. States may also prevent the expression of the minority identity on the pretext of that identity being "incompatible with national legislation".[58] The Declaration, as a General Assembly Resolution, is not *per se* binding in international law, and its potential impact on the development of customary international law is unclear. The *travaux preparatoires* of the Declaration illustrate that even in respect of an instrument of hortatory character, states were reluctant to concede any collective aspect of minority rights. Concern for state sovereignty and territorial integrity resurfaced frequently and, as a consequence, attempts to incorporate the right to autonomy proved futile.[59]

Many of the difficulties which have characterised the United Nations approach towards minorities have been reflected at the regional level in the work of the Council of Europe. The European Convention on Human Rights, as the oldest and most successful of regional human rights treaties, has been at the vanguard of protecting individual human rights for nearly half a century. It is also the case that a positive construction of the provisions of the ECHR has proved to be of great value in protecting the rights of individual members of minority groups as individuals. On the other hand the substantive provisions of the Convention, as well as the jurisprudence of the Court and the Commission, reflect an inability or unwillingness to advance the cause of minorities as distinct entities. Again a refusal to recognise group rights becomes problematic.[60]

Several of the recent initiatives by the Council of Europe tend to address the subject of minorities more directly, although the lacuna in the recognition of collective group rights remains conspicuous. The Council of Europe's Framework Convention on the Rights of National Minorities 1994,[61] the first binding instrument which has an exclusive focus on minority rights, does not detract much from the path of individual rights,[62] a point reiterated in the Explanatory Report which accompanies the Convention, which notes that the Convention itself "does not imply the recognition of collective rights".[63] The Explanatory Report further points out that the issue of collective rights is separate and distinct from the issue of the enjoyment of rights by individuals who belong to minority groups.[64]

There is little in the Framework Convention for minorities from a standpoint of autonomous development. The closest the Convention comes to indulging in the issue is in Article 15, which provides that "[t]he Parties shall create the conditions necessary for the effective participation of persons belonging to national minorities in cultural, social and economic life and in public affairs, in particular those affecting them".[65] The attenuated nature of obligations contained in this article have been the subject of criticism,[66] as the provision represents a retreat from the statements already advanced in Recommendation 1201 (1993) of the Parliamentary Assembly of the Council of Europe.[67]

From the standpoint of the present discussion, another of the Council of Europe's documents, the European Charter for Regional or Minority Languages (1992),[68] deserves attention. In the controversial domain of language, the invaluable nature of the Charter cannot be denied. It deals with the use of minority languages, *inter alia*, in schools, before public authorities and the Courts, and in the media. The 1992 Charter nonetheless is designed for a limited purpose and that is what it manages to achieve, providing a limited 'undertaking' on the part of states to recognise minority languages rather than an attempt to accord specific linguistic rights to minority groups.[69]

In addition to work done by the Council of Europe, the significant contributions in the field of minority rights made by another inter-governmental organisation, the Organisation for Security and Co-operation in Europe (OSCE),[70] requires consideration.[71] The concern shown for the subject of minority rights within the OSCE stretches back to the Helsinki Final Act 1975, with further progress made during the course of the "Follow-up meetings" – including the significant Copenhagen Document,[72] which provided:

> The participating States *note* the efforts undertaken to protect and create conditions for the promotion of the ethnic, cultural, linguistic and religious identity of certain minorities by establishing, as one of the possible means to achieve these aims, appropriate local and autonomous administrations corresponding to the specific historical and territorial circumstances of such minorities and in accordance with the policies of the State concerned (Copenhagen Document, para. 35).

From the point of the development of norms relating to autonomy, the provision contains greater promise, although critics would question even this show of optimism. The states merely "note" the "efforts undertaken" in the direction of autonomy.[73] Autonomy, itself is recognised as a means to an end (i.e. protecting and creating conditions for the promotion of minority identity) and not as an end in itself. The overall contribution of the provision is further weakened when analysed in the context of the OSCE regime which, *per se*, is of a non-binding character in international law.

While occasional references have been made to indigenous claims to autonomy and self-determination, the scope of the present chapter has been limited to analysing the relationship of autonomy with minority rights. Indigenous peoples in a number of countries occupy the position of minorities, and indeed many of their demands coincide with those of the other minorities. However, there are major differences between minorities and indigenous peoples arising from distinct claims of the indigenous peoples to their historic titles to territory. Indigenous Peoples have put forward substantial claims, with the rights to autonomy and self-determination at the centre of their demands. Their key demands relate to claims for self-governance and collective property rights to land and natural resources.

In response, state practice (both in constitutional applications and in international arrangements) has been equivocal, although more recent international instruments indicate a greater recognition of autonomy claims. The ILO Convention Concerning the Protection of Indigenous and Tribal Peoples (1989)[74] provides an exhaustive catalogue of the rights of indigenous peoples. Recent initiatives within the United Nations have also looked favourably at establishing a regime of autonomy for indigenous peoples and on the national level, important developments in Australia and the Americas may contribute to the establishment of a healthy precedent from which indigenous peoples in Europe could benefit.[75]

CONCLUSIONS

Professor Josef Kunz once commented that "[h]e who dedicates his life to the study of international law in these troubled times is sometimes struck by the appearance as if there were fashions in international law just as in neckties".[76] It would appear that, at the threshold of a new millennium, the issue of collective rights for minority groups is becoming fashionable. Nevertheless the debate surrounding a proposed right to autonomy is extremely complex. The concept of autonomy involves more than a mere recognition of collective existence. The overlap between autonomy, self-governance and self-determination has led governments, fearful of generating secessionism, to resist not only claims to self-determination (including secession) but also aspirations of autonomy (within existing national boundaries). As Klebes notes:

> The sensitivity with regard to autonomy in whatever form is still very strong in quite a number of Member States of the Council of Europe. There is a widespread fear of the spiral 'cultural autonomy, administrative autonomy, secession'.[77]

There is an overlap, as well as a linkage, between autonomy and self-determination. Whilst it is possible that claims of autonomy could be transformed into radical demands of self-determination, it is also not inconceivable to foresee a reverse course of action. It may be contended that a more accommodating and conciliatory approach on the part of governments could in fact persuade many minorities and indigenous peoples to look towards autonomy within the framework of existing national boundaries rather than taking the path of confrontation, rebellion and fragmentation of existing state structures. There is, however, reason to be optimistic. International law, having exhausted the phase of 'external' self-determination, is now beginning to develop the 'internal' or democratic aspect of the right to self-determination.[78] This 'internal' aspect of self-determination places emphasis on representative and democratic government, in which members of the majority as well as those from minorities are able to participate. Democratic and representative governments are not necessarily favourable towards minorities, although there is a greater likelihood of a conciliatory and more accommodating approach on claims presented by minority groups and indigenous peoples.

NOTES

*Javaid Rehman, Law Faculty, University of Leeds. The author would like to thank Professor Clive Walker (Leeds Law Faculty) and Dr Istvan Pogany (Warwick Law School) for their encouraging and extremely helpful comments on an earlier draft of this paper.

1. See P. Thornberry, "International and European Standards on Minority Rights", in H. Miall (ed.), *Minority Rights in Europe: The Scope for a Transnational Regime* (1994) 14–21, at 20.
2. ". . . [T]he right to autonomy is not a specific right of minorities in contemporary international law": P. Thornberry *supra* n. 1, at 20; "Self-determination is not a right of minorities:" P. Thornberry, *Minorities and Human Rights Law* (1991), at 10; ". . . [M]inorities as such do not have a right to self-determination": R. Higgins, "General Course in Public International Law", *Rec. des cours,* (1991), at 170.
3. The historic and enduring nature of disputes on the part of such groups as the Kurds, the Tamils, the Southern Sudanese, the Basques and the Miskito Indians evidence this struggle between minorities on the one hand and the state authorities on the other. See Minority Rights Group (ed.), *World Directory of Minorities* (1997).
4. See H. Hannum, *Autonomy, Sovereignty and Self-Determination: The Accommodation of Conflicting Rights* (1990).
5. See Minority Rights Group (ed.), *Minorities and Autonomy in Western Europe* (1991); M. Thatcher, "A Family of Nations", in B. Nelsen and A. Stubbs (eds.), *The European Union: Readings on the Theory and Practice of European Integration* (1994) 45–50; M. Keating, "Europeanism and Regionalism", in B. Jones and M. Keating (eds.), *The European Union and the Regions* (1995) 1–22.
6. N. Vakhtin, *Native Peoples of the Russians Far North* (1992); M. Jones, *The Sami of Lapland* (1982).
7. See Y. Dinstein, "Autonomy", in Y. Dinstein (ed.), *Models of Autonomy* (1981) 291–303, at 291.
8. Cited in H. Hannum and R. Lillich, "The Concept of Autonomy in International Law", 74 *American Journal of International Law* (1980) 858, at 858.
9. H. Hannum and R. Lillich, "The Concept of Autonomy in International Law", in Y. Dinstein (ed.). *supra* n. 7, 215–254, at 218.
10. R. Berndhart, "Federalism and Autonomy", Y. Dinstein (ed.), *supra* n. 7, 23–28, at 26.
11. Article 6 of the *Declaration of the Granting of Independence to Colonial Countries and*

Peoples, United Nations General Assembly Resolution 1514 (XV) adopted on 14 December 1960.

12. H. Hannum, *supra* n. 4, at 473.
13. R. Berndhart, *supra* n. 10, at 27.
14. See C. Palley, *Constitutional Law and Minorities* (1987).
15. See P. Thornberry, *International Law and the Rights of Minorities* (1991), at 28; H. Heinz, *Indigenous Populations, Ethnic Minorities and Human Rights* (1988), at 22.
16. See L. Gross, "The Peace of Westphalia", 42 *American Journal of International Law* (1948) 20, at 22.
17. 14 *Parrys Treaty Series* 441.
18. 22 *Parrys Treaty Series* 5.
19. 42 *Parrys Treaty Series* 320.
20. See V. Van Dyke, *Human Rights, Ethnicity and Discrimination* (1985), at 74; J. A. LaPonce, *The Protection of Minorities* (1960), 84–85.
21. V. Van Dyke, *ibid.*, at 74.
22. Note, for example, President Wilson's fourteen points programme, point twelve of which declared that non-Turkish minorities of the Empire should be "assured of an absolute unmolested opportunity of autonomous development", in D. McDowall, *The Kurds* (1991), at 15–16.
23. See P. Thornberry, *supra* n. 15, at 50.
24. See H. Hannum, *supra* n. 4, 370–384.
25. See I. Claude, *National Minorities: An International Problem* (1955); J. Robinson *et al, Were the Minorities Treaties a Failure?* (1943). Indeed some states, particularly Germany, exploited the minority issue to further their own expansionist ambitions: see J. Kelly, "National Minorities in International Law", 3 *Journal of International Law and Policy* (1973) 253, at 258.
26. Adopted 10 December, 1948; General Assembly Resolution 217, UN Doc A/810, 71.
27. The *Convention on the Prevention and the Punishment of the Crime of Genocide* (1948) fails to make any reference to the term "minorities", although the provisions of the Convention clearly apply to "national, ethnical, racial or religious" minorities. For the text of the Convention see 78 *United Nations Treaty Series* 277; 58 *United Kingdom Treaty Series* (1970).
28. Adopted 4 November 1950. For the text of the Convention see 213 *United Nations Treaty Series* 221; 71 *United Kingdom Treaty Series* (1953).
29. Article 14 of the ECHR provides: "The enjoyment of the rights and freedoms set forth in this Convention shall be secured without discrimination on any ground such as sex, race, colour, language, religion, political or other opinion, national or social origin, association with a national minority, property, birth or other status".
30. See Articles 1(2) and 55 of the United Nations Charter.
31. See the Constitution of Belgium (1993) Articles 1–4; for a commentary on the constitutional reforms see J. Fitzmaurice, *The Politics of Belgium: A Unique Federalism* (1996).
32. See Article 99.
33. Article 54.
34. See Articles 127–128; for a detailed list of the responsibilities of regional institutions see Article 6 (1) of the Special Law of 8 August, 1980.
35. These regions are Sicily, Sardinia, Trentino-Alto Adige, Friuli-Venetia Julia and Valle d'Aosta. See Title V (Section 115) the Constitution of Italy, (1948).
36. See A. Alcock, "South Tyrol", in H. Miall (ed.), *supra* n. 1, 46–55, at 46.

37. Article 2 of the Constitution of Spain (1978).
38. R. Hoffman, "The New Territorial Structure of Spain: The Autonomous Communities", 55 *Nordic Journal of International Law* (1986) 136–141; H. Hannum, *supra* n. 4, 263–279.
39. Minority Rights Group (ed.), *supra* n. 3, 136–138; J. Sigler, *Minority Rights: A Comparative Analysis* (1983), at 112–113.
40. See the Northern Ireland Act 1982; B. Hadfield, "The Northern Ireland Act 1982–Do it Yourself Devolution", 33 *Northern Ireland Legal Quarterly* (1982), 301–325.
41. See Cmnd. 9657; H. Hannum (ed.), *Documents on Autonomy and Minority Rights* (1993), at 422; B. Hadfield, "The Anglo-Irish Agreement – Blue Print or Green Print", 37 *Northern Ireland Legal Quarterly* (1986) 1, at 19.
42. H. Hannum, *supra* n. 4, at 241.
43. See Cm. 2442; C. Walker, "The Downing Street Declaration: Olive Branch or Fig Leaf", 12 *Irish Law Times* (1994), 80–84.
44. See A. Rosas and J. Helgesen, "Introduction: The Challenges of Change", in A. Rosas and J. Helgesen (eds.), *The Strength of Diversity: Human Rights and Pluralist Democracy* (1992) 1–4; V. Dimitrijevi, "Political Pluralism in the aftermath of the Eastern European Upheavals", in A. Rosas and J. Helgesen (eds.), *ibid*, 5–25.
45. P. Dunay, "Nationalism and Ethnic Conflicts in Eastern Europe: Imposed, Induced or (Simply) Re-emerged", in I. Pogany (ed.), *Human Rights in Eastern Europe* (1995) 17–45, at 21.
46. UN General Assembly Resolution 2200 (XXI), GAOR 21st Session 16, 49.
47. 993 *United Nations Treaty Series* (1966).
48. See Part 1 of the International Covenants.
49. Article 27 provides: "In those States in which ethnic, religious or linguistic minorities exist, persons belonging to such minorities shall not be denied the right, in community with other members of their group, to enjoy their own culture, to profess and practice their own religion, or to use their own language".
50. See T. Modeen, *The Protection of National Minorities in Europe* (1969), at 108; C. Tomuschat, "Protection of Minorities under Article 27 of the International Covenant on Civil and Political Rights", *Volkerrecht als Rechtsordnung Internationale Gerichtbarkeit Menscherrechte Festschrift Fur Herman Mosler* (1983) 949, at 954; L. Sohn, "Protection of Minorities", in L. Henkin (ed.), *International Bill of Rights: The Covenants on Civil and Political Rights* (1981) 270–289, at 274; *cf.* Y. Dinstein, "Freedom of Religion and Protection of Religious Minorities", in Y. Dinstein and M. Tabory (eds.), *The Protection of Minorities and Human Rights* (1992) 145–170.
51. UN. Doc A/Res/47/135.
52. See B. Dickson, "The United Nations and Freedom of Religion", 44 *International and Comparative Law Quarterly* (1995) 327, at 354.
53. Article 2(1) of the Declaration.
54. See Articles 2 and 3 of the Declaration.
55. Article 4(2) of the Declaration.
56. P. Thornberry, "The UN Declaration on Minority Rights of Persons belonging to National or Ethnic, Religious and Linguistic Minorities", in A. Phillips and A. Rosas (eds.), *The UN Minority Rights Declaration* (1993) 11–71, at 27.
57. See, for example, the German Position as adopted in its statement to the Human Rights Commission working group. UN Doc E/CN. 4/1991/53, para 17.
58. See Articles 2(3) and 4(2) of the Declaration.

59. P. Thornberry, "International and European Standards on Minority Rights", in H. Miall (ed.), supra n. 1, 14–21, at 17.
60. See D. J. Harris, M. O'Boyle and C. Warbrick, *Law of the European Convention on Human Rights* (1995), at 487; S. Poulter, "The Rights of Ethnic, Religious and Linguistic Minorities", 3 *European Human Rights Law Review* (1997), 254–264.
61. For the text of the Convention see the Appendix.
62. "The Framework Convention is predicated upon the rights of individuals and not collective rights of the minority group. . .", S. Wheatley, "The Framework Convention for the Protection of Minorities", 6 *European Human Rights Law Review* (1996) 583 – 590, at 584.
63. See the *Framework Convention for the Protection of National Minorities and Explanatory Report* (1995) para 13, at 22.
64. See E. Aarnia, "Minority Rights in the Council of Europe: Current Developments", in A. Phillips and A. Rosas (eds.), *Universal Minority Rights* (1995) 123–133, at 131.
65. See Article 15.
66. Gilbert treats the provisions of Article 15 as "some what timid": G. Gilbert, "The Council of Europe and Minority Rights", 18 *Human Rights Quarterly* (1996) 160, at 186.
67. Article 11 of the Recommendation provided that: "In the regions where they are in a majority the persons belonging to a national minority shall have the right to have at their disposal appropriate local or autonomous authorities or to have a special status, matching the specific historical and territorial situation and in accordance with the domestic legislation".
68. For the text, see 14 *Human Rights Law Journal* (1993), at 152.
69. See P. Thornberry, "The United Nations Declaration on the Rights of Persons Belonging to National or Ethnic, Religious and Linguistic Minorities: Background, Analysis, Observations and an Update", in A. Phillips and A. Rosas (eds.), *supra* n. 64, 13, at 61.
70. Formerly the Conference on Security and Co-operation in Europe (CSCE).
71. See J. Wright, "The OSCE and the Protection of Minority Rights", 18 *Human Rights Quarterly* (1996) 190–205.
72. See the Copenhagen Document on the Human Dimension of the CSCE (June 1990) 11 *Human Rights Law Journal* (1990) 232.
73. P. Thornberry, "Contemporary Legal Standards on Minority Rights", in Minority Rights Group (ed.), supra n. 3, 692–705, at 698.
74. 72 *ILO* (1989) 59; 28 *ILM* (1989) 1382.
75. See P. Thornberry, "Contemporary Legal Standards on Minority Rights", in Minority Rights Group (ed.), *supra* n. 3, 692–705, at 700.
76. J. Kunz, "The Present Status of International Law for the Protection of Minorities", 48 *American Journal of International Law* (1954) 282, at 282.
77. H Klebes, "The Council of Europe's Framework Convention for the Protection of National Minorities", 16 *Human Rights Law Journal* (1995) 92, at 96.
78. See T. Franck, "The Emerging Right to Democratic Governance", 86 *American Journal of International Law* (1992) 46–91; P. Thornberry, "The Democratic or Internal Aspect of Self- Determination with some Remarks on Federalism", in C. Tomuschat, (ed.), *Modern Law of Self-Determination* (1993) 101–138.

New Nations and National Minorities: Ukraine and the Question of Citizenship

*Bill Bowring**

INTRODUCTION

Following Russia's accession to membership of the Council of Europe,[1] the 'New' Europe now reaches from the Atlantic to the Bering Straits. This 'New' Europe does not represent a merging or integration of national identities but is defined by a recognition of universal values which may be described as post-national.[2] This 'New' Europe seems, to a number of influential observers,[3] to represent a model within which nationalist conflict, ethnic cleansing and genocide may be avoided. Although the intellectual formation of these scholars could not be more disparate, their conclusions nevertheless converge to a remarkable extent. This chapter will examine this European model against a set of circumstances whose intricacies resemble the successive layers of a Russian *matrioshka* doll: the predicament of the new state of Ukraine.

Ukraine is one of a number of new states to have emerged from the ruins of the former Soviet Union. Each of these states has inherited more or less numerous minorities, and all face acute problems concerned with the incorporation of members of those minorities into a new national identity. One pressing issue is that of citizenship, with a wide variation in the policies adopted by each state in dealing with the problem. In the Baltic States, for example (particularly in Latvia), the Russian-speaking minority has effectively been excluded from citizenship and the rights associated with it.[4] In Ukraine, by contrast, the new state has adopted an inclusive approach to the question of citizenship.

This is in part because Ukraine now seeks to establish itself as an independent modern state, rather than a Russian province; witness Ukraine's accession in November 1995 to the Council of Europe and the Constitution, adopted by the *Verkhovna Rada* (Parliament) on 28 June 1996.[5]

Nevertheless, Ukraine faces a number of difficulties generated by its demographic complexity. Within Ukraine exists a large ethnic Russian population, concentrated in the eastern part of the country, and a Russian

233

P. Cumper and S. Wheatley (eds.), Minority Rights in the 'New' Europe, 233–250
© 1999 *Kluwer Law International. Printed in Great Britain.*

province (or, rather, Autonomous Republic – Crimea, whose population is 61.6 per cent ethnic Russian[6]) whose population has regularly expressed its desire for re-assimilation into Russia. Within Crimea are the Crimean Tatars,[7] a people deported *en masse* in 1944, in an act of genocide in which 40 per cent of the population died. But a people who are now returning. Three hundred thousand Crimean Tatars, more than 10 per cent of Crimea's population of some 2,500,000, have come home since 1989. Thus, there is not only a grave historical injustice to be remedied, but complex issues of citizenship, rights and obligations to be resolved. The question posed by this chapter is whether the European model, transposed into the Ukrainian legal order, is adequate to the tasks – in particular in resolving the difficulties posed by the question of citizenship for the Crimean Tatars.

PROBLEMS OF CITIZENSHIP

Problems of citizenship are once more at the 'leading edge' of constitutional and public international legal discourse. It is contended that the "nation and nationalism remain the only realistic basis for a free society of states in the modern world", and yet while nationalism is patently not a democratic or liberal movement, "the denial of nationalism's central tenets is likely to impede progress to human rights and democracy".[8] On the other hand, it has been pointed out that there is a trend towards a new model of membership, "anchored in deterritorialised notions of personal rights".[9] According to this view, the postnational model differs from the national model in three respects: first, there is a new territorial dimension of citizenship, since individuals can make claims independent of national boundaries, whether or not they have formal citizenship; second, rights and privileges are no longer linked to the single status of citizenship – there is a plurality of membership forms; and third, universal human rights are tending to replace national rights.

Much recent work on the issue of citizenship[10] seeks to update and transcend T. H. Marshall's 1949 essay on "Citizenship and Social Class".[11] Marshall, as is well known, distinguished between three types of citizenship emerging incrementally over three centuries of social struggle: civil citizenship, establishing the rights of personal freedom; political citizenship, winning the right to participate in the exercise of political power; and, social citizenship, following the establishment of the welfare state (in Western Europe), conferring the right to economic and social security. Of course, many of the characteristics which Marshall attributed to citizenship have now been enshrined as human rights, to be applied equally to citizens or non-citizens.[12]

The renovation of citizenship theory raises fundamental political and philosophical issues, including the conflict, sometimes more apparent than real, between liberals and communitarians, and the vexed question, particularly in the North American context, of multiculturalism and the politics of recognition.[13] Will Kymlicka has, more than anyone, developed a sophisticated elaboration of liberalism to take account of the human need for a 'societal culture'.[14] He asks "How can we construct a common identity in a country where people not only belong to separate political communities but also belong in different ways – that is, some are incorporated as individuals and others through membership of a group?".[15] Defending a more traditional liberalism, John Packer sharply criticises Kymlicka for permitting arguments of cultural relativism – which can lead to nationalism. Human rights, according to Packer, are necessarily liberal and individualist; any tendency to communitarianism leads to nationalism, which itself is 'inherently conflict-creating'.[16]

My own position is that social being – the ways in which groups and collectivities, in contrast to individuals, act and are acted upon – cannot be ignored. I agree with the critique by Bikhu Parekh of the very term 'minority rights':

> [T]he terms minority and majority are numerical concepts, and individualistic in their orientation and implications. Strictly speaking, they apply to individuals, not to organised groups and communities.

He gives a British example. Afro-Caribbean culture has a distinct bearer, the Afro-Caribbean people, and a distinct social basis and geographical origin. It is a product of that peoples' unique history and experience of oppression and struggle. Their community is "not a matter of choice, but one into which its adherents are born".[17] This is even more the case for the Crimean Tatars 'Nation'.

Furthermore, nationalism in the context of the former Soviet Union cannot be avoided, as Packer desires. It is obdurately present, for reasons connected with the nationalities policy of Stalin and others. As Brubaker has pointed out in relation to national minorities, " . . . their quality as specifically *national* minorities is not an objective fact of ethnic demography, but a subjective precipitate of their self-understanding, as channelled and shaped by the national scheme of social classification that was so pervasively institutionalised in the Soviet Union".[18] Brubaker also notes, correctly, that despite Stalin's murderous repression of particular national groups, "he did not attack the social or legal foundations of institutionalised multinationality as such".[19]

The predicament of the Crimean Tatars exemplifies the consequences of the Soviet approach to minorities. Thus, their leader, Mustafa Djemilev, regrets the fact that the designation 'nationality' (which appeared in all Soviet internal and external passports) has been left out of the new Ukrainian passports.[20] This is perhaps to be regretted, but its significance cannot be ignored.

LIBERALISM, INDIVIDUALISM AND THE WESTERN EUROPEAN MODEL

John Packer's views are of particular interest, since he is Legal Adviser to the High Commissioner on National Minorities, appointed by the Organisation for Security and Co-Operation in Europe (OSCE). He combines, more than most, theory and practice. He stands four-square on the liberal foundation mapped out by Carlos Nino,[21] and concludes that belonging to a group or minority must be a matter of individual free choice, based on equality and non-discrimination. It is noteworthy that for Packer, the individual is free and plural, while the group is monolithic and static. In his writing, Packer comments[22] on the range of instruments, international and European, which deal with minority rights.[23] Minority rights add a social dimension to existing human rights law, within which persons belonging to minorities can seek to realise their ideals and plans in those aspects of life which are permitted by majority (democratic) rule, and which do not require conformity. For Packer, therefore, the European instruments on minority rights (the 1990 *Copenhagen* Document of the OSCE and the 1994 *Framework Convention for the Protection of National Minorities*), in particular, are able to reduce sources of conflict and may sustain and enhance peace, precisely because they contribute to the maximising of freedom, and both contribute to and in fact constitute tolerance.

Packer's views converge with those of scholars proceeding from a wide range of positions. The post-structuralist philosopher Jacques Derrida holds that while it is necessary to

> make sure that a centralising hegemony (capital) not be reconstituted, it is also necessary . . . not to multiply the borders . . . . It is necessary not to cultivate for their own sake minority difference, untranslatable idiolects, national antagonisms, or the chauvinisms of idiom.[24]

This implies for him a *duty* to assume "the European, and *uniquely* European, heritage of an idea of democracy". This duty "dictates respecting difference, idioms, minorities, singularities, but also the universality of formal law, the desire for translation, agreement and univocity, the law of the majority, opposition to racism, nationalism and xenophobia".[25] Renata Salecl, applying psychoanalytic theory from an Eastern European standpoint, argues that the goal of democratic politics is the creation of a political space "in which racist fantasies would not have any real effect". Only a society which 'believes' in democratic institutions and has "mechanisms of 'self-binding' of power" is able to avoid the fear that the democratic order will collapse.[26] These institutions include "a constituent assembly, a division of the legislative, executive and judicial powers, an independent banking system, and, above all, independent media".[27] In this Salecl agrees with Claude Lefort who concludes that "human rights are one of the essential elements of democracy precisely because they are grounded on the idea of the abstract individual".[28] The unspoken but unmistakable assumption is that these desirable results are to be found in the West, not the East.

The political scientist Ernesto Laclau is an exponent of the post-modern left politics of fluidity and pluralism. He insists that the constitution of the identity of an ethnic minority can only be fully achieved within the context of a nation-state, and its demands cannot be made in terms of difference, but "of some universal principles that the ethnic minority shares with the rest of the community".[29] The construction, he says, of "differential identities on the basis of total closure to what is outside them is not a viable or progressive political alternative".[30] He concludes that the universal values of the Enlightenment "do not need to be abandoned but need, instead, to be presented as pragmatic social constructions and not as expressions of a necessary requirement of reason". This clearly means that minorities can only achieve an identity by means which are progressive within a Western European context. In Eastern Europe, on the other hand, we witness the closure of ethnic identities around fully-fledged identities that can "only reinforce their most reactionary tendencies"; this, he says, poses the real danger for democracy.[31]

Fourthly, the sociologist Jürgen Habermas, writing from the German heartland of the 'New' Europe, sets out the most explicit formulation of the message which unites these disparate thinkers, who have in common only that they are European.[32] This is his controversial argument in favour of a "European constitutional patriotism", which will "grow together from various nationally specific interpretations of some universalist principles of law".[33] His hopes for a future European citizenship are founded on a belief that greater horizontal mobility, and immigration from Eastern Europe and the Third World, will "heighten the multicultural diversity of society" and "strengthen the relevance that public issues have for the lifeworld". His prescription is that "[o]ne's own tradition must in each case be appropriated from a vantage point relativised by the perspectives of other traditions, and appropriated in such a manner that it can be brought into a transnational, Western European constitutional culture".[34]

Each of these scholars, therefore, is alarmed by the unexpected consequences of the collapse of the USSR, by the proliferation of self-determination claims accompanied by nationalist rhetoric, and in many cases conflict and bloodshed. Indeed, it has been argued that the birth of nationalism in Europe was linked with the failure of the three major empires (Austrian, Ottoman and Russian) to accept genuine federalism, so that only state-reinforcing and state-subverting nationalism could develop. Federal representative government, democratically regulating the relations between regions, was not possible.[35] This theory is congruent with the positions presented above.

The four authors all see current developments in Europe from their differing perspectives as tending towards the hoped-for democratic federalism. This is a position which seems at odds with recent history, since it was the Cold War and the continuation of the Soviet 'Empire' which kept the peace for several decades. The end of the Cold War signals a new symbolic and institutional order, though one which has proved, in Yugoslavia and Chechnya, unable to cope with the new realities.

THE WESTERN EUROPEAN LEGAL ORDER

It is instructive to note how closely the key Western European legal instruments and systems rest upon the theoretical foundations described above. Western Europe has, since the human disaster of the Second World War, invested heavily in models of integration, such as the European Communities, the European Union, the OSCE, and, most importantly for the purposes of this chapter, the Council of Europe. This has meant the breaking down of traditional barriers of state sovereignty, and the encouragement of civil society and the kind of 'constitutional patriotism' for which Habermas argues.

This new Europe is to be plural, with diversity prized. Its spirit is best summed up in the 29 June 1990 *Document of the Copenhagen Meeting of the Conference on the Human Dimension of the CSCE*.[36] At paragraph 30, the participating States recognised that "the questions relating to national minorities can only be satisfactorily resolved in a democratic political framework based on the rule of law. . .[and reaffirmed] that respect for the rights of persons belonging to national minorities as part of universally recognised human rights is an essential factor for peace, justice, stability and democracy". The Document insists that belonging to a national minority is a matter of individual choice;[37] but also recognises that persons who so belong must be free of any attempts at assimilation, and assures the protection of the ethnic, cultural, linguistic and religious identity of such a minority, by special measures if necessary. Packer notes that the *Copenhagen Document* and the OSCE documents in general address 'persons belonging to national minorities' reflecting the clear intention of the participating States not to recognise group rights, or at least the absence of the political will to do so.[38]

The Council of Europe's 1994 *Framework Convention for the Protection of National Minorities*, opened for signature on 1 February 1995, is an attempt to operationalise the principles of the *Copenhagen Document*. As the Explanatory Report attached to the Convention makes clear, the Convention contains programmatic provisions "setting out objectives which the Parties undertake to pursue", and which will not be directly applicable.[39] Packer, amongst others, notes the evident reluctance of the European States to confer significant rights on persons belonging to national minorities, exemplified by the number of provisions containing qualifications or clawback clauses in favour of States, for example those contained in the provisions on education and language.[40]

The Copenhagen Document and the Framework Convention, then, reveal a Europe opposed to assimilation, open to difference, but, for reasons wholly connected with the political interests of the states concerned, conferring rights only upon individuals who are members of minorities; the instruments strikingly lack the theoretical, analytical resources to apprehend or regulate the actions of groups.

The Ukrainian test-bed

The Ukrainian Constitution and legal order represent an unprecedented attempt to combine adherence to Western European standards, with a recognition of group rights. Ukraine declared its independence from the USSR on 24 August 1991, and the USSR itself ceased to exist in December 1991. Largely because of the complex relations between the Russian-speaking and Ukrainian-speaking sections of the population, the Constitution of Ukraine was not adopted until 1996. Nevertheless, the Preamble states that the Constitution is adopted on behalf of "Ukrainian citizens of all nationalities". It refers to the "right to self-determination realised by the Ukrainian nation, [and] all Ukrainian people".[41] By Article 1, Ukraine is a sovereign and independent, democratic, social and legal state; by Article 2 it is unitarian, and its territory is indivisible and inviolable; and by Article 4 it has a single citizenship.

These provisions are contradicted in Chapter X of the Constitution, which provides for an "Autonomous Republic of Crimea" – albeit an inseparable and integral part of Ukraine. To add to this complexity, two further categories of difference are introduced: 'national minorities' and 'indigenous peoples'. Ukraine has, by Article 10, a state language, Ukrainian, although the free development, use and protection of Russian and other languages of 'national minorities' is guaranteed. Article 11 provides that the state shall assist in the consolidation and development of the Ukrainian nation, its historical consciousness, traditions and culture, as well as in the development of the ethnic, cultural, linguistic and religious features of all national minorities and – as a result of intense lobbying by the Crimean Tatars and their Ukrainian nationalist supporters – of its 'indigenous peoples'.

The Constitution thus enshrines a 'Ukrainian nation', as well as 'national minorities' and 'indigenous peoples'. 'National minorities' and 'indigenous peoples' make two further appearances in the Constitution. Article 92 provides that the rights of national minorities and indigenous peoples are to be determined by the laws of Ukraine exclusively, while Article 119 provides that "[l]ocal state administrations in the relevant territory shall ensure. . .the execution of state and local programmes of social and economic development, programmes for environmental protection, and, in places of compact settlement of national minorities and indigenous peoples, programmes for their national and cultural development as well". It is important for the purposes of this chapter to note that a number of rights and freedoms set out in Chapter II are held only by citizens. These include rights to: association in political parties and public organisations, and membership in them (Article 36); participation in public affairs and access to state and local government services (Article 38); peaceful assembly and demonstration (Article 39); use of objects of state and municipal property (Article 41); social security, and pensions (Article 46); free education in state and municipal higher education, with special rights for citizens belonging to national minorities (Article 53); and rights of ownership of intellectual property (Article 54). All other rights belong to all persons irrespective of their citizenship. However, it is clear that non-citizens are deprived of a significant range of crucial civil and political, and social and economic, rights.

Ukraine has also ratified a wide range of international instruments,[42] and has already given persons within its jurisdiction the opportunity of resorting to an international organ by ratifying the Optional Protocol to the International Covenant on Civil and Political Rights. It has ratified (on 26th January 1998) the Framework Convention on the Protection of National Minorities and has acceded to the European Cultural Convention 1954. On joining the Council of Europe it undertook to develop policies towards ethnic minorities on the basis of the Framework Convention and according to the principles of Council of Europe Parliamentary Assembly

Recommendation 1201 (1993), and pledged to sign and ratify, within one year of accession to the Council of Europe, the 1992 European Charter for Regional or Minority Languages.[43]

It may be concluded that the new Ukraine, while properly asserting its new statehood, is making admirable efforts to accommodate its minorities in accordance with international standards. Unfortunately, neither domestic law, nor the Constitution, nor, indeed, the various Council of Europe instruments already mentioned, have proved adequate to the first significant challenge confronted by them: the problem of citizenship.

CITIZENSHIP AND THE CRIMEAN TATARS

On 13 November 1991, very shortly after the declaration of independence on 14 August 1991, Ukraine enacted a *Law on Ukrainian Citizenship*. This adopted the so-called 'zero option', based on both the *jus soli* and *jus sanguinis* principles.[44] According to Article 2(1), all persons who "at the moment of enactment of this Law resided in Ukraine. . .who are not citizens of other states and who do not refuse to acquire Ukrainian citizenship" would be Ukrainian citizens. As Shevchuk points out, this law "made it possible to extend citizenship of Ukraine practically to everyone who was registered as resident at the time the law was adopted".[45]

However, for those not resident on 13 November 1991, including those who had been deported, or their descendants, Article 17 imposed the following requirements: proof that at least one parent or grandparent was born in Ukraine; that they were not citizens of another state; had sufficient knowledge of the Ukrainian language for communication; and had legal means of support.

In this way a significant group were excluded. They are the peoples deported from Crimea in 1944, including the Crimean Tatars, the 'primordial' inhabitants of Crimea, a Muslim Turkic people. During the 16th and 17th centuries there was an independent Crimean Khanate, until Russia invaded Crimea during the Russo-Turkish wars of 1735-39 and 1768-74. In 1783, Catherine the Great proclaimed Crimea to be Russian; Crimean Tatar land was confiscated and Russian settlers were introduced. The response of many Crimean Tatars was to leave. From 1783 to 1791 some 100,00 Crimean Tatars, out of a total of half a million, emigrated. This process continued into the 19th century. By the 1897 census the Crimean Tatars registered in Crimea numbered just 188,000, or one third of the total Crimean Tartar population; by 1921 this figure had fallen to 26 per cent.[46]

The Crimean Tartars' greatest catastrophe, though, followed World War

II. On 10 May 1944 Beriya proposed to Stalin that all Crimean Tatars, with other minority groups, should be deported from Crimea, on account of their alleged activities against Soviet power.[47] Within two months, 225,009 people, including Crimean Tatars, Bulgarians, Greeks, Armenians and others had been deported., with 115,604 being sent to Uzbekistan. Crimean Tatars maintain that 46 per cent of their population died during and after the deportation.

The Crimean Tatars had to wait a long time to return. By an unpublished decree of 28 April 1956, 'special settlement' restrictions were lifted from Crimean Tatars. But whereas deported Kalmyks, Chechens, Ingush, Karachay and Balkars were able to return to reconstituted autonomous territories, this was not the case for the Crimean Tatars. Moreover, on 19 February 1954, matters were greatly complicated when Crimea was transferred from the Russian Federation of the USSR to the Ukraine (Republic). The Crimean Tatars were politically rehabilitated by decree on 5 September 1967, but return only became feasible for large numbers following a Declaration of the Supreme Soviet of the USSR on 14 November 1989, which declared "illegal and criminal" all acts connected with the 1944 deportations.[48] By 13 November 1991, the date of the enactment of new *Law on Citizenship*, 73,981 Tatars had registered their presence in Crimea; by 9 January 1996 this figure had risen to 220,555, although it has been estimated that as many as 100,000 Tatars reside in Crimea without registration.[49]

A high proportion of those Crimean Tatars who returned after 13 November 1991 have not yet received Ukrainian citizenship. Estimates of the numbers concerned have varied between 60,000 (the Ukrainian government's figure) and 176,000 (Crimean Tatar estimates).[50] According to more reliable recent figures, some 146,000 Crimean Tatars are now citizens of Ukraine, with some 93,600 remaining non-citizens[51] – an issue a great cause of concern for inter-governmental and international organisations concerned to avoid the statelessness which is already a feature of Crimean Tatar life.[52]

The Ukrainian authorities responded to complaints that the language and means requirements imposed on applicants were too stringent, and on 16 April 1997 President Kuchma signed a Law of Ukraine *On the Introduction of Amendments and Additions to the Law of Ukraine On Ukrainian Citizenship*.[53] Article 2 (as amended) extended citizenship to all who were born or resided in Ukraine prior to 1944 and to their descendants who resided outside Ukraine on 13 November 1991, and who were not citizens of another state, and submitted an application before 31 December 1997. That is, the language and means requirements do not apply in this context.

The remaining barrier has been the requirement that an applicant is not a citizen of another state. The applicant must prove termination of any previous citizenship. For most of the Crimean Tatars concerned, they were citizens of the USSR, and, if they were resident in Uzbekistan, they became Uzbek citizens automatically on 2 July 1992.[54] The Uzbek *Law on Citizenship* provides that withdrawal from citizenship requires petition to the President.[55] An application must be submitted to the Uzbek Embassy with a fee of 3 dollars (US). The applicant must then wait for one year, and then pay 100 dollars (US) if the application is successful.[56] The delay, and cost involved has rendered application for Ukrainian citizenship practically impossible, even for those who would have automatically become Ukrainian citizens on 13 November 1991, but for the fact that they or their families had been unlawfully deported in 1944.

In this way, despite the Government's apparent concessions, the aspirations of the Crimean Tatars have not been met. The main obstacle now is Ukraine's determination that there should be no possibility of dual citizenship of a kind that would threaten Ukrainian statehood. Of course, the Crimean Tatars would argue that the only reason they were not resident in Ukraine on 13 November 1991 was that they had been unlawfully deported. Justice therefore requires that they should be recognised as citizens *en bloc*. It follows that the Constitution is not adequate to resolve this problem; nor are the Council of Europe's instruments. Perhaps for this reason, amongst others, the Crimean Tatars now increasingly seek recognition beyond the Ukrainian state, or indeed the Council of Europe, for recognition as an indigenous people, claiming the group rights associated with this status.

DEMANDS BEYOND THE NATION-STATE – AND BEYOND THE EUROPEAN LEGAL ORDER

Amongst the Crimean Tatars' demands[57] is for Ukraine to ratify the International Labour Organisation Convention No.169 (27 June 1989) *Concerning Indigenous Peoples and Tribal Peoples in Independent Countries*.[58] Ukraine has not yet done so.[59] The provisions of the Convention of greatest interest to the Crimean Tatars are those contained in Part II – on the issue of "Land". According to Article 14, rights of ownership and possession over the lands which the peoples concerned traditionally occupied "shall be recognised". Furthermore, measures shall be taken to safeguard the right to use the lands not exclusively occupied by such peoples, but to which they have traditionally had access. The rights to the natural resources pertaining to the lands concerned shall be "specially safeguarded".[60] Article

15 provides the mechanism for indigenous populations to safeguard their access to resources. Article 16 provides that the peoples concerned shall not be removed from the lands that they occupy. Their 'free and informed consent' is necessary if they are to be relocated as an exceptional measure, when necessary. They must be allowed to return as soon as the reason ceases to exist. If this is not possible, then equivalent land or appropriate compensation shall be provided.

A further focus of Crimean Tatar attention is the United Nations *Draft Declaration on the Rights of Indigenous Peoples*,[61] adopted by the UN Sub-Commission on Prevention of Discrimination and Protection of Minorities in 1993. Crimean Tartar representatives attend the 'open-ended inter-sessional working group' to elaborate a draft declaration on the basis of the Sub-Commission's draft.[62]

The 1993 Draft goes further than previous instruments and provides that indigenous peoples have the right to self-determination, while ensuring, by reference to a 'right of autonomy', that this is not taken to include secession or the possibility of the creation of a new state. Further, it states that an indigenous people has the right to own lands, territories and resources, "which they have traditionally owned or otherwise occupied or used (Article 26)", but this does not mean that they have the right to own all the territory once used or occupied by them, including land that was taken from them and occupied long ago by others. Article 27 makes it clear that where it is not possible for them to regain ownership, then they have the right to land equal in quality, size and legal status, or, if they consent, to financial compensation.

The primary problem of the Crimean Tatars, which differentiates them from indigenous peoples of North America and Scandinavia, is that they have over two centuries lost all of their 'ancestral territories', and have little prospect of regaining them. There is no realistic prospect of Tatar independence or political autonomy in Crimea. Although the Crimean Tatars seek to define themselves as a 'people', entitled to the right to self-determination,[63] these recent international instruments, as Thomas Musgrave points out, "have created a situation in which indigenous populations can be characterised neither as minorities nor as peoples".[64]

THE SIGNIFICANCE OF A UKRAINIAN DEFINITION

In any event, the distinction between minorities and indigenous peoples is, as Thornberry puts it, "slippery",[65] and this has meant that some groups which are 'clearly' minorities have claimed indigenous status. For example, at the 1994 UN Working Group on Indigenous Peoples, the Boers of South

Africa identified themselves as indigenous and claimed the indigenous right to self-determination.[66] Representatives of a number of indigenous peoples were hostile to this claim. Conversely, although minority rights instruments plainly apply to indigenous peoples, these peoples "may not wish to use the limited route of minority rights to advance their claims".[67] As the Chairperson-Rapporteur of the Working Group, Mrs Erica-Irene Daes, insisted, international law is faced by a major logical and conceptual problem: differentiating 'indigenous peoples' from 'minorities'. In her view, that distinction is strict: "indigenous peoples are indeed peoples and not minorities or ethnic groups".[68]

Such a distinction does not, however, provide a definition. Mrs Daes insisted that "no single definition could capture the diversity of indigenous people world-wide, and all past attempts to achieve both clarity and restrictiveness in the same definition had resulted in greater ambiguity".[69]

It is significant and ironic that whilst Ukraine has objected to the draft Declaration on the ground that it contains no definition of indigenous peoples, it is seeking to introduce one. This is set out in the 6th draft of a "Concept of the National Policy of Ukraine in Relation to Indigenous Peoples":[70]

> (a) descent from the populations which from time immemorial inhabited certain geographical regions of Ukraine in its present state boundaries; (b) preserving cultural, linguistic, religious group identity different from the identity both of the dominant nation and national minorities in Ukraine, and desire to maintain and develop such identity; (c) existence of own historical traditions, social institutions, self-government systems and bodies; (d) non-existence of the ethnically congener (sic) national state or homeland beyond Ukraine's boundaries.

According to this definition, the Crimean Tatars would be the only indigenous people in Ukraine. Indeed, the definition would seem to be expressly designed to exclude any group other than the Crimean Tatars, and it is arguable that it has more political than jurisprudential intent. It is interesting to set this definition against the others now in circulation. The ILO Convention No.169 (1989) extends, by virtue of Article 1 (1)(b), to:

> . . . peoples in independent countries who are regarded as indigenous on account of their descent from the populations which inhabited the country, or a geographical region to which the country belongs, at the time of conquest or colonisation or the establishment of the present state boundaries and who, irrespective of their legal status,

retain some or all of their own social, economic, cultural and political institutions.

This definition also applies, plausibly, to the Crimean Tatars. Article 1(2) provides that "Self-identification as indigenous or tribal shall be regarded as a fundamental criterion for determining the groups to which the provisions of this Convention apply", and goes further than its predecessor.[71]

CONCLUSION

The Ukrainian State is at present anxious to be seen to adopt and apply Western European standards. At the same time, it wishes to accommodate the demands of the Crimean Tatars to indigenous status. There are obvious political reasons why both should be desirable in the context of building a viable Ukrainian State. However, European standards, as exemplified in Council of Europe and OSCE instruments and mechanisms, are, as I have shown, resolutely individualistic and liberal in content. The Crimean Tatars do not wish to be treated as a 'national minority', and therefore turn their attention to the more recent international law concerning the rights of indigenous peoples. Indigenous status is, though, unlikely to satisfy their demands. Where, then, is a solution to be found?

I have argued in this chapter that the 'New' Europe possesses neither the intellectual nor the legal resources adequate to the problems I have described. All of the scholars referred to are committed to the rule of law or at any rate the universality of formal law, and to some version of human rights. Each is more or less vehemently opposed to the notion of group rights. Habermas in particular, argues that even if group rights could be granted in the democratic constitutional state, "they would be not only unnecessary but questionable from a normative point of view. For in the last analysis the protection of forms of life and traditions in which identities are formed is supposed to serve the recognition of their members: it does not represent a kind of preservation of the species by administrative means".[72] The shortcomings of existing legal instruments are manifest.

The demands of the Crimean Tatars, however, based as they are on a strong complaint of historical injustice, can only be addressed as group demands. This is especially true of the claim that citizenship should be granted to them *en bloc*. The crucial question for Ukraine is whether, open as it is to claims for group status by its indigenous peoples, including the Crimean Tatars, it will be able to accommodate a national minority which wishes to be a nation, albeit within Ukraine's borders. More such questions will be posed across the 'New' Europe. If answers are to be found, a radical transformation and extension of existing legal instruments will be required, one which takes account of group rights and group demands, and provides a framework in which there is a prospect of success.

NOTES

*Senior Lecturer and Director, Pan European Institute, Essex University.

1. This occurred on 28 February 1996; Ukraine acceded on 9 November 1995.
2. There is an excellent discussion of this process in Y. N. Soysal, "Changing Citizenship in Europe: Remarks on postnational membership and the national state", in D. Cesarani & M. Fulbrook (eds.), *Citizenship, Nationality and Migration in Europe* (1996).
3. These include Jacques Derrida, Renata Salecl, Ernesto Laclau, and Jürgen Habermas – discussed later in this chapter.
4. See A. Gwiazda, "National Minorities in Poland and the Baltic States", *International Relations* (1994), at 71–80; A. Hanneman, "Independence and Group Rights in the Baltics: A Double Minority Problem", *Virginia Journal of International Law* (1995), at 485; B. Bowring, "Whose Rights, What People, Which Community? The Rule of Law as an Instrument of Oppression in the New Latvia", in P. Fitzpatrick (ed.), *Nationalism, Racism and the Rule of Law* (1995).
5. Translation into the Russian language, Official Publication of the *Verkhovna Rada*, 1996.
6. M. Guboglo & S. Chervonnaia, "The Crimean Tatar Question and the Present Ethnopolitical Situation in Crimea", *Russian Politics and Law* (1995), at 31; see also V. Yevtoukh, "The Dynamics of Interethnic Relations in Crimea", in M. Drohobycky (ed.), *Crimea: Dynamics, Challenges and Prospects* (1995).
7. Information about the Crimean Tatars may be found in: A Fisher, *The Crimean Tatars* (1978); *The Crimean Tatars, Volga Germans and Meskhetians* (Minority Rights Group, 2nd ed., 1980); E. Allworth (ed.), *The Tatars of Crimea: Their Struggle for Survival* (1988); M Guboglu and Chervonnaia, "The Crimean Tatar Question and the Present Ethnopolitical Situation in Crimea", *Russian Politics and Law* (1995), at 31; A. Wilson *The Crimean Tatars: A Situation Report* (International Alert, 1994); J. Burke "Crimean Tatars: Repatriation and Conflict Prevention" (Forced Migration Projects of the Open Society Institute, 1996).
8. A. Smith, *Nations and Nationalism in a Global Era* (1995) 147, at 152.
9. Y. N. Soysal, *supra* n. 2, at 21–22.
10. See, in particular, B. van Steenbergen, *The Condition of Citizenship* (1994); and R. Beiner (ed.), *Theorising Citizenship* (1995).
11. T. H. Marshall, "Citizenship and Social Class", in S. M. Lipset (ed.), *Class, Citizenship and Social Development: Essays by T. H. Marshall* (1964), at 78.
12. E. Guild, "The Legal Framework of Citizenship of the European Union", in D. Cesarani & M. Fulbrook (eds.), *supra* n. 2, at 34; see also B. Turner "Outline of a Theory of Citizenship", 24 *Sociology* (1990), at 189; and B. Turner, "Postmodern Culture/Modern Citizens", in B. van Steenbergen, *The Condition of Citizenship* (1994), at 153.
13. See A. Gutmann (ed.), *Multiculturalism. Examining the Politics of Recognition* (1994).
14. W. Kymlicka, *Multicultural citizenship A Liberal Theory of Minority Rights* (1995); see also W. Kymlicka (ed.), *The Rights of Minority Cultures* (1995).

15. W. Kymlicka and W. Norman, "Return of the Citizen: A Survey of Recent Work on Citizenship Theory", in R. Beiner (ed.), *Theorising Citizenship* (1995) 283, at 309.

16. J. Packer, "On the Content of Minority Rights", in J. Räikkä, *Do We Need Minority Rights?* (1996).

17. B. Parekh, "British Citizenship and Cultural Difference", in G. Andrews (ed.), *Citizenship* (1990), at 183.

18. R. Brubaker, *Nationalism Reframed: Nationhood and the national question in the New Europe* (1996), at 48; see also A. Smith, *supra* n. 8.

19. *Ibid.*, at 37.

20. "We understand that things change now very slowly, but soon, possibly, there will be a new variant of the Ukrainian passport with this designation. I very much hope that things will proceed according to our opinion in the Ukraine *Verkhovna Rada* (Parliament), all the more since this concerns not only the Crimean Tatars". M. Djemilev, "The adoption of the Ukrainian Constitution is an exceptional event!", 33 *Polemika* (9/1996), at 2–3.

21. C. Nino, *The Ethics of Human Rights* (1993).

22. See generally, J. Packer, *supra*, n.16.

23. See (1) the 1966 *International Covenant on Civil and Political Rights*, Article 27; (2) the *UN Declaration on the Rights of Minorities*, adopted without a vote on 18 December 1992; (3) the 1994 Council of Europe's *Framework Convention for the Protection of National Minorities*, opened for signature on 1 February 1995; and (4) the Conference on Security and Co-operation in Europe's 1990 *Document of the Copenhagen Meeting of the Conference on the Human Dimension*.

24. J. Derrida, *The Other Heading: Reflections on Today's Europe* (1992), at 44.

25. *Ibid.*, at 78–9.

26. R. Salecl, *The Spoils of Freedom. Psychoanalysis and Feminism after the Fall of Socialism* (1994), at 37.

27. *Ibid.*, at 94.

28. *Ibid.*, at 119.

29. E. Laclau, *Emancipation(s)* (1996), at 28.

30. *Ibid.*, at 29.

31. *Ibid.*, at 103–4.

32. J. Habermas, "Citizenship and National Identity", Appendix II to *Between Facts and Norms* (1996); see also B. van Steenbergen, *The Condition of Citizenship* (1994), at 20; and R. Beiner (ed.), *Theorising Citizenship* (1995), at 235.

33. *Ibid.*, at 507.

34. *Ibid.*, at 500.

35. M. Mann, "A Political Theory of Nationalism and Its Excesses", in S. Peril (ed.), *Notions of Nationalism* (1995), at 44–64.

36. The full text may be found at *Human Rights in International Law* (Council of Europe 1992), at 424; and at 11 *Human Rights Law Journal* (1990), at 232–246.

37. Paragraph 32 states that "[t]o belong to a national minority is a matter of a person's individual choice and no disadvantage may arise from the exercise of such a choice".

38. J. Packer, *supra* n. 16, at 164.

39. The Explanatory Report (and the Convention) can be found at 2 *International Human Rights Reports* (1995) 217, at 225.

40. J. Packer, *supra* n. 16, at 159.

41. Unofficial translation into English by The International Foundation for Election Systems.

42. All details of ratification are taken from (Winter 1995) 9.4 *Interights Bulletin*, at 140.

43. Strasbourg, 5 November 1992; European Treaty Series No.148.

44. See Y. Shevchuk, "Dual citizenship in old and new states", XXXVII, 1 *Arch. Euroat Sociol.* (1996), at 47–73.

45. *Ibid.*, at 54.

46. See A. Wilson, *supra* n. 7.

47. I. Pribytkova, "Repatriatsiya Deportirovannikh Narodov: Organizatsionno-khozaistvenni i politicheski aspekti (The repatriation of deported peoples: organisational, economic and political aspects)", in UNHCR *Problemi Bezhentsev i Migratsii v Krymu (Problems of Refugees and Migrants in Crimea)*. Materials from the Round Table held at Yalta, 20 November 1996, at 31.

48. For a good account of the history of this period, see Mustafa Cemiloglu (Djemilev), "A History of the Crimean Tatar National Liberation Movement: A Sociopolitical Perspective", in M. Drohobucky (ed.), *Crimea: Dynamics, Challenges and Prospects* (1995), at 87–105.

49. *Crimea: Base-Line Socio-Economic Survey with Emphasis on Returning Refugees* (UNDP, UNOPS, January 1996).

50. Crimean Integration and Development Programme, Interim Report of W. Bowring, Legal Adviser (UNDP, 1996), cited by C. Bierwirth, "International Legal Principles and the Activities of the UNDP in Ukraine", in UNHCR *Problemi Bezhentsev i Migratsii v Krymu (Problems of Refugees and Migrants in Crimea)*, Materials from the Round Table held at Yalta, 20 November 1996, at 51.

51. Report of W. Bowring, Legal Adviser to CIDP for *Kyiv Seminar on Ukrainian Citizenship Issue*, hosted and chaired by the OSCE Mission to Ukraine on 24 July 1996.

52. See C. Bierwirth, *supra* n. 50.

53. No.210/97-VR.

54. The date of entry into force of the *Law of the Republic of Uzbekistan on Citizenship of the Republic of Uzbekistan*.

55. *Ibid.*, Article 20.

56. Attachment No.3 to the *Decision of the Cabinet of Ministers of Uzbekistan* of 19 August 1993, No.423. In September 1998, agreement was reached between Ukraine and Uzbekistan to waive this requirement. It is disputed whether all problems have now been resolved.

57. See the "Communication of the Crimean Tatar People" to the President of Ukraine, the Supreme Soviet of Ukraine, the UN, and the OSCE", 1996.

58. Convention (No.169) Concerning Indigenous and Tribal Peoples in Independent Countries, adopted by the General Conference of the ILO, Geneva, June 27, 1989. Entered into force 5 September 1991.

59. This came into force in 1991 when Norway and Mexico ratified it. Even at the time of writing, only 10 States have ratified: Bolivia, Colombia, Costa Rica, Denmark, Guatemala, Honduras, Mexico, Norway, Paraguay and Peru. "Discrimination Against Indigenous Peoples", *Report of the Working Group on Indigenous Populations, on its Fourteenth Session* (Geneva, 29 July – 2 August 1996), UN Doc. E/CN.4/Sub.2/1996/21, at 22. The ILO representative stated that several other countries are considering ratification, while others, for example the Russian Federation, have sought ILO assistance in drafting their own legislation.

60. Convention 169, Article 14(1). This is set out in S. Anaya, *Indigenous Peoples in International Law* (1996), at 197.

61. U.N.Doc.E/CN.4/Sub.2/1994/2/Add.1, 20 April 1994.

62. See, for example, the Draft Report of the Second Session of the Working Group Established in Accordance with the Commission on Human Rights Resolution 1995/32 of 3 March 1995, UN Doc: E/CN.4/1996/WG.15/CRAT 7, 1 November 1996.

63. As in common Articles 1 in the 1966 *International Covenant on Civil and Political Rights* and *International Covenant on Economic, Social and Cultural Rights.*

64. T. Musgrave, *Self Determination and National Minorities* (1997), at 177.

65. P. Thornberry, "The UN Declaration on the Rights of Persons Belonging to National or Ethnic, Religious and Linguistic Minorities: Background, Analysis, Observations and an Update", in A. Phillips and A. Rosas (eds.), *Universal Minority Rights* (1995) 13, at 55.

66. Statement of the Afrikaner Volksfront, 26 July 1994, cited in P. Thornberry, *ibid.*

67. *Ibid.* at 55. See also P. Thornberry *International Law and The Rights of Minorities* (1992), Part VI.

68. Working Paper by the Chairperson-Rapporteur, Mrs Erica Irene A. Daes, "On the concept of "indigenous people". Commission on Human Rights; Sub-Commission on Prevention of Discrimination and Protection of Minorities. Working Group on Indigenous Populations, 14th session, 29 July – 2 August 1996. Doc: E/CN.4/Sub.2/AC.4/1996/2, at 16.

69. Her only solution, based on the experience of the Working Group, was a procedural one. *Supra* n. 59.

70. This document has been prepared by a Working Group led by the Ukraine Ministry of Justice. English translation received from the *Pilip Orlyk Institute for Democracy*, Kyiv, in October 1996.

71. "Indigenous communities, peoples and nations are those which, having a historical continuity with pre-invasion and pre-colonial societies that developed on their territory, consider themselves distinct from other sectors of the societies now prevailing in those territories, or parts of them. They form at present non-dominant sectors of society and are determined to preserve, develop and transmit to future generations their ancestral territories, and their ethnic identity, as the basis of their continued existence as peoples, in accordance with their own cultural patterns, social institutions, and legal systems". UN Subcommission on Prevention of Discrimination and Protection of Minorities, *Study of the Problem of Discrimination against Indigenous Populations.* UN Doc. E/CN.4/Sub.2/1986/7/Add.4, para. 379 (1986).

72. J. Habermas, "Struggles for Recognition in the Democratic Constitutional State", in A. Gutmann (ed.), *Multiculturalism: Examining the Politics of Recognition* (1994) 107–148 , at 130.

The Rights of National Minorities in Ukraine: An Introduction

Myroslava Antonovych*

INTRODUCTION

The issue of national minorities, and the question as to how to deal with such groups, is of particular importance to Ukraine, a state within which more than 100 nationalities exist. According to a census of the population held in the Ukrainian Soviet Socialist Republic in 1989 (prior to independence), as well as the 37.5 million ethnic Ukrainians, the territory was then inhabited by 11.3 million ethnic Russians; half a million Jews; 400,000 individuals of Belarus extraction; 300,000 ethnic Moldovans; 200,000 each of ethnic Bulgarians and Poles; and numerous other national minorities. The figures are representative of present day statistics. It should consequently come as little surprise that developing an appropriate state policy towards ethnic minorities has been given a high priority by the authorities, in order to deal both with the needs and requirements of the national minority populations, and to remove the potential for intra-ethnic conflict within Ukraine.

THE HISTORY OF MINORITY RIGHTS IN UKRAINE

Ukraine as a 'nation' has experienced a loss of statehood and independence on several occasions, and for long periods, in its history during which time the Ukrainian people could be considered as having direct experience of being persons belonging to a national minority – that is, they have been a non-dominant 'minority' in a land which they consider their own. This experience, it may be argued, has, presently and traditionally, helped the Ukrainian nation to understand the particular problems and concerns of national minorities,[1] and recognise the need to provide for effective protection of minority rights. Evidence of this may be found in the action of the Ukrainian Central Rada, or Council, the highest political body of Ukraine in 1917-1918. In 1917, the Central Rada issued its Second Universal

251

P. Cumper and S. Wheatley (eds.), Minority Rights in the 'New' Europe, 251–257
© 1999 *Kluwer Law International. Printed in Great Britain.*

(Proclamation),[2] guaranteeing equality to all national minorities in Ukraine, and passed the Act on the Council of Peoples and National-Personal Autonomy,[3] granting the right of persons belonging to a particular ethnic group to organise themselves for the purpose of representation of the group with the state authorities. Further, the Third Universal of the Ukrainian Central Rada, which proclaimed the Ukrainian National Republic on 7 November 1917, guaranteed national minorities the right to use their native language in dealing with all administrative agencies and further granted, *inter alia*, to Russian, Jewish and Polish national minorities living in Ukraine a degree of autonomy and self-government in matters of their national life.[4] At the beginning of the twentieth century, no other European state enjoyed comparable minority protection legislation. Indeed, the first Deputy Secretary on Jewish Affairs in the General Secretariat of Ukraine, Moshe Zilberfarb, argued that whereas the French Revolution had declared human rights, Ukrainian Law 'On National-Personal Autonomy' had declared the rights of minority nations.[5]

Official government policy in the early part of the century was in line with the legislative regime. The Deputy Minister of Foreign Affairs, Arnold Margolin, asserted that the Ukrainian Government was consistent in its opposition to massacres of any part of its population and had neither participated in, nor bore responsibility, for such atrocities.[6] However, weak government meant that the posited laws could not guarantee the protection of minorities during the brief existence of the Ukrainian National Republic; the Jewish population, in particular, was persecuted during the Pogroms and following the seizure of power by the Bolsheviks in Russia, persons belonging to minorities enjoyed no protection from the State.

The early years of Soviet control in the 1920's saw a brief period of national revival for Ukraine and its national minorities who, at this time, constituted one fifth of the total population of the Ukrainian Soviet Socialist Republic. The development of the Ukrainian language and culture was accompanied by the opening of schools for other nationalities, who were also able to produce newspapers and journals in their own languages. However, this all ended with the introduction of a centralised government, a planned economy and the accompanying genocidal policies of the Soviet Communist regime between 1928-1936. These policies resulted in the great famine in Ukraine, from 1932-1933, in which (according to Soviet statistics) five million people died.[7]

Whilst the Constitution of the Ukrainian SSR formally recognised the existence of human rights for nations (including the right to self-determination), these were not observed in practice. The initial enterprise of a Soviet people of nations, merging into a newly created historical community, rapidly became the forced assimilation of nations, with the resultant decay of national cultures, traditions and customs, and the repression of those who sought to maintain their national character. In Ukraine, Roman Smal-Stocki claims that the systematic pogrom which was organised against Ukrainian language, literature and culture was carried out with such severity that all previous Russian Tsarist persecutions appeared almost insignificant by comparison.[8]

LEGISLATION ON MINORITY RIGHTS IN MODERN UKRAINE

Since the 1990 Declaration on State Sovereignty of Ukraine, and the adoption of the Act of Independence on 24th August 1991, much work has been undertaken concerning the provision of human rights to persons belonging to national minorities. For example, the Declaration of the Rights of Nationalities of Ukraine 1991,[9] and the Law On National Minorities in Ukraine 1992,[10] incorporate into Ukrainian law international agreements on the rights of ethnic minorities, with the former guaranteeing all nationalities equal political, economic, social, and cultural rights.

The 1992 Law On National Minorities in Ukraine provides that national minorities will be defined as those citizens of Ukraine who are not ethnic Ukrainians, but who display a sense of national self-identification and unity among themselves (Article 3). Those persons (belonging to the national minority) are entitled, *inter alia*, to use the minority language and to receive an education in that language in state educational institutions, or through national cultural societies; to develop and nurture national cultural traditions; to use national symbols; to the recognition of national holidays; to practise their religion; to satisfy their needs in terms of literature, the arts and mass media; to create national, cultural and educational institutions; and to engage in any other activity that does not contradict legislation in force (Article 6). Whilst the provisions on 'national-cultural autonomy' are encouraging, Buromenskyi notes that the law contains neither a definition of such national-cultural autonomy, nor the procedure and conditions of its existence.[11]

In the parts of the state where the national minority constitutes a majority of the population, the minority language may be used alongside the Ukrainian state language in dealings with public bodies (Article 8). The state budget of Ukraine presupposes special allocations for the development of the cultures of the national minorities (Article 16) and a Ministry of Nationalities and Migration was created with responsibility for dealing with issues relating to inter-ethnic relations (subsequently, in 1996, this was reorganised into the State Committee of Ukraine on Nationalities and Migration). Moreover, within the Verkhovna Rada (Ukrainian Parliament) there exists a standing committee on human rights, national minorities and inter- ethnic relations.

A new stage in the development of legislation on national minorities began with the adoption of the Constitution of Ukraine on 28 June 1996,[12] which defines the Ukrainian people to include citizens of all nationalities. The *preamble*, adopted by the Verkhovna Rada, notes that the Constitution is based upon Ukraine's centuries-old experience of state-building (i.e. the process of creating a civic society), and on the right to self-determination realised by the Ukrainian nation and all the Ukrainian people. Article 11 of the Constitution provides that the Ukrainian state will promote the consolidation and development of the Ukrainian nation, its historical consciousness, traditions and culture, and also the development of the ethnic, cultural, linguistic and religious identity of all national minorities and indigenous peoples of Ukraine, the later of which include the Crimean Tatars,[13] the Caraims and the Crymchaks.[14]

The state language of Ukraine is, predictably, Ukrainian; the state ensures the comprehensive development and functioning of the Ukrainian language in all spheres of social life throughout the entire territory of Ukraine, although, notably, the free development, use and protection of Russian, and the other national minority languages, is guaranteed under the constitution (Article 10). Moreover, citizens who belong to national minorities are guaranteed, in accordance with the law, the right to receive instruction in their native language, or to study their native language in state and communal educational establishments, and through cultural societies (Article 53).

IMPLEMENTATION OF THE RIGHTS OF NATIONAL MINORITIES

As well as the legislative provisions discussed previously, Ukraine has undertaken a number of measures in support of its minority languages and in the provision of education to minority groups. In over five thousand schools, children are taught in their 'Mother tongue', or a combination of Ukrainian and the national minority language; books are available in over 20 minority languages, as are dozens of newspapers; the number of TV and radio programmes in minorities languages has also seen a significant increase in recent years.[15] Furthermore, in excess of one hundred and fifty regional and district cultural societies, representing the interests of most ethnic groups, have been formed, including the Russian Pushkin Society in Lviv; the Association of Jewish Organisations and Communities of Ukraine; the Society of Jewish Culture of Ukraine; the Eminesku Society of Romanian Culture; the Polish Cultural and Educational Society in Ukraine; the Republican Society of Armenian Culture; the Society of Crimean Tatars in Kherson region; the Society of Germans of Ukraine "Vidergeburt"; the Assyrian Organisation of Ukraine; the Republican Society of Greeks in Ukraine; the Slavic Fund of Ukraine; and the Republican Cultural Centre of Turkic Language Peoples of Ukraine.[16]

Whatever advances have been made in Ukraine, a number of urgent problems relating to national minorities remain. The most difficult of these, according to Ukrainian President Leonid Kuchma, is the resettling of citizens deported under the Soviet regime and the guarantee to these 'returnees' of their legal, political, social, cultural rehabilitation.[17] Most prominent amongst these groups are the Crimean Tatars, forcibly deported to Central Asia more than 50 years ago by Stalin who had accused them of disloyalty during the Second World War. In November 1989 the Supreme Soviet of the former USSR adopted a Declaration which declared illegal all acts connected with the 1944 deportations. This was followed by the 1990 Decree of the Presidium of the Supreme Soviet of the USSR, condemning any deportations of the minority peoples of the Soviet Union, although the Decree did not provide for any concrete mechanism which would facilitate the return of deported people to their homeland. However, the issue of the deported peoples remained unresolved upon Ukrainian independence. On the 28th January 1992, the Cabinet of Ministers of the newly independent Ukraine issued the 'Decree On Some Problems Connected with the Returning of Crimean Tatars to the Crimean Autonomous Republic';[18] it provided for special allocations, from the state budget, to finance measures for the return of the Crimean Tatars. At the time of writing proposed legislation on the "Rehabilitation and Guarantee of Rights of Persons from National Minorities who Suffered from Oppression and were Deported from the Territory of Ukraine" is being drafted by the Ministry for Nationalities and Migration for adoption by the Verkhovna Rada.

The proposed legislation recognises that the Crimean Tatars were not the only minority people to suffer oppression and deportation during the Stalinist period: ethnic Bulgarians, Greeks, Armenians, Germans, Poles, Karaims, Romanians, and Hungarians all suffered. In the proposed legislation, the State accepts its responsibility for ensuring the protection of the rights of persons belonging to such minorities. In particular, the legislation proposes that those who suffered oppression and were deported should be "rehabilitated" (Article 2), and compensation would be paid to those who suffered or lost property as a result of the deportation (Article 7). This payment would have to take into account the economic resources of the state, but first priority would be given to those persons who were disabled as a result of deportation and forced labour, including those who had formed part of the notorious 'working columns' of the NKVD (the Ministry of Internal Security for the former Soviet Union, and the forerunner of the KGB). Compensation would not necessarily be monetary, but could include the provision of accommodation; improvements in living conditions; the granting of vouchers for use in private medical establishments; and priority in obtaining medical treatment in state medical establishments. In excess of one million individuals could be eligible for assistance under the proposed legislation, the adoption of which, it is contended, would promote social justice and equality among all ethnic groups in Ukraine.[19]

The problem of the Crimean Tatars continues to cause particular problems. According to Dzhemilev, the leader of the Crimean Tatar Medzhlis (national assembly), of the 250,000 Crimean Tatars who have returned to Crimea since the break-up of the Soviet Union, half are homeless and unemployed, and the mortality rate amongst members of the group is increasing.[20] It is estimated that a resettlement programme would cost 1.5 billion dollars (US). However, Ukraine, suffering the same financial difficulties as all states of the former Soviet Union, has allocated only 100 million dollars (US), and has received little in the way of support from other states, including those states from which many of the Crimean Tatars are returning, which are also former member states of the Soviet Union, with similar economic and other problems. The OSCE High Commissioner has confirmed that, without outside financial assistance, Ukraine is unlikely to be able to solve the problem of resettling Crimean Tatars.[21]

CONCLUSION

Despite the difficulties outlined in this chapter, Ukraine has succeeded in its efforts to avoid serious internal conflict between its majority and minority populations, and between the national minority groups themselves. Ukraine has, therefore, been able to avoid a problem which has afflicted most of the other states of the former Soviet Union. This is an achievement in which the Ukrainian government and people may feel a certain degree of pride.

NOTES

*Associate Professor of International Law at the University of Kyiv-Mohyla Academy and at the Centre for Legal Studies, Ukranian Legal Foundation, Kyiv, Ukraine.

1. See Z. Kohut, *Russian Centralism and Ukrainian Autonomy. Imperial Absorption of the Hetmanate 1760s–1830s* (1988).
2. *Natsionalni Vidnosyny v Ukrayini u XX st.* (1994), at 48.
3. *Ibid.*, at 51–52.
4. *Ibid.*, at 56. The Fourth Universal of the Ukrainian Central Rada reaffirmed the rights to national-personal autonomy of all ethnic groups in Ukraine, *ibid.*, at 71.
5. E. Tsherikover, *Antisemitizm un pogromen in Ukraine, 1917–1918* (1923), at 73.
6. The Jewish Chronicle (1919, May 16). See also T. Hunchak (ed.), *The Ukraine, 1917–1921: A Study in Revolution* (1977); *The Annals of the Ukrainian Academy of Arts and Sciences in the U.S.* (1956), at 1167–1168.
7. M. Mishchenko, "My Testimony on the Genocide in Ukraine", VI *Ukrainian Quarterly*.
8. R. Smal-Stocki, *The Nationality Problem of the Soviet Union and Russian Communist Imperialism (1952)*, at 104.
9. *Supra* n. 2, at 474–475.
10. *Ibid.*, at 491–493.
11. M. Buromensky, "Is It Possible to Implement the Law 'On National Minorities' in Ukraine?", 6 *Human Rights in Ukraine* (1994) 38.
12. Constitution of Ukraine, adopted at the Fifth Session of the Verkhovna Rada of Ukraine on 28 June 1996, *LII The Ukrainian Quarterly* (1996) 223.
13. See W. Bowring, "New Nations and National Minorities: Ukraine and the Question of Citizenship" (this work).
14. The law on "The Indigenous Peoples of Ukraine" is, at the time of writing, being drafted.
15. "Radiozvernennya Prezydenta Ukrayiny Leonida Kuchmy", 212 *Uryadovyi Curyer* (1996), at 2.
16. See Karta respublicanskykh, regionalnykh, oblasnykh kulturolohichnykh tovarystv natsionalnykh menshyn Ukrayiny (1992).
17. *Supra* n. 15.
18. *Supra* n. 2, at 482–483.
19. "Ukraine" (1996, Seat) 1 EELM.
20. L.Budzhurova, "Special to Intelnews", Intelnews, 23 April 1996.
21. ITAR-TASS reported on 25 January 1996.

Conflict Resolution and National Minorities

The Dayton Peace Accords: Lessons From the Past and for the Future

*Julie Mertus**

INTRODUCTION

After the First World War, the victorious allies used international law to rearrange the European landscape, parcelling out the losses of Germany, the Ottoman Empire, Bulgaria, and the successor states of the Habsburg Empire – Austria and Hungary. The nascent principle of self-determination insisted that these new states created were, as far as possible, ethnically homogenous. As Claude notes:

> The principle 'one nation, one state' was not realised to the full extent permitted by the ethnographic configuration of Europe, but it was approximated more closely than ever before.[1]

Protections, designed as a counter-balance for those millions left out of 'their' nation-state and unable to exercise their right to national self-determination, were introduced for religious, cultural, language and ethno-national minorities.[2] However, whatever the humanitarian motives advanced for the exercise of the right of national self-determination, under these inter-war agreements "the victors [still] took the spoils, but with the stipulations often clothed in the idealistic language of national self-determination and justice". [3]

More than half a century later, the peace settlement negotiated for the former Yugoslavia at Dayton, Ohio, made a similar compromise: the territorial victors were rewarded and, at the same time, the peace process trumpeted self-determination and justice. Affirmation, in the Dayton accord,[4] of the integrity of the internationally-recognised state of Bosnia-Herzegovina[5] accorded respect for the state's earlier act of self-determination. Yet, at the same time, the peace settlement divided Bosnia-Herzegovina roughly in two – giving the Bosnian Serbs what they wanted all along, a semi-autonomous state.

Under the Dayton accord, international human rights provisions were

261

P. Cumper and S. Wheatley (eds.), Minority Rights in the 'New' Europe, 261–283
© 1999 *Kluwer Law International. Printed in Great Britain.*

introduced as the mechanism through which tensions between states, ethno-national groups, and nationalisms could be addressed. Nevertheless, despite changes in international law and policy, the grand scheme to protect ethno-national groups embodied in the Dayton accord bears marked similarities to the minority rights guarantees created after the First World War. The 'minorities treaties'[6] concluded under the auspices of the League of Nations (and other inter-war minority rights measures[7]) failed both to protect the rights of ethnic, religious and linguistic minorities and to create a long-lasting peace. The Dayton accord appears predestined to make the same mistakes.

Examination of the historical underpinnings of the Dayton agreement has been absent from policy discussion on the protection of members of the various ethno-national minority groups in Bosnia-Herzegovina, Croatia, and other troubled parts of Central and Eastern Europe. Yet Dayton was not concluded in a policy vacuum; it was influenced by earlier international and regional responses to crumbling states, nationalism and the need to protect the rights of members of minority groups. Understanding the potential stumbling blocks to Dayton's effective enforcement requires an inquiry into earlier international frameworks designed to construct peace. Additionally, Dayton's attempt to address the question of 'national minorities' must reconcile itself with previous Yugoslav efforts to manage and construct ethno-national identities. Thus, an assessment of Dayton also necessitates an analysis of the ways in which Dayton attempts to foster notions of identity in a society in which deep-rooted cultural and legal identity tags have already been deployed.

This chapter explores the Dayton accord through two historical inquiries: first, it analyses the ways in which Dayton responds to the question of national identity, as framed by earlier notions of group identity; second, it examines Dayton in light of the minority rights agreements of the inter-war years. Whilst the similarities between Dayton and the treaties of the inter-war period spell potential disaster for minority groups (and the wider international community), the differences could provide their salvation.

ADDRESSING THE PROBLEM OF ETHNO-NATIONAL IDENTITY

Given the Communist regime's attempts to enforce a Yugoslav national identity over all other senses of belonging, it was inevitable perhaps with the collapse of communism that the issue of national identity should became increasingly important. Although ethno-national identity was not the cause of the wars in Croatia and Bosnia-Herzegovina, it provided the soil in which the elites' struggle for power could take root. In turn, this soil was fertilised by a combination of ingredients: the actions and inaction of international financial institutions (which led Yugoslavia to the brink of disaster); tremendous fear and uncertainty among the general populace; heavy state and party control over the broadcast media; a "heritage of authoritarianism";[8] and a lack of a civil society that could challenge government and support a diversity of opinions. Although commentators have recognised the role of nationalism in fanning the flames of war in the Balkans, few have analysed how the Dayton accord responds to (national) 'identities' hardened by years of war. To be viewed as legitimate by the people of the region, the Dayton agreement must, at the very least, address the past ways of naming identities; in order to promote long-term peace, it must somehow take steps to break-down the virulent national divides which have become a reality in Bosnia-Herzegovina. As this section will illustrate, Dayton accomplishes neither of these tasks.

This section will first examine the development of national identity in the former Yugoslavia over three periods: the formal naming of groups in the constitutional developments between 1946 and 1974; the impact of the collapse of Yugoslavia; and the impact of war (1992-1995). Against this backdrop, the response of the drafters at Dayton will be considered.

DEVELOPMENT OF NATIONAL IDENTITY IN YUGOSLAVIA

Constitutional Developments

Yugoslavia had three major constitutional revisions between 1945 and its collapse:[9] the 1946, 1963 and 1974 versions. Through arranging the legal and social terms with which people were to operate, each of these constitutions had an impact on shaping national identity.[10] Everyone enjoyed Yugoslav nationality, united in 'brotherhood and unity', although by the time of the 1946 constitution, the Yugoslavia people were *de facto* divided into two categories – the "hosts and the historical guests".[11] The hosts, or nations (*narod*), were the Serbs, Croats, Slovenes, Macedonians and Montenegrins. The guests were called national minorities.

Under the 1963 constitution, national minorities were re-designated as 'nationalities' (*narodnosti*), as the term 'minority' was perceived to be demeaning. *Narodnosti* was understood to include all those with a national homeland elsewhere; such people included (ethnic) Albanians, Hungarians, Italians, Bulgarians, Turks, Slovaks, Czechs and Russians. Those without a homeland elsewhere, such as the Romany and Vlachs, were seemingly ignored by the constitution. Perhaps the most significant development, in hindsight, in the 1963 constitution, was the fact that Muslims were elevated in status from a nationality to a nation.[12]

The 1974 Constitution provided a turning point in which national differences became "constitutionally enshrined".[13] Article 1 of the 1974 Constitution defined Yugoslavia as "a federal state having the form of a state community of voluntarily united nations and their Socialist Republics".[14] Unlike earlier constitutions, sovereignty did not rest with the people but in the 'sovereign rights' that the "nations and nationalities shall exercise in the socialist republics, and in the socialist autonomous provinces – and in the SFRY when in their common interests".[15] Each republic of Yugoslavia, with the exception of Bosnia-Herzegovina, was dominated by one national group (i.e. Serbia was mainly Serb and Croatia was mainly Croat). However, the *fit* between 'homeland' and nation was never complete, with many people living outside their 'national homeland'. Thus, with its emphasis on national divisions tied to republic lines, the 1974 Constitution created a potentially explosive mix of national tensions.

In a development that lent more importance to national identity, power under the 1974 Constitution was decentralised from the federal to the republic level, giving each of Yugoslavia's six republics and two provinces their own central bank and police force and control over the educational and judicial systems. These units, with the exception of Bosnia-Herzegovina, were *de facto* organised around national identity, based on the majority nation of that region (for example, government in Serbia was dominated by Serbs, etc.). Through such arrangements, national status, "which had seemingly been buried by the 1971 intervention [Tito's squelching of nationalist movements in Croatia], returned by the back door".[16] Reward and advancement became conditional on nationality and national status; a 'nationality key' system (of proportional representation) pushed national identity into the forefront, and became a means for many incompetent and/or corrupt party members to achieve positions of importance simply because they were of the right national status, leading to a widespread backlash and the widening of national divides.[17]

However, even after the adoption of the 1974 constitution, Yugoslavia continued to operate as a unitary state. The 'consensus' system, which officially "prevented any decisions from being adopted if opposed by any single federal unit (including the autonomous provinces)",[18] weakened the federation "by paralyzing the decision making process and removing real authority of federal decisions",[19] placing government back in the hands of the Communist Party. With everything under the control of the Party, individuals had little incentive to become involved in politics. In these circumstances a civil society could not develop.

The Collapse of Yugoslavia[20]

During the years after Tito's death, Yugoslavia increasingly divided along grounds of national identity.[21] In the first democratic elections, nationalism became the mechanism for political differentiation, and few alternative categories existed to distinguish the candidates.[22] Political and economic structures swayed under the weight of internal bickering as new leaders struggled for power and international financial institutions pressed Yugoslavia to restructure its economy.[23] This situation fostered intense bureaucratic competition and corruption, often conducted along national lines.[24] Nationalism was not the only force pushing Yugoslavia toward collapse, but, manipulated by politicians, it became a crucial ingredient.

The Impact of War: Closing Ranks

The war impacted on national identity in three ways. First, it accomplished the complete demonisation of other nations and national groups. Initially, state-controlled propaganda machines broadcast stories of the 'Other's' inhumanity. Over time, many witnesses and victims of acts of great cruelty began to tell their story – and their neighbours listened. The Diaspora often played an important role in this demonisation process. Far away from the region, living in nationally homogeneous marriages (at least at a rate much higher than their kin back home), the Diaspora had an easier time painting the 'Other' as evil.[25]

Secondly, war precipitated national segregation. People who had been forced to leave their villages and cities because of their national background crowded into enclaves of 'their own people'.[26] Segregation exploited and reinforced 'Otherness'.

Finally, war forced the closing of ranks. In Bosnia, individuals were characterised as being a member of one of three groups: Serb, Croat or Muslim. This left four categories of people without any identity: those of mixed parentage or marriage; those who were of another national identity; those who wanted to identify themselves as something else, either above the nation (such as European), or below (such as a member of a particular neighbourhood or organisation); and those who wanted out of the labelling process. Those who failed to make a choice usually left the country (if they could) or fell silent. A few stubbornly fought back, despite the extreme backlash against anything different and potentially challenging to the Nation.[27]

DAYTON'S RESPONSE: CEMENTING THE ETHNO-NATIONAL DIVIDES

The Dayton accord jettisons the terminology of nation (*narod*) and nationalities (*narodnosti*) utilised by the most recent Yugoslav constitutions, except in references to international documents and in a section on the rights of refugees to return. Instead, Dayton, and the Preamble to the Constitution of the Republic of Bosnia-Herzegovina (an annex to Dayton), refer to three groups: Bosniacs,[28] Croats and Serbs, as being the "constituent peoples. . .(along with Others)". Those who do not fall within this 'group of three' see their status reduced from nation (*narod*) or national minority (*narodnosti*) to invisibility.

Dayton further cements the national divide by creating a system of nation-based governance. Under the agreed scheme, two smaller sub-entities are drawn within the state of the Republic of Bosnia-Herzegovina (according to battle lines), which reflects national identity: Republika Srpska (the Bosnian Serb controlled area) and the Federation of Bosnia-Herzegovina (the Croat and Muslim/Bosniac controlled entity). These two entities are held together by a "thin roof",[29] a central government with so little power that it "makes the American Articles of Confederation of two centuries ago look like a centralised, unitary form of government".[30] The central government, 'the Republic of Bosnia-Herzegovina', is responsible for the following: foreign policy; foreign trade; customs; monetary policies; immigration, refugee and asylum policy; international and inter-entity criminal law enforcement; the establishment of international communication facilities; regulation of inter-entity transportation; air traffic control; enacting legislation to carry out the decisions of the Presidency or responsibilities of the federal assembly; and funding and budgeting for federal institutions.[31] The remaining responsibilities of government, including the promulgation and enforcement of local civil and criminal laws and control over the courts (except for the joint Constitutional Court, the only federal court), are given to the entities.

The entire federal government is divided on a tripartheid basis along ethno-national lines: Serb, Croat and Muslim (Bosniac). The executive arm of the government has three presidents, one from each group; even the armed forces is decentralised in threes.[32] Given that each ethno-national group has at least one army, this provision effectively creates three armies divided along ethno-national lines. Similarly, the bi-cameral legislature is proportioned equally into the three national categories. The upper house (House of Peoples) has five representatives from each group; the lower house (House of Representatives) has fourteen from each.[33]

Dayton moreover perpetuates the rule of consensus that had previously worked so well to block any chance of democratic decision making and served to promote national splintering. Fred Morrison explains:

> The three-member Presidency is supposed to act by consensus. If that fails, two members may adopt a decision, but the dissenting member may then declare that decision "destructive of a vital interest of the Entity from the territory from which he was elected". In that case, the matter is referred to the legislature of the ethnic [nation] group from which the dissenting member of the Presidency was elected. If they uphold "their" member of the Presidency by a two-thirds vote, the challenged action does not take effect.[34]

In either house of Parliament, therefore, block voting by a single national group, and in some cases the simple failure of a group to show up at Parliament, can defeat legislative proposals. In the upper house, for example, any action can fail if opposed by two-thirds of a national group. These complex consensus provisions were adopted at Dayton, not because they will work, but because Serbian President Milosevic refused to consent to the agreement without them.[35] Milosevic was well aware that if the government had been permitted to operate through some form of majority vote, a coalition of Muslim and Croat representatives (allies against the Serbs during the war) could have always out-voted the Serbs. On the other hand, the present compromise grants any national group the power to make the central governments unworkable, a *de facto* delegation of all State power to the entities.

'Kin-states', that is states composed primarily of the same ethno-national group as one within Bosnia-Herzegovina, are recognised as having special status under the Dayton plan. The Constitution for the Federation of Bosnia-Herzegovina explicitly permits each entity to "establish special parallel relationships with neighbouring states consistent with the sovereignty and territorial integrity of Bosnia-Herzegovina".[36] This is in contrast to most federal constitutions which forbid their smaller units from entering into treaties or other agreements with foreign governments. Among the foreseeable arrangements, this provision will permit Republika Srpska to enter into agreements with the 'rump' Yugoslavia (predominantly ethnic Serb), thus effectively achieving the Serb nationalists' goal of creating a 'Greater Serbia'.

On what appears to be a more positive note for ethno-national minorities, outsiders play a creative and key role in the new government, particularly with respect to those bodies considering questions of human rights and related issues. The Constitutional Court is made up of nine members, two from each national group and three foreign 'neutrals', appointed by the

European Court of Human Rights.[37] The European Court of Human Rights also appoints three outsiders to join the six local members (again two from each group) of a Commission that will consider the claims of refugees.[38] The Organisation for Security and Co-Operation in Europe (OSCE) appoints the Human Rights Ombudsman, an individual who in the beginning will be a citizen of another state, to investigate and make reports on the existing human rights violations (but not those committed during war).[39] The Committee of Ministers of the Council of Europe appoints eight outside members to complement the six local members (again, two from each group) to a Human Rights Chamber, a body that reviews complaints filed by individuals or by the Human Rights Ombudsman.[40] Similarly, UNESCO appoints two outside members to a five member Commission to Preserve National Monuments.[41]

The Dayton accord further establishes an extensive structure for human rights protection, with the Constitution declaring: "Bosnia-Herzegovina and both Entities shall ensure the highest level of internationally recognised human rights and fundamental freedoms".[42] To accomplish this goal, Dayton both creates new mechanisms, such as the Human Rights Chamber, Office of the Ombudsman, and Refugee Commission, and incorporates an array of existing international and regional human rights instruments and mechanisms.[43] Of these, the European Convention on Human Rights[44] is considered supreme, with the Convention and its protocols applying "directly in Bosnia-Herzegovina" and having "priority over all other law".[45]

Dayton includes numerous protections for people of minority nations, albeit for the most part of an individualistic and not of a collective nature. At the same time, the Constitution of Bosnia-Herzegovina grants citizenship regardless of "association with a national minority",[46] and the Annexed Agreement on Refugees and Displaced Persons calls for the prosecution of persons in the military, paramilitary and police forces who are "responsible for serious violations of the basic rights of persons belonging to ethnic or minority groups".[47] In addition, many of the regional and international guarantees referred to in the document safeguard the rights of minorities.[48] Also, the Dayton accord contains extensive provisions requiring co-operation with international human rights organisations,[49] including the United Nations Commission on Human Rights, the UN High Commissioner on Human Rights, the OSCE, the supervisory bodies of human rights treaties and the International War Crimes Tribunal for the Former Yugoslavia and Rwanda.

To be effective, these human rights guarantees must be enforced. Without enforcement, the operation of the Dayton Plan may well serve to legitimise nationalist interests under the guise of protection of minority rights and the securing of peace. In this context it must be questioned whether the measures undertaken to promote human rights will provide a sufficient counterbalance to the seemingly inoperable system of government created by Dayton. As we will see from the discussion below, the legal approach to minority protection adopted at Dayton had much in common with that adopted in the inter-war period which, as history attests, proved insufficient to protect religious, national and linguistic minorities.

THE INTER-WAR PLANS: DAYTON'S GHOST

After World War I, despite the radical rearrangement of European boundaries in line with the principle of nationality, and despite widespread movements of populations to conform with those definitions, it proved impossible to eviscerate the problem of religious, ethno-national, and linguistic minorities. Twenty to twenty-five million people who remained 'outside of their nation-state' were placed under the protection of the League of Nations to enable them to "live side by side in one and the same state, without succumbing to the temptation of each trying to force his own nationality on the other".[50]

By design, the League of Nations system for the international protection of minority groups was exceptional; it applied to a limited set of states a limited set of rights. Claude notes:

> It purported not to establish a general jurisprudence applicable wherever racial, linguistic, or religious minorities existed, but to facilitate the solution of problems of minority groups in countries where 'owing to special circumstances, these problems might present particular difficulties'.[51]

States subject to the provisions – the so-called 'Minorities States' – felt unjustly discriminated against as differential obligations had been imposed on them by the Great Powers than had been required of other states. The selective nature of the system eroded its legitimacy and hindered adherence to its terms.

In general, the system consisted of three types of obligations: multi-partite minorities treaties and the special chapters of peace treaties dealing with minority groups; declarations made by certain states before the Council of the League of Nations; and regional, bi-partite agreements, notably the German – Polish Convention of May 15, 1922, relating to Upper Silecia.[52]

The term of obligation varied according to the status of the state.[53] Defeated states – Austria, Hungary, Bulgaria and Turkey – were bound by minority provisions inserted into the various peace treaties. New or enlarged states – Poland, Czechoslovakia, Yugoslavia, Rumania, and Greece – concluded special minority treaties with the Principal Allies and the Associated Powers (France, Japan, the United Kingdom and the United States). Some states that fell within or between these two categories made declarations to the Council of the League of Nations, including Albania, Lithuania, Latvia, Estonia, Finland (in respect of the Åaland Islands) and Iraq. Germany was treated somewhat differently as a Great Power. Instead of agreeing to general minorities clauses for all of its territories and populations, Germany signed a bilateral treaty with Poland which created a special minority regime for Upper Silesia.

The instruments purported to safeguard certain rights of 'racial, religious or linguistic minorities', but the framers of the system made clear that they regarded this terminology as synonymous with 'national minorities'. The obligations contained in the minorities treaties and declarations fell into four general categories: nationality provisions; negative rights; positive rights; and specific minority provisions. With the exception of the latter category, the exact wording of the articles varied little from treaty to treaty. These obligations shall be considered in turn.

Nationality Provisions

The nationality provisions concerned the acquisition of nationality by persons belonging to minority groups. For example, the Treaty Between the Principal Allied and Associated Powers and the Serb-Croat-Slovene State provided that citizenship of the Serb-Croat-Slovene State would be granted to "Austrian, Hungarian or Bulgarian nationals habitually resident or possessing the rights of citizenship. . .",[54] and those "born in the said territory of parents habitually resident or possessing the right of citizenship. . .".[55] Furthermore, the treaty provided that "persons referred to above who are over eighteen years of age will be entitled under the conditions contained in said treaties to opt for any other nationality which may be open to them".[56]

Negative Rights

Individuals belonging to minority groups were granted non-discrimination and negative equality rights, unimpaired by their membership in the minority group. The treaties demanded, with only minor variations, the following rights: to life and liberty;[57] to freedom of religion;[58] to equality before the law and enjoyment of the same civil and political rights "without distinction as to race, language or religion";[59] and to freedom from interference with the "enjoyment of civil and political rights, as for instance admission to public employment, functions and honours, or the exercise of professions and industries" because of "differences of religion, creed or confession".[60]

Positive Rights

The treaties also included provisions which promoted 'positive equality', to enable minority groups to "preserve and develop their national culture and consciousness".[61] These included the right to the use of their own language in private relations; the use of their own language before the courts; adequate facilities for a public education in primary schools in their own language whenever there was a 'considerable proportion' of minority students; the establishment of religious and welfare institutions, schools and other educational facilities under their own control and with their own language; and the right to an equitable proportion of state and communal expenditures for educational, religious and welfare purposes.

Specific Minorities Provisions

For the most part, provisions applied equally to members of all minority groups within the jurisdiction of a particular treaty. However, Muslims received special protection in the treaty within the Kingdom of Serbs, Croats and Slovenes,[62] as did the Jewish minority population in treaties between the Allied Powers and Greece, Poland and Romania, as well as in the Lithuania declaration.[63] Stipulations for the Magyar and Saxon communities in Transylvania were included in the treaty with Romania; Czechoslovakia provided for an autonomous territory for Ruthenians; and Greece accepted special obligations for the Vlachs of the Pindus region and for the non-Greek communities of Mount Athos.[64]

As worded, most minorities clauses provided protection for the rights of individual members of minorities and not the minority groups in a collective aspect.[65] This was intentional; the drafters deliberately avoided most terminology that would have given minorities some form of corporate status, except for the purpose of allocation of an equitable share of public funds for schools and the like.[66] To recognise minorities *per se*, the drafters feared, would be to recognise 'states within states', a concept at odds with then prevalent absolute notions of state sovereignty. Thus, even the positive rights were framed in individual terms, as arising out of membership of a minority and facilitating the maintenance and development of group life.[67] At the same time, however, the minorities treaties included references to group-based rights, such as stipulations concerning proportional representation and political and cultural autonomy.

INNOVATIONS OVER EARLIER TIMES

Three interrelated elements differentiated the minorities clauses of the inter-war period from the previous systems: *who* established and *who* guaranteed the provisions; the *methods* by which it was to maintain peace and protect the rights of ethno-national minority groups; and the *assumptions* upon which it rested. Each of these will be addressed briefly in turn.

For the first time, enforcement was not left merely to the signatories or to the prerogative of an interested state (usually a 'kin-state'); instead the League of Nations guaranteed the agreement, intending to give a "more disinterested character to the performance of international obligations toward minorities".[68] Unlike previous attempts to guarantee minority protection, disputes were to be settled by an independent judicial institution, the Permanent Court of International Justice, and not by the state that had the most political power (or the highest degree of self-interest).[69] Outside 'neutrals' played a special role in other aspects of minority protections. The plan for Upper Silesia, for example, envisaged the establishment of a Mixed Commission and an Arbitral Tribunal (both presided over by neutrals) to which members of minority groups could address complaints.[70]

Not only were 'neutrals' brought in to guarantee minority rights, but also the methods at their disposal were revolutionary in admitting the right of individual minority groups – who were not then recognised as subjects of international law – to appeal directly to an international body. Although individual complaints were not provided for in the treaties, through a series of interpretative documents, members of minority groups gained the right to petition for redress in cases of alleged discrimination.[71]

The assumptions on which the minorities treaties were grounded also demonstrated a dramatic change in the use of international policy. In contrast with the previous *ad hoc* system of opposing alliances, collective security was viewed as essential for maintenance of peace.[72] The treaties also rested on the belief that people of different nationalities could live in peace, side by side, in the same state. Moreover, the system recognised a need for both external and internal guarantees for national minority protection. As Inis Claude explains:

> The operation of the treaties and declarations depended heavily upon the compliance of minority states with the obligation to treat the

stipulations as fundamental laws and to implement them by internal legislation. However, it was deemed essential to supplement internal provisions by an external guarantee, based on the premise that the treatment of minorities in the treaty-bound states was a problem of international concern.[73]

By implicitly and explicitly providing for both external and internal guarantees, the inter-war plans posed a challenge to the then accepted notion of sovereignty. The "intervention of an external agency in the relationship between a state and its own nationals was clearly incompatible with the concept of absolute sovereignty",[74] the invalidation of which the inter-war plans demanded as part of an overall peace settlement.[75]

Despite these innovations, the minorities treaties proved insufficient to protect the rights of minority groups and preserve peace. The explanation may lie in the lack of political will on the part of the international community to support the League of Nations and enforce the provisions, and the lack of the will of the 'Minorities States' to stand by their agreements. It must be noted, however, that weaknesses within the system (exacerbated by a lack of political will) crippled it from the outset by giving the impression that the scheme was of a temporary nature. Enforcement mechanisms were weak, the treaties were not enforceable in domestic courts, and the Council of the League of Nations established no effective rules of enforcement. At the same time, 'Minorities States' frequently did everything within their power to block enforcement[76] and forestall petitions alleging abuses by imposing obstacles intended to intimidate and discourage complainants. While individual minorities filed few complaints, self-interested kin-states that were members of the Council of the League of Nations tended to take the initiative in implementing League guarantees. The provisions within the treaties were vague and schematic, failing to account for differing needs and claims to education and autonomous institutions among minority groups, and failing to settle major, explosive issues such as language rights. Finally, the minorities provisions applied only to a select number of states. Ultimately, these drawbacks outweighed the treaties' innovations, and the agreements failed to safeguard the rights of members of minority groups.

LOOKING FORWARD: FOREBODING AND HOPE

The Dayton accord displays a persistent faith in some of the underlying assumptions and practices of the inter-war international legal policy proposals but, at the same time, shows a pragmatic shift to address today's conflicts between members of different ethno-national groups in the context of post-war regional and international human rights systems and mechanisms. This section examines the similarities and differences between the Dayton agreement and the inter-war minorities treaties, and asks whether members of minority groups could fare better under Dayton.

SIMILARITIES WITH INTER-WAR SCHEMES

The discredited schemes, designed to protect minority rights in the inter-war period, evinced a "paradoxical 'alliance' between turbulent nationalist passion and a newly autonomous international law".[77] In contrast, today's international law, grounded in a host of post-Second World War agreements and practices, no longer can be said to be newly autonomous. The place of law in the regional and international contexts has taken hold; human rights can now be said to be "universal, indivisible and interdependent and interrelated".[78] Regional and international systems and mechanisms designed to protect human rights are in place. Yet still, with its own paradoxical alliance with nationalism, the Dayton accord has much in common with the minority protections spawned by the Treaty of Versailles. These similarities will now be considered.

First, the Dayton accord, like the minority rights protections of the inter-war period, approaches nationalism with a "mixture of desire and terror".[79] The carving up of the newly recognised state of Bosnia-Herzegovina along ethno-national lines re-enforced the concept of the 'Nation', an imaginary community defined in opposition to the 'Other' by reference to real and imagined differences in history, culture, language and tradition. Granted, Dayton did not create the nationalisms, or the battle lines; it only recognised territories already controlled by the parties – a situation that no state had the will to reverse. Nevertheless, in doing so, ethno-nationalism was not only tolerated by the Dayton accord, but once again in European history, the nation became part of the 'solution' for peace.

Secondly, international diplomacy in the former Yugoslavia may have begun with a call for human rights, but it culminated in the same legal pragmatism of the inter-war period, accepting that those with power to act as the state *were* the state. Whether and how the powerful gained their power became less and less relevant. The United States Assistant Secretary of State Richard Holbrook's guiding principle for diplomacy was simple: negotiate with those who have power and stop the war at all cost. At one time, this strategy brought accused Bosnian Serb war criminals Karadzic and Mladic to the bargaining table and then, ultimately, Serbian President Slobodan Milosevic as the negotiator for the Bosnian and Croatian Serbs – populations which had never elected Milosevic as their leader. Croatian

President Franjo Tudjman became the negotiator for the Bosnian Croats, a group from which he enjoyed no formal legal mandate.

Holbrook and other diplomats cannot be blamed for adopting a strategy that merely reflected political and military realities. Indeed, Holbrook's negotiations only became potent when the balance of power shifted – in particular when Croatia destroyed the Krajina Serbs and threatened to drive the Bosnian Serbs out of Banja Luka, and when, after Srebrenica, NATO finally became involved in the conflict. The fact that negotiations divided the peoples by nationalist groupings was of little concern to Holbrook and his team. The success of the Dayton accord, like the inter-war agreements, *required* the support of and co-operation by nationalist leaders.

Thirdly, many of the fundamental assumptions underlying both Dayton and the inter-war minorities schemes were the same. Both saw a need for collective security, the promotion of political democracy and economic liberalism, external and internal guarantees for minority rights, and the limited right of external bodies to interfere in the relationship between a state and its own nationals.

Just as in the inter-war years, in the former Yugoslavia "the problem of nationalism came to be perceived as a primal 'clamouring' to which one should respond with a sophisticated and heterogeneously composed 'Plan'".[80] Nationalisms, supported by myth and history, *are* firmly rooted in the culture of the Balkans. Economic crisis and political and social insecurity laid the foundations for chauvinist ideologies in the then Yugoslavia. However, far from being a primal clamouring, nationalism in the former Yugoslavia spread as the direct result of a deliberate political plan crafted by political and academic elites. The emergence of nationalist ideologies was far from inevitable. In a calculated series of manoeuvres, political and academic elites tapped nationalist undercurrents, squelched alternative voices and pitted national groups against each other. It is of some concern, therefore, that the Dayton accord does nothing to challenge the position of those in positions of power, but instead entrenches that power.

Fourthly, both in the inter-war years and under Dayton, bilateral treaty relationships with neighbouring kin-states are permitted, and even encouraged. In the inter-war years, bilateral treaties with kin-states, although initially bolstering the minorities agreements, eventually led to their demise.[81] There is every reason to believe that, unless preventive steps are taken, the same problem with bilateral agreements will reoccur in the Balkans.

Fifthly, the Dayton Plan contains many of the specific attributes of the inter-war plans; in particular it is reminiscent of the plans designed to resolve the disputes over the Saar, Danzig, and Upper Silesia. Similarities include minority guarantees; provisions for emigration and the restitution of property; provisions for self-determination of the peoples, including popular elections; limited supranational integration; and, inter-nationalisation of the settlement. Without political will these measures failed.

The core similarities between the Dayton accord and the inter-war schemes may prove foreboding. The possibility that the rights of minority groups will be better safeguarded under the Dayton agreement than in inter-war times will be determined, though not by technical innovations, as there are very few such innovations, but rather by shifts or changes in international law and diplomacy.

INTERNATIONAL LAW AND DIPLOMACY

The inter-war minorities treaties and the Dayton accord were concluded during times of complex changes in international law and diplomacy. In both periods, lawyers and diplomats struggled to reconcile international law with emerging nationalisms. The inter-war lawyers bypassed "the dichotomy between statist positivism and liberal nationalism in favour of a simultaneous affirmation of the autonomy of international law and an openness to the vital forces of nationalism".[82] This meant reshaping nationalism by endowing it with legal form. At the same time, "the constraints of the stable legal order grounded in sovereignty were rejected in favour of an autonomous, 'experimental' exploration of specifically legal international techniques, doctrines and institutions".[83] Similarly, the Dayton lawyers endowed the nationalisms of the former Yugoslavia with legal form, setting up a system under which nationalisms would be checked by today's international human rights techniques, doctrines, and institutions. The main difference between the two approaches has reflected changes in the global legal environment. Recent years have seen a shift in emphasis away from states as the primary actors in international affairs, to regional and international systems and mechanisms. While this shift may be seen as cause for alarm (states may be presupposed as necessary enforcers of rights[84]), it may also provide a cause for optimism.

On its face, the Dayton agreement acts as if it supports statist positivism. It trumpets the legal fiction of an independent, functioning state of Bosnia-Herzegovina, yet creates entities formed through battle and takes steps to encourage the development of a government within the resulting structure. In doing so, the Dayton agreement bows to the thinking of many of the (ethnic) leaders of the former Yugoslavia, that every nation must have a state and that state must include all members of the nation.

The state created by the Dayton accord, though, is at odds with the statist paradigm. Each of the two internal entities of the state of Bosnia-Herzegovina has more power than the federal unit and, as a result of formal and informal agreements with kin-states, the boundaries of the state are *de facto* porous. Moreover, and also contrary to the traditional statist paradigm, the international community is invited to make decisions and take actions normally within the sovereignty of a state, including issues of international policing and the choice of members of the Constitutional Court. In addition, to the extent that self-determination is seen as the right of a State, the Dayton agreement's recognition of a Bosnia created on the battle field runs squarely against this principle. Today's Bosnia-Herzegovina does not operate like a state, but rather more akin to an interim arrangement, enforced from above by the international community.

In moving away from the statist paradigm, the Dayton agreement is influenced by the environment in which it finds itself.[85] As Falk notes:

> The essence of the new order is the globalisation of capital and the power of market forces, bypassing even the strongest states. States are now unable really to control interest rates or the value of their own currencies, the most elemental aspects of traditional notions of territorial sovereignty.[86]

Residents of Europe, especially in areas of conflict, look to regional and international legal institutions for protection, jobs, and goods. Their leaders look to international bodies for markets, military support and other assistance.

Where the inter-war period witnessed a shift in international law from states to nations (and to individuals as well), Dayton demonstrates a double shift. Global power, and the reach of international law, has moved both outward to international and regional actors (such as financial institutions, security arrangements, and mechanisms and institutions to protect human rights) and down to transnational social forces (including environmental, human rights and community groups).[87] Leaders of nation-states today enjoy a reduced level of power as they must answer to both of these levels if they are to survive. At the same time, with the decline of the nation-state, responsibility for rights enforcement has shifted increasingly from the state to regional and international entities. Both today's problems and tomorrow's solutions must recognise a new concept of state sovereignty and the limitations and opportunities posed by these new developments.

CONCLUSION

The main failing of the Dayton agreement lies in its attempt to impose a firm set of ethno-national categories on the people of Bosnia-Herzegovina on the one hand, whilst on the other perpetuating much of what went wrong in the old Yugoslav government, in particular the charade that an ethno-nationally divided government could function by 'consensus'. The Dayton plan offers few technical innovations over those schemes introduced to protect minorities of the inter-war years. However, the legal, economic and political landscape has changed greatly since the time of the inter-war minorities treaties. Today's proposals for dealing with the tensions between states, ethno-national groups and nationalisms are framed within the context of increased global interdependence, accelerated regionalisation and marked development of the international legal systems. It is within these changes that we may find salvation.

The Dayton accord reflects an understanding that in today's Europe, nation-state boundaries have become more fluid and less relevant for the purpose of fashioning guarantees for regional and international security and minority rights. International and local elites influence regional and international law and policy on the treatment of minority groups. This process in turn influences the identity of national groups and the range of acceptable solutions to their problems. Ultimately, as in the inter-war period, enforcement of the Dayton peace accord will depend not only on legal technique but also on political will. Given the shifts in the global landscape, it will be actors above and below the state who are called upon to take this action.

NOTES

*Julie Mertus is an assistant professor at Ohio Northern University, Pettit College of Law. Research for this chapter was made possible with the support of the Stable Foundation and the Human Rights Program at Harvard Law School. The author wishes to thank Henry Steiner, Barnett Rubin, Nathaniel Berman, Paul Hunt, Steven Wheatley and Peter Cumper for their comments and suggestions. An expanded version of this work is published in 23 (3) *Brooklyn Journal of International Law* (1998) 793.

1.   I. Claude, *National Minorities: An International Problem* (1955), at 12.
2.   I use the term "ethno-national" minorities and members of "national" minority groups interchangeably to refer to groups united not necessarily by geography (as a state is bounded by physical territory), but by a sense of sentiment, that is a sense of identity based on such factors as common myths, history, language, and traditions.
3.   B. Jelavich, *The History of the Balkans: Twentieth Century, Volume 2* (1983), at 122.
4.   The General Framework Agreement for Peace in Bosnia-Herzegovina is reproduced in UN Doc. A/50/790–S/1995/999 in the form initialed in Dayton on November 21,

1995, and it appears in 35 *ILM* (1996) 89 in the form signed on December 14, 1995, in Paris. The latter version corrects minor errors in the UN printing. All references herein to "Dayton" or the "Dayton accord" are to the latter. The Constitution of the Federation of Bosnia-Herzegovina is an annex to the Dayton accord.

5. The Constitution of Bosnia-Herzegovina at Article 1 provides that "The Republic of Bosnia-Herzegovina . . . shall continue its legal existence under international law as a state, with its internal structure modified as provided herein . . .".

6. "Minorities treaties" were included in the Peace Treaties of St. Germain, Triano, Neuilly and Lausanne and the Albanian and Lithuanian Declarations. See *Protection Of Linguistic, Racial And Religious Minorities By The League Of Nations, Provisions Contained In The Various International Instruments At Present In Force*, League of Nations Publications IB Minorite 1927. The Minorities Treaties empowered the League of Nations to receive petitions, conduct fact-finding investigations and issue directives to those nations in violation of the treaties. See A.T. de Azcarate y Florez, *The League of Nations and National Minorities* (1945); also, F. Capotorti, "Study on the Rights of Persons Belonging to Ethnic, Religious, and Linguistic Minorities", U.N. Doc. E/CN.4/Sub.2/384/Rev. 1, U.N. Sales No. E.78.XIV.1 (1979).

7. In particular the German-Polish Convention on Upper Silesia (known as the "Geneva Convention" at the time) (15 May 1922) contained minority rights protections and even permitted individuals to bring cases against their own state. See G. Kaeckenbeeck, *The International Experiment of Upper Silesia: A Study in the Working of the Upper Silesian Settlement, 1922–1937* (1942).

8. D. Janjic, "Resurgence of Ethnic Conflict in Yugoslavia: the Demise of Communism and the Rise of the 'New Elites' of Nationalism", in A.T. Akhavan (ed.), *Yugoslavia: The Former and the Future: Reflections from Scholars from the Region* (1995), at 33.

9. The exact date of the collapse is open to dispute. Some would set the beginning of the collapse before Tito's death in May 1980; others would point to the eruptions in Kosovo in March 1989, after the Serbian Parliament stripped Kosovo and Vojvodina of their autonomous status; others point to January 1991, when the Assembly of the Republic of Slovenia adopted the Charter announcing that it would initiate the procedure of disassociation from Yugoslavia; and still other dates can be found. Many books exist on the destruction of Yugoslavia – one of the best is L. Silber and A. Little, *The Death of Yugoslavia* (1995).

10. This does not of course settle the question of which came first, the identity or the constitution.

11. Z. Paijic, "Bosnia-Herzegovina: From Multiethnic Coexistence to 'Apartheid' and Back", in A.T. Akhavan (ed.), *supra n. 8*, at 162.

12. F. Hondius, *The Yugoslav Community of Nations* (1968), at 248.

13. The term is used by K. Verdery in "Nationalism and National Sentiment in Post-Socialist Romania", 52(2) *Slavic Review* (1993), at 179–203; and by Mary Kaldor in "Cosmopolitanism Versus Nationalism: The New Divide?", in R. Caplan and J. Feffer (eds.) *Europe's New Nationalism: States and Minorities in Conflict* (1996), at 42–58.

14. *Ustav Socijalisticke Federativne Republike Jugoslavije* [The Constitution of the Socialist Federal Republic of Yugoslavia] (1974).

15. *Ibid.* To confuse matters more, Article 244 of the 1974 Constitution provided that "nations, nationalities, working people and citizens shall realize and exercise sovereignty".

16. G. Schopflin, "The Rise and Fall of Yugoslavia", in J. McGarry and B. O'Leary (eds.),

The *Politics of Ethnic Conflict Regulation: Case Studies of Protracted Ethnic Conflicts* (1993), at 190.

17. Other key attributes of the Yugoslav constitutional system pertaining to national minorities included poly-ethnic rights, such as the right to use one's own language in public and for primary education in one's own language, counterbalanced by constitutional prohibitions *against* propagating or practicing national inequality and incitement of national, racial or religious hatred and intolerance.

18. V. Dimitrijevic, "The 1974 Constitution and the Constitutional Process as a Factor in the Collapse of Yugoslavia", in Akhavan (ed.), *supra n.* 8, 45–74, at 60.

19. *Ibid.*, at 71.

20. This section is condensed in interests of space. An examination of the process of collapse can be found in this author's book *National Truths* (1998).

21. A prime example of this tactic is the Memorandum of the Serbian Academy of Sciences and Arts which warned of attacks on "the status of Serbia and the Serb nation". An English version of the Memorandum can be found in K. Mihajlovic and V. Krestic, *Memorandum of the Serbian Academy of Sciences and Arts: Answers to Criticisms* (1995).

22. For a summary of election results, see J. Bugajski, *Ethnic Politics in Eastern Europe: A Guide to Nationality Policies, Organizations and Parties* (1995), at 3–192.

23. For one review of the economic situation, see L. Cohen, *Broken Bonds: Yugoslavia's Disintegration and Balkan Politics in Transition* (1995), at 45.

24. See S. Woodward, *Balkan Tragedy: Chaos and Dissolution After the Cold War* (1995), at 47–81.

25. Those who experienced wartime atrocities tend to be much less likely to seek revenge against an entire group of people, although they may want to avenge the death or torture of a particular family member. See J. Mertus, *et al.* (eds.), *The Suitcase: Refugees Voices from Bosnia and Croatia* (1997).

26. For documentation of this process, see Helsinki Watch, *War Crimes in Bosnia-Hercegovina, Vols. I and II* (1993, 1994).

27. See generally, A. Milic, "Nationalism and Sexism: Eastern Europe in Transition", in R. Caplan and J. Feffer (eds.), *Europe's New Nationalism: States and Minorities in Conflict* (1996), at 169–183.

28. According to some observers and participants in the peace process, the term Bosniacs has become "a euphemism for Muslim". Speech of Paul Szasz, at Yale Law School, "A Year After Dayton: Has the Bosnian Peace Process Worked?", Conference of the Orville Schell Center for International Human Rights and the Council on Foreign Relations, November 15–6, 1996. However, Bosniac could also mean all who do not identify with the earlier two categories.

29. This term has been used by Muhamed Sacirbey and others involved in the Dayton negotiations. Remarks of Ambassador Muhamed Sacirbey at Yale Law School, "A Year After Dayton: Has the Bosnian Peace Process Worked?", *Ibid.*

30. F. Morrison, "The Constitution of Bosnia-Herzegovina", 13 *Constitutional Law Commentary* (1996), at 145.

31. Constitution of Bosnia-Herzegovina at Article III, 1 and Article IV, 4.

32. Each member of the Presidency shall, by virtue of the office, have civilian command authority over armed forces. *Ibid.*, Article V, 5(a).

33. *Ibid.*, Article IV, 1, 2, 3(b).

34. F. Morrison, *supra n.* 30, at 149.

35. L. Silber and A. Little, *supra n.* 9, at 308.

36. Constitution of Bosnia-Herzegovina at Article III, 2(a).
37. *Ibid.*, Article VI, 1. The Constitutional Court has appellate jurisdiction over cases involving constitutional issues and original jurisdiction in cases arising between the Entities, between the Entities and the Central government, or among the organs of the central government (Constitution of Bosnia-Herzegovina at Article VI, 3(a), (b)). Significantly, in human rights cases, the court can hear legal questions referred from the courts of either Entity. However, referral is strictly in the discretion of the local courts.
38. Dayton accord, Annex 7, Article IX, 1.
39. *Ibid.*, Annex 6, Article V.
40. *Ibid.*, Annex 6, Article V, 7.
41. *Ibid.*, Annex 8, Article II.
42. Constitution of Bosnia-Herzegovina at Article II, 1.
43. These agreements are listed in Annex I to the Constitution and in the Appendix to the Human Rights Agreement (Dayton accord, Annex 6).
44. Convention for the Protection of Human Rights and Fundamental Freedoms (1950) ETS 5, UKTS 7.
45. Constitution of Bosnia-Herzegovina at Article II, 2.
46. *Ibid.*, Article I(7)(b).
47. Dayton accord, Annex 7, Article I(3)(e).
48. While nearly all of these guarantees apply to individuals and not collectives, two of the regional instruments provide particularly extensive guarantees for national minorities: the 1992 European Charter for Regional and Minority Languages and the 1994 Framework Convention for the Protection of National Minorities. These agreements are listed at the end of both the Convention of Bosnia-Herzegovina and the Dayton accord, Annex 6.
49. Dayton accord, Annex 6, Article XIII.
50. J. Robinson et. al, *Were the Minorities Treaties a Failure?* (1943), at 35.
51. I. Claude, *supra n.* 1, at 17.
52. See J. Stone, *Regional Guarantees of Minority Rights* (1933).
53. See I. Claude *supra n.* 1, at 16.
54. Treaty Between the Principal Allied and Associated Powers (the British Empire, France, Italy, Japan and the United States), and the Serb-Croat-Slovene State, signed at St. Germain-en-Laye, Sept. 10, 1919, ch. 1, art. 3, 226 Consol. T.S. 8, 182–191 (1919) (hereafter Serb-Croat-Slovene Minorities Treaty at x).
55. Serb-Croat-Slovene Minorities Treaty, at ch. 1, art. 4.
56. *Ibid.*, at ch. 1, art 3. The Treaty further provided: "Option by a husband will cover his wife and option by parents will cover their children under eighteen years of age", (ch. 1, art. 3) and that "All persons born in the territory of the Serb-Croat-Slovene State who are not born nationals of another State shall *ipso facto* become Serb-Croat-Slovene nationals" (ch. 1, art. 6).
57. See, for example, Serb-Croat-Slovene Minorities Treaty, at ch. 1, art. 2.
58. *Ibid.*
59. *Ibid.*, ch. 1, art. 7.
60. *Ibid.*
61. A.T. Azcarate, *supra n.* 6, at 82.
62. The Serb-Croat-Slovene State agreed "to grant the Musulmans [sic] in the matter of family law and personal status provisions suitable for regulating these matters in accordance with Musulman usage", to ensure protection for "mosques, cemeteries

and other Musulman religious establishments", and to grant full recognition to "Musulman pious foundations (Wakfs) and religious and charitable establishments. . .", Serb-Croat-Slovene Minorities Treaty, ch. 1, art. 10.

63. C.A. Macartney, *National States and National Minorities* (1934), at 230–252.
64. *Ibid.*
65. I. Claude *supra n.* 1, at 19; J. Robinson, *supra n.* 50, at 71.
66. H.W.V. Temperley, (ed.) *A History of the Peace Conference of Paris* (1920), at 137.
67. E. Chaszar, *The International Protection of National Minorities* (1988), at 3.
68. J. Robinson *supra n.* 50, at 40. Nevertheless, the system could not become politically sanitised. As Robinson notes, " . . . even the new system could not completely eliminate dissatisfaction on the part of those governments which were bound by minority obligations. Moreover, the collective will still have to find expression through the medium of individual powers. It was impossible to completely eradicate the political aspect from public law".
69. See F. Capotorti, *supra n.* 6, at 24–25.
70. See G. Kaeckenbeeck, *The International Experiment of Upper Silesia: A Study in the Working of the Upper Silesian Settlement, 1922–1937* (1942).
71. The 1929 report of the Council of the League which specifies its operating procedures (known as the "Adatci Report"); see also A.T. de Azcarate, *Protection of National Minorities*, Occasional Paper No. 5, Carnegie Endowment for International Peace, June 1967.
72. For historical background, see J.A.S. Grenville, *The Major International Treaties 1914–1945: A History and Guide with Texts* (1987).
73. I. Claude *supra n.* 1, at 20.
74. *Ibid.* at 21. Indeed, the Serb-Croat-Slovene State, Rumania and Poland fought against the minorities treaties largely on these grounds. "They characterized the minorities clauses as a violation of the principle of equality of states, an attack upon their sovereignty, and an indication of a lack of confidence and good faith. . .They claimed that an international guarantee was a source of potential danger, because the minorities would feel that their status rested upon the support of foreign powers", J. Robinson, *supra n.* 50, at 154–55.
75. "In the Versailles peace system, the minorities provisions constituted a corollary and corrective to the principle of national self-determination. They became possible only through the restriction of absolute state sovereignty. Insofar as the disturbance of external peace was caused by internal discord, the minorities provisions, as a means of regulating the relations between national groups, were a part of the general peace structure", *ibid.*, at 41.
76. States could enact provisions that would undermine the intention of the treaties. For example, although minority groups were allowed schools in their own language, a state could deprive private schools of the right to issue diplomas. Also, economic measures that would have a particular impact on a national minority could be enacted as long as the provisions did not single out the minority.
77. N. Berman, "But the Alternative is Despair: European Nationalism and the Modernist Renewal of International Law", 106 *Harvard Law Review* (1993), at 1798.
78. World Conference on Human Rights, *The Vienna Declaration and Platform for Action, June 1993*, United Nations Dept. of Public Information DPI/1394–39399–August 1993–20M.
79. N. Berman, *supra.* n. 77, at 1805.
80. *Ibid.*, at 1800.

81. J. Robinson, *supra n.* 50, at 50.
82. Berman, *supra n.* 77, at 1803.
83. *Ibid.*, at 1805.
84. For this observation, I am indebted to Yash Ghai. He has elaborated his ideas in "Globalization and the Politics of Rights", paper and talk presented at Harvard Law School, Human Rights Program, December 4, 1996.
85. L. Chen, *An Introduction to Contemporary International Law* (1989), at 26.
86. R. Falk, comments in "Teaching International Relations and International Organizations in International Law Courses", 87 *American Society of International Law Proceedings* (1993), at 398.
87. *Ibid.*

International Legal Order and Minority/Government Conflict

Nedzad Basic, Donald J. Fleming and William M. Vaughn[*]

INTRODUCTION

Recent observers such as the former UN Secretary-General and the Organisation for Security and Co-Operation in Europe (OSCE) have noted that minority interests expressed as self-determination and considerations of sovereignty pose problems in both domestic and international law and politics:[1]

> The sovereignty, territorial integrity and independence of States within the established international system, and the principle of self-determination for peoples, both of great value and importance, must not be permitted to work against each other in the period ahead. Respect for democratic principles at all levels of social existence is crucial: in communities, within States and within the community of States. Our constant duty should be to maintain the integrity of each while finding a balanced design for all.[2]

Disputes involving claims of minority rights and sovereignty may arise in any multi-ethnic state, which outnumber uni-national states by nearly nine to one.[3] Many conflicts have arisen in politically unstable multi-ethnic states, notably former socialist states, such as the former Yugoslavia, or less-developed countries such as Rwanda. But supposedly stable, developed countries also experience tension or violence such as the United Kingdom in Northern Ireland, and Canada in Québec.

Contemporary assertions of minority interests and state sovereignty continue to present challenges to peace that neither current legal nor political principles seem likely to resolve. We focus on one issue: the potential of a dispute between a minority and a government to become armed conflict. We shall explain how the *relationship* between two principles of international law in the current international legal order – self-determination and respect for territorial integrity – discourages a peaceful resolution of a dispute, and, in practice, encourages each party – the minority and the

P. Cumper and S. Wheatley (eds.), Minority Rights in the 'New' Europe, 285–304
© 1999 *Kluwer Law International. Printed in Great Britain.*

government – to have recourse to violence to 'solve' the dispute. We believe the methodology we adopt will contribute to a clearer understanding of why this occurs in the current international legal order. We begin with a hypothesis, based largely on observation of minority and government behaviour, that conflicting claims based on the legal principles of self-determination and territorial integrity often tend to promote armed conflict. This hypothesis includes the corollary that a modification in the existing relationship between the principles will affect the decisions the parties make in light of the new relationship between self-determination and territorial integrity. Consequently, if this relationship can be modified, it will encourage the parties to make decisions that will lead them to co-operation rather than conflict.

We formulate the problem of the relationship between the principles of self-determination and territorial integrity in terms of game theory models.[4] In Model 1, the 'Current International Legal Order', we will demonstrate how the application of the principles of self-determination and territorial integrity can force a minority and a government (neither of which neces-sarily wishes to trigger violent confrontation) to make rational choices that result in armed conflict between the two. In this model, no other international legal principle affects the decisions as directly and as immediately as do these two. The resulting armed conflict usually leads to human rights violations by both parties which each cites as justification for the previous use of violence against the other.

In Model 2, the 'Developing International Legal Order', we seek to demonstrate how a resolution of the conflict between the two principles and the parties may be induced. In the second model, the relationship between the principles of self-determination and territorial integrity continues to underlay the conflict between the disputing sides, but the hypothetical application of an overriding principle, the respect for international human rights law, introduces the condition that the realization of both self-determination and territorial integrity must include respect for human rights law.[5] As a result, the rational choices each party makes will differ from the previous model. In the 'Developing International Legal Order' their choices induce them to co-operate.

We suggest that the international community can govern claims of self-determination and territorial integrity by ensuring that their employment fosters a respect for human rights. In so doing, international law can help to reduce armed conflict between a minority and a government. The logical implication and the intended political result would be that peace is no longer associated with the application of one of the principles to the exclusion of the other. Instead, while both principles remain in effect, peace becomes associated with the principle of respect for human rights.

Although disputes between minorities and governments have been so divisive in our generation, in the 'Developing International Legal Order' there is potential for the creation of civil and international peace.

THE RELATIONSHIP BETWEEN THE PRINCIPLES OF TERRITORIAL INTEGRITY AND SELF-DETERMINATION

While assessments, like the former UN Secretary-General's, allude to the dangers arising from the contemporary application of the legal principles of self-determination and territorial integrity, they fail to explain why those dangers exist. Historically, each principle arose during different epochs in international relations to address specific threats to international peace and order. The principle of territorial integrity developed during the evolution of the state in the seventeenth and eighteenth centuries and sought to preserve the state system itself.[6] Self-determination is a twentieth century principle that sought the peaceful disintegration of multi-ethnic empires, first after World War I as the basis for the dissolution of the Austro-Hungarian and Ottoman European empires, and then after World War II as the legal basis of decolonisation.[7] The significance of self-determination as the basis of decolonisation culminated in 1966 in the statement of self-determination as a legal obligation in Common Article 1 of the UN Covenants onCivil and Political, and Economic Social and Cultural Rights.[8]

Since the end of the era of decolonisation, the principle of self-determination has influenced minority claims in non-colonial states. In at least one account, it has become so central in international law and politics that it has fully encompassed the principle of territorial integrity so that self-determination now means democratic government over the territory inhabited by a people[9] who may wish to exercise their right to democratic government within a separate state entity. Such an assertion of the right would lead to the break-up of multi-ethnic states given its lack of respect for the territorial integrity of existing states.[10]

Decolonisation unintentionally laid the basis for the current problem of the relationship between the two principles. At present, and at least since the end of the era of decolonisation, as Boutros-Boutros Ghali noted, there has been an inherent conflict in the relationship between the two principles. In a typical dispute between a minority and a government, each claims one principle to justify its position and seeks to regulate the outcome of the dispute according to that principle. Armed conflict threatens to occur because self-determination would lead to secession, thus threatening territorial integrity, while territorial integrity prohibits self-determination, commonly associated with the party asserting the right as statehood.[11] Rather than contribute to peace, as was the original intention of each, the two principles appear to exacerbate internal conflict, leading to external support and intervention on one side or the other.

The international community has neither managed to establish norms which would resolve the conflict between these legal principles, nor has it settled outstanding disputes between minorities and governments where the triumph of one is the defeat of the other.[12] External states appear content to deal politically with each dispute and any armed conflict which may arise from it on an *ad hoc* basis, with the international community remaining aloof from internal disputes until they threaten international peace.

Similar to the well-recognised political principle in international relations of the permissive use of force, this global legal and political context allows political leaders of many national, ethnic, linguistic, religious, and other minority groups to claim the right to an independent state regardless of the human rights violations and international instability their claims may produce. In addition, governments threatened by such claims usually respond through strong measures of centralisation and repression, which also result in violations of human rights.[13] It is an irony of the post-war period that neither principle has contributed to peace, unless it is valid to assert that violence in the name of either principle leads, in the long run, to peace.

THE MODEL OF THE 'CURRENT INTERNATIONAL LEGAL ORDER'

Diagram 1 (below) represents the relationship between the principles of self-determination and territorial integrity in the current international legal order according to the argument in the previous section. The following points may be made: at present, the principles have equal status; historically, depending on the epoch in international politics and law, respect for one or the other of the principles has contributed to peace; simultaneous claims under each principle, not having been foreseen, and not having occurred until recently, are incapable of legal resolution; self-determination has acquired the status of a human right; there is no direct legal relationship between respect for human rights and territorial integrity.

Diagram 1

Conflict: Relationship of Principles in the Current International Legal Order

HR

/

SD   =   TI

\   /

PC

Key

SD = principle of self-determination   HR = human rights
TI = principle of territorial integrity   PC = peace

If one adds to this representation of the legal order, considerations of a minority making a claim under self-determination that could lead to secession and of a government defending itself against that claim under the principle of preservation of its territorial integrity, the conflict between the two principles can be formulated as a problem in game theory. Model 1 below of the 'Current International Legal Order' represents the choices of a minority and of a government acting in light of the principles of self-determination and territorial integrity as a game theory matrix.

Model 1: The Current International Legal Order

	government	
	B-1 Decentralisation	B-2 Centralisation
minority		
	(−10)	(+50)
A-1 autonomy	Co-Operation (HR>SD, TI)	Hegemony (TI>SD, HR)
	(−10)	(−100)
	(−100)	(−50)
A-2 secession	Disintegration (SD>TI, HR)	Conflict (HR<SD, TI)
	(+50)	(−50)

Key

HR = principle of human rights
SD = principle of self-determination
TI = principle of territorial integrity

In this model the minority can adopt a strategy of seeking autonomy within the state (A-1) or of secession (A-2); the government can pursue policies of decentralisation (B-1) or centralisation (B-2). The relationship between the participants depends on the combination or outcomes of strategies chosen. Strategies of autonomy and decentralisation produce co-operation; hegemony (rule by the dominant group) results from strategies of autonomy and centralisation; disintegration from secession and decentralisation; and conflict from secession and centralisation.

The first of the numerical values (illustrated) for each outcome represents the value of the outcome for the minority; the second for the government (i.e. under A-1/B-2 (Autonomy/Centralise), the value for the minority is represented as -100, and that to the government as +50). The numbers are insignificant in themselves. They are chosen to indicate the relative position of the participants in each outcome and to represent the relative position of each participant for the four outcomes. As long as these two relative positions are respected, the model meets the criteria of the particular game theory model we use.[14]

As mentioned, the numerical values reflect the relative position of the parties for each outcome, and the relative position of each participant for the four outcomes. A standard consideration in game theory is whether participants choose their "best" or their "best possible" outcome. In Model 1, the best outcome for the minority (+50) is disintegration, and the best outcome of the government (+50) is hegemony. For reasons to be discussed below, neither one of these outcomes will result. Although each may adopt the strategy appropriate for its desired outcome, the exact outcome will be dependent on the strategy the other adopts. In some cases, again to be discussed below, the parties may choose the "best possible" outcome, which in Model 1 is Co-Operation, represented by a value of (-10) for each.

In game theory, participants behave according to their rational self-interest. Those unfamiliar with the use of game theory to analyse decision-making often object that leaders do not always behave rationally. Rational behaviour is, they contend, that which the observer considers to be reasonable. Further, game theory limits the matters that decision-makers take into account to only those variables in the model. This a necessary abstraction from "reality" if each case is not to be considered unique. Game theory does not consider whether or not the aims pursued by the leaders are reasonable in the first place; rather, it assumes that given those aims, any decision-maker will pursue policies of rational self-interest. Often, the objection to game theory reflects an opinion that international politics and law puts decision-makers in unreasonable positions, or that their aims are unreasonable. But among those who make this mistake, few would object to the proposition that, the circumstances notwithstanding, leaders behave in their rational self-interest. Game theory abstracts from 'real-life' decision-making contexts the variables in play, and models decision-making in light of them. The more the variables capture actual situations, the more the theory allows us to understand such situations. That understood, one can go further, as we do in this chapter, and hypothesise, based on international legal political developments, a change in those variables. Then one can analyse how such a change affects the choices leaders make in their rational self-interest.

THE MODEL AND THE DECISIONS THAT LEAD TO CO-OPERATION

As mentioned, participants in game theory models behave rationally. But what is the rational choice for the minority and for the government in Model 1? In terms of the values of the outcomes, the minority should try to secede (+50), but this outcome results only if the government decides on measures of decentralisation. If the government was to decide on measures of centralisation, the minority would have to fight to secede, an outcome represented by the value of (-50). But the minority could choose to try to achieve autonomy within the state, which, were the government to adopt a policy of decentralisation, it could achieve, resulting in an outcome of (-10). While this is not its best outcome (+50), it is certainly better than ending up in a civil war (-50).

The government is in an identical situation. Choosing a policy of centralisation would lead to the best outcome (+50), but only if the minority choose to seek autonomy within the state. If the group decided to secede, the government would have to contest it (-50). However, the government could avoid this by choosing to decentralise (-10), which although it is not the best outcome (+50), it is preferable to conflict (-50). The minority and the government each choose the strategy that leads to their best possible rather than their best outcome.

Model 1 indicates that, in this context, leaders acting in rational self-interest would tend to co-operate. If they choose opposing strategies – secession and centralisation – they end up in conflict (-50). If self-defeating strategies are chosen-autonomy while the government centralises, or decentralisation while the minority secedes-they risk their worst outcome (-100). Although each party would like the other to choose a self-defeating strategy so it could achieve its best outcome (+50), each party attributes rational choice to the other. Realising these possibilities, the government will seek to decentralise and the minority will seek autonomy. As a result, as a matter of rational self-interest they both choose strategies which will result in their best possible outcome. As a result they co-operate with each other knowing each would like to achieve its best outcome but that neither can achieve it.

THE BREAKDOWN IN CO-OPERATION IN THE 'CURRENT INTERNATIONAL LEGAL ORDER'

The co-operation the parties accept as the best possible relationship between them under the circumstances is unlikely to last – for two reasons. First, the risks of co-operation are immense. Given the strategies the minority and the government have adopted (autonomy and decentralisation), if either was to change its strategy, the other would face its worst outcome. If the minority was to abandon co-operation and seek to secede, the government would face the disintegration of the state. On the other hand, if the government was to discontinue co-operation and adopt measures of centralisation, the minority would be subjected to government hegemony.

The adoption of strategies that result in (on-going) policies of co-operation and the maintenance of co-operation require initial and deepening mutual confidence. Such confidence is hard to come by in most cases. Historical, political, constitutional, and economic conflicts all contribute to the difficulty of its development. In such circumstances each participant tends to choose the strategy appropriate to the realization of its best outcome: secession for the minority and centralisation for the government. But neither the minority nor the government would be irrational and allow the other to achieve its best outcome. Their strategies consequently lead them into conflict, whose value (-50 for both) they accept, although it represents a worse outcome than the co-operation they cannot maintain. In the circumstances, each participant not only protects itself against its worst outcome by accepting conflict, it also denies the best outcome to the other. Minority groups and governments have to avoid the respective risks of domination or dissolution; each will adopt the strategy that prevents the potentially most damaging outcome for it. The government will choose to centralise, since if it does not, it may contribute to the successful secession of the minority. The minority will choose to secede, since if it does not, it may contribute to the development of government hegemony.

The second reason co-operation is unlikely to last is that the relationship between the two apparently conflicting principles of self-determination and territorial integrity creates an additional dilemma for the participants. The government will tend to think its allies and the United Nations will recognise its right to protect its territorial sovereign rights over domestic affairs.[15] In this case, the government would rationally discontinue co-operation and adopt a policy of centralisation. It does this knowing the minority will not allow its centralisation (represented by a value of +50 for the government) to go uncontested. But lacking confidence in the co-operation of the minority, it prefers to take its chances to preserve the state through violence rather than to lose it through disintegration, an outcome whose value for the government is -100.

The minority will make a calculation similar in logic to the government's. It will postulate that its allies and the UN will initially support its claim of self-determination, and, given the actions of the government, many states will eventually support secession.[16] It will also count on United Nations intervention in the event of internal armed conflict, which it will also consider as support for its secession. In addition, the minority knows the government lacks confidence in its co-operation. Realising the government will adopt measures of centralisation, the minority will conclude that should the government succeed in the establishment of a high degree of constitutional, political and economic centralisation, it will lose any chance of external recognition of its right to self-determination. As a result, the minority will fear the loss of whatever political, cultural and economic independence it has achieved within the state. In this case the minority would rationally discontinue co-operation and adopt a strategy of secession. It does this knowing the government will not allow its attempt to separate to go uncontested (represented by a value of +50 for the minority). But lacking confidence in the co-operation of the government, it prefers to take its chances to realise independence through violence, rather than to lose any chance of it through being subjected to the hegemony of the government, an outcome whose value for the minority is -100.

The dilemma created by the 'Current International Legal Order' is that due to the possibility of an appeal to conflicting norms, each participant is uncertain whether the other will choose to co-operate and continue to co-operate if it does. This uncertainty deepens their mistrust, and both will tend to abandon co-operation and seek their best outcomes. In the circumstances, neither can count on the other being foolish and adopting a self-defeating strategy that would allow its rival to achieve its best outcome.[17] Neither has any choice but to adopt the strategy they both know, when paired with the other's strategy, leads to armed conflict. Thus, the parties have recourse to violence to settle an issue on one or the other of the conflicting principles of international law. On the one hand, the government tries, with external support, to defeat the minority and preserve its territorial integrity. On the other hand, the minority tries, with external support, to defeat the government in order to secede. Each side is steadfast in pursuing a policy that will bring them into conflict.[18] In general, the 'Current International Legal Order', far from creating order, lacks incentives or guarantees which would encourage the parties to co-operate.[19] As a result of the impotence of the legal constraints, a political practice has developed whereby the parties often view armed conflict as the only way to establish a new state through secession or to maintain the integrity of an existing state. Indeed, armed conflict is the process which determines the outcome of the conflict of legal principles. While one can predict from the model lack of stability in minority-government co-operation and movement towards an armed resolution, one cannot predict in the event whether self-determination in the form of secession and recognition of a new state, or preservation of the territorial integrity of the existing state and defeat of the minority will result. The model does demonstrate however, why peace is unattainable, and why, in the predictable resort to armed conflict, any hope whatsoever for state-wide respect for human rights is groundless. Ironically, this is something to which the 'Current International Legal Order' directly contributes.

MODIFYING INTERNATIONAL LAW TO PROMOTE INTERNAL CO-OPERATION

We have demonstrated (above) the irrationality of the adoption of strategies that would lead to co-operation between a minority and a government and the rationality of the adoption of strategies that result in violence. In an effort to find a solution to this problem we introduce a third legal principle – respect for international human rights law – into the relationship between the principles of self-determination of the people and the territorial integrity of the state, and analyse the effect it has on the rationality of recourse to violence. Diagram 2 (below) represents the change as the 'Developing International Legal Order'. This version of international legal order (as does the former) assumes domestic and regional violence resulting from the conflict between the principles of self-determination and territorial integrity to be a major threat to peace and security.

In this version of the international legal order, the principles of self-determination and territorial integrity continue to be respected. Unlike in the 'Current International Legal Order' however, neither self-determination nor territorial integrity can be realised to the exclusion of the other as a result of armed conflict. Rather, each finds expression to the extent that it does not exclude the other. At the same time, respect for each contributes to the observance of human rights standards. The former conflict between self-determination and territorial integrity is no longer an internal matter to be decided by marshalling external support on opposite sides and resorting to violence to settle the issue of the conflict between the principles. As articulated in the *preamble* of the United Nations Charter, observation of human rights serves the cause of peace.[20] Arguably, as the Charter originally intended, an international guarantee of the domestic observation of international human rights law becomes the focus of efforts to maintain international peace. Diagram 2 below represents this version of an international legal order.

Diagram 2

Peace: Relationship of Principles of Self-Determination and Territorial Integrity in the Developing International Legal Order

```
        HR

     /       \

SD      ||      TI

    \       /

        PC
```

Key

SD = principle of self-determination
TI = principle of territorial integrity
HR = human rights law
PC = peace

As in the previous discussion of the 'Current International Legal Order', the addition of a minority and of a government making claims under the principles of self-determination and territorial integrity can be formulated as a problem in game theory. Model 2 (below) of the 'Developing International Legal Order' is similar to Model 1 of the 'Current International Legal Order' in that the participants are motivated by the principles of self-determination and territorial integrity and in that the minority may choose to seek autonomy or to secede while the government may decide either to decentralise or centralise. The essential difference is that the introduction of an international guarantee of domestic observation of international human rights law changes the value of the outcomes for two of their decisions. If a government attempts to centralise and achieve hegemony at the expense of the minority's enjoyment of human rights, it faces its worst rather than its best outcome. Similarly, if a minority attempts to secede and uses means that violate the internationally guaranteed human rights of the government side, it too faces its worst rather than its best outcome. This effect of the changed relationship between principles of self-determination and territorial integrity is indicated by the change in values of the outcomes of disintegration and hegemony in Model 1(from +50, -100 to -50, +100, and from -100, +50 to +100, -50 respectively). As a result, as will be explained, the outcomes switch positions. What was hegemony becomes disintegration, and what was disintegration becomes hegemony.

Model 2: The Developing International Legal Order

	government	
	B-1 Decentralisation	B-2 Centralisation
minority		
	(−10)	(−50)
A-1 autonomy	Co-Operation (HR>SD, TI) (−10)	Disintegration (TI<HR, SD) (+100)
	(+100)	(−50)
A-2 secession	Hegemony (SD<HR, TI) (−50)	Conflict (HR<TI, SD) (−50)

Key
HR = principle of human rights
SD = principle of self-determination
TI = principle of territorial integrity
PC = peace

The analysis of decision-making in the 'Developing International Legal Order' might begin with the above observation of the change in values for two of the outcomes. As in the model of the 'Current International Legal Order', the combination of strategies that result in hegemony and disintegration – secession/decentralisation and autonomy/centralisation – are self-defeating, but for a different reason.

In the model of the 'Current International Legal Order', if a minority was to adopt a policy of autonomy and a government a policy of centralisation, the minority would be swallowed up in a centralised state. Thus, the values of (-100, +50). On the other hand, if the government was to adopt a self-defeating strategy and pursue measures of decentralisation while the minority sought to secede, the government would lose territory and the minority would achieve independence. Thus, the values of (+50, -100). In the model of the 'Developing International Legal Order' the signs for these outcomes are reversed to indicate the dramatic change produced by the obligation on both parties to respect international human rights law.

In the model of the 'Developing International Legal Order' the principles of self-determination and territorial integrity are no longer mutually exclusive. A minority will continue to seek self-determination and a government territorial integrity, but neither can be realised without concurrent respect for international human rights law. Rather than the realisation of one of the principles at the expense of the other through recourse to violence, the parties will co-operate to determine the extent each can be fulfilled on the condition of mutual respect for international human rights law. Thus, if a government adopts measures of centralisation while the minority seeks something less than its own state, the government does so at the expense of the rights of that minority. This results in a negative outcome for the government under international law and a positive outcome for the minority. The changed values of the outcome reflect the changed relationship between the international legal principles of the self-determination of people and the territorial integrity of the state. Whatever the minority decides, the government can attain its best outcome only if it adopts a policy of decentralisation (-10 or +100) rather than pursue measures of centralisation (-50). In practice, the government would be obligated to back away from measures of centralisation that violate the minority's human rights. In the extreme, should the government insist upon such centralisation, the pre-eminence of an international guarantee of human rights would allow the minority to secede without recourse to violence. This value of (-50) reflects the punishing loss of territory and population to a government that insists upon centralisation at the expense of the human rights of a minority.

The same logic applies to a minority which would secede and establish its own state in the wake of violations of the human rights of the government side. The minority would be obligated to back away from efforts to secede that violate the government's human rights. In the extreme, should the minority insist upon such secession, the pre-eminence of an international guarantee of human rights would allow the government to centralise without the threat or use of violence by the minority. The value of (-50) for the minority reflects the punishing loss of the benefits of self-determination through secession to a minority that insists upon violent secession at the expense of the human rights of the government. A minority, due to the changed values, would realise that a policy of secession is self-defeating. It would understand that, regardless of the strategy of the government, it is better to adopt a strategy of autonomy rather than a strategy of secession, since only then can it obtain its best outcome (-10 or +100), as opposed to its worst outcome (-50).

While it is clear the minority may opt for autonomy rather than attempt to secede and that the government is likely to offer to decentralise rather than to centralise, neither does so thinking that such a course of action will accomplish its best outcome. Either group can only achieve its best outcome (+100) if the other chooses a self-defeating strategy; either autonomy/centralisation or secession/decentralisation. Either party could adopt the strategy appropriate to achieving its best outcome and try to persuade the other to adopt the self-defeating strategy on which its realisation depends, but this ploy will not work since, as argued above, the other will see it as a self-defeating strategy for itself. Thus, as rational decision-makers, the minority decides upon autonomy realising it will be within the state, and the government decides upon decentralisation, realising it will have to accommodate the minority. This leads them to co-operation, although each realises it cannot accomplish its true aim, an independent state or the elimination of those that threaten territorial integrity.

THE STABILITY OF CO-OPERATION IN THE 'DEVELOPING INTERNATIONAL LEGAL ORDER'

But why in this model do the parties not abandon co-operation and end up in conflict, as they did in the model of the 'Current International Legal Order'? We have just established that both parties will avoid strategies that could lead to conflict: secession for the minority and centralisation for the government. We have also seen that each party will avoid these strategies since they could lead to their worst outcomes. In addition, we have seen that in adopting strategies which could lead to their best outcome (+100), autonomy for the minority and decentralisation for the government, neither can count on the other to adopt the self-defeating strategy that would produce its best outcome. If, contrary to the above two reasons, one party was to adopt a self-defeating strategy or a strategy that could lead to its worst outcome, centralisation for the government and secession for the minority, then, indeed, conflict would ensue. However, as we have seen, both of these are irrational choices. As a result, the rational choice, and, as it turns out, the best possible choice is autonomy/decentralisation (-10, -10) which results in co-operation. This outcome is not only the rational settlement of the issue between parties who embrace conflicting principles, but, since no other options exist, it is also the necessary choice.

It turns out that each party can influence the other only by continuing to co-operate. Neither can count on the other to adopt a self-defeating strategy. Thus, the co-operation that begins albeit reluctantly, on the basis of the realisation that one cannot reasonably expect any better relationship, serves as the basis for the realisation of the right to self-determination for the minority people or the preservation of territorial integrity of the state. However, the one has to be realised in the context of the accommodation of the other. This is precisely the effect desired in reforming the international legal order.

Compared to the model of the 'Current International Legal Order' in which the parties would either fail to begin to co-operate, or would discontinue co-operation due to their lack of mutual confidence, neither party would abandon co-operation in the 'Developing International Legal Order'. As demonstrated, neither the minority nor the government thinks the other will adopt a self-defeating strategy. And unlike in the 'Current International Legal Order', the temptation to settle the issue of self-determination or territorial integrity by force is removed since in the 'Developing International Legal Order', the possibility of an appeal for external support no longer exists. The international community assumes a unified position. It will not tolerate a secession that inevitably violates the human rights of those on the government side, nor will it allow a process of centralisation, which violates the human rights of the minority, to preserve territorial integrity. The participants have no rational choice other than co-operation. They will have to work out some combination of self-determination and territorial integrity, most likely through measures of decentralisation and democratisation. Thus, while a minority and a government may not like each other, and both may have a "past", they both understand the other will co-operate initially and will continue to do so.

If the minority and the government are given to understand that self-determination and territorial integrity can only be realised if human rights are observed, then negotiation between them is not about their mutually exclusive claims, but rather about how each can attain its goals within a context of respect for and observation of human rights. Thus, in theory and in practice, neither self-determination, nor the maintenance of territorial integrity should undermine the human rights of either. Rather, co-operation should expand the scope of enjoyment of human rights and lead to democratisation. As the former Secretary-General remarked in *An Agenda for Peace*, peace in the modern world requires respect for both sovereignty and self-determination in a context of respect for human rights and democratisation.

CONCLUSION

Several aspects of the argument in this chapter bear noting in conclusion: first, if self-determination and territorial integrity are put in the service of another principle as they are in the model of the 'Developing International Legal Order', then the conflict between them disappears and the rationality of conflict between parties motivated by them necessarily disappears. Thus, if a government decentralises to maintain its territorial integrity and introduces protection for the human rights of a minority seeking self-determination, its territorial integrity is preserved by international law. If a minority was to seek autonomy within the state to realise self-determination and to respect the human rights of the government seeking to preserve its territorial integrity, its claim to self-determination would be more highly respected. As argued, the combination of the strategies in the 'Developing International Legal Order' if perhaps counter-intuitive, results in the fullest extent of the realisation of both principles in the context of full enjoyment of human rights by the minority and the government. Secondly, since the principles of self-determination and territorial integrity are no longer mutually exclusive (as each contributes to the common goal of the state-wide observation of human rights), the conclusion that it is necessary to fight to establish one's "self", as a new state or to preserve the state as an integral state, is obviated. Thirdly, as the conflict between the two principles is subordinated to the realisation of respect for human rights, each obviously contributes to this third principle, and less obviously, indirectly preserves and protects the other. And, finally, mutual confidence in stable co-operation is the key to peace. Although stable co-operation between a minority and a government probably cannot be realised in the 'Current International Legal Order', it probably could be in the 'Developing International Legal Order'. The developments we discuss in international human rights law and in the re-assessment of the principles of self-determination and territorial integrity are well under way and need to be emphasised.

NOTES

*Nedzad Basic is Associate Professor of International Public Law and International Relations, University of Bihac, Republic of Bosnia and Herzegovina; Donald J. Fleming is a Professor in the Faculty of Law, University of New Brunswick; and William M. Vaughn is Associate Professor of Political Science at St. Thomas University. The authors are grateful for research grants and support by the Atlantic Human Rights Centre, St. Thomas University, the University of New Brunswick, Association of Universities and Colleges of Canada and the Canadian Centre for Foreign Policy Development.

1. See in general, C. Brölmann and others (eds.), *Peoples and Minorities in International Law* (1983); B.S. Jackson and D. McGoldrick, *Legal Visions of the New Europe* (1993); for the United Nations General Assembly's formulation of minority interests, see the General Assembly, *Declaration on the Rights of Persons Belonging to National or Ethnic, Religious, and Linguistic Minorities* (18 December 1992), A/RES/47/135.

2. United Nations, *An Agenda for Peace*, Report of the Secretary-General pursuant to the statement adopted by the Summit Meeting of the Security Council on 31 January 1992, A/47/277-5/24/11, 17 June 1992, para. 19.

3. J. Rourke, *International Politics* (1997), at 152. In this chapter we consider minorities to be relatively large and geographically concentrated groups such as Albanians in Kosovo, Serbs in Croatia, and Serbs and Croats in the Republic of Bosnia and Herzegovina.

4. In the social sciences, economics was the first to use game theory. The seminal work is J. von Neumann and O. Morgenstern, *The Theory of Games and Economic Behaviour* (1945). Using an analysis of co-operative and non-co-operative behaviour, the perspective we take in this chapter, the classic text is R.D. Luce and H. Raiffa, *Games and Decisions* (1957). Recent works that account for mathematical and analytic developments and remain introductory and readable include: P.C. Ordeshook, *Game Theory and Political Theory* (1986); P.C. Ordeshook, *A Political Theory Primer* (1992); K.A. Shepsle and M.S. Bonchek, *Analyzing Politics* (1997). Its use in law is rare and apparently limited to domestic law. Our work appears to pioneer its use in international law. On domestic legal contexts see D.G. Baird *et al*, *Game Theory and the Law* (1994).

5. The function of this chapter is not to define rights. It presumes them to be the international human rights, including minority rights (however specifically defined by the appropriate international bodies), contained in the Universal Declaration of Human Rights, UNGA Res. 217 (III), UN GAOR, 3rd Sess., Supp. No. 13, at 71, UN Doc. A/810 (1948), the International Covenant on Economic, Social and Cultural Rights (1966) 993 U.N.T.S. 3, and the International Covenant on Civil and Political Rights (1966) 999 U.N.T.S. 171.

6. On the historical development, see in general, J. Bartelson, *The Geneology of Sovereignty* (1995). For the development of the principle of the preservation of the territorial integrity of the state from the principle of sovereignty see C. Weber, *Simulating Sovereignty: Intervention, the State and Symbolic Exchange* (1995).

7. A. Cassese, *Self-Determination of Peoples: A Legal Reappraisal* (1995), at 48.

8. Consistent with our view on rights, *supra* n. 5, self-determination has come to be considered a human right. *The Vienna Declaration and Programme of Action* considers a denial of the right to self-determination as a violation of human rights: UN Doc. A/Conf. 157/23, 12 July 1993, para 2.

9. See Cassese, *supra* n. 7.

10. The distinction between colonial and non-colonial is historical and geographic rather than analytic. Colonial means the states which came to independence during the era of decolonisation. The trend in the incidence of self-determination appears to be as stated. For the incidence in non-colonial states, see W. Ofustey-Kadjoe, "Self-Determination", in *The United Nations Legal Order*, Vol. 1, O. Schachter and C. Joyner (eds.) (1994), at 385.

11. See Cassese, *supra* n. 7, at 11 and 52 *et seq*. For a view that insists upon democratic governance however the relationship of the principles is worked out, see *supra* n. 1.

12. H. Hannum, *Autonomy, Sovereignty, and Self-Determination: The Accommodation of Conflicting Rights* (1990).

13. There appears to be no consensus on the legal meaning of self-determination in non-colonial states. For an overview of self-determination, see E. Laing, "The Norm of Self-Determination 1941–91", 22 *California Western International Law Journal* (1991–92), at 209. For the view that relations between a minority and a government are within domestic jurisdiction see Y. Inoue, "United Nations' Peace-Keeping Role in the Post-Cold War Era: the Conflict in Bosnia and Herzegovina", 16 *International and Comparative Law Journal* (1994), at 264. On the question of territory see L. Wildhaber, "Territorial Modifications and Breakups in Federal States", *Canadian Yearbook of International Law* (1995). On aspects the titles indicate, see A. M. O'Connel, "Commentary on International Law: Continuing Limits on UN Intervention in Civil War", 67 *Indian Law Journal* (1989), at 903; Etzioni, "The Evils of Self-Determination", *Foreign Policy* (1992–93), at 21; R. Amer and others, "Major Armed Conflicts", *SIPRY Yearbook* (1993), at 81.

14. We consider the decisions a minority and a government make in the context of international legal orders. As we formulate the problem in the current international legal order, it is an example of decision-making in which in their mutual interest they should co-operate, but as a matter of rational behaviour they do not. We represent this in the text as the breakdown in co-operation. The current international legal order, as far as the principles of self-determination and territorial integrity are concerned, is one in which, as a matter of rational choice, a minority and a government will not co-operate. In game theory, the prisoners' dilemma is perhaps the most discussed example of non-co-operative behaviour. The literature is vast. The standard work to begin with is A.M Chammah, *Prisoners' Dilemma* (1965). A crucial question that occurs relative to minority/government relations is whether repeated contacts and negotiations make a difference in the outcome. This is known as finitely and infinitely repeated prisoners' dilemma. In this chapter, since it is an initial formulation of the problem of non-co-operative behaviour in an international legal order, we assume "one" play. We are not unaware of the possibility that negotiations can be seen as finite and perhaps infinite play. In our model, the participants tend towards mutual co-operation; nevertheless they face the dilemma of not knowing whether the other will co-operate and decide not to co-operate. In the prisoners' dilemma, there is a possibility that, with repeated play, the participants will learn how to predict whether the other will co-operate. We would argue that (space forbids developing the point) even with repeated play, the 'Current International Legal Order' rules out any co-operation whatsoever. Nigel Howard has developed an argument in response to the problem of predicting whether the other participant will co-operate: N. Howard, *Paradoxes of Rationality: Theory of Metagames and Rational Behavior* (1971). On the question of infinitely repeated play see M. Taylor, *Anarchy and Co-operation* (1976). The entire issue of *The Journal of Economic Theory* (1989) is devoted to finitely repeated play (with various concepts and in various combinations). In our model of the Developing International Legal Order the minority and the government co-operate as a matter of rational choice. This model is not therefore based upon the prisoners' dilemma although for ease of understanding in the text the discussion makes it appear as if it is since it approaches the problem as a change in values of two of the outcomes. It is however a co-operative game. On co-operative games, see J. von Neumann and O. Morgenstern, *supra* n. 4.

15. In the case of the dissolution of the former Yugoslavia the last Yugoslavian Federal Minister of Defence said, "We very certainly had information and opinion that the international community would not intervene in the case of civil war in Yugoslavia."

V. Kadijevic, *Moje vidjenje raspada, Vojska bez drzava*, Politika (Beograd) (1993). At the time, Western countries pressed the coalition of Slovenia and Croatia to stop secessionist activities and gave the green light for Federal authorities to undertake measures against the separatist movements in Croatia and Slovenia: *International Herald Tribune*, January 16, 1991.

By refusing to recognise secession as an option and by not standing strongly and clearly against re-centralisation and the use of force to reunify Yugoslavia, the international community actually supported the forcible reunification of Yugoslavia. This in turn provoked a strengthening of separatism and violations of human rights and the rights of minorities: *International Herald Tribune*, February 23, 1991. In late April, 1991, the British Prime Minister, John Major, emphasised that Western countries would not accept any act to cause the disintegration of Yugoslavia and refused to recognise any support given to the separation of Croatia: *Borba* (Beograd), April 20, 1991. The US Ambassador in Belgrade told the international weekly *Politika* that the US strongly opposed the separation of the Yugoslav Republics and told Slovenia and Croatia that they would meet difficulties in case of their separation: *Politika* (Beograd), June 1, 1991.

16. In March 1991, the Austrian Foreign Minister, Alois Mock, advised Western countries to consider the crisis in Yugoslavia and emphasised their responsibility to prevent civil war in Yugoslavia "even if this includes the recognition of the right of self-determination", *ORF* (Vienna), March 13, 1991.

17. M. Shubik, *Game and Related Approaches to Social Behavior* (1964), at 20–25, 30–32.

18. A. Rapaport and A. Chammah, *Prisoners' Dilemma* (1965), at 9–30; J. Nash, "Non-cooperative Games", 54 *Annals of Mathematics* (1951), at 286.

19. R. Macdonald and D. Johnton (eds.), *Structure and Process in International Law: Essays in Legal Philosophy, Doctrine and Theory* (1983), at 1–15.

20. It seems reasonable to propose the thesis, in light of conclusions drawn about the causes of the Holocaust and the geo-political outlook in the immediate aftermath of WWII, that the allies (the United Nations) intended the reference to "self-determination of peoples" and "human rights and for fundamental freedoms for all without distinction" to refer to the non-discriminatory enjoyment of rights within each of the signatory member states, each being a separate people. The United Nations attributed the Holocaust in part to the lack of human rights protection (and democratic government) in Germany. In addition, the overall structure of the Charter distinguishes non-self governing territories, trusteeship territories and former enemy states from the original member states (the wartime United Nations with a few exceptions). Logically, the reference to "self-determination of peoples" and "human rights . . . without distinction" in Article 1 can be read as a principle of international relations and as the same set of rights for all within each of the actual nation-states, that is, the original members, which, with the exception of the former enemy states, were nearly all of the independent states at the time. In this reading, the political development expected was for non-self governing territories and trusteeship territories to become independent on the basis of provisions in the relevant Chapters rather than on the basis of Article 1. Then, they would enjoy the benefits as unified nation-states, each comprising a "people", of domestic non-discriminatory enjoyment of human rights and of international relations based on "self-determination". (The former enemy states, which were already independent, would also enter the United Nations and enjoy the benefits of Article 1 as soon as the Charter restraints on them were removed.) In this view, gradual independence and democratisation were foreseen as coming in the

near political future. The era of decolonisation and the application of the concepts of Article 1 within nation-states, especially the original members, thus confounded the original meaning of the Charter. The relevance of this thesis to the current debate is that it re-emphasises the significance of the international context and of non-discriminatory domestic human rights enjoyment, which is exactly the change we propose in our model of the 'Developing International Legal Order'.

Minority Rights and Conflict Resolution in Northern Ireland

*Christine Bell**

INTRODUCTION

Although many commentators acknowledge the importance of human rights discourse in the context of the Northern Ireland conflict, the issue is often presented as secondary to the prior difficulty of accommodating competing territorial claims – that is dealing with the 'constitutional question' of whether sovereignty should lie with Britain or Ireland. This would seem to be the approach of political parties, commentators and the British and Irish governments (although the degree of emphasis placed by the respective parties on the issue of human rights varies).[1]

There are two problems created by considering human rights as a secondary issue. First, it underestimates the link between specific human rights violations and conflict (not the main focus of this chapter); second, it ignores the substantial area of international law relating to group accommodation and minority rights which can be applied to the situation in Northern Ireland. The issues of self-determination and minority rights link the politics of group accommodation with human rights standards. This forms a different approach to the question of conflict resolution from that of addressing constitutional divisions directly.

In this chapter I will outline, in attenuated form, the international law relating to self-determination, group accommodation and minority rights, and discuss its possible application to Northern Ireland. In the concluding third section of the chapter I suggest the types of 'solutions' that begin to emerge from such a discussion and debate the advantages and disadvantages of using international law as a starting point in the search for such 'solutions', and consider any implications for international human rights law itself.

305

P. Cumper and S. Wheatley (eds.), Minority Rights in the 'New' Europe, 305–323
© 1999 *Kluwer Law International. Printed in Great Britain.*

SELF-DETERMINATION

The international law dealing with self-determination has two aspects: a core settled meaning which grants a right to self-determination most clearly in a traditional 'colonial' situation, and a more uncertain application based on an attempt to apply the principle to a broader range of political situations, for example that of minorities *within* a state. It is clearly stated, in the international documents on self-determination, that the right is a right of 'peoples',[2] and is subject to respect for the principle of territorial integrity.[3] When examples are turned to, the most accepted application of the right to self-determination is in the situation of a colony or non-self-governing trust. This is supported by consistent State practice and was accepted by the International Court of Justice in the *Namibia* case.[4] In the situation of former colonies there is little tension between independence as an acceptable outcome and the principle of territorial integrity as the 'people' leaving the state are territorially defined. Similarly, territorial integrity is not implicated in situations where all parties within a state consent to a change in sovereignty, such as with the dissolution of the Union of Soviet Socialist Republics (USSR), the dissolution of Czechoslovakia into its two constituent republics, and the reunification of Germany.[5] Ambiguities in the definition, however, have led other groups – notably ethnic or national minority groups within states – to claim 'a right to self-determination'. Minority groups have tried to argue that they constitute 'peoples' within the definition of self-determination, despite the fact that international instruments seem to contemplate a distinction between 'peoples' and 'minorities'.[6] As explained by Epseill, a Special Rapporteur of the Sub-Commission on Prevention of Discrimination and Protection of Minorities:

> Self-determination is essentially a right of peoples. . . It is peoples as such which are entitled to the right to self-determination. Under contemporary international law minorities do not have this right.[7]

Several factors, however, suggest that the definition of a 'people' does not require an attachment to territory, a position which gives some support to the self-determination claims of groups such as minorities. First, the international instruments do not support limiting the definition of a 'people' to colonial situations.[8] Second, instruments relating to indigenous peoples have blurred the distinction between peoples and minorities by their use of the term 'peoples'.[9] Finally, definitions of 'peoples' do not suggest that a pre-determined territory is an essential requirement.[10]

Minority groups and commentators have also based claims for self-determination on the argument that territorial integrity attaches only to 'representative' government, suggesting that an unrepresentative government cannot rely on this principle. The Friendly Relations Declaration 2623 states that territorial integrity attaches to

> sovereign and independent States conducting themselves in compliance with the principle of equal rights and self-determination of peoples as described above and thus possessed of a government representing the whole people belonging to the territory without distinction as to race, creed or colour.[11]

This has led to debate on how 'representative' such a government has to be to qualify for the 'right' of territorial integrity, and whether in the absence of such government, the right to self-determination would include a right to secession, or merely a right to a more representative form of government. On this issue, Cassese suggests that the notion of self-determination as a remedy for unrepresentative government cannot be pushed too far, and can only be seen to apply to a few peoples living under racist regimes.[12] Epseill suggests that the notion of representative government indicates self-determination may be a right of persons who are not technically under colonial and alien domination where "beneath [a] guise of ostensible national unity, colonial and alien domination does in fact exist, whatever legal formula may be used in an attempt to conceal it".[13] Finally, Eide suggests that the right of the people of an independent State to self-determination is "a right to have an inclusive, representative and democratic government". Rather than a right to a specific sovereignty "[It is] . . . a right to democracy and respect for human rights".[14] However other writers have suggested a stronger relationship between human rights and self-determination claims whereby the more unrepresentative the government the broader the self-determination claims that will be tolerated by other states (if not embraced by them):

> One can discern degrees of self-determination, with the legitimacy of each tied to the degree of representative government, on one hand, and the extent of destabilization that the international community will tolerate in a self-determination claim on the other.[15]

Clearly, such a relationship would tend to support the self-determination claims of certain minority groups (and reject others).

The self-determination norm is unsatisfactory, both conceptually and in practice, for resolving territorial disputes as it falsely assumes homogeneity of peoples within territorial boundaries. In so doing it fails to deal with the issues raised by minority groups who are not adequately accommodated within existing boundaries, or indeed those minority groups created by a successful secession claim and a new state boundary. In both denying the secessionist claims of minority groups and failing to provide the amelioration of their condition within the state boundary, the norm paradoxically fuels the claims of such groups that they are denied effective participation in government and public life, in turn strengthening the merits of their self-determination claim. Thus "[m]inorities appropriate the vocabulary of self-determination whether governments approve or not".[16] This instability is further perpetuated by the fact that the political realities of a self-determination claim are on occasion endorsed even when the strict legal right is not present, such as in the former Yugoslavia.

This instability has led commentators to explore possible re-interpretations of the 'breadth' of the notion of self-determination through the idea of 'internal self-determination',[17] where groups which are somewhat less than the whole 'peoples' of a defined territory should be given a right to self-determination that is somewhat less than independent government or secession. The rhetoric and underlying rationales of the notion of self-determination are used to support the development of policies of group accommodation – such as autonomy regimes, or other minority protection less than secession. Self-determination is linked to effective participation in government, and rather than assuming homogeneity within territories, is responsive to the political reality of heterogeneous societies with minority populations. Despite these developments, it is certainly too early to talk of an existing legal 'right' to internal self-determination.

Self-determination and Northern Ireland

Politically, discussion on the issue of self-determination in Northern Ireland has focused around the question as to what is the appropriate territorial unit to self-determine its future. There are two main options: Northern Ireland, or the island of Ireland as a whole. Other possible options – of the British Isles (of Britain and Ireland), the United Kingdom (as a whole) or perhaps a European unit – are relatively unsupported by politicians and by any application of international law, and will not be considered in detail.[18] The question of the unit is important. It dictates who are the 'people' and what is the 'territory', thus affecting the outcome of a self-determination claim. If the island of Ireland as a whole is the unit to which the right applies then an all Ireland, Irish Nationalist majority will decide the future status of Northern Ireland. If Northern Ireland is the unit, the 'people' will mean that population alone, that is, at present, a British/Unionist majority.

International law standards on self-determination must be considered in the light of the (likely) possible units of self-determination.

(i) Northern Ireland as Unit of self-determination: Arguments and Outcomes.

Given that the border between Northern Ireland and the remainder of Ireland was established in 1920 and has persisted without successful international challenge, it can be argued that Northern Ireland (as part of the United Kingdom) should command respect for its borders, as a territory. Further, the Unionist majority in Northern Ireland can also argue that they constitute a 'people' on the criteria of a shared culture and history.[19] Although in 1920 the situation in Ireland could be defined as colonial, self-determination, while existing as a principle at that time, did not exist as a fully blown right under international law. Northern Ireland is further supported as the unit of self-determination given that "[a]ll the relevant states and bodies have committed themselves, as might be expected from established state practice in these matters, to the acceptance of Northern Ireland as presently constituted".[20] This is not just (arguably) the international legal position, but is consistent with the British Constitutional law position.[21] Interestingly, it is also implied by *Frameworks for the Future* (a joint British/Irish proposal for a framework for political talks hereinafter, the 'Framework Document'), which affirms that Northern Ireland is a part of the United Kingdom as the "present reality, in fact and in international law".[22]

If Northern Ireland is the requisite unit of self-determination, this then leaves the question of what it could self-determine? Theoretically permutations include secession from the United Kingdom leading to unity with Ireland; 'Ulster Independence'; increased integration with Britain; or some special status with a degree of association with either Britain or Ireland, or possibly both. It must be noted, however, that whichever option is agreed upon it would have to enjoy the free choice of the people of Northern Ireland, and there are other possible limitations. Commentators have suggested that size and viability should be additional criteria of independence, raising doubts about an independent status for Northern Ireland. The option of Irish unity would only be available with the consent of the people of the Republic of Ireland, and similarly increased integration with Britain may need the additional consent of those in the United Kingdom, although this is less clear. Finally, there are restrictions on any possible exercise of self-determination by the 'people' of Northern Ireland which would have the effect of denying rights to any minority group (such as the present Irish Nationalist minority in Northern Ireland, or indeed a future British Unionist minority in Northern Ireland). Such restriction may be implicit within the notion of self-determination itself, but is underpinned primarily by the proliferating international documents on minority rights protection.

*(ii) The Island of Ireland as the Unit of self-determination: Arguments
and Outcomes.*

Northern Ireland emerged as a result of the particular political contingencies
of the early 20th century. It can be argued that the colonial situation of
Ireland had no clear ending in Northern Ireland, where the coloniser
retained ultimate power – a power that was to be used directly from 1972
onwards.[23] During its entire 70 year history, partition has been challenged
both politically and militarily. The maintenance of the border has been at
the price of constant emergency legislation and systematic discrimination
against the Irish Nationalist minority with respect to civil and political,
and social and economic rights. Thus, there are two elements to the claim
that the island of Ireland (including Northern Ireland) should determine
its (and Northern Ireland's) future. First, it contains a 'people' within a
specific territory. Irish Nationalists within Northern Ireland are not in a
similar position to minorities created by the independence of colonies
within colonial borders, for the colonial power is still in power.

The argument that self-determination did not exist as a right in 1920,
and therefore that the border emerging at the time should be accepted
to-day can be criticised. Many colonial governments resisted arguments
for decolonisation based on self-determination (arguing that it was a
principle and not a right), and yet after independence accepted that the
right of self-determination had in fact applied. The British government,
in the context of the Falklands/Malvinas dispute, for example, stated to
the Security Council:

> It is true that we took the position in the 1960s that self-determination
> was a principle and not a right. . . Not only has my country [now]
> endorsed the right to self-determination in the sense of the Charter,
> the [International Human Rights] Covenants and the Friendly
> Relations Declaration [1970], but we have gone a great deal
> further to disprove the allegation that we are a colonial power *par
> excellence.*[24]

It can, therefore, be argued that a right to self-determination (established
clearly in contemporary international instruments and documents) was
denied in 1920 undermining the legitimacy of the border then established.

A second argument for self-determination on an all island basis lies in
the notion of representative government. It could be argued that the
consistent experience of nationalists in Northern Ireland is one of
unrepresentative government; therefore, the principle of territorial integrity
for Northern Ireland is not applicable. Indeed this is an argument which
could be used to support a right to self-determination for the Irish

Nationalist people even if Northern Ireland is taken to be the unit of self-determination – although here it would raise the problem of whether secession was an appropriate remedy as it would implicate the rights of the Unionist majority.

If the island of Ireland is taken to be the unit of self-determination then the main options seem to be some form of Irish unity or some form of association of Ireland with Britain (for example through joint authority over Northern Ireland), again with the caveat of the need for minority protection.

There remains a question as to whether the island of Ireland as a whole, as the unit of self-determination, could determine a status for Northern Ireland contrary to the wishes of a majority of the people of Northern Ireland. This suggests a counter argument, that even if the 1920 partition is accepted as illegitimate, it does not necessarily follow that the unit for self-determination is the island of Ireland. In 1996 Asbjørn Eide produced a report, commissioned by the Irish Forum for Peace and Reconciliation (established by the Irish government after the first IRA cease-fire), which examined the areas of both self-determination and minority rights. In submissions made to Eide during the course of preparing this report, Sinn Fein argued that Northern Ireland "could be seen as the remaining part of a non-self-governing territory, resulting from the disruption of territory at the time when the Republic of Ireland gained independence".[25] Eide responded:

> Even if Northern Ireland is held to be non-self-governing, it would be for the majority of the population of that territory, in line with the relevant resolutions of the United Nations. . . to decide on the future of the territory. Should the majority decide in favour of a united Ireland, they could do so, which amounts to British Government policy as stated in the Anglo-Irish Agreement, the Joint Declaration and *A New Framework for Agreement* [part of the Framework Document].[26]

Self-determination: Conclusions

A black-letter law analysis of the right to secession through self-determination would seem to permit the exercise of the right in only two situations: non-self-governing territories (of which there is a finite list as produced by the Decolonisation Committee[27]) and, in exceptional cases (of which there are few practical examples), when the population of a part of a State has been subjected to consistent and systematic discrimination and when the government of the State is not representative of that part of the population.[28] This analysis would support the claim that Northern Ireland as a unit enjoys territorial integrity and that its people must agree to any change in its status, with the consent of any other implicated state, such as Britain, and, depending on the change contemplated, Ireland. However, international law in this area is not static and given the ambiguities in the legal position of self-determination and the pressure exerted by the political realities of divided societies, it is still possible to coherently argue for a different application of the right to self-determination based on the underlying principles of colonial government and unrepresentative government. These arguments give some support to claims for self-determination by the Irish Nationalist people within Northern Ireland.

The situation of Northern Ireland illustrates the internal instability of a self-determination norm created by an assumption of homogeneity which does not reflect the political reality of divided societies. Possible 'solutions' which application of the norm may produce are undermined by its very failure to address the group which may find itself to be a minority, whether it be an Irish Nationalist minority within Northern Ireland, or a British Unionist one within a United Ireland. The self-determination norm needs to adapt to be relevant and helpful to situations of group conflict.

In contrast, a proliferating area of minority rights protection has evolved from a narrow position of non-discrimination to increasingly pro-active measures to further group accommodation and ensure that policies are not those of homogenisation (that is the elimination or assimilation of the group), but rather ones which ensure 'effective participation' of minorities in all the institutions of society. There is a clear overlap between the concept of internal self-determination and minority rights protection which suggests either territorial or institutional autonomy as a way to accommodate competing cultures and identities.

MINORITY RIGHTS AND NORTHERN IRELAND

At the core of minority rights protection are the ideas of freedom and equality,[29] and the prohibition of discrimination (placing a duty on states not to discriminate).[30] From this point there is a continuum which moves through to measures and suggestions for the preservation and promotion of group culture and identity, and arguably autonomy. Specialist Conventions impose a pro-active duty on states to take steps to ensure the elimination of discrimination. The International Convention on the Elimination of All Forms of Racial Discrimination (1966), for example, talks of "eliminating discrimination in all its forms and *promoting understanding among all races*".[31] To this end each state party is required among other things to "prohibit and bring to an end, by all appropriate means . . . racial discrimination *by any persons, group or organization*".[32] Thus the state's duty is not just a negative one, constraining its own role as a discriminator, but may necessitate positive intervention in the private sphere to prevent discrimination. Still further along the 'continuum of rights' are provisions which contemplate a group identity to be protected or accommodated (albeit with a debate as to whether rights attach to groups or to individual members of the group). Article 27 of the International Covenant on Civil and Political Rights laid the foundation for this approach providing:

> [i]n those States in which ethnic, religious or linguistic minorities exist, persons belonging to such minorities shall not be denied the right, in community with the other members of their group, to enjoy their own culture, to profess and practice their own religion, or to use their own language.

Minority rights protection is most fully articulated and extended in the UN Declaration on the Rights of Persons Belonging to National or Ethnic, Religious and Linguistic Minorities (1992), and by the Council of Europe's Framework Convention on the Protection of National Minorities (1994). Both contemplate policies of recognition and accommodation as opposed to assimilation – illustrated by continual reference to a "right to participate effectively".[33] States have obligations not just to prevent discrimination, but "to create favourable conditions to enable persons belonging to minorities to express their characteristics and to develop their culture, language, religion, traditions and customs".[34] Interestingly, as well as preserving rights to inter-group contacts within the territory, the Convention and the Declaration refer to the right of ethnic groups to maintain cross-border contacts with ethnic counterparts in other jurisdictions. The UN Declaration provides a right of minorities to maintain "contacts across frontiers with citizens of other States to whom they are related by national or ethnic, religious or linguistic ties (Article 2(5))". In Article 17(1) of the Framework Convention, States undertake "not to interfere with the right of persons belonging to national minorities to establish and maintain free and peaceful contacts across frontiers with persons lawfully staying in other States, in particular those with whom they share an ethnic, cultural, linguistic or religious identity, or a common cultural heritage". More pro-actively, Article 18 states that: "Parties shall endeavour to conclude, where necessary, bilateral and multilateral agreements with other States, in particular neighbouring States, in order to ensure the protection of persons belonging to the national minorities concerned".

In contrast with that relating to self-determination, the international

law relating to minority rights is limited less by difficulties with definitions (despite perennial debates around what is a minority, and whether
'group rights' exist), than by difficulties in implementation and enforceability. Along the 'continuum of rights' from freedom and equality and
non-discrimination, minority rights become progressively 'softer' – increasingly unenforceable due to a lack of legal status, the absence of ratifica-
tions of relevant instruments, or because of their programmatic nature.
This limits their effectiveness as a tool of conflict resolution.

Application of Minority Rights in Northern Ireland

Minority rights protection in Northern Ireland has been shown to be
inadequate, even in the narrow sense of non-discrimination in relation
to basic civil, political, social and economic rights. Moving along the
spectrum towards the recognition of group identity and other more
pro-active measures to deal with group accommodation, there has been
little progress. Such measures have not been tried explicitly. Although
bi-lateral treaties with the Republic of Ireland have been undertaken,
these efforts at reassurance of the Irish Nationalist minority have been
undermined by straightforward human rights abuses disproportionately
affecting this community. They have been further undermined by lack
of institutional change to ensure the effective participation of minority
groups in institutions of government, particularly those of the criminal
justice apparatus.

   Both the Anglo-Irish Agreement and the Framework Document, for
example, could be seen as providing minority protection through bi-lateral
agreements, cross border co-operation and internal power-sharing.[35]
Neither, however, placed the protection of rights at their centre, nor did
these documents provide clear structural guidance on how representativeness
(or 'parity of esteem') between Unionists and Nationalists could be achieved
in a broad range of political institutions.[36] Although the Framework
Document did attempt to balance institutional participation, this was
largely limited to elected institutions and would possibly have operated
through a system of vetoes. It can therefore be argued that the Anglo-
Irish Agreement, the Downing Street Declaration and the Framework
Document were overly influenced by both the prevailing view of negotiation
(the finding of wording which will mean different things to different people)
and a legal culture which is uncomfortable with the language of rights.
This left the question of rights in their usual position as peripheral to other
conflict resolution issues.

   In contrast to the inter-governmental approach, Eide's summary of his report to the Forum for Peace and Reconciliation, provides an example of what the political arrangements for minority rights protection, consistent with international instruments, might look like.[37] He overcomes the problem of enforceability by suggesting that the approach of States should be to ask, not 'what are my minimum obligations', but rather 'what is good practice with relation to minority rights, consistent with international law?' Thus, the most far reaching standards, the Council of Europe's Framework Convention on the Rights of National Minorities (1994) and the United Nations General Assembly Declaration on the Rights of Persons Belonging to National or Ethnic, Religious and Linguistic Minorities (1992), suggest, at least, that good practice and can be used to provide embryonic political models for states with divided societies. Four elements to Eide's approach can be identified:

(i) Robust protection of human rights to ensure that no negative consequences flow from ethnicity / national identification. In practice this would involve initiatives such as domestic incorporation of the European Convention on Human Rights and Fundamental Freedoms and the International Covenants (on Civil and Political and Economic, Social and Cultural Rights), perhaps through a new Northern Ireland Constitution Act. Eide also suggests the explicit recognition of separate groups or identities, with a requirement of equality of treatment.

(ii) Power-sharing and equal representation in institutions. Given that Northern Ireland is a divided society, Eide argues that power-sharing mechanisms, such as proportional representation and weighted voting, could be used to reward compromise over exclusively ethnic voting. Importantly though, he argues that these should not be implemented, and power not devolved, until adequate arrangements are in place to ensure 'equality in the common domain'; that is, stringent and positive equality measures and the "organisation of the administration of justice, security forces and others, on a basis of impartiality".[38]

(iii) Equality in the common domain and special measures to ensure 'pluralism in togetherness'. Eide argues that political arrangements should include more than the mere provision of equality, but should also "equal respect for the traditions and identities of each group, within the framework of universally recognised human rights".[39] He identifies two layers of provision to achieve this: at one level, a common identity for everyone living within the territory based on equality ('equality in the common domain'), and at the other, acceptance of the existence of separate, ethnically or culturally based national identities – with mutual respect for the two identities (the provision of a separate domain in certain areas). The first level would be established by the existence of a functioning democracy where basic civil, political and economic rights were guaranteed without discrimination. Special attention would be given to "the prevention of discrimination in the administration of justice, including the role and performance of security forces, police and agents of prosecution, as well as the judiciary". Drawing on the UN Declaration and the Framework Convention, Eide also identifies further special measures and collective rights that could be implemented so as to provide for autonomy in certain areas (notably that of identity, with provisions on language, culture and education).

(iv) Methods of securing group accommodation. A final dimension of Eide's executive summary can be categorised as methods of 'copperfastening' group accommodation, involving consideration of the possible role of the international community (through bilateral treaties, or the assistance of the institutions of the Council of Europe and Organisation for Security and Co-operation in Europe) in the development of internal legal mechanisms for group accommodation. However one of his most interesting points is that transfrontier contacts "now form a part of generally recognised human rights"[40] and amount to a right rather than a privilege in situations where the identity of the group transcends the political border. In such circumstances, individuals and communities who share a common ethnic bond should not be artificially separated by that border in their contacts with each other. In Northern Ireland, initiatives such as the Anglo-Irish Agreement, the Downing Street Declaration, the Framework Document and the most recent Belfast Agreement, all with cross border elements, can be seen, to some extent, as building on this minimum standard of a right to cross border contact. Rather than a diminution of sovereignty, or a dilution of territorial integrity, the cross border element redefines the nature of each, in the interests of minority rights protection.

INTERNATIONAL LAW AND POLITICAL THEORY

Although it is not possible to extrapolate the detail of a political settlement from international law standards, as can be seen from the above discussion, a possible political framework emerges using such standards as a basis for discussion. It is a framework within which claims for a United Ireland based on the right to self-determination are dismissed as unsupported by the rules of international law. However, it is a framework wherein notions of sovereignty are revealed as flexible and the principle of territorial integrity for Northern Ireland (a key Unionist demand) linked to robust protection of minority rights – including special measures and cross-border contacts (key Nationalist demands). As Eide points out, this model has similarities with British/Irish government policy evidenced in the Anglo-Irish agreement, the Downing Street Declaration and the Framework Document. It is also similar with those ideas advanced by political theorists, such as McGarry and O'Leary, for a form of 'consociationalism'.[41] However, there is a crucial difference in emphasis; in chief the establishment of improved human rights protection as a pre-requisite to agreement on internal power-sharing, which is, in turn, prior to constitutional questions.

In the final section of this chapter I will address the implications of dealing with the issue from an international law perspective rather than political one, considering firstly the implications for conflict resolution, and secondly, those for the international law on human rights.

IMPLICATIONS FOR CONFLICT RESOLUTION

Clearly, international legal approaches to the Northern Irish situation and those of political science are not, and should not be seen as, mutually exclusive. It is, however, worth considering the advantages in locating arguments in the application of international principles of self determination and minority rights when addressing issues of conflict resolution. It can be argued that the problem of Northern Ireland is not the lack of potential solutions, but the problem of finding a solution that the different parties and their constituents will agree to at the same point in time.[42] An international law approach has the potential to focus the processes away from the present 'zero sum' game approach, to one that is capable of envisaging 'win/win' solutions. The following discussion illustrates some of the keys to this shift.

International law articulates legitimate standards external to the parties to the conflict

International law has a claim to objectivity and legitimacy that the ideas of political theorists do not (or at least they have to earn). The advantage of using standards external to the conflict is that the 'solutions' posited have a strong claim to be non-partisan, giving a stronger claim to cross-community acceptance both morally and pragmatically. Although a full conflict resolution analysis of the recent 'peace process' cannot be attempted here, one of its persistent failures was its use of a series of trade-offs between these two communities. One of the many draw-backs of this style of negotiation is that successful interim steps can frustrate rather than further progress on the larger issues. If steps, such as proposed changes in emergency laws or the conduct of elections, are reactive to events and represented as 'concessions' to one community they will be evaluated from a 'them' and 'us' perspective – what helps them hurts us, and vice versa. Such 'concessions' establish expectations for counter-concessions regardless of the merits (in terms of human rights or justice) of the proposed action. Future action becomes increasingly difficult as it requires a balancing of the respective claims and counter-claims. Moreover, the parties are encouraged to exaggerate their demands and adopt rigid positions from which to negotiate 'concessions' rather than working to fashion solutions designed around trying to accommodate the different interests at stake. In contrast, international law cannot as easily be accused of having been shaped by 'them' and 'us' considerations, and can be used to place interests and not positions at the centre of the debate.

International law focuses on the interests underlying unnegotiable constitutional positions

Many of the 'solutions' posited to the question of the constitutional status of Northern Ireland's status attempt to 'split the difference' between the territorial claims, either conceptually (for example joint authority) or territorially (for example (re)partition). To some extent all of these solutions relate to an underlying analysis that the constitutional issue is separate from other issues, and is the primary one to be resolved. An international law perspective alters the focus – away from the question of who is the best sovereign – to consider the substantive interests which are encapsulated symbolically by different positions on the constitutional question. It does this by placing the protection of human rights at the centre of any settlement. The articulation of human rights standards of equality of treatment creates an area of common ground in which to negotiate. It does not matter who is the 'minority'. Protection is ensured for Unionists in a United Ireland and for Nationalists in Northern Ireland. Although international standards may not achieve an answer to the constitutional question (or an answer that is to everyone's satisfaction), they suggest structures for addressing the communities' fears of each other, diffusing the constitutional question and making its outcome less important to life experiences (if not to notions of identity). A framework based in principle and establishing human rights protection, rather than one based purely on balancing present group claims, seems more likely to achieve a lasting settlement, especially given possible demographic changes over time.

> *International law provides the British Government with a clear and*
> *principled basis for action in relation to Northern Ireland*

From the point of view of persuading the British government to work within such a framework, it could be argued that robust protection of minority rights – particularly that of non-discrimination – is consistent with the current British constitutional law position, and can be pursued without necessarily unravelling the present status of Northern Ireland. Further, the fact that international standards contemplate different degrees of autonomy for different categories of minority group, means that increased protection could be established within Northern Ireland without necessarily leading to irresistible pressure for increased minority rights protection within the rest of the United Kingdom. Often, the fear of the so-called 'read-across' implications (to the rest of the UK) of reform in Northern Ireland are regrettably seen as an obstacle to change.

Pessimistic counter-arguments remain. There is no culture of minority rights within the British constitutional tradition, which argues that minorities do not need positive treatment but are adequately protected by protecting everyone without discrimination.[43] However it is possible to argue that the approach with relation to Northern Ireland has been more progressive. Measures such as the Fair Employment affirmative action provisions[44] and the Policy, Appraisal and Fair Treatment Guidelines,[45] together with (failed) power-sharing initiatives and cross-border co-operation, establish a precedent at least for some expectations of creativity in minority rights protection. Yet, it still remains doubtful whether the British government will consider itself mandated to follow such 'an international legal path', if not otherwise disposed to do so. Even hard law sources, for example the European Convention on Human Rights (1950), have been disavowed and derogated from where the Northern Ireland conflict is concerned.

Likewise, parties to the conflict other than the British Government may resist internationalisation where it does not suit them. This is made more likely by ambiguities in the law on self-determination and questions as to the enforceability of minority rights standards. Why, for example, should Nationalists accept a hard rights based approach to self-determination when there are convincing moral and legal arguments for a more expansive approach, especially when the alternative international legal framework for minority rights is largely aspirational? Or indeed, why should Unionists accept minority rights obligations greater than the minimum actually required? Further, as Eide points out, different groups may see their claims differently, and for some, self-determination as a 'minority' can even be problematic.

Finally, there is a possible price to pay in linking the quest for human rights protection to party political debate. International instruments relating to minority rights protection suffer from repetition: each instrument tends to restate basic non-discrimination measures with reference to basic civil and political liberties. This can confuse the distinction between hard and soft law, and governments can be encouraged, in what is an all too present tendency, to condition basic human rights demands to political settlement. This would not be a legitimate approach; indeed much of the work of local Non Governmental Organisations in Northern Ireland has related to educating the population around the idea that human rights are for all citizens, and are not a partisan interest of one community.

IMPLICATIONS FOR INTERNATIONAL LAWYERS

The application of international law as a tool of conflict resolution has been considered elsewhere, but is nevertheless worth considering in this context. This analysis, as well as providing for discussion as to the legal status of Northern Ireland and (legal) pre-requisites for any potential solution, enables us to make several general comments in respect of international law itself. As well as providing for discussion as to the legal status of Northern Ireland and (legal) prerequisites for any potential solution, the application of international law as a tool of conflict resolution affirms conclusions about international law which have been rehearsed elsewhere, but which are worth stating in this context. First, the international law on the principle of self-determination needs to be clarified; at present it is not only unhelpful to situations of conflict, but arguably exacerbates them.[46] In seeking to prioritise territorial integrity while assuming homogeneity within territories, the law undermines strategies for group accommodation. In particular, notions of internal self-determination and autonomy could usefully be explored with a view to giving them substantive legal content.

Second, the question of enforceability of minority rights also needs addressing. Minority rights have developed largely through soft-law mechanisms and the question mark over their enforceability remains an ongoing criticism. One problem with the question of enforceability is that it is not just a question of political will, but a perennial jurisprudential debate raising questions such as 'is it possible to deal effectively with different minority rights claims, which by their nature involve specific and varying circumstances, through legally justiciable means?' If so, what are the implications for human rights discourse; are claims to basic civil and political rights diluted? With relation to Northern Ireland, even if the different parties were to accept the international positions outlined by Eide, would this really have an educative role and change how different groups perceive their differences and claims?

Despite the above reservations, the international law debate is worth engaging in. Although discussion of the possible application of the relevant standards does not provide easy answers for Northern Ireland, it does establish itself as a relevant ingredient to the political situation. This is not least because different parties to the conflict in Northern Ireland use the language of human rights, territorial integrity, self-determination and consent in support of their (political) positions; examination of the relevant international standards will, if nothing else, assess the legitimacy of these claims.

NOTES

*Lecturer and Director, Centre for International and Comparative Human Rights Law, Queen's University of Belfast.

1. See J. McGarry and B. O'Leary, *The Future of Northern Ireland* (1989), at 296: *"While we do not dissent* from the primacy of the political and constitutional problems and solutions we believe that concentration on these questions should not take place at the expense of public-policy problems surrounding discrimination and civil rights" (emphasis added). This analysis can be somewhat re-worked in the light of the "Belfast Agreement", which due to a variety of reasons moved more closely to the position argued in this paper, vindicating the analysis of the role for human rights law and provisions suggested here. Analysis of this agreement and its effect, must await further developments and will be the subject of a later piece.

2. Declaration on the Granting of Independence to Colonial Countries and People, G.A.Res. 1514, 14 Dec. 1960, para 2; Declaration on Principles of International Law concerning Friendly Relations and Co-operation among States in accordance with the Charter of the United Nations, G.A.Res. 2625, adopted without vote on 24 Oct. 1970. See also Article 2(4), and Article 55, United Nations Charter; Article 1(3) of both the International Covenant on Civil and Political Rights 1966 (ICCPR) and the International Covenant on Economic, Social and Cultural Rights 1966 (ICESCR); and Article 2(1) *The Vienna Declaration and Programme of* Action, published by the United Nations Department of Public Information, Doc. DPI/1394–39399, August 1993.

3. Colonial Declaration 1514 states that "[a]ny attempt aimed at the partial or total disruption of the national unity and the territorial integrity of a country is incompatible with the purposes and principles of the Charter of the United Nations". Friendly Relations Declaration 2623 states that, "Nothing in the foregoing paragraphs (dealing with self-determination) shall be construed as authorizing or encouraging any action which would dismember or impair, totally or in part, the territorial integrity or political unity of sovereign and independent States . . .".

4. *Advisory Opinion on the Legal Consequences for States of the Continued Presence of South Africa in Namibia (South West Africa) Notwithstanding Security Council Resolution 276 (1970)* I.C.J. Rep. 1971 16, at 31. See also R. McCorquodale,

"Self-Determination: A Human Rights Approach", 43 *International and Comparative Law Quarterly* (1994) 857, at 859–60.

5. A. Eide, *A Review and Analysis of Constructive Approaches to Group Accommodation and Minority Protection in Divided or Multicultural Societies*, Forum for Peace and Reconciliation / Forum um Schiochain agus Arthmhuintearas, Consultancy Studies No. 3, July 1996.

6. While Article 1 of International Covenant on Civil and Political Rights establishes a right to self-determination for "peoples", Article 27 gives members of minority groups only "the right, in community with the other members of their group, to enjoy their own culture, to profess and practice their own religion, or to use their own language".

7. H.G. Espeil, *The Right to Self-Determination: Implementation of United Nations Resolutions* (1980) 9, para. 56.

8. R. McCorquodale, *supra* n. 4, at 860.

9. See for example Article 1(1) and 1(2), International Labour Organisation Convention Concerning Indigenous and Tribal Peoples in Independent Countries, 1989 (No 169) (although Article1(3) denies that this has any implications as to rights, in an oblique reference to self-determination). United Nations Draft Declaration on Indigenous Peoples also refers to the holders of rights as "peoples". "[At] least verbally, it brings indigenous populations close to peoples that are undeniably holders of the right of self-determination", C. Tomuschat, "Self-Determination in a Post-Colonial World", in Tomuschat (ed.), *Modern Law of Self-Determination* (1993) 1–20, at 13.

10. See P. Thornberry, "The Democratic or Internal Aspect of Self-Determination with Some Remarks on Federalism", in C. Tomuschat (ed.), *ibid.*, 101–138, at 114–119 and 124–131; see also, L. Brilmayer, "Secession and Self-determination: A Territorial Interpretation", 16 *Yale Journal of International Law* (1991), at 177.

11. This is effectively re-stated in Article 2(3), *The Vienna Declaration and Programme of Action*, (1993) UN doc.DPI/1394–39399.

12. A. Cassese, in T. Buergenthal and Hall (eds.), *Human Rights, International Law and the Helsinki Accord* (1977), at 95 *et seq.*; see also M. Pomerance, *Self-determination in Law and Practice* (1982), at 39.

13. H.G. Epseill, *supra* n. 7, at 10 para. 60.

14. A. Eide, *supra* n. 5, at 46 para. 3.5.

15. F. Kirgis, "The Degrees of Self-determination in the United Nations Era", 88 *American Journal of International Law* (1994) 304, at 307.

16. See P. Thornberry, "Self-Determination, Minorities, Human Rights: A Review of International Instruments", 38 *International and Comparative Law Quarterly* (1989) 867, at 868.

17. See generally, R. McCorquodale, *supra* n. 4; H. Hannum, *Autonomy, Sovereignty and Self-determination* (1990); C. Tomuschat, *supra* n. 9, 11–17; and P. Thornberry, *supra* n. 10.

18. Although the British Isles option has re-entered political debate with the Unionist suggestion of a Council of the Isles as part of a settlement (adopted in the Belfast agreement).

19. T. Hadden, "The Application of the Principle of the Self-determination to Northern Ireland", Submission to Northern Ireland Human Rights Assembly (1988), unpublished. For full report on self-determination see *Broken Covenants: Violations of International Law in Northern Ireland*, Report of the Northern Ireland Human Rights Assembly 6–8 April 1992, London (1993), at 140–150.

20. T. Hadden, *ibid.*, para 4.

21. T. Hadden, "British Constitutional Constraints on a Settlement in Northern Ireland" (1995), unpublished.

22. *Frameworks for the Future* (1995), at 14 para. 2.

23. See generally, R. Harvey, "The Rights of the People of the Whole of Ireland to Self-determination, Unity, Sovereignty and Independence", 11 *New York Law School Journal of International and Comparative Law* (1990), at 167–206.

24. Statement of UK's representative in Security Council, 25 May 1982, 54 *British Yearbook of International Law* (1983), at 371–372, cited in R. McCorquodale, *supra* n. 4, at 860.

25. A. Eide, *supra* n. 5, at 7 para. 19.

26. *Ibid.*

27. Committee of 24 (set up under resolution 1514 (XV) Declaration on Decolonisation).

28. A. Eide *supra* n. 5, at 7 para. 19.

29. Article 1 of the Universal Declaration of Human Rights states that "[a]ll human beings are born free and equal in dignity and rights. They are endowed with reason and conscience and should act towards each other in a spirit of brotherhood". This can be seen as a founding principle and other rights should be viewed within this context; see A. Eide, *supra* n. 5, at 54 para. 4.1.

30. See for example Articles 2(1) and 7 of the Universal Declaration; Article 2(1) International Covenant on Civil and Political Rights, and Article 2(2) of the International Covenant on Economic Social and Cultural Rights (both 1966).

31. Article 2, International Convention on the Elimination of All Forms of Racial Discrimination 1966.

32. *Ibid.,* Article 2(d).

33. Article 5(2), Council of Europe's Framework Convention on the Rights of National Minorities, 34 *ILM* (1995) 351 (hereafter the Framework Convention); see also Article 1(1) United Nations General Assembly Declaration on the Rights of Persons Belonging to National or Ethnic, Religious and Linguistic Minorities, GA Res. 47/135, December 18, 1992.

34. Article 4(2), United Nations General Assembly Declaration on the Rights of Persons Belonging to Minorities; see also, the Council of Europe's Framework Convention, *passim.*

35. A. Eide, *supra* n. 5, at 21.

36. The Belfast Agreement did not adopt this approach and is interesting for its marked emphasis on human rights protections, an emphasis that clearly differentiates it from its predecessor the Framework Document.

37. Eide, *supra* n. 5, at 1–24.

38. *Ibid.*, at 12 para. 41.

39. *Ibid.* at 14 para. 51.

40. *Ibid.*, at 21 para 80.

41. *Supra* n. 1, at 294–300.

42. *Ibid.,* at preface.

43. Interestingly, when the British Government reports under the ICCPR to the Human Rights Committee, minorities are dealt with under Article 2 and not Article 27.

44. Section 58(1), Fair Employment Act 1989.

45. Policy, Appraisal and Fair Treatment Guidelines, Central Secretariat Circular 5/93, 22 December 1993 (available from CCRU, 20–24 Donegall Street, Belfast, BT1 2GP).

46. See A. Guelke "International legitimacy, Self-determination, and Northern Ireland", 11 *Review of International Studies* (1985), at 37-52, for a robust claim that this has been the case in Northern Ireland.

Contributors

Myroslava Antonovych is Associate Professor of International Law at the University of Kyiv-Mohyla Academy and at the Centre for Legal Studies, Ukranian Legal Foundation, Kyiv, Ukraine.

Nedzad Basic is Associate Professor of International Relations, University of Mostar, Republic of Bosnia and Herzegovina, Donald J. Fleming is a Professor in the Faculty of Law, University of New Brunswick, Canada, and William M. Vaughn is Associate Professor of Political Science at St. Thomas University, Canada.

Christine Bell is a Lecturer, and Director of the Centre for International and Comparative Human Rights Law, at Queen's University of Belfast.

Adam Biscoe is a Lecturer in European Integration in the Department of Politics at the University of Bristol.

William Bowring is a Senior Lecturer, and Director of the Pan European Institute, at Essex University.

Peter Cumper is a Lecturer in the Law Faculty at Leicester University.

John Edwards is Professor of Social Policy in the Department of Social Policy and Social Science at Royal Holloway, University of London.

María Amor Martín Estébanez, D.Phil. Research Student, Centre Socio-Legal Studies, Wolfson College, University of Oxford.

Geoff Gilbert is Professor of Law, Director, Human Rights Centre, University of Essex.

Brigid Hadfield is Professor of Public Law at The Queen's University of Belfast.

Julie Mertus is an assistant professor at Ohio Northern University, Pettit College of Law.

Wolf Mannens is a Researcher and Lecturer at the Department of Public International Law, Leiden University, the Netherlands.

Gerd Oberleitner is a Lecturer at the Institute of International Law and International Relations at the University of Graz, Austria.

P. Cumper and S. Wheatley (eds.), Minority Rights in the 'New' Europe, 325–326
© 1999 *Kluwer Law International. Printed in Great Britain.*

Istvan Pogany is a Reader in law at Warwick University.

Javaid Rehman is a Lecturer in the Law Faculty at the University of Leeds.

Patrick Thornberry is Professor of International Law at the University of Keele.

Steven Wheatley is a Senior Lecturer in the Department of Legal Studies at the University of Central Lancashire.

Selected Documents on Minority Rights

CONTENTS

These extracts are taken from the following documents:

INTERNATIONAL COVENANT ON CIVIL AND POLITICAL RIGHTS (1966), ADOPTED AND OPENED FOR SIGNATURE, RATIFICATION AND ACCESSION BY GENERAL ASSEMBLY RESOLUTION 2200 A(XXI), 16 DECEMBER 1966

. . .

Article 1

1. All peoples have the right of self-determination. By virtue of that right they freely pursue their economic, social and cultural development.

. . .

P. Cumper and S. Wheatley (eds.), Minority Rights in the 'New' Europe, 327–374
© 1999 Kluwer Law International. Printed in Great Britain.

Article 2

1. Each State Party to the present Covenant undertakes to respect and to ensure to all individuals within its territory and subject to its jurisdiction the rights recognized in the present Covenant, without discrimination of any kind, such as race, colour, sex, language, religion, political or other opinion, national or social origin, property, birth or other status.

. . .

Article 26

All persons are equal before the law and are entitled without discrimination to the equal protection of the law. In this respect, the law shall prohibit any discrimination and guarantee to all persons equal and effective protection against discrimination on any ground such as race, colour, sex, language, religion, political or other opinion, national or social origin, property, birth or other status.

Article 27

In those States in which ethnic, religious or linguistic minorities exist, persons belonging to such minorities shall not be denied the right, in community with the other members of their group, to enjoy their own culture, to profess and practice their own religion, or to use their own language.

. . .

DECLARATION ON THE RIGHTS OF PERSONS BELONGING TO
NATIONAL OR ETHNIC OR RELIGIOUS MINORITIES (1992), GENERAL
ASSEMBLY RESOLUTION 47/135, ADOPTED 18 DECEMBER, 1992

The General Assembly,
. . .

Inspired by the provisions of article 27 of the International Covenant on Civil and Political Rights concerning the rights of persons belonging to ethnic, religious or linguistic minorities,
Considering that the promotion and protection of the rights of persons belonging to national or ethnic, religious and linguistic minorities contribute to the political and social stability of States in which they live,

Emphasizing that the constant promotion and realization of the rights of persons belonging to national or ethnic, religious and linguistic minorities, as an integral part of the development of society as a whole and within a democratic framework based on the rule of law, would contribute to the strengthening of friendship and co-operation among peoples and States,

Proclaims this Declaration on the Rights of Persons Belonging to National or Ethnic, Religious and Linguistic Minorities:

Article 1

1. States shall protect the existence and the national or ethnic, cultural, religious and linguistic identity of minorities within their respective territories and shall encourage conditions for the promotion of that identity.

2. States shall adopt appropriate legislative and other measures to achieve those ends.

Article 2

1. Persons belonging to national or ethnic, religious and linguistic minorities (hereinafter referred to as persons belonging to minorities) have the right to enjoy their own culture, to profess and practise their own religion, and to use their own language, in private and in public, freely and without interference or any form of discrimination.

2. Persons belonging to minorities have the right to participate effectively in cultural, religious, social, economic and public life.

3. Persons belonging to minorities have the right to participate effectively in decisions on the national and, where appropriate, regional level concerning the minority to which they belong or the regions in which they live, in a manner not incompatible with national legislation.

4. Persons belonging to minorities have the right to establish and maintain their own associations.

5. Persons belonging to minorities have the right to establish and maintain, without any discrimination, free and peaceful contacts with other members of their group and with persons belonging to other minorities, as well as contacts across frontiers with citizens of other States to whom they are related by national or ethnic, religious or linguistic ties.

Article 3

1. Persons belonging to minorities may exercise their rights, including those set forth in the present Declaration, individually as well as in community with other members of their group, without any discrimination.

2. No disadvantage shall result for any person belonging to a minority as the consequence of the exercise or non-exercise of the rights set forth in the present Declaration.

Article 4

1. States shall take measures where required to ensure that persons belonging to minorities may exercise fully and effectively all their human rights and fundamental freedoms without any discrimination and in full equality before the law.

2. States shall take measures to create favourable conditions to enable persons belonging to minorities to express their characteristics and to develop their culture, language, religion, traditions and customs, except where specific practices are in violation of national law and contrary to international standards.

3. States should take appropriate measures so that, wherever possible, persons belonging to minorities may have adequate opportunities to learn their mother tongue or to have instruction in their mother tongue.

4. States should, where appropriate, take measures in the field of education, in order to encourage knowledge of the history, traditions, language and culture of the minorities existing within their territory. Persons belonging to minorities should have adequate opportunities to gain knowledge of the society as a whole.

5. States should consider appropriate measures so that persons belonging to minorities may participate fully in the economic progress and development in their country.

Article 5

1. National policies and programmes shall be planned and implemented with due regard for the legitimate interests of persons belonging to minorities.

2.Programmes of co-operation and assistance among States should be planned and implemented with due regard for the legitimate interests of persons belonging to minorities.

Article 6

States should co-operate on questions relating to persons belonging to minorities, inter alia, exchanging information and experiences, in order to promote mutual understanding and confidence.

Article 7

States should co-operate in order to promote respect for the rights set forth in the present Declaration.

Article 8

1. Nothing in the present Declaration shall prevent the fulfilment of international obligations of States in relation to persons belonging to minorities. In particular, States shall fulfil in good faith the obligations and commitments they have assumed under international treaties and agreements to which they are parties.

2. The exercise of the rights set forth in the present Declaration shall not prejudice the enjoyment by all persons of universally recognized human rights and fundamental freedoms.

3. Measures taken by States to ensure the effective enjoyment of the rights set forth in the present Declaration shall not prima facie be considered contrary to the principle of equality contained in the Universal Declaration of Human Rights.

4. Nothing in the present Declaration may be construed as permitting any activity contrary to the purposes and principles of the United Nations, including sovereign equality, territorial integrity and political independence of States.

Article 9

The specialized agencies and other organizations of the United Nations system shall contribute to the full realization of the rights and principles set forth in the present Declaration, within their respective fields of competence.

EUROPEAN CONVENTION FOR PROTECTION OF HUMAN RIGHTS AND FUNDAMENTAL FREEDOMS (1950), COUNCIL OF EUROPE, ROME, 4 NOVEMBER 1950

. . .

Article 14

The enjoyment of the rights and freedoms set forth in this Convention shall be secured without discrimination on any ground such as sex, race, colour, language, religion, political or other opinion, national or social origin, association with a national minority, property, birth or other status.

EUROPEAN CHARTER FOR REGIONAL OR MINORITY LANGUAGES (1992), COUNCIL OF EUROPE, STRASBOURG, 2 OCTOBER, 1992

Preamble

. . .

Considering that the protection of the historical regional or minority languages of Europe, some of which are in danger of eventual extinction, contributes to the maintenance and development of Europe's cultural wealth and traditions;

Considering that the right to use a regional or minority language in private and public life is an inalienable right . . .

Stressing the value of interculturalism and multilingualism and considering that the protection and encouragement of regional or minority languages should not be to the detriment of the official languages and the need to learn them;

Realising that the protection and promotion of regional or minority languages in the different countries and regions of Europe represent an important contribution to the building of a Europe based on the principles of democracy and cultural diversity within the framework of national sovereignty and territorial integrity;

Have agreed as follows:

Article 1
Definitions

For the purposes of this Charter:
(a) "regional or minority languages" means languages that are:
(i) traditionally used within a given territory of a State by nationals of that State who form a group numerically smaller than the rest of the State's population; and
(ii) different from the official language(s) of that State;
it does not include either dialects of the official language(s) of the State or the languages of migrants;
(b) "territory in which the regional or minority language is used" means the geographical area in which the said language is the mode of expression of a number of people justifying the adoption of the various protective and promotional measures provided for in this Charter;
(c) "non-territorial languages" means languages used by nationals of the State which differ from the language or languages used by the rest of the State's population but which, although traditionally used within the territory of the State, cannot be identified with a particular area thereof.

Article 2
Undertakings

1. Each Party undertakes to apply the provisions of Part II to all the regional or minority languages spoken within its territory and which comply with the definition in Article 1.

2. In respect of each language specified at the time of ratification, acceptance or approval, in accordance with Article 3, each Party undertakes to apply a minimum of thirty-five paragraphs or sub-paragraphs chosen from among the provisions of Part III of the Charter, including at least three chosen from each of the Articles 8 and 12 and one from each of the Articles 9, 10, 11 and 13.

Article 3
Practical arrangements

1. Each Contracting State shall specify in its instrument of ratification, acceptance or approval, each regional or minority language, or official language which is less widely used on the whole or part of its territory, to which the paragraphs chosen in accordance with Article 2, paragraph 2, shall apply.

. . .

Part II

Article 7
Objectives and principles

1. In respect of regional or minority languages, within the territories in which such languages are used and according to the situation of each language, the Parties shall base their policies, legislation and practice on the following objectives and principles:
(a) the recognition of the regional or minority languages as an expression of cultural wealth;
(b) the respect of the geographical area of each regional or minority language in order to ensure that existing or new administrative divisions do not constitute an obstacle to the promotion of the regional or minority language in question;
(c) the need for resolute action to promote regional or minority languages in order to safeguard them;
(d) the facilitation and/or encouragement of the use of regional or minority languages, in speech and writing, in public and private life;
(e) the maintenance and development of links, in the fields covered by this Charter, between groups using a regional or minority language and other groups in the State employing a language used in identical or similar form, as well as the establishment of cultural relations with other groups in the State using different languages;
(f) the provision of appropriate forms and means for the teaching and study of regional or minority languages at all appropriate stages;
(g) the provision of facilities enabling non-speakers of a regional or minority language living in the area where it is used to learn it if they so desire;
(h) the promotion of study and research on regional or minority languages at universities or equivalent institutions;
(i) the promotion of appropriate types of transnational exchanges, in the fields covered by this Charter, for regional or minority languages used in identical or similar form in two or more States.
2. The Parties undertake to eliminate, if they have not yet done so, any unjustified distinction, exclusion, restriction or preference relating to the use of a regional or minority language and intended to discourage or endanger the maintenance or development of it. The adoption of special measures in favour of regional or minority languages aimed at promoting equality between the users of these languages and the rest of the population or which take due account of their specific conditions is not considered to be an act of discrimination against the users of more widely-used languages.
3. The Parties undertake to promote, by appropriate measures, mutual

understanding between all the linguistic groups of the country and in particular the inclusion of respect, understanding and tolerance in relation to regional or minority languages among the objectives of education and training provided within their countries and encouragement of the mass media to pursue the same objective.

4. In determining their policy with regard to regional or minority languages, the Parties shall take into consideration the needs and wishes expressed by the groups which use such languages. They are encouraged to establish bodies, if necessary, for the purpose of advising the authorities on all matters pertaining to regional or minority languages.

5. The Parties undertake to apply, *mutatis mutandis*, the principles listed in paragraphs 1 to 4 above to non-territorial languages. However, as far as these languages are concerned, the nature and scope of the measures to be taken to give effect to this Charter shall be determined in a flexible manner, bearing in mind the needs and wishes, and respecting the traditions and characteristics, of the groups which use the languages concerned.

Article 8
Education

1. With regard to education, the Parties undertake, within the territory in which such languages are used, according to the situation of each of these languages, and without prejudice to the teaching of the official language(s) of the State:

(a)
(i) to make available pre-school education in the relevant regional or minority languages; or
(ii) to make available a substantial part of pre-school education in the relevant regional or minority languages; or
(iii) to apply one of the measures provided for under i and ii above at least to those pupils whose families so request and whose number is considered sufficient; or
(iv) if the public authorities have no direct competence in the field of pre-school education, to favour and/or encourage the application of the measures referred to under i to iii above;

(b)
(i) to make available primary education in the relevant regional or minority languages; or
(ii) to make available a substantial part of primary education in the relevant regional or minority languages; or
(iii) to provide, within primary education, for the teaching of the relevant regional or minority languages as an integral part of the curriculum; or

(iv) to apply one of the measures provided for under i to iii above at least to those pupils whose families so request and whose number is considered sufficient;

(c)

(i) to make available secondary education in the relevant regional or minority languages; or

(ii) to make available a substantial part of secondary education in the relevant regional or minority languages; or

(iii) to provide, within secondary education, for the teaching of the relevant regional or minority languages as an integral part of the curriculum; or

(iv) to apply one of the measures provided for under i to iii above at least to those pupils who, or where appropriate whose families, so wish in a number considered sufficient;

(d)

(i) to make available technical and vocational education in the relevant regional or minority languages; or

(ii) to make available a substantial part of technical and vocational education in the relevant regional or minority languages; or

(iii) to provide, within technical and vocational education, for the teaching of the relevant regional or minority languages as an integral part of the curriculum; or

(iv) to apply one of the measures provided for under i to iii above at least to those pupils who, or where appropriate whose families, so wish in a number considered sufficient;

(e)

(i) to make available university and other higher education in regional or minority languages; or

(ii) to provide facilities for the study of these languages as university and higher education subjects; or

(iii) if, by reason of the role of the State in relation to higher education institutions, sub-paragraphs i and ii cannot be applied, to encourage and/or allow the provision of university or other forms of higher education in regional or minority languages or of facilities for the study of these languages as university or higher education subjects;

(f)

(i) to arrange for the provision of adult and continuing education courses which are taught mainly or wholly in the regional or minority languages; or

(ii) to offer such languages as subjects of adult and continuing education; or

(iii) if the public authorities have no direct competence in the field of adult education, to favour and/or encourage the offering of such languages as subjects of adult and continuing education;

(g) to make arrangements to ensure the teaching of the history and the culture which is reflected by the regional or minority language;

(h) to provide the basic and further training of the teachers required to implement those of paragraphs a to g accepted by the Party;

(i) to set up a supervisory body or bodies responsible for monitoring the measures taken and progress achieved in establishing or developing the teaching of regional or minority languages and for drawing up periodic reports of their findings, which will be made public.

2. With regard to education and in respect of territories other than those in which the regional or minority languages are traditionally used, the Parties undertake, if the number of users of a regional or minority language justifies it, to allow, encourage or provide teaching in or of the regional or minority language at all the appropriate stages of education.

Article 9
Judicial authorities

1. The Parties undertake, in respect of those judicial districts in which the number of residents using the regional or minority languages justifies the measures specified below, according to the situation of each of these languages and on condition that the use of the facilities afforded by the present paragraph is not considered by the judge to hamper the proper administration of justice:

(a) in criminal proceedings:

(i) to provide that the courts, at the request of one of the parties, shall conduct the proceedings in the regional or minority languages; and/or

(ii) to guarantee the accused the right to use his/her regional or minority language; and/or

(iii) to provide that requests and evidence, whether written or oral, shall not be considered inadmissible solely because they are formulated in a regional or minority language; and/or

(iv) to produce, on request, documents connected with legal proceedings in the relevant regional or minority language, if necessary by the use of interpreters and translations involving no extra expense for the persons concerned;

(b) in civil proceedings:

(i) to provide that the courts, at the request of one of the parties, shall conduct the proceedings in the regional or minority languages; and/or

(ii) to allow, whenever a litigant has to appear in person before a court, that he or she may use his or her regional or minority language without thereby incurring additional expense; and/or

(iii) to allow documents and evidence to be produced in the regional or minority languages, if necessary by the use of interpreters and translations;

(c) in proceedings before courts concerning administrative matters:

(i) to provide that the courts, at the request of one of the parties, shall conduct the proceedings in the regional or minority languages; and/or

(ii) to allow, whenever a litigant has to appear in person before a court, that he or she may use his or her regional or minority language without thereby incurring additional expense; and/or

(iii) to allow documents and evidence to be produced in the regional or minority languages, if necessary by the use of interpreters and translations;

(d) to take steps to ensure that the application of sub-paragraphs i and iii of paragraphs b and c above and any necessary use of interpreters and translations does not involve extra expense for the persons concerned.

2. The Parties undertake:

(a) not to deny the validity of legal documents drawn up within the State solely because they are drafted in a regional or minority language; or

(b) not to deny the validity, as between the parties, of legal documents drawn up within the country solely because they are drafted in a regional or minority language, and to provide that they can be invoked against interested third parties who are not users of these languages on condition that the contents of the document are made known to them by the person(s) who invoke(s) it; or

(c) not to deny the validity, as between the parties, of legal documents drawn up within the country solely because they are drafted in a regional or minority language.

3. The Parties undertake to make available in the regional or minority languages the most important national statutory texts and those relating particularly to users of these languages, unless they are otherwise provided.

Article 10
Administrative authorities and public services

1. Within the administrative districts of the State in which the number of residents who are users of regional or minority languages justifies the measures specified below and according to the situation of each language, the Parties undertake, as far as this is reasonably possible:

(a)

(i) to ensure that the administrative authorities use the regional or minority languages; or

(ii) to ensure that such of their officers as are in contact with the public use the regional or minority languages in their relations with persons applying to them in these languages; or

(iii) to ensure that users of regional or minority languages may submit oral or written applications and receive a reply in these languages; or

(iv) to ensure that users of regional or minority languages may submit oral or written applications in these languages; or

(v) to ensure that users of regional or minority languages may validly submit a document in these languages;

(b) to make available widely used administrative texts and forms for the population in the regional or minority languages or in bilingual versions;

(c) to allow the administrative authorities to draft documents in a regional or minority language.

2. In respect of the local and regional authorities on whose territory the number of residents who are users of regional or minority languages is such as to justify the measures specified below, the Parties undertake to allow and/or encourage:

(a) the use of regional or minority languages within the framework of the regional or local authority;

(b) the possibility for users of regional or minority languages to submit oral or written applications in these languages;

(c) the publication by regional authorities of their official documents also in the relevant regional or minority languages;

(d) the publication by local authorities of their official documents also in the relevant regional or minority languages;

(e) the use by regional authorities of regional or minority languages in debates in their assemblies, without excluding, however, the use of the official language(s) of the State;

(f) the use by local authorities of regional or minority languages in debates in their assemblies, without excluding, however, the use of the official language(s) of the State;

(g) the use or adoption, if necessary in conjunction with the name in the official language(s), of traditional and correct forms of place-names in regional or minority languages.

3. With regard to public services provided by the administrative authorities or other persons acting on their behalf, the Parties undertake, within the territory in which regional or minority languages are used, in accordance with the situation of each language and as far as this is reasonably possible:

(a) to ensure that the regional or minority languages are used in the provision of the service; or

(b) to allow users of regional or minority languages to submit a request and receive a reply in these languages; or

(c) to allow users of regional or minority languages to submit a request in these languages.

4. With a view to putting into effect those provisions of paragraphs 1, 2 and 3 accepted by them, the Parties undertake to take one or more of the following measures:

(a) translation or interpretation as may be required;

(b) recruitment and, where necessary, training of the officials and other public service employees required;

(c) compliance as far as possible with requests from public service employees having a knowledge of a regional or minority language to be appointed in the territory in which that language is used.

5. The Parties undertake to allow the use or adoption of family names in the regional or minority languages, at the request of those concerned.

Article 11
Media

1. The Parties undertake, for the users of the regional or minority languages within the territories in which those languages are spoken, according to the situation of each language, to the extent that the public authorities, directly or indirectly, are competent, have power or play a role in this field, and respecting the principle of the independence and autonomy of the media:

(a) to the extent that radio and television carry out a public service mission:

(i) to ensure the creation of at least one radio station and one television channel in the regional or minority languages; or

(ii) to encourage and/or facilitate the creation of at least one radio station and one television channel in the regional or minority languages; or

(iii) to make adequate provision so that broadcasters offer programmes in the regional or minority languages;

(b)

(i) to encourage and/or facilitate the creation of at least one radio station in the regional or minority languages; or

(ii) to encourage and/or facilitate the broadcasting of radio programmes in the regional or minority languages on a regular basis;

(c)

(i) to encourage and/or facilitate the creation of at least one television channel in the regional or minority languages; or

(ii) to encourage and/or facilitate the broadcasting of television programmes in the regional or minority languages on a regular basis;

(d) to encourage and/or facilitate the production and distribution of audio and audio-visual works in the regional or minority languages;

(e)

(i) to encourage and/or facilitate the creation and/or maintenance of at least one newspaper in the regional or minority languages; or

(ii) to encourage and/or facilitate the publication of newspaper articles in the regional or minority languages on a regular basis;

(f)

(i) to cover the additional costs of those media which use regional or minority languages, wherever the law provides for financial assistance in general for the media; or

(ii) to apply existing measures for financial assistance also to audio-visual productions in the regional or minority languages;

(g) to support the training of journalists and other staff for media using regional or minority languages.

2. The Parties undertake to guarantee freedom of direct reception of radio and television broadcasts from neighbouring countries in a language used in identical or similar form to a regional or minority language, and not to oppose the retransmission of radio and television broadcasts from neighbouring countries in such a language. They further undertake to ensure that no restrictions will be placed on the freedom of expression and free circulation of information in the written press in a language used in identical or similar form to a regional or minority language. The exercise of the above-mentioned freedoms, since it carries with it duties and responsibilities, may be subject to such formalities, conditions, restrictions or penalties as are prescribed by law and are necessary in a democratic society, in the interests of national security, territorial integrity or public safety, for the prevention of disorder or crime, for the protection of health or morals, for the protection of the reputation or rights of others, for preventing disclosure of information received in confidence, or for maintaining the authority and impartiality of the judiciary.

3. The Parties undertake to ensure that the interests of the users of regional or minority languages are represented or taken into account within such bodies as may be established in accordance with the law with responsibility for guaranteeing the freedom and pluralism of the media.

Article 12
Cultural activities and facilities

1. With regard to cultural activities and facilities – especially libraries, video libraries, cultural centres, museums, archives, academies, theatres and cinemas, as well as literary work and film production, vernacular forms of cultural expression, festivals and the culture industries, including inter alia the use of new technologies – the Parties undertake, within the territory

in which such languages are used and to the extent that the public authorities are competent, have power or play a role in this field:

(a) to encourage types of expression and initiative specific to regional or minority languages and foster the different means of access to works produced in these languages;

(b) to foster the different means of access in other languages to works produced in regional or minority languages by aiding and developing translation, dubbing, post-synchronisation and subtitling activities;

(c) to foster access in regional or minority languages to works produced in other languages by aiding and developing translation, dubbing, post-synchronisation and subtitling activities;

(d) to ensure that the bodies responsible for organising or supporting cultural activities of various kinds make appropriate allowance for incorporating the knowledge and use of regional or minority languages and cultures in the undertakings which they initiate or for which they provide backing;

(e) to promote measures to ensure that the bodies responsible for organising or supporting cultural activities have at their disposal staff who have a full command of the regional or minority language concerned, as well as of the language(s) of the rest of the population;

(f) to encourage direct participation by representatives of the users of a given regional or minority language in providing facilities and planning cultural activities;

(g) to encourage and/or facilitate the creation of a body or bodies responsible for collecting, keeping a copy of and presenting or publishing works produced in the regional or minority languages;

(h) if necessary, to create and/or promote and finance translation and terminological research services, particularly with a view to maintaining and developing appropriate administrative, commercial, economic, social, technical or legal terminology in each regional or minority language.

2. In respect of territories other than those in which the regional or minority languages are traditionally used, the Parties undertake, if the number of users of a regional or minority language justifies it, to allow, encourage and/or provide appropriate cultural activities and facilities in accordance with the preceding paragraph.

3. The Parties undertake to make appropriate provision, in pursuing their cultural policy abroad, for regional or minority languages and the cultures they reflect.

Article 13
Economic and social life

1. With regard to economic and social activities, the Parties undertake, within the whole country:

(a) to eliminate from their legislation any provision prohibiting or limiting without justifiable reasons the use of regional or minority languages in documents relating to economic or social life, particularly contracts of employment, and in technical documents such as instructions for the use of products or installations;

(b) to prohibit the insertion in internal regulations of companies and private documents of any clauses excluding or restricting the use of regional or minority languages, at least between users of the same language;

(c) to oppose practices designed to discourage the use of regional or minority languages in connection with economic or social activities;

(d) to facilitate and/or encourage the use of regional or minority languages by means other than those specified in the above sub-paragraphs.

2. With regard to economic and social activities, the Parties undertake, in so far as the public authorities are competent, within the territory in which the regional or minority languages are used, and as far as this is reasonably possible:

(a) to include in their financial and banking regulations provisions which allow, by means of procedures compatible with commercial practice, the use of regional or minority languages in drawing up payment orders (cheques, drafts, etc.) or other financial documents, or, where appropriate, to ensure the implementation of such provisions;

(b) in the economic and social sectors directly under their control (public sector), to organise activities to promote the use of regional or minority languages;

(c) to ensure that social care facilities such as hospitals, retirement homes and hostels offer the possibility of receiving and treating in their own language persons using a regional or minority language who are in need of care on grounds of ill-health, old age or for other reasons;

(d) to ensure by appropriate means that safety instructions are also drawn up in regional or minority languages;

(e) to arrange for information provided by the competent public authorities concerning the rights of consumers to be made available in regional or minority languages.

. . .

Article 15
Periodical reports

1. The Parties shall present periodically to the Secretary General of the Council of Europe, in a form to be prescribed by the Committee of Ministers, a report on their policy pursued in accordance with Part II of this Charter and on the measures taken in application of those provisions

of Part III which they have accepted. The first report shall be presented within the year following the entry into force of the Charter with respect to the Party concerned, the other reports at three-yearly intervals after the first report.

2. The Parties shall make their reports public.

Article 16
Examination of the reports

1. The reports presented to the Secretary General of the Council of Europe under Article 15 shall be examined by a committee of experts constituted in accordance with Article 17.

2. Bodies or associations legally established in a Party may draw the attention of the committee of experts to matters relating to the undertakings entered into by that Party under Part III of this Charter.

3. On the basis of the reports specified in paragraph 1 and the information mentioned in paragraph 2, the committee of experts shall prepare a report for the Committee of Ministers. This report shall be accompanied by the comments which the Parties have been requested to make and may be made public by the Committee of Ministers.

4. The report specified in paragraph 3 shall contain in particular the proposals of the committee of experts to the Committee of Ministers for the preparation of such recommendations of the latter body to one or more of the Parties as may be required. The Secretary General of the Council of Europe shall make a two-yearly detailed report to the Parliamentary Assembly on the application of the Charter.

Article 17
Committee of experts

1. The committee of experts shall be composed of one member per Party, appointed by the Committee of Ministers from a list of individuals of the highest integrity and recognised competence in the matters dealt with in the Charter, who shall be nominated by the Party concerned.

2. Members of the committee shall be appointed for a period of six years and shall be eligible for reappointment.

3. The committee of experts shall adopt rules of procedure. Its secretarial services shall be provided by the Secretary General of the Council of Europe.

PARLIAMENTARY ASSEMBLY OF THE COUNCIL OF
EUROPE, FORTY-FOURTH ORDINARY SESSION,
RECOMMENDATION 1201 (1993), ON AN ADDITIONAL PROTOCOL
ON THE RIGHTS OF NATIONAL MINORITIES TO THE EUROPEAN
CONVENTION ON HUMAN RIGHTS

. . .

Preamble

. . .

3. Considering that only the recognition of the rights of persons belonging to a national minority within a state, and the international protection of those rights, are capable of putting a lasting end to ethnic confrontations, and thus of helping to guarantee justice, democracy, stability and peace;
4. Considering that the rights concerned are those which any person may exercise singly or jointly;

. . .

Have agreed the following:

Section 1 – Definition

Article 1

For the purpose of this Convention, the expression "national minority" refers to a group of persons in a state who:
a. reside in the territory of that state and are citizens thereof;
b. maintain long-standing, firm and lasting ties with that state;
c. display distinctive ethnic, cultural, religious or linguistic characteristics;
d. are sufficiently representative, although smaller in number than the rest of the population of that state or of a region of that state;
e. are motivated by a concern to preserve together that which constitutes their common identity, including their culture, their traditions, their religion or their language.

Section 2 – General Principles

. . .

Article 3

1. Every person belonging to a national minority shall have the right to express, preserve and develop in complete freedom his/her religious, ethnic, linguistic and/or cultural identity, without being subject to any attempt at assimilation against his/her will.
2. Every person belonging to a national minority may exercise his/her rights and enjoy them individually or in association with others.

. . .

Article 5

Deliberate changes to the democratic composition of the region in the which a national minority is settled, to the detriment of that minority, shall be prohibited.

Section 3 – Substantive Rights

. . .

Article 7

. . .

3. In the regions in which substantial numbers of a national minority are settled, the persons belonging to a national minority shall have the right to use their mother tongue in their contacts with the administrative authorities and in proceedings before the courts and legal authorities.
4. In the regions in which substantial numbers of a national minority are settled, the persons belonging that minority shall have the right to display in their language local names, signs, inscriptions and other similar information visible to the public. . . .

Article 8

1. Every person belonging to a national minority shall have the right to learn his/her mother tongue and to receive an education in his/her mother

tongue at an appropriate number of schools and of state educational and training establishments, located in accordance with the geographical distribution of the minority.

. . .

Article 9

If a violation of the rights protected by this protocol is alleged, every person belonging to a national minority or any representative organisations shall have an effective remedy before a state authority.

. . .

Article 11

In the regions where they are in a majority the persons belonging to a national minority shall have the right to have at their disposal appropriate local or autonomous authorities or to have a special status, matching the specific historical and territorial situation and in accordance with the domestic legislation of the state.

FRAMEWORK CONVENTION FOR THE PROTECTION OF NATIONAL MINORITIES (1994), COUNCIL OF EUROPE, STRASBOURG, 8 NOVEMBER, 1994

Preamble

The member States of the Council of Europe and the other States, signatories to the present framework Convention,
Considering that the aim of the Council of Europe is to achieve greater unity between its members for the purpose of safeguarding and realising the ideals and principles which are their common heritage;

. . .

Being resolved to protect within their respective territories the existence of national minorities;

Considering that the upheavals of European history have shown that the protection of national minorities is essential to stability, democratic security and peace in this continent;

Considering that a pluralist and genuinely democratic society should not only respect the ethnic, cultural, linguistic and religious identity of each person belonging to a national minority, but also create appropriate conditions enabling them to express, preserve and develop this identity;

. . .

Having regard to the Convention for the Protection of Human Rights and Fundamental Freedoms and the Protocols thereto;

Having regard to the commitments concerning the protection of national minorities in United Nations conventions and declarations and in the documents of the Conference on Security and Co-operation in Europe, particularly the Copenhagen Document of 29 June 1990;

Being resolved to define the principles to be respected and the obligations which flow from them, in order to ensure, in the member States and such other States as may become Parties to the present instrument, the effective protection of national minorities and of the rights and freedoms of persons belonging to those minorities, within the rule of law, respecting the territorial integrity and national sovereignty of states;

Being determined to implement the principles set out in this framework Convention through national legislation and appropriate governmental policies,

Have agreed as follows:

Section I

Article 1

The protection of national minorities and of the rights and freedoms of persons belonging to those minorities forms an integral part of the international protection of human rights, and as such falls within the scope of international co-operation.

Article 2

The provisions of this framework Convention shall be applied in good faith, in a spirit of understanding and tolerance and in conformity with the principles of good neighbourliness, friendly relations and co-operation between States.

Article 3

1. Every person belonging to a national minority shall have the right freely to choose to be treated or not to be treated as such and no disadvantage shall result from this choice or from the exercise of the rights which are connected to that choice.

2. Persons belonging to national minorities may exercise the rights and enjoy the freedoms flowing from the principles enshrined in the present framework Convention individually as well as in community with others.

Section II

Article 4

1. The Parties undertake to guarantee to persons belonging to national minorities the right of equality before the law and of equal protection of the law. In this respect, any discrimination based on belonging to a national minority shall be prohibited.

2. The Parties undertake to adopt, where necessary, adequate measures in order to promote, in all areas of economic, social, political and cultural life, full and effective equality between persons belonging to a national minority and those belonging to the majority. In this respect, they shall take due account of the specific conditions of the persons belonging to national minorities.

3. The measures adopted in accordance with paragraph 2 shall not be considered to be an act of discrimination

Article 5

1. The Parties undertake to promote the conditions necessary for persons belonging to national minorities to maintain and develop their culture, and to preserve the essential elements of their identity, namely their religion, language, traditions and cultural heritage.

2. Without prejudice to measures taken in pursuance of their general integration policy, the Parties shall refrain from policies or practices aimed at assimilation of persons belonging to national minorities against their will and shall protect these persons from any action aimed at such assimilation.

Article 6

1. The Parties shall encourage a spirit of tolerance and intercultural dialogue and take effective measures to promote mutual respect and understanding and co-operation among all persons living on their territory, irrespective of those persons' ethnic, cultural, linguistic or religious identity, in particular in the fields of education, culture and the media.

2. The Parties undertake to take appropriate measures to protect persons who may be subject to threats or acts of discrimination, hostility or violence as a result of their ethnic, cultural, linguistic or religious identity.

Article 7

The Parties shall ensure respect for the right of every person belonging to a national minority to freedom of peaceful assembly, freedom of association, freedom of expression, and freedom of thought, conscience and religion

Article 8

The Parties undertake to recognise that every person belonging to a national minority has the right to manifest his or her religion or belief and to establish religious institutions, organisations and associations.

Article 9

1. The Parties undertake to recognise that the right to freedom of expression of every person belonging to a national minority includes freedom to hold opinions and to receive and impart information and ideas in the minority language, without interference by public authorities and regardless of frontiers. The Parties shall ensure, within the framework of their legal systems, that persons belonging to a national minority are not discriminated against in their access to the media.

2. Paragraph 1 shall not prevent Parties from requiring the licensing, without discrimination and based on objective criteria, of sound radio and television broadcasting, or cinema enterprises.

3. The Parties shall not hinder the creation and the use of printed media by persons belonging to national minorities. In the legal framework of

sound radio and television broadcasting, they shall ensure, as far as possible, and taking into account the provisions of paragraph 1, that persons belonging to national minorities are granted the possibility of creating and using their own media.

4. In the framework of their legal systems, the Parties shall adopt adequate measures in order to facilitate access to the media for persons belonging to national minorities and in order to promote tolerance and permit cultural pluralism.

Article 10

1. The Parties undertake to recognise that every person belonging to a national minority has the right to use freely and without interference his or her minority language, in private and in public, orally and in writing.

2. In areas inhabited by persons belonging to national minorities traditionally or in substantial numbers, if those persons so request and where such a request corresponds to a real need, the Parties shall endeavour to ensure, as far as possible, the conditions which would make it possible to use the minority language in relations between those persons and the administrative authorities.

3. The Parties undertake to guarantee the right of every person belonging to a national minority to be informed promptly, in a language which he or she understands, against him or her, and to defend himself or herself in this language, if necessary with the free assistance of an interpreter.

Article 11

1. The Parties undertake to recognise that every person belonging to a national minority has the right to use his or her surname (patronym) and first names in the minority language and the right to official recognition of them, according to modalities provided for in their legal system.

2. The Parties undertake to recognise that every person belonging to a national minority has the right to display in his or her minority language signs, inscriptions and other information of a private nature visible to the public.

3. In areas traditionally inhabited by substantial numbers of persons belonging to a national minority, the Parties shall endeavour, in the framework of their legal system, including, where appropriate, agreements with other States, and taking into account their specific conditions, to display traditional local names, street names and other topographical indications intended for the public also in the minority language when there is a sufficient demand for such indications.

Article 12

1. The Parties shall, where appropriate, take measures in the fields of education and research to foster knowledge of the culture, history, language and religion of their national minorities and of the majority.

2. In this context the Parties shall inter alia provide adequate opportunities for teacher training and access to textbooks, and facilitate contacts among students and teachers of different communities.

3. The Parties undertake to promote equal opportunities for access to education at all levels for persons belonging to national minorities.

Article 13

1. Within the framework of their education systems, the Parties shall recognise that persons belonging to a national minority have the right to set up and to manage their own private educational and training establishments.

2. The exercise of this right shall not entail any financial obligation for the Parties.

Article 14

1. The Parties undertake to recognise that every person belonging to a national minority has the right to learn his or her minority language.

2. In areas inhabited by persons belonging to national minorities traditionally or in substantial numbers, if there is sufficient demand, the Parties shall endeavour to ensure, as far as possible and within the framework of their education systems, that persons belonging to those minorities have adequate opportunities for being taught the minority language or for receiving instruction in this language.

3. Paragraph 2 of this article shall be implemented without prejudice to the learning of the official language or the teaching in this language.

Article 15

The Parties shall create the conditions necessary for the effective participation of persons belonging to national minorities in cultural, social and economic life and in public affairs, in particular those affecting them.

Article 16

The Parties shall refrain from measures which alter the proportions of the population in areas inhabited by persons belonging to national minorities and are aimed at restricting the rights and freedoms flowing from the principles enshrined in the present framework Convention.

Article 17

1. The Parties undertake not to interfere with the right of persons belonging to national minorities to establish and maintain free and peaceful contacts across frontiers with persons lawfully staying in other States, in particular those with whom they share an ethnic, cultural, linguistic or religious identity, or a common cultural heritage.

2. The Parties undertake not to interfere with the right of persons belonging to national minorities to participate in the activities of non-governmental organisations, both at the national and international levels.

Article 18

1. The Parties shall endeavour to conclude, where necessary, bilateral and multilateral agreements with other States, in particular neighbouring States, in order to ensure the protection of persons belonging to the national minorities concerned.

2. Where relevant, the Parties shall take measures to encourage transfrontier co-operation.

Article 19

The Parties undertake to respect and implement the principles enshrined in the present framework Convention making, where necessary, only those limitations, restrictions or derogations which are provided for in international legal instruments, in particular the Convention for the Protection of Human Rights and Fundamental Freedoms, in so far as they are relevant to the rights and freedoms flowing from the said principles.

Section III

Article 20

In the exercise of the rights and freedoms flowing from the principles enshrined in the present framework Convention, any person belonging to a national minority shall respect the national legislation and the rights of others, in particular those of persons belonging to the majority or to other national minorities.

Article 21

Nothing in the present framework Convention shall be interpreted as implying any right to engage in any activity or perform any act contrary to the fundamental principles of international law and in particular of the sovereign equality, territorial integrity and political independence of States.

Article 22

Nothing in the present framework Convention shall be construed as limiting or derogating from any of the human rights and fundamental freedoms which may be ensured under the laws of any Contracting Party or under any other agreement to which it is a Party.

Article 23

The rights and freedoms flowing from the principles enshrined in the present framework Convention, in so far as they are the subject of a corresponding provision in the Convention for the Protection of Human Rights and Fundamental Freedoms or in the Protocols thereto, shall be understood so as to conform to the latter provisions.

Section IV

Article 24

1. The Committee of Ministers of the Council of Europe shall monitor the implementation of this framework Convention by the Contracting Parties.

2. The Parties which are not members of the Council of Europe shall participate in the implementation mechanism, according to modalities to be determined.

Article 25

1. Within a period of one year following the entry into force of this framework Convention in respect of a Contracting Party, the latter shall transmit to the Secretary General of the Council of Europe full information on the legislative and other measures taken to give effect to the principles set out in this framework Convention.

2. Thereafter, each Party shall transmit to the Secretary General on a periodical basis and whenever the Committee of Ministers so requests any further information of relevance to the implementation of this framework Convention.

3. The Secretary General shall forward to the Committee of Ministers the information transmitted under the terms of this Article.

Article 26

1. In evaluating the adequacy of the measures taken by the Parties to give effect to the principles set out in this framework Convention the Committee of Ministers shall be assisted by an advisory committee, the members of which shall have recognised expertise in the field of the protection of national minorities.

2. The composition of this advisory committee and its procedure shall be determined by the Committee of Ministers within a period of one year following the entry into force of this framework Convention.

Article 27

This framework Convention shall be open for signature by the member States of the Council of Europe. Up until the date when the Convention enters into force, it shall also be open for signature by any other State so invited by the Committee of Ministers. It is subject to ratification, acceptance or approval. Instruments of ratification, acceptance or approval shall be deposited with the Secretary General of the Council of Europe.

Article 28

1. This framework Convention shall enter into force on the first day of the month following the expiration of a period of three months after the date on which twelve member States of the Council of Europe have expressed their consent to be bound by the Convention in accordance with the provisions of Article 27.

2. In respect of any member State which subsequently expresses its consent to be bound by it, the framework Convention shall enter into force on the first day of the month following the expiration of a period of three months after the date of the deposit of the instrument of ratification, acceptance or approval.

Article 29

1. After the entry into force of this framework Convention and after consulting the Contracting States, the Committee of Ministers of the Council of Europe may invite to accede to the Convention, by a decision taken by the majority provided for in Article 20.d of the Statute of the Council of Europe, any non-member State of the Council of Europe which, invited to sign in accordance with the provisions of Article 27, has not yet done so, and any other non-member State.

2. In respect of any acceding State, the framework Convention shall enter into force on the first day of the month following the expiration of a period of three months after the date of the deposit of the instrument of accession with the Secretary General of the Council of Europe.

Article 30

1. Any State may at the time of signature or when depositing its instrument of ratification, acceptance, approval or accession, specify the territory or territories for whose international relations it is responsible to which this framework Convention shall apply.

. . .

Article 31

1. Any Party may at any time denounce this framework Convention by means of a notification addressed to the Secretary General of the Council of Europe.

2. Such denunciation shall become effective on the first day of the month following the expiration of a period of six months after the date of receipt of the notification by the Secretary General.

. . .

DOCUMENT OF THE COPENHAGEN MEETING OF THE CONFERENCE ON THE HUMAN DIMENSION OF THE CSCE (1990)

. . .

[T]he participating States agree on the following:

. . .

(2) They are determined to support and advance those principles of justice which form the basis of the rule of law. They consider that the rule of law does not mean merely a formal legality which assures regularity and consistency in the achievement and enforcement of democratic order, but justice based on the recognition and full acceptance of the supreme value of the human personality and guaranteed by institutions providing a framework for its fullest expression.

(3) They reaffirm that democracy is an inherent element of the rule of law. They recognize the importance of pluralism with regard to political organizations.

. . .

(5.7) human rights and fundamental freedoms will be guaranteed by law and in accordance with their obligations under international law;

. . .

(7.8) . . . no legal or administrative obstacle stands in the way of unimpeded access to the media on a non-discriminatory basis for all political groupings and individuals wishing to participate in the electoral process;

. . .

(9.4) everyone will have the right to freedom of thought, conscience and religion. This right includes freedom to change one's religion or belief and freedom to manifest one's religion or belief, either alone or in community with others, in public or in private, through worship, teaching, practice and observance. The exercise of these rights may be subject only to such restrictions as are prescribed by law and are consistent with international standards;

(9.5) they will respect the right of everyone to leave any country, including his own, and to return to his country, consistent with a State's international obligations and CSCE commitments. Restrictions on this right will have the character of very rare exceptions, will be considered necessary only if they respond to a specific public need, pursue a legitimate aim and are proportionate to that aim, and will not be abused or applied in an arbitrary manner;

. . .

(23) The participating States reaffirm their conviction expressed in the Vienna Concluding Document that the promotion of economic, social and cultural rights as well as of civil and political rights is of paramount importance for human dignity and for the attainment of the legitimate aspirations of every individual. In the context of continuing their efforts with a view to achieving progressively the full realization of economic, social and cultural rights by all appropriate means, they will pay special attention to problems in the areas of employment, housing, social security, health, education and culture.

. . .

(25.4) . . . measures [derogating from human rights obligations] will not discriminate solely on the grounds of race, colour, sex, language, religion, social origin or of belonging to a minority.

. . .

Part IV

(30) The participating States recognize that the questions relating to national minorities can only be satisfactorily resolved in a democratic political framework based on the rule of law, with a functioning independent

judiciary. This framework guarantees full respect for human rights and fundamental freedoms, equal rights and status for all citizens, the free expression of all their legitimate interests and aspirations, political pluralism, social tolerance and the implementation of legal rules that place effective restraints on the abuse of governmental power.

They further reaffirm that respect for the rights of persons belonging to national minorities as part of universally recognized human rights is an essential factor for peace, justice, stability and democracy in the participating States.

(31) Persons belonging to national minorities have the right to exercise fully and effectively their human rights and fundamental freedoms without any discrimination and in full equality before the law.

The participating States will adopt, where necessary, special measures for the purpose of ensuring to persons belonging to national minorities full equality with the other citizens in the exercise and enjoyment of human rights and fundamental freedoms.

(32) To belong to a national minority is a matter of a person's individual choice and no disadvantage may arise from the exercise of such choice.

Persons belonging to national minorities have the right freely to express, preserve and develop their ethnic, cultural, linguistic or religious identity and to maintain and develop their culture in all its aspects, free of any attempts at assimilation against their will. In particular, they have the right

(32.1) to use freely their mother tongue in private as well as in public;

(32.2) to establish and maintain their own educational, cultural and religious institutions, organizations or associations, which can seek voluntary financial and other contributions as well as public assistance, in conformity with national legislation;

(32.3) to profess and practise their religion, including the acquisition, possession and use of religious materials, and to conduct religious educational activities in their mother tongue;

(32.4) to establish and maintain unimpeded contacts among themselves within their country as well as contacts across frontiers with citizens of other States with whom they share a common ethnic or national origin, cultural heritage or religious beliefs;

(32.5) to disseminate, have access to and exchange information in their mother tongue;

(32.6) to establish and maintain organizations or associations within their country and to participate in international non-governmental organizations.

Persons belonging to national minorities can exercise and enjoy their rights individually as well as in community with other members of their group. No disadvantage may arise for a person belonging to a national minority on account of the exercise or non-exercise of any such rights.

(33) The participating States will protect the ethnic, cultural, linguistic and religious identity of national minorities on their territory and create conditions for the promotion of that identity. They will take the necessary measures to that effect after due consultations, including contacts with organizations or associations of such minorities, in accordance with the decision-making procedures of each State.

Any such measures will be in conformity with the principles of equality and non-discrimination with respect to the other citizens of the participating State concerned.

(34) The participating States will endeavour to ensure that persons belonging to national minorities, notwithstanding the need to learn the official language or languages of the State concerned, have adequate opportunities for instruction of their mother tongue or in their mother tongue, as well as, wherever possible and necessary, for its use before public authorities, in conformity with applicable national legislation.

In the context of the teaching of history and culture in educational establishments, they will also take account of the history and culture of national minorities.

(35) The participating States will respect the right of persons belonging to national minorities to effective participation in public affairs, including participation in the affairs relating to the protection and promotion of the identity of such minorities.

The participating States note the efforts undertaken to protect and create conditions for the promotion of the ethnic, cultural, linguistic and religious identity of certain national minorities by establishing, as one of the possible means to achieve these aims, appropriate local or autonomous administrations corresponding to the specific historical and territorial circumstances of such minorities and in accordance with the policies of the State concerned.

(36) The participating States recognize the particular importance of increasing constructive co-operation among themselves on questions relating to national minorities. Such co-operation seeks to promote mutual understanding and confidence, friendly and good-neighbourly relations, international peace, security and justice.

Every participating State will promote a climate of mutual respect, understanding, co-operation and solidarity among all persons living on its territory, without distinction as to ethnic or national origin or religion, and will encourage the solution of problems through dialogue based on the principles of the rule of law.

(37) None of these commitments may be interpreted as implying any right to engage in any activity or perform any action in contravention of the purposes and principles of the Charter of the United Nations, other obligations under international law or the provisions of the Final Act, including the principle of territorial integrity of States.

(38) The participating States, in their efforts to protect and promote the rights of persons belonging to national minorities, will fully respect their undertakings under existing human rights conventions and other relevant international instruments and consider adhering to the relevant conventions, if they have not yet done so, including those providing for a right of complaint by individuals.

(40) The participating States clearly and unequivocally condemn totalitarianism, racial and ethnic hatred, anti-semitism, xenophobia and discrimination against anyone as well as persecution on religious and ideological grounds. In this context, they also recognize the particular problems of Roma (gypsies).
They declare their firm intention to intensify the efforts to combat these phenomena in all their forms and therefore will;

(40.1) take effective measures, including the adoption, in conformity with their constitutional systems and their international obligations, of such laws as may be necessary, to provide protection against any acts that constitute incitement to violence against persons or groups based on national, racial, ethnic or religious discrimination, hostility or hatred, including anti-semitism;

(40.2) commit themselves to take appropriate and proportionate measures to protect persons or groups who may be subject to threats or acts of discrimination, hostility or violence as a result of their racial, ethnic, cultural, linguistic or religious identity, and to protect their property;

(40.3) take effective measures, in conformity with their constitutional systems, at the national, regional and local levels to promote understanding and tolerance, particularly in the fields of education, culture and information;

(40.4) endeavour to ensure that the objectives of education include special attention to the problem of racial prejudice and hatred and to the development of respect for different civilizations and cultures;

(40.5) recognize the right of the individual to effective remedies and endeavour to recognize, in conformity with national legislation, the right of interested persons and groups to initiate and support complaints against acts of discrimination, including racist and xenophobic acts;

(40.6) consider adhering, if they have not yet done so, to the international instruments which address the problem of discrimination and ensure full compliance with the obligations therein, including those relating to the submission of periodic reports;

(40.7) consider, also, accepting those international mechanisms which allow States and individuals to bring communications relating to discrimination before international bodies.

REPORT OF THE CSCE MEETING OF EXPERTS ON NATIONAL MINORITIES, GENEVA 1991

. . .

Part I.

Recognizing that their observance and full exercise of human rights and fundamental freedoms, including those of persons belonging to national minorities, are the foundation of the New Europe,

Reaffirming their deep conviction that friendly relations among their peoples, as well as peace, justice, stability and democracy, require that the ethnic, cultural, linguistic and religious identity of national minorities be protected, and conditions for the promotion of that identity be created,

Convinced that, in States with national minorities, democracy requires that all persons, including those belonging to national minorities, enjoy full and effective equality of rights and fundamental freedoms and benefit from the rule of law and democratic institutions,

Aware of the diversity of situations and constitutional systems in their countries, and therefore recognizing that various approaches to the implementation of CSCE commitments regarding national minorities are appropriate,

Mindful of the importance of exerting efforts to address national minorities issues, particularly in areas where democratic institutions are being consolidated and questions relating to national minorities are of special concern,

Aware that national minorities form an integral part of the society of the States in which they live and that they are a factor of enrichment of each respective State and society,

Confirming the need to respect and implement fully and fairly their undertakings in the field of human rights and fundamental freedoms as set forth in the international instruments by which they may be bound,

Reaffirming their strong determination to respect and apply, to their full extent, all their commitments relating to national minorities and persons belonging to them in the Helsinki Final Act, the Madrid Concluding Document and the Vienna Concluding Document, the Document of the Copenhagen Meeting of the Conference on the Human Dimension of the CSCE, the Document of the Cracow Symposium on the Cultural Heritage as well as the Charter of Paris for a New Europe, the participating States present below the summary of their conclusions.

The representatives of the participating States took as the fundamental basis of their work the commitments undertaken by them with respect to national minorities as contained in the relevant adopted CSCE documents, in particular those in the Charter of Paris for a New Europe and the Document of the Copenhagen Meeting of the Conference on the Human Dimension of the CSCE, which they fully reaffirmed.

Part II.

The participating States stress the continued importance of a thorough review of implementation of their CSCE commitments relating to persons belonging to national minorities.

They emphasize that human rights and fundamental freedoms are the basis for the protection and promotion of rights of persons belonging to national minorities. They further recognize that questions relating to national minorities can only be satisfactorily resolved in a democratic political framework based on the rule of law, with a functioning independent judiciary. This framework guarantees full respect for human rights and fundamental freedoms, equal rights and status for all citizens, including persons belonging to national minorities, the free expression of all their legitimate interests and aspirations, political pluralism, social tolerance and the implementation of legal rules that place effective restraints on the abuse of governmental power.

Issues concerning national minorities, as well as compliance with international obligations and commitments concerning the rights of persons belonging to them, are matters of legitimate international concern and consequently do not constitute exclusively an internal affair of the respective State.

They note that not all ethnic, cultural, linguistic or religious differences necessarily lead to the creation of national minorities.

Part III.

Respecting the right of persons belonging to national minorities to effective participation in public affairs, the participating States consider that when issues relating to the situation of national minorities are discussed within their countries, they themselves should have the effective opportunity to be involved, in accordance with the decision-making procedures of each State. They further consider that appropriate democratic participation of persons belonging to national minorities or their representatives in decision-making or consultative bodies constitutes an important element of effective participation in public affairs.

They consider that special efforts must be made to resolve specific problems in a constructive manner and through dialogue by means of negotiations and consultations with a view to improving the situation of persons belonging to national minorities. They recognize that the promotion of dialogue between States, and between States and persons belonging to national minorities, will be most successful when there is a free flow of information and ideas between all parties. They encourage unilateral, bilateral and multilateral efforts by governments to explore avenues for enhancing the effectiveness of their implementation of CSCE commitments relating to national minorities.

The participating States further consider that respect for human rights and fundamental freedoms must be accorded on a non-discriminatory basis throughout society. In areas inhabited mainly by persons belonging to a national minority, the human rights and fundamental freedoms of persons belonging to that minority, of persons belonging to the majority population of the respective State, and of persons belonging to other national minorities residing in these areas will be equally protected.

They reconfirm that persons belonging to national minorities have the right freely to express, preserve and develop their ethnic, cultural, linguistic or religious identity and to maintain and develop their culture in all its aspects, free of any attempts at assimilation against their will.

They will permit the competent authorities to inform the Office for Free Elections of all scheduled public elections on their territories, including those held below national level. The participating States will consider favourably, to the extent permitted by law, the presence of observers at elections held below the national level, including in areas inhabited by national minorities, and will endeavour to facilitate their access.

Part IV.

The participating States will create conditions for persons belonging to national minorities to have equal opportunity to be effectively involved in the public life, economic activities, and building of their societies.

In accordance with paragraph 31 of the Copenhagen Document, the participating States will take the necessary measures to prevent discrimination against individuals, particularly in respect of employment, housing and education, on the grounds of belonging or not belonging to a national minority. In that context, they will make provision, if they have not yet done so, for effective recourse to redress for individuals who have experienced discriminatory treatment on the grounds of their belonging or not belonging to a national minority, including by making available to individual victims of discrimination a broad array of administrative and judicial remedies.

The participating States are convinced that the preservation of the values and of the cultural heritage of national minorities requires the involvement of persons belonging to such minorities and that tolerance and respect for different cultures are of paramount importance in this regard. Accordingly, they confirm the importance of refraining from hindering the production of cultural materials concerning national minorities, including by persons belonging to them.

The participating States affirm that persons belonging to a national minority will enjoy the same rights and have the same duties of citizenship as the rest of the population.

The participating States reconfirm the importance of adopting, where necessary, special measures for the purpose of ensuring to persons belonging to national minorities full equality with the other citizens in the exercise and enjoyment of human rights and fundamental freedoms. They further recall the need to take the necessary measures to protect the ethnic, cultural, linguistic and religious identity of national minorities on their territory and create conditions for the promotion of that identity; any such measures will be in conformity with the principles of equality and non-discrimination with respect to the other citizens of the participating State concerned.

They recognize that such measures, which take into account, *inter alia*, historical and territorial circumstances of national minorities, are particularly important in areas where democratic institutions are being consolidated and national minorities issues are of special concern.

Aware of the diversity and varying constitutional systems among them, which make no single approach necessarily generally applicable, the participating States note with interest that positive results have been obtained by some of them in an appropriate democratic manner by, *inter alia*:

–advisory and decision-making bodies in which minorities are represented, in particular with regard to education, culture and religion;

–elected bodies and assemblies of national minority affairs;

–local and autonomous administration, as well as autonomy on a territorial basis, including the existence of consultative, legislative and executive bodies chosen through free and periodic elections;

–self-administration by a national minority of aspects concerning its identity in situations where autonomy on a territorial basis does not apply;

–decentralized or local forms of government;
-bilateral and multilateral agreements and other arrangements regarding national minorities;

–for persons belonging to national minorities, provision of adequate types and levels of education in their mother tongue with due regard to the number, geographic settlement patterns and cultural traditions of national minorities;

–funding the teaching of minority languages to the general public, as well as the inclusion of minority languages in teacher-training institutions, in particular in regions inhabited by persons belonging to national minorities;

–in cases where instruction in a particular subject is not provided in their territory in the minority language at all levels, taking the necessary measures to find means of recognizing diplomas issued abroad for a course of study completed in that language;

–creation of government research agencies to review legislation and disseminate information related to equal rights and non-discrimination;

–provision of financial and technical assistance to persons belonging to national minorities who so wish to exercise their right to establish and maintain their own educational, cultural and religious institutions, organizations and associations;

–governmental assistance for addressing local difficulties relating to discriminatory practices (e.g. a citizens relations service);

–encouragement of grassroots community relations efforts between minority communities, between majority and minority communities, and between neighbouring communities sharing borders, aimed at helping to prevent local tensions from arising and address conflicts peacefully should they arise; and

–either inter-State or regional, to facilitate continuing dialogue between the border regions concerned.

The participating States are of the view that these or other approaches, individually or in combination, could be helpful in improving the situation of national minorities on their territories.

Part V.

The participating States respect the right of persons belonging to national minorities to exercise and enjoy their rights alone or in community with others, to establish and maintain organizations and associations within their country, and to participate in international non-governmental organizations.

The participating States reaffirm, and will not hinder the exercise of, the right of persons belonging to national minorities to establish and maintain their own educational, cultural and religious institutions, organizations and associations.

In this regard, they recognize the major and vital role that individuals, non-governmental organizations, and religious and other groups play in fostering cross-cultural understanding and improving relations at all levels of society, as well as across international frontiers.

They believe that the first-hand observations and experience of such organizations, groups, and individuals can be of great value in promoting the implementation of CSCE commitments relating to persons belonging to national minorities. They therefore will encourage and not hinder the work of such organizations, groups and individuals and welcome their contributions in this area.

Part VI.

The participating States, concerned by the proliferation of acts of racial, ethnic and religious hatred, anti-semitism, xenophobia and discrimination, stress their determination to condemn, on a continuing basis, such acts against anyone.

In this context, they reaffirm their recognition of the particular problems of Roma (gypsies). They are ready to undertake effective measures in order to achieve full equality of opportunity between persons belonging to Roma ordinarily resident in their State and the rest of the resident population. They will also encourage research and studies regarding Roma and the particular problems they face.

They will take effective measures to promote tolerance, understanding, equality of opportunity and good relations between individuals of different origins within their country.

Further, the participating States will take effective measures, including the adoption, in conformity with their constitutional law and their international obligations, if they have not already done so, of laws that would prohibit acts that constitute incitement to violence based on national, racial, ethnic or religious discrimination, hostility or hatred, including anti-semitism, and policies to enforce such laws.

Moreover, in order to heighten public awareness of prejudice and hatred, to improve enforcement of laws against hate-related crime and otherwise to further efforts to address hatred and prejudice in society, they will make efforts to collect, publish on a regular basis, and make available to the public, data about crimes on their respective territories that are based on prejudice as to race, ethnic identity or religion, including the guidelines used for the collection of such data. These data should not contain any personal information.

They will consult and exchange views and information at the international level, including at future meetings of the CSCE, on crimes that manifest evidence of prejudice and hate.

Part VII.

Convinced that the protection of the rights of persons belonging to national minorities necessitates free flow of information and exchange of ideas, the participating States emphasize the importance of communication between persons belonging to national minorities without interference by public authorities and regardless of frontiers. The exercise of such rights may be subject only to such restrictions as are prescribed by law and are consistent with international standards. They reaffirm that no one belonging to a national minority, simply by virtue of belonging to such a minority, will be subject to penal or administrative sanctions for having had contacts within or outside his/her own country.

In access to the media, they will not discriminate against anyone based on ethnic, cultural, linguistic or religious grounds. They will make information available that will assist the electronic mass media in taking into account, in their programmes, the ethnic, cultural, linguistic and religious identity of national minorities.

They reaffirm that establishment and maintenance of unimpeded contacts among persons belonging to a national minority, as well as contacts across frontiers by persons belonging to a national minority with persons with whom they share a common ethnic or national origin, cultural heritage or religious belief, contributes to mutual understanding and promotes good-neighbourly relations.

They therefore encourage transfrontier co-operation arrangements on a national, regional and local level, *inter alia*, on local border crossings, the preservation of and visits to cultural and historical monuments and sites, tourism, the improvement of traffic, the economy, youth exchange, the protection of the environment and the establishment of regional commissions.

. . .

CSCE HELSINKI DOCUMENT 1992, THE CHALLENGES OF CHANGE

Helsinki Decisions

I. Strengthening CSCE Institutions and Structures

. . .

High Commissioner on National Minorities

(23) The Council will appoint a High Commissioner on National Minorities. The High Commissioner provides "early warning" and, as appropriate, "early action" at the earliest possible stage in regard to tensions involving national minority issues that have the potential to develop into a conflict within the CSCE area, affecting peace, stability, or relations between participating States. The High Commissioner will draw upon the facilities of the Office for Democratic Institutions and Human Rights (ODIHR) in Warsaw.

. . .

II CSCE High Commissioner on National Minorities

(1) The participating States decide to establish a High Commissioner on National Minorities.

Mandate

(2) The High Commissioner will act under the aegis of the CSO and will thus be an instrument of conflict prevention at the earliest possible stage.

(3) The High Commissioner will provide "early warning" and, as

appropriate, "early action" at the earliest possible stage in regard to tensions involving national minority issues which have not yet developed beyond an early warning stage, but, in the judgement of the High Commissioner, have the potential to develop into a conflict within the CSCE area, affecting peace, stability or relations between participating States, requiring the attention of and action by the Council or the CSO.

(4) Within the mandate, based on CSCE principles and commitments, the High Commissioner will work in confidence and will act independently of all parties directly involved in the tensions.

(5a) The High Commissioner will consider national minority issues occurring in the State of which the High Commissioner is a national or a resident, or involving a national minority to which the High Commissioner belongs, only if all parties directly involved agree, including the State concerned.

(5b) The High Commissioner will not consider national minority issues in situations involving organized acts of terrorism.

(5c) Nor will the High Commissioner consider violations of CSCE commitments with regard to an individual person belonging to a national minority.

(6) In considering a situation, the High Commissioner will take fully into account the availability of democratic means and international instruments to respond to it, and their utilization by the parties involved.

(7) When a particular national minority issue has been brought to the attention of the CSO, the involvement of the High Commissioner will require a request and a specific mandate from the CSO.

Profile, appointment, support

(8) The High Commissioner will be an eminent international personality with long-standing relevant experience from whom an impartial performance of the function may be expected.

(9) The High Commissioner will be appointed by the Council by consensus upon the recommendation of the CSO for a period of three years, which may be extended for one further term of three years only.

(10) The High Commissioner will draw upon the facilities of the ODIHR in Warsaw, and in particular upon the information relevant to all aspects of national minority questions available at the ODIHR.

Early warning

The High Commissioner will:

(11a) collect and receive information regarding national minority issues from sources described below (see Supplement paragraphs (23)-(25));

(11b) assess at the earliest possible stage the role of the parties directly concerned, the nature of the tensions and recent developments therein and, where possible, the potential consequences for peace and stability within the CSCE area;

(11c) to this end, be able to pay a visit, in accordance with paragraph (17) and Supplement paragraphs (27)-(30), to any participating State and communicate in person, subject to the provisions of paragraph (25), with parties directly concerned to obtain first-hand information about the situation of national minorities.

(12) The High Commissioner may during a visit to a participating State, while obtaining first-hand information from all parties directly involved, discuss the questions with the parties, and where appropriate promote dialogue, confidence and co-operation between them.

Provision of early warning

(13) If, on the basis of exchanges of communications and contacts with relevant parties, the High Commissioner concludes that there is a prima facie risk of potential conflict (as set out in paragraph (3)) he/she may issue an early warning, which will be communicated promptly by the Chairman-in-Office to the CSO.

(14) The Chairman-in-Office will include this early warning in the agenda for the next meeting of the CSO. If a State believes that such an early warning merits prompt consultation, it may initiate the procedure set out in Annex 2 of the Summary of Conclusions of the Berlin Meeting of the Council ("Emergency Mechanism").

(15) The High Commissioner will explain to the CSO the reasons for issuing the early warning.

Early action

(16) The High Commissioner may recommend that he/she be authorized to enter into further contact and closer consultations with the parties concerned with a view to possible solutions, according to a mandate to be decided by the CSO. The CSO may decide accordingly.

Accountability

(17) The High Commissioner will consult the Chairman-in-Office prior to a departure for a participating State to address a tension involving

national minorities. The Chairman-in-Office will consult, in confidence, the participating State(s) concerned and may consult more widely.

(18) After a visit to a participating State, the High Commissioner will provide strictly confidential reports to the Chairman-in-Office on the findings and progress of the High Commissioner's involvement in a particular question.

(19) After termination of the involvement of the High Commissioner in a particular issue, the High Commissioner will report to the Chairman-in-Office on the findings, results and conclusions. Within a period of one month, the Chairman-in-Office will consult, in confidence, on the findings, results and conclusions the participating State(s) concerned and may consult more widely. Thereafter the report, together with possible comments, will be transmitted to the CSO.

(20) Should the High Commissioner conclude that the situation is escalating into a conflict, or if the High Commissioner deems that the scope for action by the High Commissioner is exhausted, the High Commissioner shall, through the Chairman-in-Office, so inform the CSO.

(21) Should the CSO become involved in a particular issue, the High Commissioner will provide information and, on request, advice to the CSO, or to any other institution or organization which the CSO may invite, in accordance with the provisions of Chapter III of this document, to take action with regard to the tensions or conflict.

(22) The High Commissioner, if so requested by the CSO and with due regard to the requirement of confidentiality in his/her mandate, will provide information about his/her activities at CSCE implementation meetings on Human Dimension issues.

Supplement

Sources of information about national minority issues

(23) The High Commissioner may:
(23a) collect and receive information regarding the situation of national minorities and the role of parties involved therein from any source, including the media and non-governmental organizations with the exception referred to in paragraph (25);

(23b) receive specific reports from parties directly involved regarding developments concerning national minority issues. These may include reports on violations of CSCE commitments with respect to national minorities as well as other violations in the context of national minority issues.

(24) Such specific reports to the High Commissioner should meet the following requirements:
– they should be in writing, addressed to the High Commissioner as such and signed with full names and addresses;
– they should contain a factual account of the developments which are relevant to the situation of persons belonging to national minorities and the role of the parties involved therein, and which have taken place recently, in principle not more than 12 months previously. The reports should contain information which can be sufficiently substantiated.

(25) The High Commissioner will not communicate with and will not acknowledge communications from any person or organization which practises or publicly condones terrorism or violence.

Parties directly concerned

(26) Parties directly concerned in tensions who can provide specific reports to the High Commissioner and with whom the High Commissioner will seek to communicate in person during a visit to a participating State are the following:

(26a) governments of participating States, including, if appropriate, regional and local authorities in areas in which national minorities reside;

(26b) representatives of associations, non-governmental organizations, religious and other groups of national minorities directly concerned and in the area of tension, which are authorized by the persons belonging to those national minorities to represent them.

Conditions for travel by the High Commissioner

(27) Prior to an intended visit, the High Commissioner will submit to the participating State concerned specific information regarding the intended purpose of that visit. Within two weeks the State(s) concerned will consult with the High Commissioner on the objectives of the visit, which may include the promotion of dialogue, confidence and co-operation between the parties. After entry the State concerned will facilitate free travel and communication of the High Commissioner subject to the provisions of paragraph (25) above.

(28) If the State concerned does not allow the High Commissioner to enter the country and to travel and communicate freely, the High Commissioner will so inform the CSO.

(29) In the course of such a visit, subject to the provision of paragraph (25) the High Commissioner may consult the parties involved, and may receive information in confidence from any individual, group or organization directly

concerned on questions the High Commissioner is addressing. The High Commissioner will respect the confidential nature of the information.

(30) The participating States will refrain from taking any action against persons, organizations or institutions on account of their contact with the High Commissioner.

High Commissioner and involvement of experts

(31) The High Commissioner may decide to request assistance from not more than three experts with relevant expertise in specific matters on which brief, specialized investigation and advice are required.

(32) If the High Commissioner decides to call on experts, the High Commissioner will set a clearly defined mandate and time-frame for the activities of the experts.

(33) Experts will only visit a participating State at the same time as the High Commissioner. Their mandate will be an integral part of the mandate of the High Commissioner and the same conditions for travel will apply.

(34) The advice and recommendations requested from the experts will be submitted in confidence to the High Commissioner, who will be responsible for the activities and for the reports of the experts and who will decide whether and in what form the advice and recommendations will be communicated to the parties concerned. They will be non-binding. If the High Commissioner decides to make the advice and recommendations available, the State(s) concerned will be given the opportunity to comment.

(35) The experts will be selected by the High Commissioner with the assistance of the ODIHR from the resource list established at the ODIHR as laid down in the Document of the Moscow Meeting.

(36) The experts will not include nationals or residents of the participating State concerned, or any person appointed by the State concerned, or any expert against whom the participating State has previously entered reservations. The experts will not include the participating State's own nationals or residents or any of the persons it appointed to the resource list, or more than one national or resident of any particular State.

Budget

(37) A separate budget will be determined at the ODIHR, which will provide, as appropriate, logistical support for travel and communication. The budget will be funded by the participating States according to the established CSCE scale of distribution. Details will be worked out by the Financial Committee and approved by the CSO.

Index

P. Cumper and S. Wheatley (eds.), Minority Rights in the 'New' Europe, 375–385
© 1999 Kluwer Law International. Printed in Great Britain.